The Japanese Oligarchy and the Russo-Japanese War

STUDIES OF THE
EAST ASIAN INSTITUTE
COLUMBIA UNIVERSITY

The Japanese Oligarchy and the Russo-Japanese War

by SHUMPEI OKAMOTO

New York and London 1970

COLUMBIA UNIVERSITY PRESS

SHUMPEI OKAMOTO is Associate Professor
of History at Temple University.

Copyright © 1970 Columbia University Press
Library of Congress Catalog Card Number: 74-114259
ISBN: 0-231-03404-0
Printed in the United States of America

THE EAST ASIAN INSTITUTE OF COLUMBIA UNIVERSITY was established in 1949 to prepare graduate students for careers dealing with East Asia, and to aid research and publication on East Asia during the modern period. The faculty of the Institute are grateful to the Ford Foundation and the Rockefeller Foundation for their financial assistance.

The Studies of the East Asian Institute were inaugurated in 1962 to bring to a wider public the results of significant new research on modern and contemporary East Asia.

To Ellen

ACKNOWLEDGMENTS

MORE than ten years ago, a Japanese iron ore freighter left me at a little-known pier on the banks of the Columbia River in Oregon. My life in America, since then, has been filled with good fortune. No piece of good fortune, however, has been greater than my encounter with my adviser, James William Morley, Professor of Government and chairman of the Japan Studies Committee of the East Asian Institute, Columbia University. Throughout my years at Columbia, Professor Morley gave me generous guidance and encouragement and directed me by constructive pressure and criticism.

During the various stages of writing this book, I have become deeply indebted to many other scholars on the Morningside Heights campus. For his characteristically quiet, kind, and always pertinent advice, I should like to express my sincere and ever-growing appreciation to Professor Herschel F. Webb. He saved me from numerous pitfalls into which a researcher in Japanese sources can so easily fall. I should like to thank also Dr. John M. H. Lindbeck, Director of the East Asian Institute, for his personal encouragement; Dr. Dorothy Borg for the guidance she perhaps unwittingly gave me by asking questions that only an experienced and truly concerned researcher could ask; Dr. Hugh Borton for his reading of the manuscript; and Professors Alexander Dallin, Henry F. Graff, and Warner R. Schilling for their criticism of an earlier version of the manuscript.

Many people kindly and ably assisted me in my search for materials. I am particularly grateful to Miss Miwa Kai, who never failed to respond with a smile to my frequent but at times hesitant knocks at her office door, and to Dr. Philip Yampolsky, both of the East Asian Library, Columbia University; Mr. Andrew Kuroda and Mr. Key K. Kobayashi of the Library of Congress; Mr. Aoki Toshiyuki of Harvard University Library. My *gakkei*, Ikei Masaru, Professor of Far Eastern Diplomacy,

Keiō University, kindly found several vital documents at libraries and secondhand bookstores in Tokyo. Members of my family in Tokyo copied for me some important materials from the collections at the Kensei Shiryōshitsu, the National Diet Library.

For their assistance in research, editing, and typing, I am grateful to Miss Cynthia Soller, Mrs. Ann Scher, Mrs. Tamako Yorichika, and Mrs. Deborah S. Howe. I am especially thankful to Mrs. Sandy Steinhardt, who, with a competent linguist's enthusiasm and precision, spent so many of her precious hours on my manuscript. I also thank Miss Dale K. Anderson for her invaluable editorial assistance. I am deeply grateful also to Mrs. Mary Schoch, Administrative Assistant of the East Asian Institute, and the staff of Columbia University Press for their patience with an inexperienced author.

I should also like to express my sincere gratitude to the Association of American University Women for their one-way freighter fare grant; Anderson College, Indiana, where I spent my first year in this country; the Japan Society of New York for a timely and valuable scholarship; and most importantly, Columbia University, particularly the Japan Foreign Relations Project and the Contemporary Japan Studies Committee of the East Asian Institute, for vital financial assistance.

Needless to say, I alone am responsible for the shortcomings in this book. I wish, however, to share with these individuals and institutions whatever success this work may enjoy.

Finally, my sons, Karl and Eugene, who watched their father's snail-like progress with only slightly less interest than they watched their favorite television programs, have helped me in the way that only two growing, healthy sons can help their father. I shall not even attempt to thank my wife for what she has been to me all these years. I simply dedicate this book to her with my love and respect.

Philadelphia   SHUMPEI OKAMOTO
April 1970

CONTENTS

The Japanese
Oligarchy
and the Russo-
Japanese War

INTRODUCTION

THIS STUDY attempts to examine a singularly successful instance of foreign policy making under an oligarchic system. The study treats the formation and execution of Japan's foreign policy during the Russo-Japanese War in terms of those factors that contributed to the successful prosecution of the war; it also explores the limitations of those factors.

The study is conducted in the hope that it will contribute to the answering of two questions: First, what are the strengths and weaknesses of oligarchic control of foreign policy? Second, what bearing did such strengths and weaknesses have on the conduct of Japan's prewar foreign policy?

One valuable development in recent studies of foreign policy is an increasing attention to the interactions between domestic politics and foreign policy. A growing number of studies, both theoretical and empirical, have been published in this field.[1] These studies show tantalizing ambiguities and are far from realizing a general theory; nevertheless, they present more refined approaches to, and hypotheses on, the interrelationships between domestic political process and foreign policy.

This painfully slow but important progress has already shed new light on the time-honored debate on the comparative capabilities of democratic and nondemocratic systems in the realm of foreign policy making. Abstractness, the traditional feature of the debate, has gradually been replaced with more concrete, empirical investigation. As a result, pessimism about the capabilities of democratic foreign policy making, expressed by Alexis de Tocqueville and shared by many others, is being modified.[2]

On the one hand, the exaggerated view has been corrected that, because policy making in a democracy is decentralized, it is therefore inefficient. Our growing knowledge of what is called public opinion in foreign policy making has revealed that foreign policy making in a democracy is much more elite-oriented than has been widely assumed and that this tendency is particularly pronounced in crisis situations.[3] On the other hand, the advantages in an authoritarian system of centralized decision making have come to be regarded with suspicion. An increasing number of studies have asserted that foreign policy in a totalitarian or authoritarian system, while less affected by the direct impact of public opinion, is influenced by internal politics as much as, if not more than, in a democracy.[4]

Thus R. Barry Farrell concludes his comparative study of the capabilities of constitutional democracy and totalitarianism in foreign policy making: "Both the open and closed societies have marked advantages and disadvantages. . . . The disadvantages do not seem so clearly assigned to one side or the other."[5] Carl J. Friedrich endorses this relative view. He still concedes, "How to structure the process of foreign affairs decision-making in a nation which is democratically organized so as to insure an effective conduct of its foreign policy is an unsolved problem." Nevertheless, he now maintains:

Totalitarian governments, while somewhat freer from a general public opinion and its gyrations, are demonstrably subject to the push and pull of party divisions. Hence in both democratic and totalitarian regimes the people may force a bad policy, they may prevent a good policy from being adopted, they may allow special interests to deflect national policy, and they may even provide the government with ready excuses for a policy which is unpalatable to other powers.[6]

Some of the underlying assumptions of the debate on the advantages and disadvantages of an oligarchic foreign policy can be summarized as follows:

First, foreign policy is, in the final analysis, the work of political leaders, and its success or failure depends upon the quality of political leadership and its working conditions.

Second, the basic interdependent attributes of competent leadership in foreign policy making must include:

(a). The ability to set sensible foreign policy goals for the nation. Leadership must keep the objectives and methods of its foreign policy in harmony with the national power available to support the policy with a maximum chance of success. In order to achieve this, leadership must be equipped with a sense of realism and imagination, flexibility, firmness, vigor, and moderation.[7] It must also enjoy a basic unity, without destroying the possibility of discussion on broad policy alternatives among the leaders themselves. It must have access to reliable information about domestic and international conditions.

(b). The ability to lead, not to follow, public opinion. This requires candid recognition that "the conflict between the requirements of good foreign policy and the preferences of public opinion is in the nature of things and, hence, unavoidable."[8] Leadership must therefore be firm enough to maintain what it believes to be good foreign policy and to resist public demands. At the same time, it must avoid unnecessarily intensifying its conflict with the public. It must avoid alienating the public or driving the public to outright resistance against it.

(c). The ability to arouse and maintain popular support for its policy. Leadership must endeavor to cultivate public opinion favorable to the policy it wishes to pursue. It must avoid creating opportunities for the opposition or demagogues to mislead the public.

Third, an effective political process for foreign policy making must therefore possess: (a) the capability to produce and keep producing the kind of leadership described above; and (b) the capability, broadly stated, to nurture a domestic setting that will enable competent leadership to exert its best efforts with minimum interference.

The qualities listed above are intended to be neither exhaustive nor conceptually elegant. Rather, the aim is to present a useful yardstick with which to measure the capabilities of oligarchic foreign policy making.

It may also be useful to state here our basic position in selecting the case of Japan's foreign policy making in the Russo-Japanese War. While the Japanese leaders concerned, both civilian and military, humbly and assiduously attributed their success in the war to the august glory of the Emperor Meiji and the benevolent guidance and protection of the spirits of his divine ancestors, scholars have cited as one major reason for victory successful coordination between the Japanese civilian and military leaders in the policy-making process.[9] Although we have no quarrel with this view, we should, however, like to go one step further and ask several questions. For instance, how good was this coordination in reality? What were the basic factors that made such coordination possible? Were these factors particularistic to Japan at the time of the Russo-Japanese War? What were their limitations? What were the costs of good coordination?

It is our hope that in seeking answers to such questions as these we shall find some clues to the capabilities of oligarchic foreign policy making. While this study does not purport, except by indirection, to participate in the debate on the relative capabilities of various foreign policy-making processes, and while it is not possible for one case study such as this to arrive at a general theory of the capabilities of oligarchic foreign policy making, we hope this study will serve as an initial step in that direction and that it will contribute to the development of the study of the interactions between domestic political process and foreign policy.

Our second interest in this study is related to the question of political development. In his Epilogue to *Political Development in Modern Japan*, Robert E. Ward presents 14 general propositions on the process of political modernization, suggested by the Japanese experience.[10] They include the following:

...That widespread fear of foreign intervention or exploitation can be a powerful stimulus to political modernization. [I]

...That forces and institutions that are supportive of the political modernization process at one time, or on one scale, or in one set of circumstances are capable of being counterproductive in others. [II]

...That if the quality of leadership is held constant, authoritarian and oligarchic forms of government may be superior to democratic forms in the earlier stages of political development. [III]

...That, despite the existence of an authoritarian political system to begin with, significant liberalizing tendencies may be inherent in the modernization process. [IV]

...That the history of the democratization of Japan emphasizes the importance of gradual preparation and preparation in depth for the attainment of a viable democratic political system. [V]

Collective reading of these five selected propositions points us to some basic causes for the dilemma in modern Japan's political development. Here we take the liberty of shifting these propositions around. In order to make the point clear, we present one of many possible rearrangements: In Japan, fear of foreign intervention stimulated rapid political modernization (proposition I). This requirement for rapid modernization resulted in the creation of essentially oligarchic rule, and the Japanese experience indeed seems to have supported the carefully qualified proposition III. The course of modern Japanese history shows that oligarchic rule in the end could not completely forestall the trend toward liberalism (proposition IV). And if we agree with proposition V that consequently the "gradual preparation and preparation in depth for the attainment of a viable democratic political system" is important, how could such a huge stumbling block as proposition II be avoided?

This dilemma grows more complex when we consider it in the context of foreign policy making, which, as stated above, requires high quality leadership and a more skeptical view of the capability of democracy in foreign policy making. For example, how can we ensure that the quality of leadership will be constant during the period of transition? How can "a viable democracy" (from the point of view of desirable foreign policy making, this must be at least as viable as an oligarchic system with good leadership) emerge out of the original oligarchic system? If gradual liberalization and democratization are inevitable, might not an oligarchic state develop toward a situation in which no viable democracy emerges but instead a deteriorated leadership heads a government that is somewhere between the original oligarchic state and a viable democracy, without having the advantages of either? Was not this the dilemma in which modern Japan found itself, particularly in the realm of foreign policy?

We hope that the present study will provide an empirical case that will test the validity of Ward's propositions and lead us to a better understanding of the dilemma modern Japan faced, particularly in foreign policy making, as shown in our free rearrangement of these propositions. Although we confine ourselves here to the case of Japan, we believe it has relevance and interest to the study of political development in general.

The importance of this exercise will be fully attested to as we examine the nature of Japanese politics during the period under study. The Russo-Japanese War stands at the midpoint of Japan's modern century, which in both domestic and foreign affairs was one of the most crucial periods for modern Japan.[11] Internally, it was a period of transition, marked by a gradual shift and decline in Genrō politics, the rise of second-generation political elites, further development in party politics, and the emergence of more diversified interests in Japanese society as the inevitable consequence of modernization. It is also regarded as an immediate prelude to the appearance of the masses on the political scene. Externally, this period saw the island nation, which had been forced to face the vicissitudes of the outside world merely half a century before, emerge as a world power, achieve equality with the West, and embark on ambitious colonial enterprises. With these achievements, Japan's relations with other world powers naturally changed. Japan joined in the power struggles among the leading nations of the world for supremacy on the Asian continent and in the Pacific. Japan, to which Asian nationalists had looked as a source of inspiration in their struggles with the West, became instead a new menace to neighboring states. Traditionally friendly relations between Japan and the United States reached a turning point, initiating a power contest between the two nations that lasted 40 long years.

Thus an examination of the characteristics of Japan's oligarchic foreign policy making at this point in its political history is particularly significant. It will assist us in understanding the growing dilemma of Japanese political development and foreign policy in the latter half of its modern century and, at the same time, lead us to a more balanced view of the achievements of Japan's rapid modernization.

Scholars, as noted above, have cited effective coordination between the civilian and military sectors in the Japanese political process as one major reason for Japan's success in the war against Russia. They have, in turn, cited the rivalry between the two sectors as the major cause of trouble in a latter period; there are some excellent studies that deal with this issue of civil-military rivalry.[12] When and how did coordination turn into rivalry? At the time of the Russo-Japanese War, what factors prevented rivalry from emerging as the major issue? In what sense was the policy-making process during the Russo-Japanese War already a seedbed for rivalry? In this study we hope to provide a background for an understanding of the later period of civil-military rivalry.

This study is divided into five parts. Part One first discusses the constitutional structure and components of Japan's oligarchic foreign policy making at the time of the Russo-Japanese War, then examines Japanese attitudes toward foreign relations during the Meiji period to discover their general tendency and the nature of the dichotomy between the attitudes of the oligarchy, on the one hand, and the political activists, on the other. The domestic political setting having been described, Part Two traces how and why the oligarchs decided to go to war and how the political activists worked for war, in order to determine the role of the political activists and their impact on the oligarchs' decision for war. Part Three examines how the oligarchs prepared for the conclusion of peace, how the political activists looked at the progress of the war, and what they expected out of it. The Portsmouth Conference is described primarily to see how the differences in views between the oligarchy and the political activists were exposed.

Part Four deals with domestic repercussions to the concluded peace. How was the public mobilized for the anti-treaty movement? How did the Hibiya anti-peace treaty riot develop and what occurred? This part of the study is particularly interesting for several reasons. First, a survey of the available literature on the interrelationships between domestic political process and foreign policy shows that most of these studies stop at the point at which a policy has been reached. They do not extend their investigations to a study of the formulation or the impact of foreign policy on the domestic political scene. In other words, domestic reaction to a policy is rarely examined. As long as we regard a state as an ongoing entity, the picture is not complete unless we cover domestic repercussions within the purview of our study. For domestic reaction to a previous policy is remembered by both the public and the decision-makers and thus forms an internal setting for ensuing policy formulation that will in turn influence decisional outcomes. The importance of this aspect of the study is obvious when we consider a case study in a nondemocratic system. For the capabilities of such a system cannot be adequately measured until we observe the domestic reactions to a policy, which often constitute a delayed payment for the seemingly smooth operation of the system during the process of policy formulation.

Second, the domestic repercussions of the Portsmouth Treaty resulted in major rioting in the city of Tokyo on the day the treaty was signed, the first violent urban mass demonstration arising from popular opposition to an international treaty concluded by the Japanese government. The second occurrence was in May and June of 1960 over the question of the revised United States-Japan Security Treaty. These episodes together provide useful materials for the study of the nature of the Japanese political process at two different points in time and under two different political systems. They raise many questions; for example, what caused these uproars and why did those protesting resort to extra-parliamentary tactics? Fully analyzed and compared, the two incidents might reveal both constant and changing features of Japan's political process. They might provide valuable material for the study of political violence in general. The fact that these episodes occurred, one under a nondemocratic system and the other under a working democracy, provides interesting material for a comparative study of the impact of domestic political processes upon foreign policy making in two different systems. The 1960 "Security Treaty crisis" has been the subject of several comprehensive studies in both English and Japanese.[13] The earlier episode still awaits such a study. It has been dealt with in a few articles and several police studies, all in Japanese. For these reasons, the September 1905 "antitreaty riot" is examined here, not only as a case study of the capabilities of oligarchic foreign policy making, but also as an independent subject of interest to the study of the political process in modern Japan. To clarify the causes and nature of the riot, we shall compare our findings with some widely held views of this particular riot and with the conclusions expressed in some leading studies of riots in general.

Part Five summarizes the characteristics of oligarchic foreign policy making as revealed in this study and draws some conclusions as to the strengths and weaknesses of the system. These conclusions will, in turn, point to some of the causes of the dilemma in foreign policy making in prewar Japan.

PART ONE
Structure and Attitudes

CHAPTER ONE

THE OLIGARCHIC STRUCTURE OF JAPAN'S FOREIGN POLICY MAKING

ON February 11, 1889, the 2549th anniversary of the legendary founding of the Japanese state, the Meiji Emperor, as a token of imperial benevolence to his subjects, promulgated a constitution. The constitution, which had been drafted and ratified in strict secrecy by his trusted advisers, climaxed two decades of political consolidation and experimentation following the Meiji Restoration,[1] and until 1945 it determined the basic political structure of Imperial Japan. From the point of view of the drafters, the constitution was an instrument by which they intended to regularize and solidify the structure and functioning of their political authority. It made some limited concessions to the principle of modern constitutionalism by providing for a national parliament and guaranteeing "within the limits of law" the rights of subjects. One striking feature of the Meiji Constitution, however, was that the conduct and control of a broad area of state affairs were exclusively vested in the hands of the Emperor.[2] One of the more important of these imperial prerogatives was the making of foreign policy. Thus, according to the provisions of the Meiji Constitution, the Emperor was to formulate and execute Japan's foreign policy with the assistance of his advisers but without consulting the Diet at all. In short, the Meiji Constitution created a dualism in Japan's policy-making process. In domestic policy making, limited but significant popular participation was guaranteed by the establishment of the Diet. In foreign policy making, however, no provision was made for direct popular participation. This chapter will describe this oligarchic structure and the components of Japan's foreign policy making at the time of the Russo-Japanese War (1904–1905).

The Emperor's Prerogatives

The Meiji Constitution stipulates that the reigning Emperor is the sovereign of the state and the sole ultimate repository of all state powers: executive, legislative, and judicial. Thus the Preamble to the constitution declares: "The rights of sovereignty of the State, We have inherited from Our Ancestors, and We shall bequeath them to Our descendants." Article I provides: "The Empire of Japan shall be reigned over and governed by a line of Emperors unbroken for ages eternal."

Under the constitution the power to make wars and treaties was exclusively that of the Emperor. Article 13 reads: "The Emperor declares war, makes peace, and concludes treaties." Itō Hirobumi, the drafter of the constitution, commented on the provision as follows:

Declaration of war, conclusion of peace and of treaties with foreign countries are the exclusive rights of the Sovereign concerning which no consent of the Diet is required.

He then gives two prime reasons for the stipulation:

For, in the first place, it is desirable that a Monarch should manifest the unity of the sovereign power that represents the State in its intercourse with foreign powers; and in the second, in war and treaty matters, promptness in forming plans according to the nature of the crisis is of paramount importance.

In concluding his commentary on the basic article on the control of Japan's foreign policy making, he reiterates:

The principal objective of the present Article is to state that the Emperor shall dispose of all matters relating to foreign intercourse, with the advice of His ministers, but allowing no interference by the Diet therein.[3]

Scholars, liberal as well as conservative, agree unanimously as to the unlimited character of the imperial prerogative to conclude treaties and declare war.[4] Hozumi Yatsuka, professor of constitutional law at Tokyo Imperial University, who is regarded as the representative of the conservative interpreters of the basic law, states: "The conclusion of treaties is reserved to the personal sanction and autocratic action of the Emperor." Minobe Tatsukichi of the same university, who is regarded as a champion of a liberal interpretation of the constitution, admits: "Power to declare war, conclude peace, and make treaties belongs to the Emperor unconditionally, Article XIII so provides."[5]

In practice, however, the "personal rule of the Emperor" was largely fictitious. Not only was the Emperor to act only on the counsel of his constitutional and extra-constitutional advisers, but furthermore, he rarely exercised his personal power in policy making. Emperor Meiji, who is believed to be politically and militarily the most active of the three emperors of modern Japan, was no exception to this rule.[6] It may be closer to reality to state that the Emperor's authority was delegated to a complex array of advisers. In other words, the essential role of the Emperor was not so much to render his personal decisions on policy matters as to legitimize with his prestige and ritualized acts the political decisions his advisers made in his name. It was this complex advisory system, the coordination of which it was originally expected would be maintained by imperial moral leadership, that changed the disarmingly succinct constitutional provision for the control of Japan's foreign policy making into a maze of political power struggles. At the time of the Russo-Japanese War, the following elements, of varying degrees of importance, constituted the Emperor's advisory system: the Genrō (elder statesmen), the ministers of state, the military leadership, and the Privy Council.

Emperor Meiji, born in 1852, ascended to the imperial throne in the eventful year of 1867, when he succeeded his conservative father Emperor Kōmei. He was quickly made the symbol of national unity and independence by the modernizing Meiji oligarchs. His role in this new Japan, however, did not remain in the realm of morality and spiritual aspiration. As Herschel Webb puts it, "The Meiji Emperor was not only near the government; he was a member of it."[7] In fact, he was head of the government and supreme commander of the army and navy. More important, in practice he was the sanctifier of the political authority the modernizing oligarchs wielded in their desperate efforts to build a moderinized Japan. Emperor Meiji's stature grew in the eyes of the public throughout those turbulent years, as political consolidation of the nation was accomplished in his name and as the national power of his imperial state rapidly increased, overcoming both internal and external obstacles. Now, in 1904, Emperor Meiji stood at the pinnacle of his personal prestige and national aspiration. During the Russo-Japanese War, an official biography of the Emperor reports, he worked assiduously, going through military reports day and night.[8]

The Genrō

It is ironic and at the same time indicative of the nature of Japan's political process that it is possible to describe this informal, extra-constitutional, and extra-legal group of elders as the most influential of the Emperor's advisers.[9]

This informal advisory body had two basic functions. First, being regarded as the Emperor's highest advisory organ by virtue of political experience and past achievements, it was to advise the Emperor on crucial problems facing the nation, both internal and external: the selection of prime ministers and decisions concerning war and peace, to name but two. Second, the Genrō, with its prestige and power, was to assist the Emperor to unify and coordinate the various elements of the imperial decision-making structure. This function of the group came to be of vital importance once the Emperor's moral leadership alone proved insufficient to maintain unity and coordination among the various organs of the state, for the constitution provided no specific instrument to assume this task for the Emperor.

Varying opinions have been expressed about the qualifications for Genrō membership. It is equally difficult to pinpoint exactly when this informal advisory body emerged, but as Roger F. Hackett points out, it is important to note "that the institution took shape at the time that the new political structure [under the constitution] had been completed."[10] In other words, this informal body was not to be abolished with the establishment of constitutional government. Rather, it might even be said that the constitution was predicated on the continued existence of this powerful group of political leaders. One might go one step further and say that the drafters of the constitution had consciously or unconsciously written the Genrō into the constitution with invisible ink as a continuing organ to unify and coordinate the various overlapping and competing elements of the state under the "immutable fundamental law."

Who were the five Genrō in 1904? What were their characteristics? First, let us look briefly at their biographies.

Marquis Itō Hirobumi was born in 1841 into a poor peasant family of Chōshū. Later, together with his parents, he was adopted into a family of the lowest samurai rank (*keisotsu*) named Itō. He studied under the loyalist Yoshida Shōin and learned some Western military techniques from the Dutch in Nagasaki. He joined the loyalist movement under the leadership of Kido Takayoshi and Takasugi Shinsaku, participated in the attack on the British legation in 1862, and was promoted to upper samurai rank (*shibun*) for his loyalist activities. In 1863, while studying in London with Inoue Kaoru, he became convinced of the folly of the "expel the barbarians" (*jōi*) policy and, in 1864, tried in vain to dissuade the Chōshū clan leaders from fighting the squadron of the four Western powers. In 1868 he joined the new Meiji government and thereafter held a wide variety of offices in foreign relations, finance, and industry. In 1870 he studied banking and financial policy in America and in the following year joined the Iwakura Mission, traveling in both America and Europe. In the 1873 "Korean debate" he sided with Ōkubo Toshimichi.

Following Ōkubo's assassination in 1878, Itō became one of the most important members of the government and, when Ōkuma Shigenobu of Hizen was ousted from the government in 1881, assumed the most influential position in the Meiji regime. In 1882 he traveled to various European nations, studying their constitutional systems. In 1885 he concluded the Treaty of Tientsin with Li Hung-chang over the Korean issue and in the same year became the first prime minister under the new cabinet system that he had created. Meanwhile, he drafted the Imperial Constitution and in 1888, as president of the Privy Council, presided over the final discussions of the constitution that had been drafted. In 1892 he made his first abortive efforts to form a political party but instead formed the second Itō Cabinet, under which Japan fought the Sino-Japanese War. During the war he attended the Imperial Headquarters conferences to ensure coordination between military and foreign policies. Itō represented Japan at the Shimonoseki Peace Conference in 1895. In 1898 he formed the third Itō Cabinet and tried a second time to form a political party. When he failed, he recommended the establishment of a "party cabinet" under the leadership of Ōkuma Shigenobu and Itagaki Taisuke. In 1900 he established a political party, the Rikken Seiyūkai (Association of Friends of Constitutional Government), and in September formed the fourth Itō Cabinet. In 1901, during the first Katsura Cabinet, Itō traveled to America and Europe. His efforts to reach an agreement with Russia failed when the Katsura government concluded the first Anglo-Japanese Alliance early in 1902. In July 1903, by imperial order, Itō reassumed the presidency of the Privy Council and left the

Seiyūkai. He forsook his earlier belief in a "transcendental cabinet" and compromised with the party politicians. Generally regarded as pro-Russian, Itō is considered to have been the "most trusted adviser of the Emperor."[11]

Field Marshal Marquis Yamagata Aritomo, also a Chōshū man, was born in 1838 into a family of the lowest samurai rank. He studied under Yoshida Shōin and participated in the loyalist movement. In 1863 he became a commander of the Chōshū Kiheitai (irregular troop units composed of samurai and commoners); in 1864 he was wounded during the bombardment of the coastal defenses of Chōshū. During the anti-Tokugawa campaigns, he commanded the loyalist forces that defeated the Aizu clan troops in northern Japan. He held various important military positions in the new Meiji government and in 1869 went to Europe for a year and a half of study. In 1872 he became the commander of the Imperial Guards (konoehei) and prepared the conscription law issued in January 1873. In June 1873, he was appointed minister of the army and commanded the government forces during the 1877 Satsuma Rebellion. In December 1878, he adopted the German general staff system, establishing the principle that in matters of miltiary command the chief of staff was under the direct command of the Emperor, with the right of direct access to him and completely independent of the minister of the army and the civilian government. In the same year he issued the Gunjin Kunkai (Admonition to the Military), stressing the traditional virtues of loyalty, bravery, and obedience. In 1882 the Emperor, at Yamagata's request, issued the Gunjin Chokuyu (Imperial Rescript to Soldiers and Sailors), emphasizing the "supreme command" of the Emperor over the army and navy.

In 1883 Yamagata became minister of home affairs and, from 1885 on, as minister of home affairs in the first Itō Cabinet, he reorganized the police and local government systems. He was instrumental in the issuance of the Peace Preservation Law of 1887. In October 1888 he traveled to Europe and America to make a study of local government. The first Yamagata Cabinet was formed in December 1890, the year he was promoted to the rank of general of the army. He also promoted the drafting and issuance of the 1890 Imperial Rescript on Education. In 1892 he joined the second Itō Cabinet as minister of justice but in March 1893 was appointed president of the Privy Council.

During the Sino-Japanese War, Yamagata assumed command of the

First Army and in March 1895 again became minister of the army. He represented Japan at the coronation of the Russian emperor in 1896 and in June concluded an agreement with Russian Foreign Minister Lobanov, placing the two contracting powers on an equal footing as to rights and privileges in Korea. Promoted to the rank of field marshal in 1898, he became a member of the *Gensuifu* (Board of Field Marshals and Fleet Admirals). In November 1898, he formed the second Yamagata Cabinet. In 1900 he expanded the power of the Privy Council, issued peace preservation police laws (*chian keisatsu hō*) to suppress labor and peasant movements, and stipulated that only officers of the two highest ranks in active service could be appointed army or navy ministers. During 1901 and early 1902, he assisted Premier Katsura Tarō in concluding the Anglo-Japanese Alliance. In July 1903, he became a member of the Privy Council. A year later he succeeded Ōyama Iwao, who became commander of the Manchurian forces, as army chief of staff and remained in that position throughout the Russo-Japanese War. Regarded as the founder of the modern Japanese army, he enjoyed great personal power, both in the army and in the home ministry. He was a literal believer in the principle of imperial rule and in a transcendental cabinet and was very reluctant to make any concessions to party politicians.[12]

Count Matsukata Masayoshi was born in 1835 into a low-ranking samurai family of Satsuma. He participated in the anti-Tokugawa campaigns and in 1868 joined the new government, in which he held various positions in the home ministry as well as in financial affairs. He traveled to several European countries in 1878. In 1880 he was appointed minister of home affairs and, in 1881, became minister of finance, remaining in that position until 1892. He succeeded in restoring and consolidating the financial base of the regime; in 1882 he founded the Bank of Japan. The first Matsukata Cabinet was formed in 1891. In 1896 he resumed the premiership and brought about the monetary reforms following the conclusion of the Sino-Japanese War. In 1898 he became minister of finance for a second time, this time in the second Yamagata Cabinet. In July 1903, he was appointed to the Privy Council. Regarded as a financial genius, during the Russo-Japanese War he assisted the minister of finance in solving the special budgetary problems caused by the war.[13]

Count Inoue Kaoru was another Chōshū man, born in 1836 into a samurai family. Like Itō, he joined the loyalist movement and in 1862 participated in the attack on the British legation. In 1863 he went to London to study with Itō Hirobumi and others; there he came to believe that the *jōi* policy was nonsense. In 1864 he and Itō tried in vain to prevent the Chōshū clan from fighting the squadron of the four Western powers. Thereafter he tried to persuade the clan to focus on anti-Tokugawa policy and was attacked by an assassin for his views. He hovered between life and death for several days, but finally survived and participated actively in the anti-Tokugawa campaign.

In 1868 he joined the new government, in which he held a wide variety of positions in foreign relations and finance. He left the government temporarily in 1873 to engage in private business, but returned in 1875 as a member of the *Genrōin* (Senate). In 1876 he helped Kuroda Kiyotaka to conclude the Treaty of Kanghwa that "opened" Korea. In June of that year he traveled to Europe to study financial and economic policy. On his return to Japan in July 1878, he was appointed minister of industry, then became minister of foreign affairs in September 1879. In 1884 he went to Korea as ambassador. As minister of foreign affairs in the first Itō Cabinet, he tried in 1885, by means of an extreme pro-Western policy, to effect treaty revisions. In 1888 he became minister of agriculture and commerce in the Kuroda Cabinet; then in 1892, he became minister of home affairs in the second Itō Cabinet. During the Sino-Japanese War he was in Korea, where he promoted Korean domestic reforms. In 1898 he became minister of finance in the third Itō Cabinet. In May 1901, after the fall of the fourth Itō Cabinet, he received an imperial order to form a cabinet but was unsuccessful. During the Anglo-Japanese Alliance negotiations, he sided with Itō in favoring an agreement with Russia. He joined Matsukata in assisting the minister of finance during the Russo-Japanese War. Regarded as "the dean of Japanese business circles," he acted in close concert with Itō Hirobumi.[14]

Field Marshal Marquis Ōyama Iwao, a Satsuma man, was born in 1842 into a samurai family. He was the cousin of Saigō Takamori, whom he resembled. Ōyama participated in the fight against the British fleet that bombarded Kagoshima in 1863, and during the anti-Tokugawa campaigns he commanded a Satsuma gunnery troop. After joining the new government, he was sent to Europe in 1870 to observe the Franco-

Prussian War. He returned to Japan in March 1871 and was promoted first to the rank of colonel and then to major general. In November, however, he resigned his government position in order to study in France. He returned in 1874 and resumed his rank of major general. For a short time in 1876 he was commander of the Kumamoto Garrison, then fought in Kyushu as a brigade commander during the 1877 Satsuma Rebellion, and in 1878 was promoted to the rank of lieutenant-general and appointed vice-chief of staff of the army. In 1880 he became minister of the army and in 1882 army chief of staff. After traveling to Europe in 1884 to study military systems there, he was appointed minister of the army in the first Itō Cabinet in 1885, remaining in the post during several succeeding cabinets. In 1891 he was promoted to the rank of general of the army and for a short time was a member of the Privy Council. In 1892 he returned to active service and again became minister of the army. During the Sino-Japanese War, he commanded the Second Army. In 1898 he was promoted to the rank of field marshal and joined the Gensuifu (Board of Field Marshals and Fleet Admirals). In 1899 he was appointed army chief of staff, remaining in that position until he became commander of the Manchurian Army in June 1904. He considered himself a soldier and showed little interest in politics.[15]

Several general characteristics can be ascertained from these brief biographies: (1) The five Genrō came from either Satsuma (Matsukata and Ōyama) or Chōshū (Itō, Inoue, and Yamagata). (2) All except Itō, who was of peasant origin, were of lower samurai background. (3) They were old men—their average age in 1904 was 66 years. (4) All had participated in the loyalist movement and in the anti-Tokugawa campaigns during the last years of the Shogunate. (5) Because of a youthful encounter with the overwhelming power of the West—Itō and Inoue during their study trips to London in 1863, the others during the Western powers' bombardment of their coastal defenses in 1863 and 1864—all had early realized the folly of the *jōi* policy. (6) They had all joined the new Meiji government at its inception and had accumulated wide administrative and executive experience at different levels in the bureaucracy, in civil and/or military affairs. (7) All had repeatedly held cabinet posts, and three of them—Itō, Yamagata, and Matsukata— had held the premiership (Itō four times, Yamagata and Matsukata

twice each). With Kuroda Kiyotaka, who died in 1900, they monopolized the post of prime minister until 1901, except for the brief period
of the Ōkuma-Itagaki Cabinet in 1898. (8) They had all traveled extensively abroad, acquired solid, first-hand knowledge of the West, and
accumulated, in varying degrees, personal experience in dealing with
the Western powers.

The high qualifications and impressive credentials of the Emperor's
highest advisory body are apparent. But several other points should be
particularly noted.

First, their political experience, achievement in both civil and military
affairs, concurrent appointments in high military positions and in the
Privy Council, long lists of personal followers serving in the government, and the confidence placed in them by the Emperor should have
been powerful assets to them in the control, unification, and coordination of the various elements in the power structure under the Meiji
Constitution.[16]

Second, the group should not be regarded as monolithic. There were
causes for actual and potential disunity and even rivalry; for instance,
conflict between the Satsuma and Chōshū forces and personal friction
among the Genrō because of individual differences in political beliefs
and policy priorities, notably between Itō and Yamagata. And yet one
should not overstress this point. As Edwin O. Reischauer observes:[17]

There was no concealing the divergence of views between Yamagata, determined to keep what he viewed as the emperor's own military forces and
bureaucracy free from control by petty-minded businessmen, and Itō, the
agile politician, prepared to make any compromises necessary to win the support of the parliament he had created. But neither Itō, with his strong following in the bureaucracy, nor Yamagata, with his even more powerful
following in the military establishment as well as the bureaucracy, attempted
to use his base of power against the other. The interests uniting them were
greater than those dividing them. Both were devoted to the same dream of
creating a strong and rich Japan, and Itō's hopes for a powerful military and
firm leadership by the Elder Statesmen differed only in degree from those of
Yamagata. They both did their best to continue the cooperation that had
started in their revolutionary youth in Chōshū, making what concessions they
could to each other.

Finally, and more important than the question of the group's internal
unity, the power position of the Genrō vis-a-vis other elements in the

state must be considered. The position of the Genrō in this situation was far from static. More precisely, it was in transition and, at the time of the Russo-Japanese War, in a definite decline. This will become clearer as we discuss the next category of the Emperor's advisers, the ministers of state in the Katsura Cabinet.

The Ministers of State

The word "cabinet" (*naikaku*), like "Genrō," is nowhere found in the Meiji Constitution. The cabinet system was created in 1885, four years before the promulgation of the constitution. This measure was taken at least partly because the Meiji leaders wanted no interference from the Diet in the reorganization of the executive organ. After 1889 the cabinet as an institution was continued, with recognition in Article 76 of the constitution, as a collective body consisting of a prime minister and nine departmental ministers.[18] In this section we shall describe, first, the legal function of the cabinet in Japan's foreign policy making[19] and, second, the components and characteristics of the Katsura Cabinet.

The Meiji Constitution, on the one hand, established that the Emperor was not accountable to the law, declaring in Article 3: "The Emperor is sacred and inviolable." On the other hand, Article 55, the only article in the constitution that deals directly with the ministers of state, provides: "The respective Ministers of State shall give their advice to the Emperor, and be responsible for it. All laws, Imperial Ordinances, and Imperial Rescripts of whatever kind, that relate to the affairs of the State, require the countersignature of a Minister of State." This meant that the Emperor's prerogatives over foreign policy making could be exercised only with the advice of a minister of state.

In reality, however, the power of the cabinet in advising the throne was neither as extensive nor as complete as Article 55 might suggest. There seem to have been three basic factors that weakened the powers of the cabinet.

First, as we have already noted, the cabinet was merely one of the Emperor's advisory organs. Its advisory power was shared by the Genrō, the Privy Council, and the military. Second, as we shall see later, the doctrine of the independence of the supreme command placed matters concerning military command outside the power of the cabinet. Within the cabinet, moreover, this doctrine of the independence of the supreme command resulted in the creation of a "dual cabinet." Article 7 of the

Imperial Ordinance of the Organization of the Cabinet (*naikaku kansei*) of December 24, 1889, provides:

With the exception of those items which may be submitted to the cabinet [for deliberation] by imperial order, matters concerning military secrets (*gunki*) and military command (*gunrei*), which have been reported directly to the Emperor, shall be reported to the Prime Minister by the Ministers of the Army and the Navy.[20]

This provision did not clearly extend to the ministers of the army and the navy the "right of direct access to the throne" (*iaku jōsō*), which had originally been enjoyed only by the chiefs of staff of both services. In fact, the provision did not specify who had the "right of direct access." Nevertheless, it was used by the military to give a statutory basis to their customary practice, which gave the right of direct access to the ministers and chiefs of staff of both services. This created a situation in which military matters that had been reported to the prime minister by the service ministers would often not be divulged to other cabinet members at all. Worse yet, because many military matters were first reported directly to the Emperor by his service ministers, when they were finally referred to the prime minister, they were often *faits accomplis* that the prime minister found difficult to change even if they greatly affected the position of the cabinet in matters such as national defense planning.[21] The problem tended to grow more serious, for the exact scope of the military matters referred to in the provision was, as in the case of the "supreme command," never clearly defined and relative power positions at a specific time and circumstances were, in practice, the final arbiter. Thus, within the cabinet the service ministers held a dual role: they were heads of departments, like other civil ministers, and at the same time they were participants in the supreme command.[22]

This situation was further aggravated by the establishment in 1900, under the second Yamagata Cabinet, of the rule that only generals or lieutenant-generals on active service could be appointed minister of the army and only admirals or vice-admirals could be pointed minister of the navy. This requirement not only prohibited the appointment of a civilian to the position of service minister, but it also placed the prime minister and his cabinet at the mercy of the army and the navy. If the army or the navy refused to furnish a qualified officer, the prime minister could not form a cabinet; and even when a cabinet was formed, it could be destroyed by the resignation of one of the service ministers.[23]

Third, despite the views and wishes of liberal interpreters of the Meiji Constitution, the principle of collective responsibility of the cabinet was never established. Rather, the individual ministers of state were regarded as being directly responsible to the Emperor, and the prime minister did not have the clear power to control them. Yet it was generally agreed that cabinet decisions required unanimity; consequently one or more ministers could cause a cabinet to fall by refusing to make a cabinet decision unamimous.[24]

The Cabinet and the Diet

As we observed earlier, under the Meiji Constitution the Diet had no power to participate directly in treaty and war making. How much control could the Diet then exert over the ministers of state, whose duty it was to advise the Emperor in making foreign policy? According to Article 10 of the constitution, their primary responsibility was unquestionably to the Emperor, who had the sole power to appoint and remove them.[25]

Legal opinion was divided as to the nature of cabinet responsibility to the Diet. Whatever this responsibility was, however, it was indirect and political, not legal, responsibility.[26] Itō Hirobumi commented:

The appointment and dismissal of [the ministers of state] having been included by the Constitution in the sovereign power of the Emperor, it is only a legitimate consequence that the power of deciding as to the responsibility of Ministers is withheld from the Diet. But the Diet may put questions to the Ministers and demand open answers from them before the public, and it may also present addresses to the Sovereign setting forth its opinions. Moreover, although the Emperor reserves to Himself in the Constitution the right of appointing His Ministers at His pleasure, in making an appointment the susceptibilities of the public mind must also be taken into consideration. This may be regarded as an indirect method of controlling the responsibility of Ministers. . . . Ministers are directly responsible to the Emperor and indirectly so to the people.[27]

Thus it is clear that the Diet could resort only to indirect measures to control the ministers of state, to such measures as parliamentary interpellations, the passing of resolutions, the presentation of addresses to the throne, and representations to the government. In other words, the power of the Diet over ministers of state was limited to the power of exhortation and criticism, and the Diet had no legal authority to force the ministers to comply with its views. Actually, even this indirect power was rendered more ineffectual by virtue of the fact that the cabinet was only one of the Emperor's advisory organs and his other advisory bodies were even further beyond the reach of Diet influence. Thus, as far as the constitution was concerned, very little power over the ministers of state was given to the Diet. In the final analysis, the degree of power the Diet could exert over the ministers of state, and thus over the making of Japan's foreign policy, depended upon the political strength of the Diet in relation to the other organs of the state. We shall return to the general question of the wartime Diet and political parties later in this chapter. Let us turn now to a discussion of the components and characteristics of the first Katsura Cabinet.

The First Katsura Cabinet

On May 2, 1901, Prime Minister Itō Hirobumi, having failed to maintain unity on budgetary policy among the members of his cabinet, submitted his resignation to the Emperor. To find a successor, the Genrō had to hold more than ten conferences before the first Katsura Cabinet was formed on June 2, exactly one month later. The fall of the fourth Itō Cabinet and the unwillingness and inability of the Genrō to form a cabinet to succeed it showed clearly that the aging Genrō were unable to manage the intricate handling of political parties necessary to solve the increasingly aggravating financial problems of the nation.[28]

From a broader historical perspective, what happened during this month had far-reaching consequences in Japan's domestic politics and, as we shall see in Chapter 3, significantly affected its foreign policy during the ensuing turbulent years. The event signified the end of one era in Japanese political history and the beginning of another. Since 1885 the Genrō had practically monopolized the premiership, but from the first Katsura Cabinet on, none of the Genrō was to reassume the post of prime minister. They withdrew instead to the backstage of politics and from there tried, with increasing difficulty, to continue to control their political protégés and other members of the second generation political elite who had replaced them as standard-bearers. As long as the members of the Genrō maintained their power, without their expressed or tacit approval it was not possible to form a cabinet or to formulate and execute important domestic and foreign policy decisions. Eventually, however, the second generation political leaders began utilizing the prestige and power of the Genrō to their own advantage, rather than remain subservient and contented followers of the older men. The period of the first Katsura Cabinet, during which the Russo-Japanese War was fought, marked the clear beginning of this transition in the power relationship between the Genrō and their protégés.

The anxiety of the Genrō about the erosion of their power over state affairs and about the capabilities of the emerging second generation, to whom they had entrusted the reins of government, was revealed in a specific agreement concerning foreign policy making between the Genrō and the first Katsura Cabinet. The agreement stipulated that important foreign policy issues should be decided upon by a Genrō conference attended by various ministers of state as well as the Genrō, and that more important questions should be referred to, and decided by, an imperial conference attended by relevant ministers of state as well as the Genrō in the presence of the Emperor.[29]

Who were the members of this second generation political elite who served in the first Katsura Cabinet at the time of the war against Russia? Brief biographies of these ten cabinet members follow.

Count Katsura Tarō, Prime Minister and General of the Army, was born into a Chōshū samurai family in 1847. During his youth he joined the loyalist movement and participated in the anti-Tokugawa campaigns. In 1870 Katsura went to Germany to study the German military system and, in 1874, a year after his return, was appointed captain. From 1875 to 1878 he served in Germany as military attaché in the Japanese legation. In 1882 he was promoted to the rank of colonel. In 1884 Katsura accompanied Minister of the Army Ōyama Iwao to Europe on an inspection tour of European military systems. He was promoted to the rank of major general in May 1885 and became vice-minister of the army in March of the following year. During these years, Katsura ably assisted Yamagata and Ōyama in various reforms of the Japanese army. Made a lieutenant-general in 1890, he served during the Sino-Japanese War in Manchuria as a commander in Yamagata's army. For his performance in the campaign he was elevated to the peerage in 1895 with the title of viscount. From January 1898 to December 1900, Katsura was minister of the army in the Itō, Ōkuma, and Yamagata cabinets. Meanwhile, he was promoted to the rank of general of the army in September 1898. In June 1901, as we saw above, Katsura formed his first cabinet. He was Yamagata's protégé and, like his mentor, showed considerable talent both as a politician and as a soldier. It was during the Russo-Japanese War that Katsura began showing signs of independence of Yamagata and asserted a stronger position for the second generation political elite.[30]

Baron Yamamoto Gonnohyōe, Admiral and Minister of the Navy, was born in 1852, the third son of a Satsuma samurai. During the anti-Tokugawa campaigns, he joined the Satsuma forces and engaged in the battles of Fushimi and Toba in 1868 and the battle of Hakodate in the following year. In 1870 Yamamoto entered a naval academy and was appointed a naval cadet when he graduated from the school in 1874. In January 1877, he was assigned to a German warship in order to study navigation, thus beginning his sea service, which lasted more than ten years. In 1893 Yamamoto, by then a captain, was appointed chief secretary in the navy ministry; during the Sino-Japanese War he held the posts of aide to the navy minister at Imperial Headquarters, chief of the naval military affairs bureau, and naval staff officer at Imperial Headquarters. Meanwhile, he was promoted to the rank of rear admiral in 1895 and to vice-admiral in May 1898. In November 1898, he was appointed minister of the navy in the second Yamagata Cabinet and remained in that post until January 1906, throughout the fourth Itō Cabinet and the first Katsura Cabinet. Thus he was a lifelong naval officer and one of the most influential leaders of the Satsuma naval clique, particularly after 1902, when the Satsuma Genrō Admiral Saigō Tsugumichi died. Yamamoto made relentless efforts to safeguard and expand naval interests in Japanese military planning. In the first Katsura Cabinet he was regarded as the "deputy prime minister."[31]

Baron Komura Jutarō, the Minister of Foreign Affairs, was born in 1855 into a samurai family of the Obi clan in Kyushu. In 1869 he went to Nagasaki to learn English and in 1871 was chosen by his clan for a scholarship to a college in Tokyo, which later became Tokyo Imperial University. Upon graduating in 1874, he was sent by the Japanese government to study at Harvard Law School. When he returned to Japan in 1880 after completing his studies at Harvard and gaining some practical training in New York, he was appointed a judge in the Tokyo-Osaka area. In 1884, however, he entered the Ministry of Foreign Affairs, where for about ten years his primary responsibility was translating official correspondence. In 1893 he was discovered by Foreign Minister Mutsu Munemitsu, who appointed him first secretary of the Japanese legation in Peking. As acting minister in Peking when the Sino-Japanese War approached, Komura warned the home government that war with China was inevitable and advised the Japanese leaders to commence hostilities early. During the war he served first as the chief civil administrator of the areas under Japanese occupation in Manchuria and then as chief of the Foreign Ministry's political affairs bureau. From October 1895 to June 1896, Komura was stationed in Korea, before returning to Japan as vice-minister of foreign affairs.

In September 1898, Komura became minister plenipotentiary to the United States but was transferred to Russia in April 1900. Soon afterward, the Boxer uprising took him to Peking again, where he represented Japan as minister plenipotentiary in the international conferences that negotiated with the Ching court for a post-uprising settlement. In September 1901, Komura was ordered back to Tokyo to assume the post of foreign minister in the first Katsura Cabinet. He worked with Katsura for the conclusion of the Anglo-Japanese Alliance of 1902, in opposition to the Russo-Japanese agreement that Itō and Inoue had been trying to consummate. During those years, Komura advocated a strong policy toward Russia, anticipating early a war that was in the end inevitable. It was in this belief, as we shall see in Chapter 3, that Komura conducted prewar negotiations with Russia. He represented Japan at the peace conference in Portsmouth.

Two items in Komura's biography are noteworthy. First, he was not from one of the feudal clans from which most of the Meiji oligarchs came. This fact seems to have affected Komura's career greatly and conditioned his behavior as a policy-maker. As we have noted, until he was recognized and promoted by Mutsu, another "non-clan" Meiji politician, Komura seemed doomed to remain a useful but undistinguished official in the Foreign Ministry.[32] Like many other ambitious "non-clan" youths of his day, Komura had once aspired to destroy the clan oligarchy in the Meiji government, but he chose to work from inside rather than to attack the oligarchy from outside by joining the political opposition. His earlier aspirations seem gradually to have left him, and he died in 1911, a truly successful Meiji bureaucrat and the Emperor's loyal servant. Komura was, nevertheless, a black sheep among the Meiji decision-makers. A Komura biographer tells us that in his later years Komura viewed Japan as surrounded by the Western powers, just as he had once seen his weak native clan oppressed by the powerful clans surrounding it.[33]

This brings us to the second point. Komura advocated a markedly strong foreign policy. In the eyes of those who regard the Sino-Japanese War, the Anglo-Japanese Alliance, and the Russo-Japanese War as unequivocal victories for Japanese diplomacy, Komura was the greatest foreign minister Japan has ever produced.[34] Within the circle of decision-makers, Komura deliberately but cautiously promoted a strong policy toward the Asian continent, and his biographies reveal his extensive and close associations with those Japanese nationalists who worked for Japanese expansion on the continent.

Perhaps the best summation of Komura's career is found in a remark allegedly made by Tōyama Mitsuru, the dean of Japanese ultranationalists and the founder of the Genyōsha (Dark Ocean Society). When General Nogi Maresuke, commander of the Japanese troops that attacked Port Arthur during the Russo-Japanese War, followed the Emperor Meiji in death, Tōyama said: "His Imperial Majesty must be pleased, for he is accompanied by Komura in the front and Nogi in the rear."[35]

Minister of the Army, Lieutenant-General Terauchi Masatake was born in 1852 into a Chōshū samurai family and was later adopted by his maternal grandfather. Terauchi joined the Chōshū forces during the anti-Tokugawa campaigns. Ōmura Masujirō, who initiated the building of Japan's modern army, recognized Terauchi's ability and recommended him for study at an army academy in Osaka. In 1871 Terauchi was appointed a lieutenant in the army. During the Satsuma Rebellion, he was a captain in the Imperial Guards Regiment and engaged in the most decisive engagement of the campaign, the Battle of Taharazaka, during which he was permanently injured in his right arm. He was nevertheless retained in active service. In 1883 Terauchi was sent to France as a military attaché in the Japanese legation; thereafter he held various army posts including secretary to the minister of the army, principal of the Army Officers School, and chief of the first bureau of the Army General Staff. In 1894 Terauchi was promoted to the rank of major-general. During the Sino-Japanese War, he was in charge of military transportation and communications. In 1898 he was appointed the first inspector general of military education. After serving successively as vice-chief of the Army General Staff and president of the Army War College, in March 1902 Terauchi was appointed minister of the army in the first Katsura Cabinet, a post he held for ten years. He was the leader of the Chōshū army clique.[36]

Minister of Finance, Baron Sone Arasuke was born into a Chōshū samurai family in 1849. During the anti-Tokugawa campaigns, he engaged in several battles in northeastern Japan. Beginning in 1872, he studied in France; after his return to Japan in 1877, he held a wide variety of government posts. He conducted research in preparation for the establishment of the national parliament. Sone served as the first secretary-general of the House of Representatives from 1890, when the Diet was convened, until 1892, when he resigned to run successfully for the seat from Yamaguchi in the Diet. Soon thereafter, he was elected vice-speaker of the House of Representatives. A year later, Sone was appointed minister plenipotentiary to France, charged with negotiating with the French authorities for treaty revisions. In 1898 he became minister of justice in the third Itō Cabinet and later joined the second Yamagata Cabinet as minister of agriculture and commerce. In September 1900, Sone was appointed a member of the House of Peers. When the first Katsura Cabinet was formed in 1901, he became minister of finance. In 1902 he was given the title of baron for his role in concluding the Anglo-Japanese Alliance. During the Russo-Japanese War, it was Sone's task to grapple with the difficult problems of wartime finance.[37]

Minister of Home Affairs, Viscount Yoshikawa Akimasa was born in Tokushima in 1841. After studying in America for several years, in 1870 he joined the Meiji government and held various posts in the fields of industry and foreign affairs before he became governor of Tokyo in 1884. Thereafter he served as minister of justice and minister of communications in several cabinets. In June 1901, he became minister of communications in the first Katsura Cabinet and then was shifted to the post of minister of home affairs in February 1904.[38]

Minister of Agriculture and Commerce, Baron Kiyoura Keigo was born in 1850 into the family of a Buddhist priest and later adopted into a samurai family in Kumamoto. He joined the government service in 1873 and thereafter held various positions in the justice ministry. In 1896 Kiyoura became minister of justice in the second Matsukata Cabinet and served in the same capacity in the second Yamagata Cabinet. When the first Katsura Cabinet was formed in 1901, he held first the post of minister of justice and then, in 1903, was shifted to the post of minister of agriculture and commerce.[39]

Minister of Justice Hatano Takanao was born into a samurai family of Kojiro, Kyushu, in 1850. He entered government service in 1874. Before becoming vice-minister of justice in 1899, he held judgeships in courts of various levels. In September 1904, Hatano was appointed minister of justice in the first Katsura Cabinet.[40]

Minister of Communications Ōura Kanetake was born in 1850 into a samurai family of the Satsuma area under the jurisdiction of a branch family of the lord of Satsuma. Ōura was therefore regarded as one of the associate retainers (*baishin*) of the Satsuma clan. He began his government service in 1872 as a police officer in Tokyo, thereafter holding various police posts in such places as Tokyo, Osaka, and Shimane. In 1893 Ōura was appointed governor of Shimane prefecture. Ōura was made chief of the Metropolitan Police Board under the second Yamagata Cabinet. He left the post during the fourth Itō Cabinet, only to reassume it upon the formation of the first Katsura Cabinet.[41]

Minister of Education Kubota Yuzuru was born into a samurai family from Hyōgo in 1847. Later he studied at Fukuzawa Yukichi's Keiō Gijuku. In 1872 he entered government service and held various posts in the education ministry. In September 1903, he was appointed minister of education in the first Katsura Cabinet.[42]

The emergence of the first Katsura Cabinet signaled an important change in Japanese politics. Not only did it put an end to the tradition of Genrō premiership, but for the first time no Genrō served in the cabinet at all. For this reason, the first Katsura Cabinet was sometimes nicknamed the "second-rate cabinet" (*niryū naikaku*) or the "three-day cabinet" (*mikka naikaku*).[43] It was composed entirely of the emerging second generation, a generation that as a whole had had far less experience than the original Genrō group in dealing with the internal and external turmoil of the Meiji Restoration. In 1904 the average age of the cabinet ministers was 55 years, in contrast to the 66 years of the Genrō. An age difference of more than ten years between the two groups during this stormy era inevitably caused significant differences in the extent and quality of their experiences with the surrounding world. Moreover, five of the ten cabinet members came from clans that had been far less involved in the turbulent events of the Restoration period; consequently, the impact on this second generation of the Restoration, which had conditioned the thoughts and behavior of the Genrō, was not nearly so profound. While both groups felt fear and anguish at the prospect of a weak Japan faced with the Western onslaught, the new leaders were more aware of, and impressed by, Japan's increasingly rapid development into a strong, modern state. In other words, the second generation felt more confidence in Japan's capabilities than did the Genrō, and they were thus more forward-looking and aggressive in their dealings with the outside world than were the more cautious Genrō. This changing situation was the background of the Katsura Cabinet's agreement with the Genrō concerning the procedures for foreign policy making.

In domestic politics, of course, the second generation leaders could not totally disregard the power of the Genrō. In fact, Genrō support was still the condition for any cabinet's survival. But in the face of the gradual shift in power relations during the period of the first Katsura Cabinet, the Genrō found it increasingly difficult to maintain their control over the nation's affairs. At the same time, as the substance of control gradually shifted into the hands of the second generation, the new leaders showed that the old political forms would be retained as long as they served to support the new power balance.

This somewhat ambivalent attitude on the part of the new leaders may be observed in the composition of the first Katsura Cabinet, which was essentially under Satchō domination. Not only were five of the ten cabinet posts occupied by men from Satsuma or Chōshū, but, except for Komura, Prime Minister Katsura and the other "non-clan" members were regarded as bureaucratic followers of the Genrō Yamagata. Two alternatives, it has been noted, were open to "non-clan" political as-

pirants in the early years of the Meiji era. The first was to become one
of the "bureaucratic technicians" (*gijutsu kanryō*) whose services were
indispensable in the rapid modernization of Japan. The other was to
join the political opposition and work for the destruction of the clan
oligarchy through public criticism of governmental policies and the
promotion of party politics. Journalism and law were the professions
most commonly entered by adherents of this second approach.[44] The
"non-clan" members of the first Katsura Cabinet had chosen the first
road and successfully climbed the bureaucratic ladder, and in the
process their political outlook seems to have changed. Once they achieved
the high positions of cabinet ministers, they identified more with the
oligarchic government than with the forces working for the destruction
of that political structure and seemed more interested in expanding
their power within the framework of the existing oligarchic structure.
In this sense, the first Katsura Cabinet, without a single party member,
was a reaction against the movement toward party government.

The first Katsura Cabinet was held in low esteem in the beginning.
Several persons refused to join the cabinet when they were approached
by Katsura, and those who did join did so only reluctantly.[45] The only
exception seems to have been Foreign Minister Komura, who ignored
the warnings and advice of friends who were loath to see his rising
reputation damaged by association with a cabinet that, they thought,
would not last more than three months. In joining the cabinet, Komura
had a specific objective that was fully shared by Katsura. He is reported
to have told his advisers that he alone would take charge of the post-
Boxer Rebellion Manchurian question and that three months would be
sufficient time to conclude an Anglo-Japanese alliance checkmating
Russian expansion in Manchuria.[46]

In spite of an initial unpopularity, the prestige of the first Katsura
Cabinet gradually grew. Its public image was changed considerably by
the successful conclusion of the Anglo-Japanese Alliance in January
1902. Through a skillful use of hard- and soft-sell methods, it managed
to weather stormy Diet sessions and get finance bills passed. Whenever
necessary, it relied upon Yamagata's support and guidance and upon a
friendly House of Peers. In dealing with the Seiyūkai, the leading party
in the Diet, Katsura made use of the influence of its president, Itō
Hirobumi, as long as the latter could control the party for the benefit

of the government; when Itō's power over the Seiyūkai was widely challenged by party members, Katsura schemed to have the Emperor order Itō to reassume the presidency of the Privy Council in July of 1903. Thereafter, the Katsura Cabinet's relations with the Seiyūkai were greatly enhanced through direct dealings with the new top leadership of the party, who shared the basic aspirations of the second-generation political elite.

The Military

In the Meiji Constitution decisions concerning military command (*gunrei*) and military administration (*gunsei*) were designated as exclusive imperial prerogatives (Articles 11 and 12),[47] and no parliamentary interference was allowed in the exercise of these prerogatives.[48] Moreover, with the establishment of the general staff system in 1878, the doctrine of the independence of the supreme command (*tōsuiken no dokuritsu*) was recognized and put into practice. According to this doctrine, both the army and the navy were under the personal command of the Emperor as commander-in-chief, and the supreme military command (*gunrei*) of both services was exercised by the Emperor through military advisers who were separate from, and independent of, the civilian ministers of state who advised the throne on general affairs of state.[49]

Article 11 was generally interpreted as a confirmation of this doctrine and thus constituted an important exception to Article 55, which specified that the imperial prerogative over affairs of state could be exercised only upon the advice of a minister of state. Contrary to this, Article 12 was interpreted to mean that imperial power over the military administration (*gunsei*) was to be exercised through responsible ministers of state. However, the distinction between the supreme command (*gunrei*) and the military administration (*gunsei*) was never clearly established, and as a result, the demarcation between them had to be worked out in practice. Actual power relationships between the military and the civilian government came to be the determining factor, increasingly to the advantage of the former.[50]

At the time of the Russo-Japanese War, the Emperor's military advisers were the chief of the Army General Staff and the chief of the Navy General Staff, and the ministers of the army and of the navy, whose dual role gave them the right of direct access to the Emperor (*iaku jōsō*).[51] At the time of the Russo-Japanese War, the principle of a unified command under the chief of the Army General Staff had been discarded, and the chiefs of the army and navy general staffs were considered to be equal, individually responsible for their respective staff organizations and jointly responsible for planning and executing co-ordinated operations.[52] We must also include among the Emperor's military advisers the vice-chiefs of the general staffs of both services, for, as we shall see in Chapter 3, they played a significant role in the process of formulating policy toward the war. The two service ministers have already been discussed, but it is important to note that the post of chief of the Army General Staff was consecutively occupied by two Genrō, Ōyama Iwao and Yamagata Aritomo.

Chief of the Navy General Staff, Viscount Admiral Itō Sukeyuki was born in 1843 into a Satsuma samurai family. His experience in the British bombardment of Kagoshima in 1863 led him to choose the navy as his career. After serving in the Satsuma naval forces during the anti-Tokugawa campaigns, he entered the navy under the Meiji government. In 1881 he was promoted to the rank of vice-admiral. During the Sino-Japanese War, he was the commander of Japan's combined fleet; for his meritorious deeds in the war, Itō was elevated to the peerage with the title of viscount. He was appointed chief of the Navy General Staff in 1895 and remained in the post for about ten years, including the entire period of the Russo-Japanese War. Itō was a leading elder of the Satsuma naval clique. His prestige in the navy was considered to be equal to that of Yamagata in the army. Itō, however, remained a sailor and showed no interest in politics. In spite of the legal equality of the general staffs of the two services, Itō Sukeyuki was overshadowed by his army counterparts during the war against Russia. The strong-minded navy minister, Yamamoto, may also have contributed to this situation.[53]

Vice-Chief of the Army General Staff, Viscount General Kodama Gentarō was born in 1852 into a samurai family of the Tokuyama clan. After participating in the anti-Tokugawa campaigns, he joined the new Meiji army and for several years engaged in the suppression of rebels such as those in the Saga and Satsuma rebellions. In May 1885, he was appointed chief of the first bureau of the Army General Staff; then, in

October 1887, he became president of the Army War College. In June 1891, he traveled to Europe to study military education. Upon his return home in August 1892, he was appointed vice-minister of the army and chief of the military affairs bureau. During the Sino-Japanese War, Kodama was an army staff officer at Imperial Headquarters. In August 1895, he was given the title of baron and in the following year was promoted to the rank of lieutenant-general. Kodama became governor-general of Taiwan in February 1898 and was soon promoted to viscount. In December 1900, Kodama was appointed minister of the army in the fourth Itō Cabinet and remained in the post when the first Katsura Cabinet was formed. He later assumed the posts of minister of education and minister of home affairs.

In October 1903, when war clouds were gathering over Manchuria, Kodama, disregarding the obvious demotion in rank, assumed the post of vice-chief of the Army General Staff, which had been vacated by the sudden death of his predecessor. He was promoted to the rank of general of the army in June 1904. Kodama played an important role in the formulation of the Japanese policy for war against Russia. He left his post as vice-chief in June 1904, in order to become chief of staff of the Manchurian forces under Ōyama Iwao's command. As we shall see later, he was instrumental in facilitating coordination between the civil and military leaders for termination of the war.[54]

Vice-Chief of the Navy General Staff, Vice-Admiral Ijūin Gorō was born in 1852 to a Satsuma samurai family. After participating in various battles during the anti-Tokugawa campaigns, Ijūin entered a naval academy in 1871 and in 1883 was graduated from the British Naval Academy. He was a naval staff officer at Imperial Headquarters during the Sino-Japanese War; after the war, he was promoted to the rank of rear admiral and appointed vice-chief of the Navy General Staff. He served for several years as the commander of Japan's standing fleet before reassuming in 1902 the post of vice-chief, which he held until November 1906. As we shall observe later, during the prewar negotiations with Russia he attended some of the Genrō and imperial conferences that made the decision for war.[55]

Two additional bodies had at least the theoretical duty of advising the Emperor on important military affairs: the Gensuifu (Board of Field Marshals and Fleet Admirals) and the Gunji Sangiin (Supreme War

Council). During the Russo-Japanese War, however, they exerted little influence.[56]

With the outbreak of war, the Daihon'ei (Imperial Headquarters) was established, as it had been at the time of the Sino-Japanese War. Unlike its predecessors, however, Imperial Headquarters was not used for making important decisions during the Russo-Japanese War. Rather, it became a place where staff officers of both services reported formally to the Emperor strictly on matters concerning military operations.[57] The Genrō conference, which was usually followed by an imperial conference, continued throughout the war as the highest decision-making organ on military and foreign policy issues.

The Privy Council

The Meiji Constitution provided no procedure for the ratification of treaties. However, in accordance with Article 56 of the constitution, which stipulates in general terms the duties of the Privy Council, and with an imperial ordinance on the organization of the Council, international treaties were usually submitted to the Privy Council before receiving the Emperor's signature.[58]

Privy Councillors were appointed for life by the Emperor upon the recommendation of the prime minister. They had no responsibility to the Diet. Ministers of state, by virtue of their office, were entitled to sit in the Council and had the right to vote in plenary sessions, which required the attendance of more than ten councillors and as a rule were held in the presence of the Emperor. Recommendations of the Privy Council to the throne were adopted by a majority vote.[59]

When serious disagreements between the Privy Council and the cabinet arose, the Privy Council could significantly intervene in the cabinet's foreign policy-making activities. Some vivid examples of this occurred in the 1920s and 1930s.

At the time of the ratification of the Portsmouth Treaty in October 1905, there was no serious disagreement between the Privy Council and the cabinet. If there were any individual complaints about the treaty on the part of the councillors, they certainly had no effect on the attitude of the Council as a whole. A closer look at the composition of the Privy Council at the time of the Portsmouth Treaty clearly shows that it was unlikely that the Privy Council would raise any serious opposition to the treaty, which was supported by the Genrō, the ministers of state, and the military leaders.[60]

At the time the treaty was signed, there were 27 councillors, including the president (Itō Hirobumi) and the vice-president. Three Genrō (Itō, Yamagata, and Matsukata) were included. The councillors' domain origins were as follows:

Satsuma	8	Owari	1
Chōshū	7	Banshū (Akō)	1
[Satchō]	[15]	Mita	1
Tosa	4	Tokushima	1
Court	2	Nagasaki	1
Hizen	1		

All were high-ranking bureaucrats and a few served in the military. They were either "clan" members or "bureaucrat-technicians."[61]

The Imperial Conference and the Oligarchs

Thus far we have discussed those officials who were actually or theoretically in a position to make decisions on foreign policy under the Meiji Constitution, a total of exactly 50 individuals of different degrees of importance within the system. Some played continuing and vital roles in the policy-making process, while some had only peripheral parts as members of the Supreme War Council or, like the non-Genrō members of the Privy Council, appeared only at specific stages.

In any government it is difficult to determine precisely which individuals are the decision-makers.[62] In this study, however, we should like to propose that those who attended the imperial conferences were the foreign policy decision-makers in the oligarchic structure established by the Meiji Constitution. As we have seen, the first Katsura Cabinet agreed that important foreign policy questions were to be discussed and decided upon by the Genrō conference and/or the imperial conference—records show that the cabinet faithfully adhered to this understanding. It is true that imperial conferences in most instances were held merely to give imperial sanction to decisions already reached in the Genrō conferences. To say that those who attended imperial conferences constituted the decision-making oligarchy, however, does not omit any of the real decision-makers, for those present at imperial conferences included all those who attended the Genrō conferences.

Four major imperial conferences were held at the time of the Russo-Japanese War, each following a Genrō conference at which the real policy decision had been made: on June 23, 1903, when Japan decided to initiate negotiations with Russia; on January 12, 1904, when the Japanese government decided to send another, final proposal to the Russians; on February 4, 1904, when the decision for war was made; and on August 28, 1905, when the oligarchs decided upon the final instruction ordering plenipotentiary Komura to accept the terms of peace without indemnity.[63]

The following is a list of these foreign policy-makers:[64]

Name	Position	Place of Origin	Age
Mutsuhito	Emperor	Court	52
Itō Hirobumi	Genrō; President of the Privy Council	Chōshū	63
Yamagata Aritomo	Genrō; Chief of Army General Staff	Chōshū	66
Matsukata Masayoshi	Genrō	Satsuma	69
Inoue Kaoru	Genrō	Chōshū	68
Ōyama Iwao	Genrō; Chief of Army General Staff; Commander, Manchurian forces	Satsuma	62
Katsura Tarō	Prime Minister	Chōshū	56
Yamamoto Gonnohyōe	Navy Minister	Satsuma	52
Komura Jutarō	Foreign Minister	Obi	49
Terauchi Masatake	Army Minister	Chōshū	52
Sone Arasuke	Finance Minister	Chōshū	55
Itō Sukeyuki	Chief of Navy General Staff	Satsuma	61
Kodama Gentarō	Vice-Chief of Army General Staff; Chief of Staff, Manchurian forces	Tokuyama	52
Ijūin Gorō	Vice-Chief of Navy General Staff	Satsuma	52

At the time of the Russo-Japanese War, this foreign policy-making oligarchy contained elements contributing to both unity and disunity. It was a small group of 14 men whose average age was 58 years in 1904. Eleven of these men, including all five Genrō, came from the two western clans that dominated the political scene throughout the Meiji period. They had had similar experience in internal and external affairs during those years of kaleidoscopic change, and they shared similar aspirations to build a rich nation with a strong army as rapidly as possible. Basic unity among them was maintained by a shared sense of national crisis.

And yet signs of potential disunity also existed. The oligarchy was not a monolithic body but a collection of several parts unified by the Genrō at the top. The Genrō group itself consisted of five strong-willed men with individual specializations and policy preferences. Furthermore, a "generation gap" was noticeable between the Genrō and the younger leaders within the oligarchy, despite overall similarities in experience and geographical backgrounds.

The second-generation leadership showed more internal divergence than did the Genrō. The power position of the Genrō was in transition —more exactly speaking, in decline—to the advantage of the emerging second generation. Because the Genrō group was in actuality the sole unifier of this multigroup system of advisers to the Emperor, the growing weakness of Genrō control meant increasing cause for rivalry among the various components, for example, between the civilian and the military and between the army and the navy.

Note must also be taken of the peculiar role that the Diet and the political parties played in this oligarchic system gradually undergoing an internal transformation. The Meiji Constitution excluded the Diet from the foreign policy-making process and placed responsibility totally in the hands of the Emperor and his advisers. The Diet had no power over the appointment and removal of those foreign policy decision-makers, and at the time of the Russo-Japanese War, no party man as such was included among the oligarchs. The Diet had little formal, direct power that would allow its views to influence foreign policy decisions. Should we then completely dismiss the Diet and the political parties from the picture?

The traditional view of Japanese wartime Diets holds that, in the excited atmosphere of patriotism following the outbreak of war, the Diet immediately drops all activities opposing the government and meets only to rubberstamp whatever military expenditure bills the government proposes.[65] This view is too superficial, at least in regard to the Russo-Japanese War. We shall discuss later how the political parties took advantage of the golden opportunity provided by the war to promote their own political interests. Suffice it to say here, however, that in-fighting between the political parties and the government continued throughout the war, and the constant maneuvering and scheming had at least two major consequences. First, it contributed to a further weakening of the control of the Genrō over the second-generation leaders. Second, the political parties completely failed to provide the political communication so direly needed, particularly during the last stages of the war, in order to prevent the gap between the oligarchy and the public from widening. Along with the oligarchs, who by inclination and because of the basis of their political power, had little regard for the sentiments of the populace, the political parties helped create a dangerous situation in which, as we shall observe in the following chapters, what we term "political activists"—generally uninformed, chauvinistic groups and individuals—were given a free hand to take advantage of the situation and incite the masses.

Japan's oligarchic foreign policy-making structure at the time of the Russo-Japanese War was, then, a small group made up of many parts under the declining control of the Genrō, with internal factors conducive to both unity and disunity. This exclusive group was not free from the gradual intrusion of political parties from the outside, an intrusion that in turn accelerated the pace of the internal power transformation. Firm in the conviction that they had a monopoly on wisdom in foreign policy-making, the oligarchs acted as advisers to the throne from which they derived their political power and legitimacy.

CHAPTER TWO

THE DICHOTOMY IN ATTITUDES
ON FOREIGN RELATIONS

A NOTED student of Japanese foreign relations, Kiyosawa Kiyoshi, wrote in 1942:

What impresses one when he surveys the history of Japanese diplomacy . . . is the fact that public opinion in Japan has always demanded a strong foreign policy, while government policy has always been cautious. During ninety years of diplomatic relations between Japan and the outside world since the last days of the Tokugawa, I cannot name even one cabinet that has not been subjected to public attack for its weak diplomacy; perhaps the only exceptions are the first and second Konoe cabinets. No one would deny that Mutsu Munemitsu and Komura [Jutarō] were the ablest foreign ministers in the history of Japanese diplomacy. When we look back, however, we see that no other foreign ministers were more severely castigated by the public for their alleged incompetence than these two. Mutsu's diplomacy in the first Sino-Japanese War was rewarded by a vote of non-confidence in the House of Representatives. The consequence of Komura's diplomacy in the war against Russia was the most serious riot the city of Tokyo had ever known. In the area of foreign relations, the Japanese public's cooperation with the government has always commenced with the start of a war and ended with its termination. Diplomacy has been a synonym for weakness, and it has been the target of public rage. . . . It is a common belief, held persistently by the Japanese public since the last days of Tokugawa, that foreign policy objectives can be achieved only if the government takes a forceful stand, and that the lack of diplomatic success is always caused by government failure to take such a stand. For whatever reasons there may be, it is an undeniable fact that advocacy of strong foreign policy has always been the basic stand of our public opinion. Public opinion is by nature irresponsible and emotional. When one thinks of our foreign policy, he must always think of this peculiar national sentiment. A remarkable feature of this sentiment is that persistent expansionism constitutes its core . . . and our experience in the past tells us that only a powerful cabinet can succeed in controlling and guiding such public opinion and its demands for strong foreign policy.[1]

It is debatable whether or not Japanese government policy has always been cautious. Kiyosawa's view that Japanese public opinion has always demanded a stronger foreign policy than the government provided, however, has been shared by a number of scholars of modern Japanese history.[2] Public opinion during the period of the Russo-Japanese War was no exception to this view. This period is, in fact, a prime example of the conflict between strong public opinion and cautious government policy.

It is the purpose of this chapter to trace briefly the historical background of this dichotomy between the decision-makers and the public in their attitudes toward foreign relations and to examine the types of individuals that created and led public opinion at the time of the Russo-Japanese War.

Two points should be made clear from the start. First, the dichotomy of attitudes between the oligarchic decision-makers and the public opinion leaders was fundamentally created by the distinct differences in responsibility and experience these two segments had had in state affairs. Such a dichotomy might be expected, to a greater or lesser degree, in any nation. During the Meiji period, however, decision making had early been monopolized by the leading oligarchs. In terms of both institutions and practice, few channels existed through which those outside the government could share responsibilities and experiences in handling foreign affairs, and very little constructive exchange of opinion on foreign policy took place between the decision-makers and those outside the government.[3] In other words, very little was done to minimize the dichotomy when it emerged at the very inception of the new Meiji regime.

Second, the leading advocates of a strong foreign policy during the Meiji period tended increasingly to be those whose aspirations to high government office were less immediate or sanguine. Either as a political tactic to embarrass the oligarchy or out of ideological conviction, the liberals, party politicians, and ardent nationalists demanded that the government take a strong stand in foreign relations. Meiji political history, particularly after the promulgation of the constitution, shows, however, a gradual rearrangement within the ranks of the anti-oligarchic forces. Broadly speaking, those who had moved closer to the locus of political power, both on the national scene and within individual political parties, started to reveal a greater measure of understanding for the oligarchy and for their policy. Consequently, advocacy of a strong foreign policy came increasingly to be concentrated among journalists, intellectuals (including some university professors), not so successful party politicians, and, most important of all, members of nationalistic societies. In this study, we shall refer to this category of people as "political activists."[4]

Throughout the Meiji period, the aspiration and resolve shared by all those concerned with the fate of the nation were that Japan strive to maintain its national independence in a world dominated by the Western powers. The one point of agreement among political leaders both inside and outside the government was that, in order to achieve this objective and to regain a position of equality with the West, Japan had to pursue vigorously a policy of *fukoku kyōhei* (enrich the nation and strengthen its army).[5] In short, differences between various groups of Meiji political leaders involved only method and timing, not ultimate objectives. This was as true of foreign relations as of domestic policy.[6] Both those responsible for national policy and those critical of it shared the same slogan and aim, *fukoku kyōhei*. The policy-makers, however, because of the responsibility of office and a growing awareness of their vested interest in the existing power structure, early differentiated between program and slogan, and, as a result, differences of opinion began to emerge. Realizing that many individual steps must be taken before a destination could be reached, the policy-makers became aware that each step could not always be taken when they desired. They soon learned the necessity of waiting for the opportune moment for each forward step.

The critics of the government failed to make such a distinction between program and slogan, or they deliberately refused to do so, because of their political stand or their ignorance of reality. In any case, their opposition to government policy in the area of Japan's foreign relations derived largely from their perpetual lack of first-hand experience and of a sense of responsibility for the affairs of state. Consequently, they overlooked this step-by-step process and instead demanded that Japan at once leap forward to the ultimate goal. Their clamor for a stronger foreign policy and their attack on the "timidity" of the government enjoyed an air of legitimacy, for the early attainment of a position of security and equality among the world powers was the declared national goal of Meiji Japan.

The first instance of this conflict of opinion on foreign policy can be observed on January 1, 1868, in the reaction of a politically conscious segment of the Japanese public to the Imperial Proclamation on the Opening of International Intercourse, which announced the principle on which the new regime would conduct its foreign relations. The proclamation stated:

Relations with foreign countries being of the greatest importance, the late Emperor was long concerned about its [sic] establishment. The mistaken policy pursued by the Shogun Government had misled public opinion as to this question, with the result of the present confusion. Now that the changed condition of the country urges us to leave such a policy of seclusion, we so hereby make proclamation that henceforth international intercourse upon the basis of international rules is opened, and both Government and governed shall unite to achieve this, Our Intention.[7]

This proclamation obviously came as a great shock to many of those who had not dreamed that the new government would reverse the old order so drastically. They had expected that the new government, whose leaders had led the battle against the Tokugawa régime under the slogan *of Sonnō Jōi* (revere the Emperor and expel the barbarians), would pursue the same policy with increased vigor. The die-hard believers in *Sonnō Jōi* felt themselves betrayed by the new regime. Some of them proceeded to attack foreign residents in Japan in defiance of, and indignation at, the policy the new regime had decided so abruptly to follow.[8]

In making the proclamation, the leaders of the new regime had not intended to declare the dawn of a new era of internationalism in Japan; it was, rather, a tactical retreat. At the same time, by a deliberate distortion of historical facts, the leaders placed the entire blame for Japan's recent difficulties with the foreign powers upon the late Tokugawa government. Experiences during the last days of the Tokugawa era and rapidly increasing knowledge of the West had convinced the new leaders that the seclusion policy was impossible to enforce, and that their country urgently needed to be strengthened through westernization in order to become a unified state. Even during their campaigns against the Tokugawa regime, they had concluded that the *Jōi* policy must be modified and its execution postponed until Japan had become sufficiently strong. The *Jōi* policy then became a mere slogan that they exploited in order to rally national sentiment against the Tokugawa regime, which they accused of yielding meekly to the demands of the Western barbarians. The new government's declaration of a new principle in foreign relations was therefore nothing more than the explicit statement of a conclusion that its leaders had reached during the last days of Tokugawa rule. All the same, a precedent was established in the opening hours of the Meiji regime for a cautious and realistic diplomatic policy despite demands for a strong, unrealistic, and often chauvinistic foreign policy from that segment of the general public that was politically conscious but largely uninformed.

The *Seikan-ron* ("conquer Korea controversy") of 1873 served to widen the dichotomy. We need not go into the details of this significant episode here,[9] but three points may be noted: first, the debate within the decision-making circles of the Japanese government was not over the question of the ultimate goal. The desire to see Japan expand onto the Korean peninsula was shared both by those who demanded an immediate expedition to Korea and by those who opposed it. Second, as a consequence, the controversy was essentially over how and when such an expansionist policy should be implemented in Korea. The "internal reform faction," which placed the need for domestic consolidation and modernization ahead of an overseas adventure, won. The victors' conviction was fortified by fresh knowledge and impressions of the West, which the principal members of the faction had just visited. As may be observed in Ōkubo Toshimichi's oft-quoted opinion, the "internal reform faction" made a realistic appraisal of Japan's international position and anticipated that the nations who had such deep interests in Korea would not let Japan invade that region without protesting or intervening. Taking a long-range view, they then considered what impact this reaction on the part of the Powers might have on Japan and gave serious consideration to the financial burden such an expedition would place upon Japan. The victors clung to a rationalism and realism based on calm observation of Japan's situation, both internal and external.[10] The losers, in an excess of emotionalism, failed to see the issue in such wide perspective. Third, this "great divide" in the decision-making circles of the new Japan resulted in further concentration of governmental power in the hands of the Satchō oligarchy, which came virtually to monopolize positions of responsibility in the exercise of state power. Thus the dichotomy of opinion on foreign policy between the realistic and cautious oligarchic decision-makers and their political opponents was more firmly established.

The Satsuma Rebellion of 1877 proved the futility of armed resistance to the new regime. Some of those whom the Korean debate had turned into dissidents now began to focus their opposition to the oligarchy on the political arena. The details of the *Jiyū Minken Undō* (popular Political-Rights Movement) are not of concern here.[11] It should be noted, however, that from its inception the Political-Rights Movement was strongly tinged with nationalistic fervor. While not completely devoid of belief in political liberalism, it tended to give preference to building a strong state over securing wider political participation on the principle of individualism and freedom. This strong nationalism was manifest in the backgrounds of the leaders of the movement. It was, in fact, their argument that, in order to make a nation truly unified and strong, it was necessary to cultivate the political consciousness of the masses and to encourage their political participation. From the beginning, the movement tended to equate *minken* (popular political rights) with *kokken* (national power).[12]

Oka Yoshitake states that the exponents of the Jiyū Minken Undō viewed the international situation strictly from the standpoint of power politics (*jakuniku kyōshoku*—the strong devouring the weak) and believed that Asia was on the verge of falling prey to Western imperialism. On this point, their view was not much different from that of the oligarchic decision-makers. The sense of *taiketsu* (confrontation) with the West dominated the thinking of both the decision-makers and their opponents.[13] This same view, however, led the oligarchs down the road of caution and realism and their opponents down the road of chauvinism and adventurism. As the oligarchs' control of internal issues was solidified, their political opponents concentrated their attacks increasingly on foreign policy issues. No other issue appealed more effectively to the nationalistic sentiment of the public than foreign policy problems. The opposition could attack the government's cautious foreign policy as being contrary to declared national aspirations. During the 1880s and the first half of the 1890s, the question of treaty revision gave the opposition a constant opportunity to attack the oligarchic government.[14] In the eyes of the critics, the cautious, realistic, and conciliatory diplomacy of the government was simply too timid, clumsy, and humiliating to Japan's national honor. In the process, the opposition seems to have become convinced that the government was always too weak-kneed toward foreign powers and that, without their vigilance and warning, the oligarchs might decide upon a policy that would bring irrevocable national humiliation.

Victory in the Sino-Japanese War of 1894—1895 had several far-reaching effects upon Japan. First, it brought about a fundamental change in the Japanese attitude toward China. The Jiyū Minken Undō activists, as we have seen, anxiously viewed the countries on the Asian continent as easy prey for the Western powers. As Japan gradually grew more confident of its independence, they had cause to assert that the way to strengthen Asian solidarity vis-à-vis the West would be to conclude an alliance with China. This was, of course, a reflection of the weight of the Western threat upon the Japanese mind, but at the same time the idea of an alliance with China stemmed from the high esteem in which Japan had traditionally held China. As Japan's modernization accelerated, however, while China remained largely unmodernized, some exponents of Japan's continental policy, such as Fukuzawa Yukichi, Nakae Chōmin, and Ōi Kentarō, modified their views on China and Korea and began to urge that Japan engage in reform activities in these countries.[15] Japan's victory over China exposed the weakness of China. Now that Japan was a colonial power, people such as Fukuzawa Yukichi asserted that Japan should join the West rather than align itself with China. Japan could thereby obtain rights and interests on the continent and secure the territory necessary to guarantee its national security. This idea of *datsu-A* (cast-off Asia), in Fukuzawa's words, became dominant among the *Tairiku-ronsha* (continental activists) in Japan.[16] The same idea was readily applied to Korea. The Korean peninsula was traditionally considered a dagger pointing at the heart of Japan. At the same time, it was regarded as a foothold for Japan's continental expansion. Hence there was no disagreement between the Japanese decision-makers and their opponents about the fact that Korea, under the domination of a foreign power, would be an immediate threat to Japan's security. Now they were all the more anxious to maintain the Korean "independence" over which Japan had gone to war with China.

The results of the Sino-Japanese War were not entirely advantageous to Japan, however. Immediately after the conclusion of the Treaty of Shimonoseki, the Triple Intervention of Russia, Germany, and France occurred. This came as a great blow to Japan. Its national confidence, boosted immensely by the victorious war, was shattered. The Japanese found their country at the mercy of Western imperialism as the Liaotung

Peninsula, the "fruit of the Sino-Japanese War," was taken away. The entire nation, beginning with the Emperor, felt humiliated. To control the public outrage, the government had to resort to having the Emperor issue an imperial edict admonishing his subjects against rash actions.[17] Out of this bitter experience, a new nationalism arose. *Gashin shōtan* (suffer privation for revenge) became the slogan of the day. People such as Takayama Chogyū, Kimura Takatarō, and Inoue Tetsujirō proclaimed a new type of tradition-oriented, narrow-minded patriotism: *Nipponshugi* ("Nippon-ism"). They stressed the uniqueness of the Japanese culture and nation.

Another group, consisting of such nationalistic journalists as Shiga Shigetaka, Miyake Setsurei, Sugiura Jūkō, and Kuga Katsunan and the nationalistic Buddhist scholar Inoue Enryō, propagated *Kokusuishugi* ("national essence-ism"), which demanded an immediate solution to the unequal treaty question and endeavored to counteract the tide of westernization in Japan.[18] Tokutomi Sohō, editor (beginning in 1887) of the influential journal *Kokumin no Tomo*, editor of the liberal newspaper *Kokumin Shimbun,* and champion of *heiminshugi* (democratic liberalism and responsible cabinets), now became an ardent nationalist in bitterness over the Triple Intervention. He wrote in his autobiography: "It is no exaggeration to state that the return of the Liaotung Peninsula decided my fate. Thereafter I became a different man spiritually. Japan was forced to succumb to the Powers' will only because it was weak. I was convinced that, without power, justice and morality had no value at all."[19] As we shall see, Tokutomi Sohō became an advocate of a strong Japan before and above everything else and collaborated with the oligarchic government that had earlier been the object of his disdain.

Clearly, the Triple Intervention made Russia, whom the Japanese public believed to have spearheaded the intervention, the enemy in the war of revenge that was, they thought, sure to come in the near future. Russia had been the major threat to Japan from the north during the Tokugawa period. As early as 1871, Yamagata Aritomo, the builder of Japan's modern army, had drafted a defense plan envisaging Russia as Japan's "hypothetical enemy."[20] Some Japanese apparently remembered the Kurile-Sakhalin exchange of 1875 as a high-handed action of the northern bear against a helpless Japan.

The significance of *gashin shōtan* in modern Japanese history cannot be overemphasized. It began the rise of a frankly chauvinistic nationalism directed at one country, Russia. The Japanese government started a vigorous ten-year, arms-expansion program, aimed at a rapid and far-reaching development of land and naval forces, together with the establishment of the necessary basic industries. The total estimated expenses for the program came to 781.05 million yen, about nine times the entire national budget in 1893.[21] It consumed the bulk of the huge indemnity Japan had obtained from China and forced the government to resort to various tax increases. Because many of the new taxes were in the form of excise taxes on consumer goods, the lower-income classes suffered increased economic hardship. Yet the Japanese public somehow withstood the hardship, led by the slogan of *gashin shōtan* that kept alive their memories of the indignities Russia had visited upon their nation. In 1898 only three years after Japan was forced to return the Liaotung Peninsula to China on the grounds that Japanese control was detrimental to the peace of the Far East, Russia obtained the lease of the peninsula from China. This added insult to the injury that was still a bitter memory in the minds of the politically conscious segment of the Japanese public.

Neither the public outcry for revenge nor the arms-expansion program in anticipation of a war with Russia, however, characterized the basic foreign policy attitude of the oligarchs, who clearly differentiated slogan from program. While they prepared Japan for the worst eventuality, they sought through cautious and realistic measures to solve the problems caused in the Far East by the war with China. The conclusion of agreements on Korea with Tsarist Russia in 1896 and 1898 serves as evidence of their cautious policy.[22] It must be stressed here that, more than anything else, the Triple Intervention had an extremely sobering effect upon the oligarchic decision-makers. In the midst of national exultation over the victorious war and public outcry for revenge over the intervention, the oligarchs learned once again the need for caution and prudence, the fundamental characteristics of their foreign policy in the postwar years.

The Sino-Japanese War accelerated the trend toward compromise between the oligarchs and the party politicians. The background and development of this trend need not be discussed in detail here.[23] Suffice it to say that after initial clashes in the Imperial Diet between the political parties and the oligarchic government, a trend toward compromise gradually emerged. There were many reasons for this. The stormy Diet sessions provided opportunities for contending groups to size up both their own strengths and those of their opponents. As they learned that neither side could expect complete victory over the other, but that some compromise was required, both sides eventually came to adopt more realistic stands. The process was clearly accelerated when victory in the Sino-Japanese War enhanced the prestige of the government. By then, the political parties recognized more keenly than ever before the need for compromise with the oligarchs in order to achieve any position of power. The oligarchs, anticipating difficulties in managing the postwar government, were amenable to conciliatory overtures from the political parties.

With this trend toward compromise between the oligarchy and the political parties, a new power structure developed within the political parties also. Broadly speaking, there was a growing concentration of party leadership in the hands of those who held seats in the Diet. This might have been an inevitable result of the fact that, after 1890, the relative strengths of the political parties were measured in terms of the number of seats they held in the Diet. Diet membership thus became a prerequisite for any party politician desiring to influence governmental policy; eventually the political parties were split between those members who held Diet seats and those (*ingaidan*) who did not. As the compromising posture of the party leaders toward the oligarchy became more and more marked, vociferous attacks on the oligarchy were left to the party rank and file who were outside the Diet, or to those who may have held Diet seats but remained too low in the party hieracrhy to have benefited from the compromises between the party leaders and the oligarchs. But this tendency for the top party politicians to compromise with the oligarchs in behind-the-scenes confrontations had a wider implication. It left the field of criticism of the government's foreign policy and the leadership of anti-government public opinion increasingly in the hands of those who were more distant from the center of governmental responsibility. The government's critics therefore tended to be more unrealistic, "idealistic," and often chauvinistic. They were members of nationalistic societies, such as the Genyōsha, journalists, university professors, as well as not too successful party politicians. As noted earlier, they constituted the ranks of the political activists at the time of the Russo-Japanese War.

The Genyōsha (Dark Ocean Society), the most important nationalist group during the Meiji period, was founded in February 1881 at Fukuoka in Kyushu.[24] Its founders were all local veterans of the Korean expedition movement and included Hiraoka Kōtarō, a rich mining entrepreneur, and Tōyama Mitsuru, perhaps the best-known, ultra-nationalist in Japan. Saigō Takamori, who only a few years earlier had perished in the abortive rebellion against the central government, was the hero and guiding spirit of these dissident former samurai. The society's bylaws stressed three principles: to revere the imperial institution, to love Japan and uphold its national honor, and to defend the people's rights.[25] Its principal concern, however, was the promotion of Japanese overseas expansion. The society soon cast off its third principle, in the Genyōsha's own words, "like worn-out shoes," and participated vigorously in the Matsukata Cabinet's interference with the second national election in 1892.[26]

Doggedly demanding that the government assume a forceful stand in foreign relations, the society lodged violent protests against the oligarchs' *Ōka seisaku* (pro-westernization policy) and against the conciliatory treaty-revision proposals put forward by Foreign Ministers Inoue and Ōkuma. Kurushima Tsuneyoshi, who threw a bomb at Ōkuma, was a member of the Genyōsha; the official history of the society proudly describes the assassination attempt and Kurushima's suicide as a "righteous deed" and counts him among the society's martyrs. Some Genyōsha members, notably Uchida Ryōhei, later the founder of the Kokuryūkai (Amur River Society), became self-appointed executors of Japan's Korean policy. Their activities in Korea often caused serious international embarrassment for the Japanese government.

A strong consciousness of being members of an elite was another feature of this group of self-righteous, highly visionary adventurers, coloring their thought and behavior with a peculiar elitist heroism. The society therefore showed little interest in mass-based movement. How could this sort of society not merely survive but also grow in Meiji Japan and thereafter? The question touches upon a central issue of Japanese politics prior to the end of World War II.[27] For one thing, the society's nationalistic stand and expansionist aspirations were in essence shared also by the leaders of the government. In particular, its support for the imperial institution and the creed of *kokutai* (the divine national polity of Japan) served to forestall repression by the oligarchic government, whose claims to legitimacy were based upon the same institution and creed. Furthermore, although often unruly and troublesome, the society could at times be useful to the government. We have already mentioned how the Matsukata Cabinet made use of the society in the bloody national election. In wars such as those against China and, later, Russia, its members, with their specialized knowledge, served as interpreters, spies, and saboteurs. The society was, however, at best a *shishi shinchū no mushi* (parasite in a lion's body), its relative strength inversely proportional to the soundness of the Japanese political structure. In any event, at the turn of the century, the Genyōsha and other like-minded nationalist groups began vociferously to demand that the government formulate and implement speedy and forceful solutions to foreign policy issues.

It would be impossible to attempt here a comprehensive analysis of the extremely complex state of the Japanese press at the turn of the century. Reliable and precise data on the subject are both scant and inconclusive.[28] The briefest and most impressionistic account must, however, include the following points. First, the Japanese press in general traditionally took an anti-government stand. There were, of course, some official and semiofficial government organs. Criticism of the government, however, reflected the general attitude of the Japanese press. Journalism was one of the major channels open to non-*hambatsu* (non-clan) youth with political ambitions and served as a tool with which to attack the clan government. In every major political controversy—the popular Political-Rights Movement, treaty revision, the drafting of the constitution, the war against China, and the Triple Intervention—the press played a significant role, and repeated repression by the government through stringent press codes and libel laws, for example, merely served to antagonize the articulate segment of the public. The extreme politicization of the press hindered the development of neutral and objective news reporting.

It is true that after the Sino-Japanese War of 1894–1895 the newspapers became progressively more commercialized. Many newspapers ceased to be mere organs of political parties and began to assert their political independence. These newspapers also started to print more articles of a nonpolitical nature. This trend, however, did not greatly affect the generally anti-government stand of most leading newspapers. The positions of editorial writers on the more influential newspapers came to be occupied by well-known professional journalists who no longer regarded journalism as a stepping-stone to politics and claimed to be independent of both the government and the political parties. Many of them were extremely nationalistic, as we have already stated in discussing Japan after the Triple Intervention. With the growing tendency toward compromise between the oligarchic government and the top echelon of the political parties, these independent editorial writers assumed the role of anti-government critics.

Second, we must note the rapid increase in the circulation of newspapers and journals in Japan. After the Sino-Japanese War, the number of newspapers and their total circulation grew greatly in both metropolitan and provincial areas. In 1904 Japan was said to have 375 newspapers,[29] with perhaps as many as 160 local newspapers immediately before the outbreak of the Russo-Japanese War.[30] One source reports that at the time of the Sino-Japanese War there were 70,000 newspaper subscribers in the city of Tokyo and that the number grew to 200,000 before the outbreak of the war against Russia.[31]

There is no way to measure exactly the impact of the press on the Japanese public at the beginning of the twentieth century. It is safe to assume, however, that by the turn of the century the press played a significant role in influencing and leading the political orientation of the Japanese public. Virtually universal primary education; the resulting high literacy rate; growing urbanization; rapid developments in communications; and the restricted, yet significant, practice of suffrage must by then have made a large segment of the public politically attentive.[32]

Perhaps more important was the general character of the national ideology then being vigorously promoted among the public. A frankly nationalistic, emperor-centered educational system had been in operation for the ten years following the promulgation of the Imperial Rescript on Education in 1890.[33] The idea of Japan as a family state (*kazoku kokka*), with the Emperor as father and his subjects as children, had been effectively disseminated. This indoctrination was particularly concentrated on the lower classes, which were normally denied a more liberal higher education. The universal conscription system had had a similar effect upon the youth. They were imbued with a strong sense of loyalty to imperial Japan and the idea of *kazoku kokka* again was strongly propagated. The separation of the individual from the state, or of society and state, even became unnatural to many Japanese.[34] By the turn of the century, the emperor, whose name had been fully utilized by the oligarchs as an instrument of national mass mobilization, had become absolutely sacred and inviolable, so much so that the position of the oligarchs themselves was endangered. For the idea of the sanctity and inviolability of the emperor eventually gave rise to the doctrine of *kunsoku no kan* (evil advisers surrounding the emperor). Upholding the emperor as an infallible and always benevolent ruler, critics of the government attributed alleged misrule to the emperor's advisers. The advisers surrounding the emperor, the critics asserted, must have denied the emperor access to accurate information or, worst yet, supplied wrong information. Thus the oligarchic government, in justifying its rule and power in the name of the emperor, may have benefited from exalting the imperial institution so highly, but at the same time it invited attacks from the critics, also in the name of the emperor. The imperial institution thus proved to be a double-edged sword for the oligarchy.[35]

Early, though as yet relatively mild, evidence of this trend may be found in the frequent use made by the anti-oligarchic forces of memorials to the throne and by the oligarchs of imperial edicts or admonitions. It is important to note that the successful nationalistic indoctrination of the Japanese public by a strong central government had made a large segment of the public politically attentive. This segment was definitely more responsive to the call of vociferous nationalism than to the voice of caution and realism. Although we cannot describe here the public state of mind in more precise terms, there is no doubt that by the beginning of the twentieth century in Japan the masses were no longer the passive spectators that British Minister Alcock reported he had seen unconcernedly watching the foreign bombardment of the Chōshū batteries in 1864 and even helping the French troops dismantle the Japanese cannons.

Edward Shils has stated that an "oligarchic regime presupposes a situation of feeble public opinion. . . . Homogeneity of opinion is a desideratum of the modernizing oligarchy."[36] At the turn of the century, Japanese public opinion confronting the oligarchic formulators of foreign policy was anything but feeble and homogeneous.

PART TWO

The Decision for War

CHAPTER THREE

THE OLIGARCHS AND THE POLITICAL ACTIVISTS IN THE COMING OF WAR WITH RUSSIA

THE Russo-Japanese War broke out on the night of February 8, 1904, when the Japanese torpedo boats launched a surprise attack on the Russian fleet at Port Arthur. Diplomatic negotiations had dragged on since the previous August, but they failed to avert the final outbreak of hostilities, the culmination of steadily deteriorating relations between the two countries over a much longer period. This chapter traces the activities of both the oligarchic decision-makers and the political activists in Japan during the period of the prewar negotiations. It seeks answers to two questions: Why and how did the decision-makers decide on war, and what role did the political activists play in the process?[1]

The Political Activists and the Manchurian Question

In the summer of 1900, the Boxer Rebellion precipitated a renewed international scramble for concessions in China. Russia responded vigorously and occupied Manchuria. Other powers sent troops to China to guard their interests. After the rebellion was quelled, most of the expeditionary forces were eventually withdrawn. The Russian government, however, refused to withdraw its forces from Manchuria unless China signed an agreement that would have greatly strengthened Russia's exclusive rights in Manchuria. China resisted the Russian pressures and refused to conclude such an agreement. Russian troops therefore remained in Manchuria. Finally, on April 8, 1902, international pressures and changes in the internal power balance in Russia resulted in the Manchurian convention, in which Russia pledged to evacuate all of its troops in the region within 18 months. The withdrawal was to be carried out in three stages, the first ending on October 8, 1902, the second on April 8, 1903, and the third on October 8, 1903.[2]

The first stage was carried out as promised, but when the April withdrawal did not occur, the Japanese public reacted quickly and vehemently.

The Kokumin Dōmeikai. In 1900 a group of political activists in Japan, who were particularly interested in China, had organized a nationalistic association known as the Kokumin Dōmeikai (People's League). A total of 93 persons attended the League's inaugural meeting on September 24, 1900. They included 9 members of the House of Peers, 19 members of the House of Representatives, some leading journalists, and members of various nationalistic societies. The most important of its founding members were: Prince Konoe Atsumaro, the German-educated president of the House of Peers; Count Shimazu Tadasuke and Viscount Nagaoka Moriyoshi of the House of Peers; Sassa Tomofusa of the Teikokutō, a nationalistic minor party; Inukai Tsuyoshi, Shiba Shirō, Kōmuchi Tomotsune, and Ōishi Masami of the Kenseihontō, and Tōyama Mitsuru, the founder of the Genyōsha.[3]

The declared aim of the League was to unify Japanese public opinion without distinction for political party and official or civil standing, in support of a solution to the Far Eastern question on the basis of "maintaining the integrity of China" (*Shina hozen*) and "upholding Korea" (*Chōsen yōgo*). Its immediate objective was to urge the government to send troops to Korea to check Russian ambitions in Manchuria.[4]

The League was supported by both the Teikokutō and the Kenseihontō.[5] More than 30 newspapermen who were members, representing 16 Tokyo newspapers, organized the Zenkoku Dōshi Kisha Dōmei (National Newspapermen's League). As a result, more than two-thirds of the newspapers in Japan reportedly came to support the Kokumin Dōmeikai.[6] The Seiyūkai, which had just been formed under the presidency of Genrō Itō Hirobumi, decided not to cooperate with the League, declaring that its activities were only harmful to the conduct of Japan's foreign policy. This decision reflected Itō's conciliatory attitude toward Russia. The leaders of the Seiyūkai, which was soon to become the government party, were largely interested in supporting government policy and rejected overtures from the political activists. Consequently, some Seiyūkai members who had initially supported the League withdrew.[7] When Itō formed his fourth cabinet, the government designated the League a political association, thus placing it under the restrictions of the Political Association Law.[8]

The Kokumin Dōmeikai, nevertheless, continued its attempts to arouse public opinion by demanding that the government take forceful measures against Russia. Speeches were given throughout Japan; representatives of the League visited government leaders to urge them to adopt a strong foreign policy.[9] The Kokumin Dōmeikai welcomed the formation of the first Katsura Cabinet in June 1901, expressing particular satisfaction with the choice of Komura Jutarō as foreign minister and with the cabinet's conclusion of the Anglo-Japanese Alliance in January 1902.[10] On April 27, soon after the evacuation agreement was reached, the Kokumin Dōmeikai dissolved itself with the statement that its original objective had been successfully achieved.[11]

The Six Professors. At the time of the Boxer Rebellion, a group of university professors was also active in trying to unify public opinion against the Russian occupation of Manchuria. The group consisted of six professors of Law—Tomizu Kanjin, Terao Tōru, Kanai Noburu, Matsuzaki Kuranosuke, and Tomii Seishō from Tokyo Imperial University, and Nakamura Shingo from Gakushūin (Peers' College).[12] On September 9, 1900, the six professors were invited by Prince Konoe, then president of Gakushūin, to discuss Russian activity in Manchuria. At the meeting they decided to present a proposal on foreign policy to Prime Minister Yamagata Aritomo. Somewhat typical of a gathering of university professors, the group was, in Tomizu's words, an assembly of self-assured men (*kotengu no kaigō*). Realizing that they would be unable to formulate a position with which every participant could agree, the professors followed Prince Konoe's suggestion and requested Kuga Minoru to prepare a draft for them. Kuga, who wrote under the pen name Katsunan, was president and editor-in-chief of the nationalistic newspaper *Nihon* and an adviser to the Kokumin Dōmeikai.

After revising Kuga's draft, the six professors called on Prime Minister Yamagata on September 28 and presented to him their proposal on foreign policy. Yamagata welcomed the professors "unexpectedly cordially" and promised that, since a cabinet change was imminent, he would convey their proposal to his successor.[13] The proposal stated *inter alia:*

In the course of this incident in China, our imperial nation has expended the largest number of troops and has been remarkably successful in rescuing the foreign legations and residents in Peking from the dangers posed by the Boxer rebels. This is because our nation desires to maintain the status quo in East Asia and to share with the world the blessings of eternal peace in the region. The Powers will appreciate our desire and merit in this event and will regard our claim as important to the settlement of the incident. We should not miss this opportunity. Today our imperial nation must make the first move in a great leap forward.

Traditionally, our attitude toward the powers has shown an excessive virtue of modesty. Modesty is not necessarily bad. The Powers, however, seem to have regarded our modesty not as virtue, but as cowardice. In this incident the interests of the Powers are not in accord. It is, therefore, impossible for us to satisfy everyone. Those responsible for our imperial nation's foreign relations should keep this fact in mind. . . .[14]

The proposal urged the government not only to take positive steps to restrain Russian activities in Manchuria, but also to expand Japan's influence in China.

On November 25, 1900, the professors called on Katō Takaaki, Foreign Minister in the fourth Itō cabinet. They regarded him as an able foreign minister but entertained little hope for the cabinet as a whole. The public did not know of the professors' visits and their proposal, for the professors had agreed with Yamagata and Katō that the meetings would be kept from the public.[15]

In order to arouse public opinion, however, the six professors prepared pamphlets setting forth their individual positions on the Manchurian question. In October 1900, when international settlement of the Boxer Rebellion was being discussed in Peking, the professors privately distributed the pamphlets without obtaining a publication permit from the Ministry of Home Affairs. These opinions were hot-blooded, random exhortations rather than scholarly discourses. Their positions and emphases differed and were often mutually contradictory. On certain points they were agreed, however: Russia's eastward expansion, they were convinced, was not a temporary matter; it had a long history and would certainly continue. Russian interests in Manchuria collided with Japan's interests in the region. For this reason a Russo-Japanese agreement was impossible and war was probably inevitable. An alliance with the United States and England was in Japan's interests. The Japanese economy would certainly be able to support a war lasting one year at most. Japan should seize the present opportunity to advance into Manchuria, which was indispensable for Japan's future development. To solve the Manchurian question was to solve the Korean problem, not vice versa.[16]

Newspapers reported the professors' opinions throughout Japan but their influence upon the public is difficult to measure. The fact that such prestigious individuals had left their ivory towers to engage in political activity must have had some impact. Thereafter, the professors continued their propaganda activities through newspaper and magazine articles and speech-making.[17]

The Kokuryūkai. Another group that advocated a strong policy against Russia was the Kokuryūkai (Amur River Society, more commonly mistranslated as the Black Dragon Society), founded on February 3, 1901, by Uchida Ryōhei and more than 20 activists in Chinese and Korean affairs. According to a biography recently published by a former Kokuryūkai group, Uchida Ryōhei was born in Fukuoka on the historical date February 11, 1874. His first impression of the world reportedly was formed on December 13, 1876, when the two-year-old Uchida glimpsed from his elder sister's back the heroic figure of Imamura Momohachirō being taken in a jinrikisha to a nearby execution ground. Imamura was one of the leaders in the Akizuki Rebellion, a precursor of the Satsuma Rebellion. A nephew of Hiraoka Kōtarō, one of the founders of the Genyōsha, Uchida grew with the nationalist society into an ardent activist in Chinese and Korean affairs. The Triple Intervention, however, redirected his ambitions. Having sworn revenge upon Russia, he made several trips to Russia and as early as 1898 concluded that Japan need not fear that corrupt nation.[18]

On the day of its inauguration, the Kokuryūkai declared, "In view of the situation in East Asia and the mission of imperial Japan, and in order to check the expansion of the Western powers in the East, and to promote the development and prosperity of East Asia, it is the urgent duty of Japan to fight Russia and expel it from the East, and then to lay the foundation for a grand continental enterprise taking Manchuria, Mongolia, and Siberia as one region."[19] Thereafter the society endeavored through publications and forums to propagate to the public their argument for war, contending that Japan need not fear Russia, that war with Russia was the only way to secure eternal peace in East Asia, and that Japan's victory in such a war was assured. In March 1901, the society began to publish the *Kokuryūkai Report.* The second

issue contained a 70-page article entitled "On the Relative Merits of
War and Peace Based on the Estimated War Potential of Japan and
Russia." The government prohibited its distribution, for it deemed the
article to be detrimental to relations between the two countries. In May
the society started a monthly journal, *Kokuryū,* which described conditions in Russia with a strong assertion of the need for an early war.
Continuous government interferences soon compelled the society to
modify its editorial policy.

Meanwhile, in April 1901, the Kokuryūkai had published a map of
Manchuria. In May the society published the *Rokoku Tōhō Keiei
Bumen Zenzu,* which illustrated Russia's eastward expansion. It is said
that Foreign Minister Komura and Yamaza Enjirō[20] assisted the Kokuryūkai in its publication. In September 1901, Uchida published *Roshia
Bōkokuron* (On Decaying Russia), but its distribution was promptly
prohibited by the government, and only a revised version entitled
Roshia Ron (On Russia) was allowed to be published.[21] In this work,
Uchida stressed the necessity of a war against Russia. Although he
asserted that Japan would be victorious, he went so far as to state
that should Japan be defeated, it would be an honorable defeat that
would occupy a glorious place in the history of mankind. In December
1901, the Kokuryūkai opened a Russian and Chinese language school
in Kanda, Tokyo. While Uchida aroused public opinion for war he
worked simultaneously to establish a Japan-Russia society (Nichi-Ro
Kyōkai), envisioning the need, according to Kokuryūkai sources, to
prepare for the conduct of *postwar* relations with Russia. He therefore
desired to found an organization through which Japan would be able
to promote the restoration of close relations with, and guidance of, the
Russian people once the approaching war had ended with Japan's victory. Uchida sought support for this project from Genrō Itō, believing
that the later's well-known and highly regarded pro-Russian attitude
would add greatly to the success of such a project. For his own reasons,
Itō was quite amenable to the idea, and the Nichi-Ro Kyōkai was
founded in 1902.[22]

The Taigaikō Dōshikai. Besides failing to carry out the second
stage of the military withdrawal as promised, Russia also presented
a seven-point demand to the Chinese government, on April 8, 1903.
On the same day, the Kokumin Dōmeikai was revived and renamed

the Taigaikō Dōshikai (Comrades' Society for a Strong Foreign Policy).
Its inaugural meeting was attended by more than 140 people. Speaking despite a bronchial catarrh from which he was suffering, Professor
Tomizu Kanjin declared that war alone could solve the Manchurian
question. The Japanese population was increasing so rapidly, Tomizu
emphasized, that Japan had to find additional resources to sustain it.
The only satisfactory course was for Japan to ensure that the Asian
continent, above all Manchuria, would remain open to Japanese im-
migration. For this reason, Russia must be expelled from the region.
Moreover, he continued, China and Korea were now perplexed as to
whether they should rely on Russia or Japan. If Japan should show
weakness at this juncture, China and Korea would be lost to Russia.[23]
The following resolution was passed by acclaim:

Apart from the question whether or not Russia's evacuation procedure
constitutes any indication of the withdrawal of its troops from Manchuria,
we believe that in actuality it as yet evinces no intention to abandon its
military occupation. We therefore hope that the governments of Japan and
England will at once urge the Chinese government to take steps to recover
its administrative rights in Manchuria and to open that region to other
foreign powers, so as to secure permanent tranquillity in East Asia.[24]

The Seven Professors. In early April, Prince Konoe presented his
proposal on the Manchurian question to Foreign Minister Komura.[25]
Other Dōshikai leaders, including Kōmuchi, Tōyama, and Sassa, presented their separate proposals to both Komura and Prime Minister
Katsura.

On May 31, 1903, Prince Konoe met at the Nansa Sō in Shiba,
Tokyo, with seven university professors—Tomizu, Terao, Nakamura,
Kanai, and Tomii, all of whom, as we have seen, had been actively
promoting a strong foreign policy from the time of the Boxer Rebellion;
and two new participants, Takahashi Sakue and Onozuka Kiheiji.[26]
All except Nakamura, who was at Gakushūin, were professors of law
at Tokyo Imperial University. During the meeting, Prince Konoe
urged the professors to pressure government leaders to adopt forceful
measures against the continued Russian occupation of Manchuria and
to unite public opinion in support of such a policy. The seven professors thereupon decided to give their advice on the Manchurian
question to government leaders, as they had done during the Boxer

crisis in 1900. Again finding themselves unable to agree upon a policy statement, the professors decided first to call upon individual government leaders to advise them orally. They also decided to work independently of the Taigaikō Dōshikai and other pro-war groups, apparently concluding that they would be most effective if they capitalized on their prestige and specialized knowledge as a distinctive group.[27]

On June 1 they called on Prime Minister Katsura. Tomii, who with Onozuka constituted the moderate faction within the group, was designated the spokesman for the meeting. He urged Katsura to adopt a forceful policy against Russia, to which Katsura replied that he was as much concerned for Japan's future as were the professors. There was no need for them to worry about the Russian problem, he told them, because responsible authorities were taking the necessary steps with determination. Katsura also assured them that the government would not follow a so-called *Mankan kōkan* policy of exchanging Manchuria for Korea. Despite Onozuka's objections, Tomizu declared that, since war with Russia was inevitable, Japan should declare war right away. Katsura retorted that fighting was soldiers' business and that he never expected to hear a lecture on war from a university professor. Katsura even accused Tomizu of engaging in activities improper in his profession and demanded that he quiet down.[28]

The professors called on Foreign Minister Komura on the same day, but Komura not only declined to meet with them but also refused to make an appointment for a future meeting, pleading the pressure of state affairs. When the seven professors called on Genrō Yamagata the following day, he was not home. Frustrated by the futility of their efforts, the professors now decided to draw up a written policy to present to the government leaders. The first draft was prepared by Takahashi, who drew together those points on which the group was able to agree. A revised statement was submitted on June 10 to Prime Minister Katsura, Foreign Minister Komura, Navy Minister Yamamoto, and Army Minister Terauchi, as well as to Genrō Yamagata and Matsukata, and on June 17 to Kodama Gentarō, then governor-general of Taiwan.[29] A summary of their 3000-word statement follows.

The Japanese government in the past has often followed a policy of drift and neglect and has allowed opportunities to slip by. For instance, the government's failure to secure a nonalienation pledge from China when Japan restored the Liaotung Peninsula has resulted in the present problem in Manchuria. When the paltry German forces seized Kiaochow, a determined protest from Japan would have blocked their advance and averted the pretext upon which Russia demanded to lease Port Arthur and Dairen. Furthermore, after the Boxer Rebellion, when the withdrawal of foreign troops from North China was decided upon, had Japan grasped the opportunity to have the Powers agree upon specific procedures for the evacuation of Manchuria as well, the present complications would not have arisen. Should the Japanese government continue to pursue a policy of neglect and let the present opportunity slip by, Japan, China, and Korea will never be able to raise their heads again and everlasting calamity will be brought upon the empire. Russian expansion in East Asia has been continuous and uninterrupted. The longer it is unchecked, the more difficult it will be to check. At present, Japan is slightly superior to Russia militarily, but this military superiority will not last more than a year. Once Russia becomes master of Manchuria, how shall it be kept out of Korea? Once it becomes master of Korea, what will be its next objective? In sum, if the Manchurian question is not solved satisfactorily, the Korean problem cannot be solved. If the Korean problem cannot be solved, neither can the Japanese. The time is now. Some people claim that utmost circumspection is required in the conduct of foreign affairs, and that Japan must accurately determine the attitudes of each of the Powers beforehand. This is true. But the attitudes of the various Powers are already more or less known. Nothing could be more regrettable than that Japan not take advantage of this once-in-a-thousand-years opportunity. The policy of exchanging Manchuria for Korea is totally unwise and unacceptable. The Japanese government must strive for a fundamental solution to the Manchurian question and for the establishment of a permanent peace in the Far East.[30]

Although this statement took a stronger position than had the April 8 resolution of the Taigaikō Dōshikai, it should be noted that, in accordance with their agreement with Prime Minister Katsura, the professors' advice was given only to government leaders and was not made public. Nevertheless, the press soon learned of it, and on June 16 the *Niroku Shimpō* published a highly distorted version of the statement.

The *Niroku Shimpō* was owned by Akiyama Teisuke,[31] an independent Diet member from Tokyo who was opposed to the Katsura Cabinet and attempted in this way to embarrass the cabinet. On June 19 the professors discussed whether or not they should publish the original text to discredit the "absurd version" printed in the *Niroku Shimpō*, but they failed to come to a decision because of mutual disagreement. When Tomizu proposed that they issue a public declaration of the need for Japan to adopt a strong policy toward Russia, his proposal was opposed by the moderates in the group.[32] On June 21, however, an editorial in the *Tokyo Nichi-nichi Shimbun,* a semiofficial organ of the government, strongly condemning the professors' activities, quoted accurately from the original statement. This editorial reminded the professors of the duties incumbent upon them as professors and of their responsibilities as men of recognized learning. The paper disputed their contention that Japan would become weaker than Russia and warned the professors to consider more seriously the consequences of a war with Russia.[33]

The editorial in the *Tokyo Nichi-nichi Shimbun* led the professors to conclude that someone in the Katsura Cabinet had released the statement to the newspaper. The paper was owned by Genrō Itō's protégé Itō Miyoji, who was then cultivating closer connections with Genrō Yamagata and Prime Minister Katsura.[34] On June 24, the professors finally made the text public, rewording it only slightly to sound more like an essay. This added fuel to the heated public debate over the Manchurian question then being carried on with increasing vigor in the Japanese press, which seems to have greeted the professors' statement with more support than criticism.[35] Meanwhile, although it was rumored that the government would censure the seven professors for alleged abuse of their academic positions, no direct action was taken. Apparently at the request of the minister of education, Yamakawa Kenjirō, president of Tokyo Imperial University, advised the professors to be more prudent and not give rise to misunderstandings among the people, stating that it was unwise for university professors to engage in radical political activities in collaboration with people outside the university.[36] The professors nevertheless continued their efforts to arouse public opinion in favor of war with Russia. There is no doubt that, at a time when the prestige of university professors was particularly high, the activities of the professors, popularly called the *Kaisen Shichi Hakase* (seven pro-war doctors),[37] were influential in unifying Japanese public opinion in support of war.

The Press. We have already noted that, following the Boxer Rebellion, most of the Japanese press opposed Russian activities in Manchuria and urged the Japanese government to take decisive measures against Russia. In 1902 press criticism subsided temporarily when the diplomatic policy of the Katsura Cabinet resulted in Russia's promise to withdraw its troops from Manchuria. When the scheduled evacuation was not carried out in April 1903, the reaction of the Japanese press was far from unanimous.

Several of the nation's leading papers demanded that Japan declare war on Russia, including the *Tokyo Asahi Shimbun* (90; Kenseihontō), the *Osaka Asahi Shimbun* (200; Kenseihontō), the *Jiji Shimpō* (founded by Fukuzawa Yukichi, who had died in 1901; 55; neutral), the *Nihon* (owned by Kuga Minoru; 12; neutral), the *Yomiuri Shimbun* (15; Kenseihontō), the *Hōchi Shimbun* (140; Kenseihontō), and the *Osaka Mainichi Shimbun* (200; neutral).[38] The *Yorozu Chōhō* (160; neutral) and the *Mainichi Shimbun* (8; Kenseihontō) held to the anti-war position they had been advocating for some time. Kuroiwa Shūroku (Ruikō), owner of the *Yorozu Chōhō*, had organized in 1901 the Risōdan (Idealists' group), which called for social justice and reform in Japan; he is said to have opposed war on humanistic grounds. The well-known Christian Uchimura Kanzō, one of the paper's major contributors, opposed it on the basis of his religious convictions, while the paper's editorial writers, Kōtoku Denjirō (Shūsui) and Sakai Toshihiko (Kosen) opposed it from a socialist point of view.[39] On April 24, 1903, the *Yorozu Chōhō* published a major article entitled "A Diplomatic Question," which discussed the effect the slogan *Gaikō mondai* (diplomatic question) could have on the Japanese mind:

"Gaikō mondai!" Once this phrase is shouted, we Japanese have the habit of dashing out, forgetting everything else. The phrase "Gaikō mondai" is to Japanese ears the same as a fire alarm at midnight. . . . Indeed, whenever "Gaikō mondai" is heard, we have the habit of suddenly becoming confused and losing our rationality. The phrase "Gaikō mondai" works on the Japanese mind like an anesthetic. . . . Throughout history and everywhere in the world there have been nations like ours. There have also been many politicians who have taken advantage of this idiosyncrasy among their people and have utilized it to fulfill their own selfish desires. These demagogues, without exception, shouted loudly, "Look at our borders, a great enemy is encroaching upon us! We should cooperate with one another! We should forget our differences! Be united now! National unity is the only thing we need now!" Napoleon III often used this method. Bismarck resorted to this tactic skillfully. . . . What about our Japanese politicians?

They say that Russia is not withdrawing its forces from Manchuria. Obviously, Japan, England, and the other Powers cannot acquiesce. However, if our people, just because of this, immediately throw out every other consideration and start jumping around in confusion without seeing what is what, it will be of no benefit to our nation at all. Nay, worse still, we would only become a sacrifice to the selfish ambitions of miniature Napoleons and Bismarcks. . . .

Yet, while we are aware of a grave diplomatic question on the one hand, we should not forget the continuing rapacity of the clan autocracy on the other. We should always be aware that their dictatorial rule is still like that of a tiger. We should not forget that first of all we must overthrow the present government.[40]

The exact reason for the *Mainichi Shimbun*'s stand against the war is not known. Under its president, Shimada Saburō, the paper had been campaigning for social and political reforms; its anti-war stand may have derived from this emphasis upon the need for domestic reforms. The anti-war view of one of the paper's editorial writers, Christian socialist Kinoshita Naoe, probably had some influence upon editorial policy.[41]

The *Tokyo Nichi-nichi Shimbun* and the *Kokumin Shimbun,* both generally considered to be semiofficial government organs, remained noncommittal. The *Tokyo Nichi-nichi Shimbun*'s criticism of the seven professors has already been mentioned. The *Kokumin Shimbun* was owned by Tokutomi Sohō, who had sworn revenge on Russia for the Triple Intervention.[42] Tokutomi's close relationship with Katsura, whom he had met in Manchuria at the time of the intervention, was strengthened in 1902, when the conclusion of the Anglo-Japanese alliance convinced Tokutomi that Katsura was the man to lead Japan's war against Russia. Throughout the period of the prewar negotiations and the war with Russia, the *Kokumin Shimbun* firmly supported the Katsura Cabinet.[43]

By mid-1903, therefore, political activists in Japan were working vigorously to promote a strong policy against the continued Russian occupation of Manchuria. Public opinion, however, was still divided as to the means Japan should employ to solve the Manchurian question, even though pro-war sentiments were generally on the rise.

The Oligarchs Start Negotiations with Russia

The Murin'an Conference. On April 19, 1903, the Japanese minister at Peking, Uchida Yasuya, telegraphed his home government that Russia had not only ignored the scheduled evacuation on April 8, but had also presented China with a new seven-point demand. At about the same time, the Japanese decision-makers were alarmed by Russia's increasing activities in North Korea. Faced with these developments, Genrō Itō, Prime Minister Katsura, and Foreign Minister Komura visited Genrō Yamagata at his villa, Murin'an, in Kyoto, on April 21. As guidelines for Japan's future policy toward Russia, they agreed upon four general principles:

1. Should Russia fail to withdraw its troops from Manchuria in violation of the Russo-Chinese convention, Japan should lodge a protest with Russia.
2. Taking the opportunity of the present Manchurian question, Japan should begin direct negotiations with Russia to solve the Korean problem.
3. Japan should have Russia recognize Japan's preponderant rights (*yūetsuken*) in Korea and should make no concessions whatsoever to Russia as far as Korea was concerned.
4. With the aim of reaching a complete solution to the Korean problem, Japan should recognize Russia's preponderant rights in Manchuria.[44]

The four decision-makers thus agreed, as a general principle that, in view of Russian expansion in Manchuria, Japan should endeavor to achieve and maintain complete domination of Korea through what might be called the policy of exchanging Manchuria and Korea between Russia and Japan (*Mankan kōkan*). On one point, they were firmly agreed. Maintaining Korea as Japan's sphere of influence was so vital to the latter's security that any measures necessary to achieve that purpose should be taken.

A difference of attitudes toward the Murin'an agreement, however, seems to have existed between Itō and Yamagata, on the one hand, and

Katsura and Komura on the other. The Genrō, particularly Itō, apparently viewed the agreement as a policy guideline that would result in the peaceful solution of the Manchurian-Korean problem. For several years Itō had been championing the idea of a Manchuria-Korea exchange between Russia and Japan. On March 15, only about a month before the Murin'an conference, Itō had discussed the Manchurian question with only the other four Genrō. Itō's report of their discussion might be summarized as follows:

Since England and Germany obviously would not use military force to restrain Russia in Manchuria, Japan had no choice but to confine its action against Russia within the scope of British and German intentions. Russia seemed to wish no immediate clash with Japan on Korea; therefore Japan should endeavor to maintain the status quo and, should an opportunity arise, negotiate with Russia to reach an agreement on Korean independence and to prevent the Korean problem from becoming a cause for war between Japan and Russia.[45]

Despite the bitter experience of previous years, Genrō Itō still hoped for an entente with Russia.

In contrast, Katsura and Komura regarded the Murin'an agreement with pessimism. When Katsura formed his cabinet in 1901, two of his goals were to conclude an alliance with a European power in order to bolster Japan's position in the Far East, and to turn Korea into a Japanese protectorate.[46] The first of these objectives was realized in January 1902 with the conclusion of the Anglo-Japanese Alliance. According to Katsura's memoirs, he was convinced that Russia would not be satisfied merely to occupy Manchuria, but would certainly attempt to take Korea. He therefore promoted an alliance with England and rejected the Russo-Japanese entente that Genrō Itō and Inoue had been trying to achieve. In other words, in 1902 Katsura had concluded that an agreement with Russia based on the principle of a Manchuria-Korea exchange would produce only a temporary solution and would not bring an end to Russia's ambitions in Korea.[47] By April 1903, Katsura seems to have regarded Russia's agreement on even a Manchuria-Korea exchange nearly an impossibility. Katsura was fully aware, according to his memoirs, that Japanese dominance in Korea would be viewed as a direct threat to Russia in Manchuria, just as Russian domination of Manchuria would be a threat to the security of Korea. Katsura realized that Russia had as much reason not to let Korea slip into Japanese hands as Japan had for preventing its domination by Russia. As long as the Murin'an agreement precluded any concession by Japan on the question of Korea, Katsura saw very little hope for reaching an agreement with Russia.[48]

Komura seems to have fully shared Katsura's pessimistic view. In fact, Komura's pessimism about the future of Russo-Japanese relations seems to have been even more deeply rooted than Katsura's. Komura had worked vigorously for the realization of the alliance with England. Ever since he was minister to St. Petersburg in 1900, he is said to have been convinced that a Russo-Japanese entente would be possible only after a war between the two countries.[49] Thus Katsura and Komura apparently took their initial steps toward opening negotiations with Russia in full anticipation of, or even determination for, war. What they had achieved in the Murin'an conference, therefore, was the commitment of the Genrō to negotiations with Russia, negotiations that Katsura and Komura fully anticipated would end in war. It was with these different perspectives that Japan's top decision-makers decided to prepare to negotiate with Russia.

The Army General Staff. The majority of the division chiefs on the Army General Staff reacted to Russian activities in Manchuria with great vigor and much urgent concern. They concluded, first, that war with Russia was inevitable; second, that the military situation vis-à-vis Russia would be favorable to Japan if war broke out soon; and, third, that the government should be urged to make the final decision immediately. Spokesmen for this strongly pro-war opinion within the General Staff were the chief of the General Affairs Division, Major General Iguchi Shōgo; the chief of the First Division, Colonel Matsukawa Toshitane; and the chief of the Second Division, Major General Fukushima Yasumasa. Together they pressed Vice-Chief of the Army General Staff Major General Tamura Iyozō to request Chief of Staff Ōyama Iwao to express to the cabinet the army's desire for a quick solution of the Manchurian question, but at first both Tamura and Ōyama resisted this pressure from their subordinates and took no action.[50]

In May 1903, when Tamura received the report that Russia had begun to establish a settlement at Yongampo in north Korea, he ordered the division chiefs "to investigate matters requiring the immediate attention of the army." Reportedly the objective was not to prepare for immediate war but to improve military preparedness in general. The Army General Staff had been urging such a program for several years, and Tamura seems to have decided to take advantage of the increasingly critical situation in Manchuria and North Korea to carry it out. On May 11, Tamura presented to Ōyama a report prepared largely by Iguchi and Matsukawa on the state of Japan's military preparedness. On the basis of this report, the following day Ōyama submitted to the Emperor a "Memorial on the Replenishment of Military Preparedness," copies of which were distributed to Prime Minister Katsura, Army Minister Terauchi Masatake, and Chief of the Navy General Staff Itō Sukeyuki. In stressing simultaneously the need for both immediate action and improvement of military preparedness to meet properly the approaching crisis, the memorial was logically inconsistent.[51] The document was apparently an attempted compromise between the cautious position of Ōyama and Tamura on the one hand, and the demands of Iguchi and Matsukawa for immediate action on the other, and reveals the difference of opinions regarding the Manchurian question between the nation's two top commanding officers and their high-ranking subordinates on the Army General Staff.

The problem for the pro-war subordinates was that they had no spokesman at the key decision-making council, the Genrō conference, usually attended by the Genrō and the key cabinet members. To their intense dissatisfaction, at these conferences Chief of the Army General Staff Ōyama Iwao acted as a Genrō, not as Chief of Staff.[52] The other army representative, Army Minister Terauchi, whatever his own views might have been, could not speak for the supreme command; that was exclusively the prerogative of the Army General Staff. Furthermore, even if Terauchi had held pro-war sympathies, he would have been no match against the two cautious elders of the army, Genrō Yamagata and Ōyama. Navy Minister Yamamoto Gonnohyōe was, as we shall see, "soft" and totally "unreliable."[53]

The Kogetsukai. In order to strengthen their position, the pro-war faction on the Army General Staff contacted like-minded elements on the Navy General Staff and in the Foreign Ministry and soon formed a secret alliance of high and middle ranking officers and officials of the three bodies. In late May 1903, the group held its first secret meeting in a warehouse of the Kogetsu restaurant at Karasumori, Shiba, in Tokyo.[54] The known members of the group, which later came to be known as the Kogetsukai or Kogetsugumi from the name of the restaurant in which its first meeting was held, were as follows.

ARMY

Iguchi Shōgo, Major General; Chief of the General Affairs Division of the General Staff

Matsukawa Toshitane, Colonel; Chief of the First Division of the Army General Staff

Tachibana Koichirō, Lieutenant-Colonel; Staff Officer of the Army General Staff

Yamaguchi Masaru, Lieutenant-Colonel; Staff Officer of the Army General Staff

Tanaka Giichi, Major; Faculty member of the Army War College, formerly Chief of the Russian Section of the Army General Staff

Fukuda Masatarō, Major; Adjutant to the Chief of the Army General Staff, Field Marshal Ōyama

Horiuchi Bunjirō, Major; Adjutant to Army Minister Terauchi

Kinoshita Usaburō, Major; Staff Officer of the Army General Staff

Koike Yasuyuki, Major; Staff Officer of the Army General Staff

Satō Kōjirō, Major; Staff Officer of the Army General Staff

Ono Sanenobu, Major; Staff Officer of the Army General Staff

Nishikawa Torajirō, Major; Staff Officer of the Army General Staff

NAVY

Tomioka Sadayasu, Rear Admiral; Chief of the First Division of the Navy General Staff

Yashiro Rokurō, Captain; Commander of the cruiser *Asama*

Yamashita Gentarō, Captain; Staff Officer of the Navy General Staff

Kamiizumi Tokuya, Commander; Staff Officer of the Navy General Staff

Moriyama Keizaburō, Commander; Staff Officer of the Navy General Staff

Takarabe Akira, Commander; Staff Officer of the Navy General Staff

Akiyama Masayuki, Lieutenant-Commander; Faculty member of the Navy War College

Matsui Kenkichi, Lieutenant; Staff Officer of the Navy General Staff

FOREIGN MINISTRY

Yamaza Enjirō, Chief of the Political Affairs Bureau

Ishii Kikujirō, Chief of the Commerce Bureau

Matsui Keishirō, Secretary of the Political Affairs Bureau

Honda Kumatarō, Secretary to Foreign Minister Komura

Sakata Jūjirō, Secretary of the Political Affairs Bureau

Ochiai Kentarō, Secretary of the Political Affairs Bureau

Kurachi Tetsukichi, Counselor of the Ministry

The members differed in two ways from those whom we have termed the political activists. First, they were all military officers and government officials. Although they could not participate directly in decision making and lacked a legal structure through which they might have pressed their point of view upon the decision-making oligarchy, they were in daily personal contact with some of the decision-makers. Second, although there are indications that limited and individual liaisons existed between some Kogetsukai members and the political activists,[55] the activities of the Kogetsukai were aimed at applying direct pressure upon the oligarchic decision-makers and showed no intent of mobilizing public opinion in favor of war. On the contrary, it was a secret group whose activities, if fully revealed, would have been tantamount to insubordination.[56]

The two groups, however, did share certain similarities. Both were convinced that war with Russia was ultimately inevitable and that, the sooner the war started, the more favorable the military situation would be for Japan. Consequently, they were agreed that prolonged diplomatic negotiations, or even a peaceful solution of the Manchurian question, were undesirable, because the outcome at best would be a temporary peace that would merely provide Russia with the critical time it needed to build up its military strength in the Far East. Should Japan miss the present opportunity, they asserted, not only would it be unable to stop Russia's ambitions in East Asia, but Japan's national security would be seriously jeopardized.[57] They also shared a distrust of the ability and judgment of the government leaders in the face of Russian expansion. Above all, they distrusted the Genrō. To press the government leaders to reach an early decision for war, the Kogetsukai members decided to try to persuade the Genrō and the cabinet members directly by calling on them one by one. They divided the "targets" among themselves and began to apply tenaciously personal pressure on the government leaders. At the same time, they endeavored to create a unanimous pro-war opinion within their respective state organs and to prepare for their superiors reports and memoranda to bolster their pro-war arguments.

Unfortunately, few materials are available on the details of the Kogetsukai's activities in pressuring the government leaders individually. All we can gather is that they responded in various ways. Genrō Itō,

Yamagata, Matsukata, Inoue, and Ōyama brushed aside the Kogetsukai proposition as an "immature theory" (*shoseiron*).[58] Prime Minister Katsura reportedly rejected their argument, while Navy Minister Yamamoto adamantly refused to listen. Each time a member of the Kogetsukai approached Yamamoto, it is said, he simply repeated the question, "Where will you find two billion yen necessary to fight a war with Russia?"[59] On the contrary, the "sensible" and "able" Foreign Minister Komura from the outset was quite sympathetic toward the group. He cooperated closely with the service officers and appears to have trusted and relied on Yamaza and Honda more than upon any other members of his ministry.[60] Home Minister Kodama Gentarō also turned out to be an earnest supporter of the Kogetsukai view,[61] but he was not yet one of the oligarchic decision-makers. According to one source, War Minister Terauchi was found "not difficult to persuade."[62]

On June 8, 1903, a conference of division chiefs of the Army General Staff was held to discuss the Manchurian question. Both Chief of Staff Ōyama, who normally did not attend such conferences, and Vice-Chief Tamura participated in the meeting. Iguchi, Matsukawa, and Colonel Ōshima Ken'ichi of the Fourth Division read prepared statements in which they argued vigorously that, in opening negotiations with Russia, Japan should immediately take an uncompromising stand on both Manchuria and Korea. The comparative military strengths of the two countries were such that, should negotiations fail, Japan would still win the war if it commenced right away. The division chiefs were opposed to a Manchuria-Korea exchange policy. They wanted to see Russia clearly expelled from Manchuria, and Korea securely placed under Japanese domination. Should Japan miss the present opportunity, they asserted, there would never be another chance to defeat Russia. The cost of the war, which they estimated at five hundred million yen, they believed would readily be borne by the Japanese people in such a time of national crisis. Furthermore, the indemnity a victorious Japan would get from Russia would more than cover the cost of the war. Colonel Ōshima is reported to have stressed Japan's growing population as one reason for the inevitability of a war with Russia. The division chiefs concluded their argument with two proverbs, which they attributed to Sun Tzu and the Greeks, respectively: "If above and below are united in anger, they win," and "the small defeats the big." To the disappointment of his subordinates, Ōyama remained unconvinced. His only response was said to have been, "Rokoku wa taikoku de gowasu kara na" (Remember that Russia is a powerful nation). Tamura remained silent throughout the conference.[63]

The division chiefs' efforts, however, appear not to have been totally in vain. On June 22, Chief of Staff Ōyama submitted to the Emperor his "Opinion Regarding the Solution of the Korean Problem," written on the basis of a memorandum that Tamura had prepared on June 17. Ōyama stressed the importance of Korea to Japan's national security and urged that the government open negotiations with Russia to settle the Korean problem on the principle of a Manchuria-Korea exchange while Japan still maintained a military superiority over Russian forces in the Far East. His memorandum was also distributed to the key cabinet members. Originally, Ōyama had hoped to submit an opinion signed jointly by Navy Chief of Staff Itō. Although the most important members of the Navy General Staff, including Vice-Chief Ijūin Gorō, supported Ōyama, Itō consulted the elder statesman of the Satsuma naval clique, Navy Minister Yamamoto, who was flatly opposed, declaring, "Japan need not worry about losing Korea. All that Japan must do is to defend Japan itself." Navy Chief of Staff Itō bowed to Yamamoto's views and the memorandum was submitted to the emperor with Ōyama's signature alone.[64]

The Imperial Conference of June 23, 1903. Since early June, Katsura and Komura had been preparing a memorandum on opening direct negotiations with Russia based on the principles agreed upon at the Murin'an conference. On June 17, Katsura called upon Genrō Itō for his advice. Itō suggested that he ask the Emperor to convene an imperial conference for the purpose of formally determining Japan's position in the proposed negotiations. Accordingly, on June 23, the day after Ōyama's opinion on the Korean problem had been submitted to the Emperor, an imperial conference, attended by Genrō Itō, Yamagata, Ōyama, Matsukata, and Inoue, Prime Minister Katsura, Navy Minister Yamamoto, Foreign Minister Komura, and Army Minister Terauchi, was held to study Komura's memorandum on negotiations with Russia.

The main points of the memorandum were as follows: The major objectives of Japanese policy in the light of the situation in East Asia should be national defense and economic development. In pursuing these two objectives, Japan must pay particular attention to Korea and Fukien, where Japan possessed its most vital ties to the continent. Of these, Korea required Japan's immediate attention. The peninsula was like a dagger pointing at the heart of Japan, and its possession by a foreign power could never be tolerated by Japan. Russia's conduct in Manchuria and Korea was leading toward eventual domination of Korea. Now was the time for Japan to open direct negotiations with Russia to settle the serious problems in the Far East. Should the opportunity be missed, it would be a cause for eternal regret to Japan. The main aim of the negotiations should be to maintain the security of Korea; toward that end, Japan should endeavor to restrict the Russian conduct in Manchuria within the limits of existing treaties. As principles to guide Japan's approach to Russia, Komura suggested: (1) preservation of the independence and territorial integrity of China and Korea, and equal opportunity for commerce and industry in both countries; (2) mutual recognition of the rights that Japan and Russia, respectively, possessed in Korea and Manchuria and the measures necessary for their protection; (3) mutual recognition of the right of Japan and Russia to send forces when necessary to preserve their interests or to repel uprisings in these territories, such forces to be withdrawn as soon as the objective in sending them had been achieved (police forces needed for railways and telegraphs were not included in this); and (4) Japan's special right to advise and assist Korea in carrying out internal reform.

Komura concluded his memorandum with the statement: "Should Japan succeed in reaching an agreement with Russia on the basis of the above principles, Japan's rights and interests will have been maintained. It is expected, however, that it will be extremely difficult to obtain Russia's concurrence in such an agreement. Consequently, I believe it to be essential that, in commencing negotiations, Japan be firmly resolved to achieve its objectives whatever the costs."[65]

After several hours of deliberation, the imperial conference approved Komura's memorandum, reaffirming that Japan would make no concession whatsoever regarding Korea. Genrō Itō expressed his concern as to the implications of Komura's conclusion, but when Navy Minister Yamamoto stated that he understood Komura to mean simply that Japan was resolved to achieve its objectives through negotiations, however trying Russia might make them for Japan. Itō seemed satisfied.[66] Thus the concluding statement, which apparently meant to Komura and Katsura that Japan was willing to risk war with Russia, was interpreted differently, at least by Genrō Itō and Navy Minister Yamamoto.

Katsura's Threat to Resign. On June 24, the day after the imperial conference had sanctioned a policy of direct negotiations with Russsia, Katsura told Genrō Itō and Yamagata that he wished to resign the premiership in favor of a leading Genrō, in whose hands the responsibility for guiding the nation through the international crisis should be placed, but his sudden proposal was brushed aside. On July 1, therefore, Katsura, pleading illness, tendered his resignation directly to the Emperor.[67]

It is clear that by "a leading Genrō," Katsura meant Itō Hirobumi. In his memoirs, Katsura wrote that, as long as Itō played a double role, both as a Genrō who participated in every major government decision and as the president of the majority political party, Seiyūkai, whose attitude of course had serious bearing upon cabinet deliberations, Katsura found it impossible to assume full responsibility for leading the nation. The Emperor refused to accept Katsura's resignation. On the advice of Yamagata and Itō Miyoji, he ordered Genrō Itō to assume the presidency of the Privy Council and to cooperate fully with the Katsura Cabinet. Unable to disobey an imperial order, Itō accepted the presidency of the Privy Council on July 13 on the condition that Yamagata, Matsukata, and Inoue be appointed privy councilors. Since his new position virtually forced him to resign the presidency of the Seiyūkai, Genrō Itō selected as his successor the incumbent president of the Privy Council, Saionji Kimmochi.[68]

Whether this was Katsura's hope in tendering his resignation is difficult to say. Tokutomi Sohō, Katsura's political friend and biographer, vigorously denies it, declaring that Katsura sincerely desired to have Genrō Itō assume the premiership.[69] Itō Miyoji's diary, however, clearly indicates some collusion among Yamagata, Miyoji, and Katsura in pushing Itō up to the presidency of the Privy Council. Yamagata was more than willing to exert his anti-political party energies on this occasion to separate Itō from the Seiyūkai. Miyoji, should we accept this shrewd schemer's own justification, was concerned for the last years of his meritorious patron, believing that it would be most desirable for Itō to end his political party activities and adorn the remaining years of his glorious career, as the most esteemed of the Genrō. Consequently, according to this highly plausible conspiracy theory, when Katsura was about to commit "a sham hara-kiri," he was readily rescued by the other two men.[70] One might even conjecture that Genrō Itō himself, by then fully irked by his political party, actually found it a timely excuse, and that certain Seiyūkai members, for their own reasons, probably accepted the turn of events quite readily.[71] It is ironic that by that time the second generation of political leaders could already manipulate the Genrō by dangling the specter of the onerous job of prime minister, which the Genrō could no longer undertake even though they were still entrusted with the selection of the prime minister.

This change had far-reaching consequences. By placing the three Genrō in the Privy Council, the Katsura Cabinet obtained their fuller commitment to its policies. By removing Genrō Itō from the Seiyūkai, Katsura found the party much easier to deal with. Perhaps most important of all, by pushing the cautious Genrō to the back seat, Katsura and Komura, in particular, found more room to exercise their hard-line diplomacy toward Russia. On July 15, Katsura further solidified his position by partially reshuffling his cabinet. By the end of the month, the internal political situation was stabilized, and the Katsura Cabinet was ready to proceed with the negotiations with Russia.

The First Japanese Proposals. In compliance with the spirit of the Anglo-Japanese Alliance, Foreign Minister Komura secured British approval of Japan's proposed negotiations,[72] and then, on July 28, he instructed Kurino Shin'ichirō, the Japanese minister at St. Petersburg, to make known to Russia the wishes of his government. On August 12, after Russia had confirmed its willingness to open negotiations, Japan presented six articles as a proposed basis for an understanding between the two nations. The main thrust of these first Japanese proposals was expressed in Articles I, II, and V as follows:

    I. Mutual engagement to respect the independence and territorial integrity of the Chinese and Korean Empires and to maintain the principle of equal opportunity for the commerce and industry of all nations in those countries.

   II. Reciprocal recognition of Japan's preponderating interests in Korea and Russia's special interests in railway enterprises in

Manchuria, and of the right of Japan to take in Korea and of
Russia to take in Manchuria such measures as may be necessary
for the protection of their respective interests as above defined,
subject, however, to the provisions of Article I of the Agreement.

V. Recognition on the part of Russia of the exclusive right of Japan
to give advice and assistance in the interest of reform and good
government in Korea, including necessary military assistance.[73]

While the Japanese proposals maintained the form of the policy of a
Manchuria-Korea exchange, they proposed a clearly one-sided arrangement. Fifty-two days were to elapse before the first Russian counterproposals were presented to Japan.

When the first Japanese proposals were presented, difference of
opinion still existed among the Japanese decision-makers. The Genrō
as a whole were more optimistic and conciliatory toward the negotiations
than were second-generation leaders such as Katsura and Komura.
Within the Army and Navy General Staffs, opinions were still divided
between the Chiefs of Staffs and their subordinates. The Navy under
Yamamoto's control appeared to be least enthusiastic about a war. Although the oligarchic decision-makers were in agreement that the security of Korea must be maintained, that Japan should make no concession on Korea, and that as a general principle the policy of a Manchuria-Korea exchange should be pursued in the negotiations, a wide
range of opinions existed among them as to the precise formulation of
an exchange policy. Its narrowest interpretation, as shown in the first
Japanese proposals, was urged by Katsura and Komura. The Genrō
would exercise their utmost efforts to restrain the younger leaders and
make the exchange policy more palatable to Russia without jeopardizing
the security of Korea for Japan. In view of Japan's first demands, however, from the beginning of the negotiations very little possibility of
success existed. The success or failure of the negotiations would depend
first upon Russia's willingness to agree to some sort of Manchuria-
Korea exchange without demanding any concessions from Japan in
Korea, and second, upon how far Japan would retreat from its first
proposals in regard to Manchuria. Within the Japanese decision-making
circles, only the Genrō had the power to press for, and willingness to
maintain, a conciliatory attitude. A conciliatory posture on the part of
Russia, however, was a prerequisite to enabling them to maintain their
stand on the negotiations.

Toward a United War Cry

The Tairo Dōshikai. The imperial conference of June 23, 1903, was widely reported in the Japanese press. While the reports consisted largely of various conjectures, since the press had no way of knowing exactly what had transpired in the conference, it was correctly deduced that in view of the increasingly tense relations between Japan and Russia a decision must have been made to open direct negotiations with Russia. News of the imperial conference came as an added impetus to the political activists.[74]

On August 9, four months after Russia had violated its promise for the second stage of evacuations, the Taigaikō Dōshikai, which had been watching Russia's actions in Manchuria and impatiently awaiting some positive response from the Japanese government, held a general meeting at Kinkikan Hall in Kanda, Tokyo. The *Tokyo Asahi Shimbun* reported that more than a hundred members of the Dōshikai attended the meeting, including Sassa Tomofusa, Tōyama Mitsuru, Hiraoka Kōtarō, Kōmuchi Tomotsune, Suzuki Shigetō (an old Jiyū Minken Undō activist and former Kenseihontō Diet member from Ehime), Takeuchi Masashi (an independent-Kenseihontō line Diet member from Niigata), Nakanishi Masaki (an old China activist), Kunitomo Shigeaki (journalist and old China activist), and Kudō Kōkan (a Kenseihontō Diet member from Aomori). The hall was reported filled by an audience of about 500 other people.

In the course of the meeting the Taigaikō Dōshikai was reorganized under the new name of the Tairo Dōshikai (Anti-Russia Comrades' Society), which, needless to say, expressed more frankly the purpose of the society. Its declaration enumerated five recent occasions on which Japan had exercised great forbearance in the face of Russian activities: the retrocession of the Liaotung Peninsula in 1895, its acquisition by Russia only three years later, the Russian extension of its railway to Port Arthur and Dairen, the repeated conclusion of Russo-Japanese ententes on Korea, and Japan's patient waiting for Russian evacuation of Manchuria after the Boxer Rebellion. The following resolution was adopted with resounding applause:

It is the heaven-ordained mission of our nation to maintain eternal peace in the Far East. We must first make the Russians carry out their promised withdrawal of troops from Manchuria, and second have the Chinese government open the region to the world. We demand that our government carry out its mission without any hesitation.

Messages from Prince Konoe,[75] Count Ōkuma Shigenobu, and Count Itagaki Taisuke were read to the meeting. Konoe urged that Japan actively resist Russian recalcitrance and stressed that the complete expulsion of Russian influence from Manchuria was a prerequisite for Japan's security in Korea. He therefore rejected any idea of a Manchuria-Korea exchange. Ōkuma lamented the Japanese authorities' hesitancy in contrast to "the people's firm resolution, which is just like a volcano on the verge of erupting." Itagaki demanded that Japan check Russia's sinister ambitions, which were disturbing the peace of East Asia. Ōtake Kan'ichi then reviewed the history of the retrocession of the Liaotung Peninsula, concluding with a peculiar twist of logic that, since "history repeats itself," it was now Russia's turn to be forced to swallow the bitter pill. With 600 people standing in solemn attention, he respectfully read the Imperial Rescript on the Retrocession of the Liaotung Peninsula. Three shouts of "banzai!" and the "Kimi ga Yo" (the national anthem) concluded the meeting. The *Tokyo Asahi Shimbun* reported that the meeting proceeded peacefully, except when several policemen refused to stand up as the imperial rescript was about to be read. A storm of protest from the audience forced them to conform.[76]

The peculiar lack of incisiveness in the Dōshikai resolution appears to have reflected the fact that the Tairo Dōshikai was a highly heterogeneous assemblage of political activists. Available materials are too scant to show any details of the society's composition, but it is quite obvious that the Dōshikai included both persons unequivocally opposed to, and critical of, the government and those who at heart were as anxious to assist and encourage the government as outwardly they appeared disposed to harass it.[77] In fact, particularly in the beginning, a persistent and widespread rumor seems to have existed that the Tairo Dōshikai was merely a tool of the Katsura Cabinet.[78] Although the Dōshikai's increasingly hostile stand toward the government eventually diminished the credibility of such a rumor, there is no doubt that the Dōshikai members were more or less united by only one factor, the desire to promote a strong foreign policy against Russia. The Dōshikai was otherwise a gathering of people of various backgrounds and motives, and this heterogeneity naturally affected its course of action. It risked a complete split every time it had to make a major decision on strategy, whether it concerned publicly censuring the cabinet for its secret diplomacy of allegedly constant retreat, or a memorial to the throne requesting the Emperor to admonish his temporizing and indecisive ministers and advisers. Some members demanded that such measures be executed immediately, while others called for caution and circumspection and displayed a degree of understanding of the government's problems in the delicate negotiations with Russia.[79] Unity and eventual unanimity of action seem to have been achieved only as the diplomatic negotiations dragged on without visible signs of success.

On September 12, 1903, the Tairo Dōshikai sent Tōyama, Kōmuchi, and Hasegawa Yoshinosuke, three members of its Keikoku Iin (warning committee), to Prime Minister Katsura to deliver the society's letter of warning, which cautioned Katsura against Russian insincerity and demanded that he "take ultimate measures to solve the Manchurian question."[80] This was exactly a month after Japan had presented its first proposals to Russia. Though they were increasingly pessimistic, Japan's oligarchic decision-makers were still determined to continue negotiations and wait for Russia's counterproposals. They had not completely given up hope of reaching a conciliation with Russia through the mutual recognition of Russia's preferred position in Manchuria and Japan's paramount role in Korea. By this time, however, the Tairo Dōshikai members had apparently concluded that the negotiations would be totally futile and that the situation required Japan to resort to "ultimate measures."

Meanwhile, Russian activities in North Korea grew increasingly threatening, and there was no sign that the third withdrawal of troops, scheduled for October 8, would be carried out. Just three days before that date, on October 5, the Tairo Dōshikai, dissatisfied with the slow diplomacy of the government, held a general meeting at the Kabuki theater. The following resolution was adopted by about a thousand persons who attended: "In view of the present situation, we deem that the time has now come for us to take measures of last resort. We shall no longer permit hesitation and indecision on the part of the government."[81]

On October 9, the day after Russia ignored the scheduled evacuation, representatives of the Zenkoku Seinen Dōshisha (All-Japan Youth Comrades' Association), described as "an assemblage of the younger bloods of the Tairo Dōshikai," addressed an appeal to Prime Minister Katsura, in the name of the 37,000 members claimed by the association, stating that the reason for negotiations was over and nothing remained but a resort to the sword.[82] Independent of these groups, the Seven Pro-War Doctors continued an intense propaganda campaign through the medium of the printing press.

On November 5, representatives of the Tairo Dōshikai handed letters of warning to Genrō Itō and Prime Minister Katsura. This action was prompted by their belief that the government's indecision was due primarily to Genrō Itō's alleged interference in cabinet decision making, "abusing the special favor of the sovereign he enjoyed." The Dōshikai warned Genrō Itō of the "public indignation" that would be roused against him if he were to continue his interference. At the same time, the Dōshikai reminded Katsura that ultimate responsibility for the state affairs lay with him, and that interference by one of the Genrō would not absolve him from the immediate necessity of making the final decision.[83] It is difficult to determine whether the information that led to the Dōshikai's accusation against Itō was derived solely, as they themselves claimed, from street rumors and newspaper stories or from more authoritative sources that were anxious to see more public pressure applied upon the Genrō. In any event, the Dōshikai's letters of warning, which were made public after Genrō Itō criticized the Dōshikai in the *Tokyo Nichi-nichi Shimbun*, created such commotion and speculation that, on November 10, Katsura invited in three Dōshikai members, Sassa, Kōmuchi, and Tōyama, and declared that there was no want of unanimity between the Genrō and the cabinet ministers.[84]

The Dōshikai had also planned to present a memorial to the Emperor during the nineteenth session of the Imperial Diet, criticizing the government for its weak attitude toward Russia. This plan was forestalled by the action of Speaker Kōno Hironaka, as will be discussed below, whereupon the society submitted a memorial directly to the Emperor on December 16, 1903. The memorial stressed that the maintenance of peace in the East was Japan's sacred mission, that Russia had no intention of negotiating an agreement with Japan, and therefore the time had come to start fighting. It asked the Emperor to respond to the burning loyalty of his subjects by making the final decision immediately, for further hesitation by the government might seriously damage the nation's welfare.[85] Following the Dōshikai's action, it is said, many similar memorials were submitted to the throne by individuals and various organizations.[86]

On January 4, the Tairo Dōshikai issued another declaration calling for an immediate declaration of war, and a committee of six—Kōmuchi, Tōyama, Ōtake, Hasegawa, Kudō, and Nezu Hajime (a former army intelligence officer and an old China activist)—was appointed to visit the cabinet members and urge them to take decisive action immediately.[87] The declaration began:

It has already been nine long months since the negotiations with Russia started. In spite of the undeniable fact that our national opinion has long been united in favor of war, the government has so far drifted along, deluded by an indecisive and temporal peace with Russia. All the people of our nation are doubtful about, fearful of, and indignant over, this attitude on the part of the government.

It then traced the course of negotiations, stating that Russia had no intention of reaching an agreement with Japan, and added the familiar sentence, "Should we fail to decide the matter now, the opportunity will be gone forever." In conclusion, it discussed the responsibility of the government leaders and warned that the only choice was to take decisive action right away. The conclusion is particularly indicative of the thinking of these political activists:

We are told that a Russian reply will come soon. For what reason is our government waiting for their reply after all? We are convinced that the basic cause of the prolonged critical situation in Manchuria is negligence on the part of our government leaders. They have failed to fulfill their primary duty of assisting His Majesty's rule. Externally they have been preoccupied with the ceremonies of international relations and have meekly subjected our nation to the will of the Powers. Internally they have taken a weak-kneed attitude, hoping to transfer their basic responsibility to someone else. Since the shameful returning of the Liaotung Peninsula, nine long years have already passed. Is it not for today's opportunity that our people have borne the heavy burden and, in spite of severe economic difficulties, have approved and supported the great expansion of armaments?

Should the responsible people in our government miss this once-in-a-thousand years opportunity because of indecisiveness and hesitation, and should they as a result cause eternal harm to our nation, their crime shall never be atoned for, not even by death.

The Press. It has been stated that the *Yorozu Chōhō* and the *Mainichi Shimbun* adopted an anti-war stand. As pro-war opinion grew more and more intense, however, the *Yorozu Chōhō's* attitude began gradually to change. On September 15, 1903, less than a month before the scheduled third withdrawal of Russian troops, the *Yorozu Chōhō* published the following article criticizing the indecisive attitude of the government:

The Russian rampage has not been confined to Manchuria. It has now invaded the Korean border. Russia has demanded a lease on the strategic point of Yongampo . . . and yet, what positive action has our government taken in this critical situation? . . . . We have endured the Russians too long. Just because we have borne the unbearable, their license, rapacity, insults, and contempt have come upon us endlessly. We have now reached the limit of our endurance. Does the present situation still leave any room for discussion? Certainly not. If, in spite of this fact, our government leaders do not know what to do, it would be better to discard all the diplomatic and military organs of our nation, which consume a large portion of the national budget and the energies of the people.[88]

When Russia failed to carry out the October evacuation, Kuroiwa, the owner of the *Yorozu Chōhō*, changed his attitude completely. He fired Uchimura, Kōtoku, and Sakai and joined the ranks of the pro-war newspapers with an editorial answering affirmatively the question "Is War Inevitable?"[89] The following day, an editorial entitled "The Final Decision"[90] advocated war. Meanwhile, the tone of other newspapers and magazines was growing increasingly intense. On October 8, both the *Jiji Shimpō*, in "Our People's Forbearance," and the *Osaka Asahi Shimbun*, in "What Should We Do Hereafter?" demanded that the government make the final decision.[91] On October 14, even the pro-government *Kokumin Shimbun* issued "A Warning to the Government Leaders," stating that "should our government show signs of making further concessions to Russia, the righteous indignation of our people could not be held back even by 10,000 oxen. If this should occur, our nation would fall into confusion like a broken-up nest of a thousand bees."[92] The economics journal *Tōyō Keizai Shimpō*, discussing the inevitability of war in an editorial on November 5, said that "the possible effects of war upon the national economy are indeed grave, but the prestige and independence of our nation are of even more concern. If fighting is inevitable, we must of course bear the burden."[93] As already observed, the Tairo Dōshikai became extremely active about this time.

In this excited atmosphere, the Jikyoku Mondai Rengō Daikonshinkai (Friendly Meeting of Persons to Consider the Problem of the Current Situation) was held at the Imperial Hotel on November 10 under the joint auspices of various newspapers, magazine publishers, and news agencies. The meeting was reportedly attended by 215 "well-known people," including 70 Diet members, 30 newspapermen, and 50 businessmen, who unanimously adopted a resolution urging the government to take decisive action.[94] On November 13, when grand army maneuvers were held under the supervision of the Emperor in Hyōgo prefecture, newspapermen covering the affair met at Akashi; at the initiative of the *Osaka Asahi Shimbun* they resolved to promote immediate and decisive action against Russia.[95] On November 22, the Jikyoku Mondai Tōzai Rengō Shimbunkisha Dai Enzetsukai (Grand East-West Journalists' Forum on Current Affairs) was held at the Nakanoshima public hall in Osaka to promote unity in support of war within press circles. The main speakers included such well-known journalists as Enjōji Kiyoshi of the *Yorozu Chōhō* and Naitō Torajirō (Konan) of the *Osaka Asahi Shimbun*. It was reported that the audience numbered 2500 persons.[96] The following day a second forum was held in Osaka by representatives of several major newspapers including the *Osaka Mainichi Shimbun*, the *Hōchi Shimbun*, and the *Tokyo Asahi Shimbun*. They resolved to demand that the government declare war immediately, stating, "A peaceful solution of the Manchurian question through indecisive diplomatic measures and humiliating conditions is meaningless. This is not what our nation wants."[97]

Apparently realizing that the *Mainichi Shimbun*, which until then had been opposed to war, was going against the current trend, its president, Shimada Saburō, suddenly changed his views.[98] This left only Itō Miyoji's *Tokyo Nichi-nichi Shimbun* adhering to a generally anti-war stand in support of the government. It charged that the Tairo Dōshikai and the Seven Pro-War Doctors were mere notoriety seekers, calling them "city idlers," "spineless and frivolous people," "Russophobes," and even "noisy and crazy fellows."[99] As late as November 11,

1903, the paper still argued that "the so-called [opinion of our nation] is no more than the utterance of a few advocates of war. Our government should endeavor to defend our rights by peaceful means only and to avoid war in the Far East."[100]

Political Parties. During this period of prewar negotiations, political parties in Japan were in no position to function as intermediaries between the government and the public. As noted in Chapter 2, this was partly due to the growing tendency of the top party leadership to compromise with the government, and partly to their ignorance of the actual progress of the negotiations with Russia.[101] Not only did the political parties and the Diet have no function in foreign policy making, but, on the pretext of "diplomatic secrecy," the government repeatedly refused to answer questions on foreign policy raised by Diet members.[102]

The Seiyūkai's attitude toward the Manchurian question was very ambiguous. We have seen that it refused to cooperate with the Kokumin Dōmeikai in 1900. The party failed to make its stand clear even when the Taigaikō Dōshikai demanded on July 29, 1903, that it do so. In response to the Tairo Dōshikai's demand for cooperation, Seiyūkai president Saionji Kimmochi made a speech on October 16, which was distributed to local party members.[103] While declaring his support for strong action, Saionji at the same time acquiesced in the seemingly weak policy of the government. He stated:

Since the Meiji Restoration, it has been our nation's basic policy that internally we cultivate national strength and promote national culture, and externally we expand national interests and increase national wealth . . . . Therefore we must say that even on the current foreign question, which has been causing considerable uproar in our country, the grand policy of our nation has long been set . . . . Thus, we should provide our government with the greatest freedom of action, so that it will be able to obtain the most effective diplomatic results in accordance with the already set policy of our nation . . . .[104]

The Ingaidan (non-Diet members) group within the Seiyūkai disagreed with Saionji. At its inaugural meeting on December 1, 1903, the Ingaidan issued a strongly worded resolution: "The measures taken by our government in the negotiations with Russia have been most inappropriate. We have thereafter decided to take action to censure the government in the coming Diet session."[105] Thus the Seiyūkai was divided between its leadership and its rank-and-file.

The Kenseihontō's situation was no better. On November 24, a general meeting of party Diet members had broken up after two hours of debate "without having reached any resolution on the foreign policy question."[106] On December 2, a meeting of Diet members, former Diet members, and party councilors discussed the attitude the party should adopt in regard to the coming nineteenth Diet session. The resolution approved at the meeting stated: "In order to maintain peace in East Asia, we must make Russia withdraw its troops from Manchuria, and at the same time we must have China open that region to the world. Our imperial nation's interests will develop soundly in Manchuria and Korea only after these measures have been carried out."[107] This statement was a product of compromise among the party members. Those who demanded a strong policy wanted to insert into the resolution the following passage: "The present cabinet's indecisive and weak attitude toward Russia has harmed the welfare of our nation. The cabinet should be changed immediately." This was rejected by the opposition, which included the influential Ōishi Masami and Inukai Tsuyoshi. Thus internal disagreement prevented the Kenseihontō as well from taking a clear stand on the foreign policy question.[108]

The minor parties were in no way prepared to deal with the issue, and therefore no political party presented the government with a clearcut, independent policy.[109] The *Tokyo Nichi-nichi Shimbun*, which had not yet changed its stand, expressed its distrust of the political parties when it declared that "it is the greatest shame of the political parties that their existence seems to have nothing to do with the welfare of our state and people."[110] Only some individual party politicians, as we have seen, engaged in pro-war activities. Certain members of the Seiyūkai and the Kenseihontō were bogged down in a seemingly futile attempt to form a coalition to oppose the Katsura Cabinet; but before they could achieve any effective alignment, the nineteenth session had convened.

At the opening ceremony convening the Diet on December 10, the customary imperial message was read to the House of Representatives. The Speaker of the House for the session was Kōno Hironaka, the leader of the Jiyū Minken Undō in Fukushima and one of the leading members of the old Jiyūtō. Although not a member of the Tairo Dōshikai, he was apparently an ardent sympathizer.[111] When the time came for the House to adopt its reply to the throne, Kōno, instead of reading the ceremonial address prepared by the Chief Secretary of the House Hayashida Kametarō, pulled from his pocket a draft he himself had prepared and read it aloud to the House. The House voted for Kōno's draft with resounding applause, apparently believing that it had been merely a ceremonial address to the throne, as established by time-honored practice, and it is unlikely that many representatives had listened carefully. In fact, what Kōno had read was a memorial to the Emperor censuring the Katsura Cabinet's indecisive attitude toward Russia.[112] It stated:

We are honored with Your Majesty's gracious message which you have so kindly given us, and that you now grant us the opportunity to hold this grand ceremony at the opening of the nineteenth session of the Diet. We have been deeply moved by Your Majesty's grace.

In this period of unprecedented national uprising, the administration of our cabinet ministers does not accord with the national demands of the time. Internal policies are based simply on temporary, remedial actions, and opportunities in foreign diplomacy are being missed. We cannot help feeling the utmost anxiety for such misgovernment by our administration; and therefore we appeal to Your Majesty's wise judgment.

We, the members of the House of Representatives, who are entrusted with the duty of assisting Your Majesty in the conduct of the affairs of state, expect to be true to your gracious will above and to the trust of the people below.

Your humble subject, Kōno Hironaka, Speaker of the House of Representatives, most respectfully presents this reply to Your Majesty.[113]

Some members of the Diet belatedly realized that Kōno's second paragraph was clearly intended to censure the Katsura Cabinet's handling of the Manchurian question. Few Diet members had such an intention when they blindly approved the draft memorial. Some of the Seiyūkai and Kenseihontō members tried, in cooperation with the government, to move to reexamine the address. When this attempt failed, the government dissolved the Diet on December 11, before the memorial could reach the throne.[114] This incident caused a further increase in the popular war spirit.[115] At the same time, the unexpected dissolution of the Diet gave the Katsura Cabinet time to pursue the negotiations with Russia and to cooperate with the Privy Council unhampered by parliamentary scrutiny and criticism.[116] Kōno Hironaka had resigned his membership in the Kenseihontō before resorting to this drastic measure, and for a short time after the incident he confined himself to his home.[117] Thus the political parties and the Diet played almost no role during the period of prewar negotiations.

Business Circles. Attitudes on war in business circles in the beginning were rather diverse, reflecting the unbalanced process of Japan's economic development. While more small-scale industrialists seem to have believed that "war would offer a golden opportunity to end the long-standing depression," those connected with more modern and larger scale industries were either distinctly opposed to war or at least hesitant about it.[118] In 1903 the cotton textile industry in Japan is reported to have been very confident of its future in both the foreign and domestic markets, as sales in China had continued to increase and a great expansion of the domestic market was expected. Among some businessmen, Russia's thrust into Manchuria was even welcomed in the belief that it would result in increasing demands for Japanese products. This outlook was not particularly heretical at that time. An executive of a major shipbuilding company, commenting on the Manchurian question in May 1903, stated:

The Russian government never wants to fight. It not only has no intention of fighting but also desires peace most sincerely . . . . Therefore, so long as we do not intend to fight, the Manchurian question will be solved peacefully . . . . If unfortunately we should fail to settle the question peacefully, our economy, which has not yet completely recovered from its last illness, will be totally destroyed by the war . . . . The peaceful settlement of the Manchurian question is what Japanese business circles most earnestly wish.[119]

Even as late as September 25, 1903, the leading economics journal *Tōyō Keizai Shimpō* declared: "The people should not worry about war. They may engage in their various occupations with unburdened minds, for knowledgeable people would never join these fellows who excitedly advocate war against Russia."[120] Thus, until late 1903, businessmen, particularly those in industries that were solidly established and making steady profits, were doubtful about the desirability of war.

Their attitude, however, began gradually to change, when Russia failed to carry out the third stage of its troop withdrawal in October. On October 28, at a Ginkō Shūkaijo (Bankers Club) banquet, Shi-

busawa Eiichi, president of the Daiichi Ginkō (First National Bank)
and of the Tokyo Chamber of Commerce, declared that "Japan should
fight Russia," and Kondō Rempei of the Nihon Yūsen Kaisha proclaimed, "One day's delay means another day's advantage for Russia."[121]
Business leaders attended the "Friendly Meeting of Persons to Consider
the Problem of the Current Situation" on November 10, and "earnestly
stressed the inevitability of war with Russia and urged the government
to make the final decision."[122]

Why did the upper strata in business circles change their attitudes
toward war? There seem to have been three basic reasons. First of all,
while they did not want to go to war over Manchuria, they regarded
Korea as essential to Japan's development. Takahashi Yoshio of the
Mitsui Company stated, "If anybody ignores our nation's prestige and
interests in Korea, Japan will not shrink from fighting."[123] President
Soeda Juichi of the Nihon Kangyō Ginkō agreed with Takahashi and
urged the government to take bolder steps for the development of
Korea.[124] Thus the opinions of business leaders grew more and more
bellicose as Russian actions seemed increasingly to threaten Japan's
position in Korea.

The second reason for this gradual change in attitude was the existence of what the press of the time termed a *fuan no heiwa* (uneasy
peace). Mimura Kumpei of the Mitsubishi Ginkō described the situation as follows:

Since the diplomatic question has not been settled in favor of either war or
peace, people are afraid they may be caught in a suddenly changed situation
or in a disaster. They are, therefore, frightened without knowing what to do
to restore their sense of security. This is the cause of the business depression
today. . . . There is no way to cure the root of the sickness in our business
activities except to settle the Manchurian question quickly.[125]

On December 1 the *Tokyo Asahi Shimbun* reported the ill effects of
the "uneasy peace" on business activities: ". . . the situation today is
one of neither war nor peace. . . . Because of this, businessmen are like
farmers who anticipate the coming of rain. They have returned quickly
from their farms and are now watching the movement of the clouds
from their doorsteps." The newspaper further declared, "The ill effects
of an endless 'uneasy peace' are worse than those of a temporary war.
This is why people wish to solve the problem swiftly, even if it means

war."[126] As businessmen thus tended increasingly to link the economic depression to the Manchurian question, business circles were gradually unified in favor of war.

The third reason was the generally optimistic view many businessmen held on the outcome of a war with Russia. According to Taguchi Ukichi, a well-known social and economic critic and editor of the influential *Tokyo Keizai Zasshi*, "peace-loving" businessmen finally made up their minds by thinking, "Prosperity should follow war. A humiliating peace is not the way to invigorate business activities."[127] This attitude was partly due to the belief that some still held that Russia would not fight if Japan maintained a determined stance.[128] Thus even those businessmen who were hesitant about war in the beginning finally joined the tide of pro-war enthusiasm. Their attitudes, however, were generally passive. They did not play an active role in unifying public opinion in support of war; immediately after the war broke out, Hara Takashi observed that "above all, businessmen abhorred war the most. But they did not have the courage to speak up. . . ."[129]

The Anti-War Activists. In the face of the growing war fever, the handful of anti-war activists as then existed in Japan faced an overwhelming task. Their activities centered around the *Heimin Shimbun* (Commoners' Newspaper), which according to its official subtitle was "A Weekly Journal of Socialist Propaganda." The key figures were Sakai Toshihiko and Kōtoku Shūsui, who had lost their positions on the *Yorozu Chōhō* in October 1903, when its owner changed his attitude on the war. Uchimura Kanzō, who also left the *Yorozu Chōhō*, did not join the Heiminsha (Commoners' Society), but confined his anti-war activities largely to Christian circles. The society was, however, assisted by such well-known Christian socialists as Abe Isoo and Kinoshita Naoe. The first issue of the *Heimin Shimbun* appeared on November 15, 1903; publication continued until January 29, 1905, sixty-four issues altogether with a reported average circulation of between 3500 and 4000. Government interference then forced the Heiminsha to cease publication, although their propaganda was soon resumed with the successor paper, *Chokugen* (Speaking Straightforwardly).[130]

In the beginning, the anti-war activists were not alone in their struggle. A number of newspapers and magazines opposed the war until quite late, even though some of them were admittedly, "semiofficial" organs, and the upper strata in business circles were at least reluctant to go to war until late 1903. It is ironic that, during the negotiations with Russia, the position of the socialist anti-war activists seemed to accord with that of the oligarchic decision-makers as a whole. In fact, before the outbreak of the war, the government was extremely tolerant toward the socialists.

In order to win public support, however, the anti-war activists had to counter Japan's basic political structure, which was giving rise to particularly strong feelings of nationalism and chauvinism. Moreover, they had to formulate an effective alternative with which to oppose Russian expansion in Manchuria and Korea. And all of this had to be done in an atmosphere of traditional anti-Russian sentiment. The anti-war activists were too weak, too inconsistent in their opinions, too unrealistic, and too far removed from the public to succeed.

Their writings, however, at times showed a prophetic insight, as when the *Heimin Shimbun* warned the Japanese people against what it regarded as war hysteria:

What would you, the people, get out of a victory in this war? First, would not the interest on national loans soon amount to some tens of millions or even several billion yen? Would not you and your posterity long live in agony under this burden? Second, would not a horrible increase in taxes become necessary to meet the endless expansion of public finance? A horrible increase in taxes! Is this not more terrifying to us than a fierce tiger? Third, would it not lead to a sudden rise of militarism? Would it not result in arms expansion? Furthermore, would it not produce wild speculation? A rise in prices? The degradation of public morals? . . . This is what you, the people, can no longer endure. With what expectation, then, do you rejoice in this war? We do not hesitate to predict today that, when the war comes to an end, your joy will certainly turn into remorse.[131]

Nevertheless, they failed to present a practical program to the public, which seemed increasingly convinced of the necessity of war to solve the Manchurian question. The anti-war movement, which has received a great deal of attention from recent historians, was in actuality only a feeble voice drowned out by the nationwide cry for war.[132]

The General Public. On September 25, 1903, Erwin Baelz, the Meiji emperor's court physician, recorded in his diary:

. . . on the train I met a fashionably dressed Japanese man. He told me, 'the people's indignation toward Russia is no longer under control. The government should declare war immediately. Otherwise, there will be, I fear, a civil rebellion. In fact, even the throne is threatened.' Life is easy for such irresponsible men as this man.[133]

During those days, the Japanese possessed by a strong war fever against Russia were apparently not the only such "irresponsible people" whom the German doctor happened to meet. The young poet Ishikawa Takuboku, who a few years later showed strong socialist leanings, wholeheartedly welcomed the war against Russia. He thought "the time had come to fight the Russians under the command of the gods," for he believed that the Russian troops in the Far East were "the devil's army and were hampering the eternal progress of the world." He therefore gathered villagers at a local school and as a "pure patriot" delivered an "impassioned speech" to them. He also desired to compose a "song for patriots" for "the people who wished to sing but had no song." Writing at the outbreak of the war, he exclaimed, "I don't know why, but my blood boils and my eyes burn. What joy! What joy!"[134] The more level-headed novelist Futabatei Shimei was no different. He thought the war with Russia would "freshen the oppressive air of our society and time," and would offer "an opportunity for the common people of Japan to become masters of their nation."[135] Deluged with war cries, even the most under-privileged classes in Japanese society, normally apathetic about politics, reportedly dashed to the front with optimistic and brave shouts.[136]

It is next to impossible to gauge accurately the state of mind of the general public. Newspaper accounts inevitably present an exaggerated picture. Throughout this period of national excitement, the Japanese people must have felt a normal sense of reluctance to go to war, a feeling not expressed in print. It seems, however, that the Japanese public reacted to the Manchurian question with mixed feelings of fear and hate. An emotional public is easily swayed by effective propaganda either in the direction of "war," as in the case of Japan at the time of the present study, or "peace" at other times and places in history. It cannot be denied that, by early 1904, the political activists and the press in Japan had created a strong war fever even among the general public.

Belgian Minister d'Anethan summarized the situation in Japan in a report to his government on January 22, 1904:

During the long period of suspense and anxiety, when Japanese patriotism was awakened and overexcited to a point that cannot be appreciated from afar and that is well understood only by the foreigner who has studied the history and character of this essentially military people, the Government defied unanimous public opinion to maintain peace. The pressure has become too strong and, unless Russia capitulates, there will be war.

We know that in the history of great countries agitation and popular emotion sometimes swept the Government into an imprudent and reckless policy in spite of itself. When this happened, however, cool-headed men always thought to calm the spirits by their counsels and influence and to show the dangers of thoughtless action. For the past two years Japan has been passing through one of these fatal crises. But vainly do I look for wise and moderate counsels outside the Cabinet.[137]

American Minister in Tokyo Lloyd C. Griscom's report of January 21, 1904, supports d'Anethan's view, but with even greater alarm:

The Japanese nation is now worked up to a high pitch of excitement, and it is no exaggeration to say that if there is no war it will be a severe disappointment to the Japanese individual of every walk of life. The people are under such a strain that the present condition cannot last long.[138]

The Final Decision

As we have stated earlier, when formal negotiations with Russia commenced, Japan's oligarchic decision-makers were not a monolithic group, as they have usually been described, but were divided into two groups. One group was represented by the Genrō, who still held a relatively optimistic view of the negotiations and were sincerely anxious to reach an agreement with Russia. They were the only people within the decision-making circle both able and willing to moderate the Japanese demands. Whether or not they could effectively play such a moderating role, however, depended upon the Russian response. The one condition upon which the Japanese decision-makers were unanimously agreed was that Japan's security in Korea must be guaranteed. Unless Russia were willing to accept this precondition, the Genrō would not be able to maintain the validity of their relatively conciliatory stand with respect to others within the decision-making circle. The other group, the second-generation leaders, represented by Prime Minister Katsura and Foreign Minister Komura, held a pessimistic view of the prospects for negotiations and, fully anticipating a war with Russia, were determined to pursue a hard-line policy. Responsibility for the conduct of the negotiations rested with them, but the final decision for war could not be made without the full approval of the Genrō.

The first counterproposals, which Russia finally presented to Japan on October 3, 1903, seriously undermined the Genrō's optimism.[139] Russia not only refused to make any engagement regarding China's independence and territorial integrity, but also demanded that Japan recognize Manchuria and its littoral as being outside the Japanese sphere of interest. Russia thus sought complete freedom of action in Manchuria. At the same time, Russia proposed to restrict Japan's position in Korea, admitting Japan's right to send troops to Korea only on the condition that it was done "with the knowledge of Russia." In addition, Russia proposed that the two countries mutually agree not to use any part of Korean territory for strategic purposes and that a neutral zone be established entirely within Korean territory north of the 39th parallel. Russia's intention, therefore, was to exclude Manchuria from the negotiations and discuss only the disposition of Korea.[140]

The Genrō's position was further weakened by the sudden death on October 1, 1903, of Vice-Chief of the Army General Staff Tamura Iyozō, who had been, as we have seen, a faithful subordinate to Genrō Ōyama. Tamura was succeeded by Kodama Gentarō, then home minister and concurrently governor general of Taiwan. The selection was apparently dictated by Yamagata's and Katsura's consideration that the new vice-chief must be able to carry out his responsibilities should war with Russia break out.[141] Kodama, who was quite sympathetic toward the Kogetsukai group, is said to have accepted the appointment willingly, despite the definite demotion in rank. He took the post on October 13, it is believed, with a view to preparing Japan for the coming war against Russia, and to the great joy of the Kogetsukai members in the army, embarked vigorously on war preparations.[142]

Meanwhile, Foreign Minister Komura began discussion with Baron Rosen, the Russian Minister to Tokyo, with the Japanese proposals and the Russian counterproposals as the starting point. They met several times during the month of October, but little was achieved.[143] On October 30, Komura presented a second set of Japanese proposals to Russia. These proposals contained some definite concessions. While insisting upon a mutual engagement to respect the independence and territorial integrity of China as well as Korea, Japan proposed to recognize Manchuria as being outside its sphere of special interest in return for the recognition by Russia that Korea was outside Russia's sphere of interest. Japan proposed also to recognize Russia's special interests in Manchuria (the phrase "in railway enterprises" was deleted) and its right to take such measures as might be necessary to protect those interests. Furthermore, Japan did not completely reject the idea of a neutral zone, suggesting that it should extend 50 kilometers on each side of the Korea-Manchuria frontier. Japan reserved the right to use Korean territory for strategic purposes, but offered to promise not to undertake any military works on the Korean coast capable of menacing freedom of navigation in the Korean Straits.[144]

These amended proposals were prepared in two Genrō conferences held on October 14 and 24. Unfortunately, no materials are available to give details of these conferences, but it seems safe to assume that the concessions were largely the result of Genrō insistence. Just about the time the second Japanese proposals were presented, we may recall, the rumor was widespread that the Genrō were forcing the cabinet ministers to take a conciliatory stand. The new proposals shifted from a clearly one-sided position to an approximately fifty-fifty bargain.

Russia's second counterproposals, which Rosen presented to Komura on December 11, virtually rejected the Japanese amendments. Reaffirming most of its previous proposals on Korea, including a neutral zone north of the 39th parallel and a mutual engagement not to use any part of Korean territory for strategic purposes, the new Russian counterproposals contained no reference to Manchuria, which was thus absolutely excluded from discussion.[145]

On December 16, a Genrō conference was convened, attended by Itō, Yamagata, Matsukata, Inoue, Ōyama, Katsura, Komura, Yamamoto, and Terauchi. A letter of December 21 from Yamagata to Katsura indicates that the Genrō apparently made some feeble efforts to continue the conciliatory policy.[146] In the end, however, the arguments of Komura and other cabinet ministers won out, and the conference decided that Japan should request Russia "to reconsider its position on the subject" and reinject Manchuria into the negotiations. This decision marks the end of any moderating role played by the Genrō, and of any hope for a peaceful solution of the Manchuria-Korea problem, unless Russia were to accept Japan's new proposals. The third set of Japanese proposals, actually constituting Japan's final position, were presented to Russia on December 21 in the form of a note verbale. There was little hope for Russian acceptance. Having given up almost all hope for reaching an agreement with Russia, the oligarchic decision-makers thereafter regarded the negotiations more as a means to earn time for military preparations than as serious efforts for a peaceful solution.[147]

The Genrō, whose stand had been seriously undermined by the two Russian counterproposals, were now forced to accept the situation. In the middle of December, Genrō Itō was still privately expressing the wish that war with Russia might be averted. On December 21, Katsura wrote to Yamagata reiterating the policy Japan would follow: first, that it would endeavor to solve the Manchurian question through diplomatic negotiations and would not resort to war for the sake of Manchuria; and second, that unless Russia accepted the Japanese amendments on Korea, Japan should take the last resort. Yamagata replied on the same day that he was not yet convinced of the need for Japan to go to war with Russia to solve the Korean problem.[148] The Genrō's reluctance, however, was not accompanied by any effective alternative policy. On December 24, after consulting with Kodama and Terauchi, Katsura called on the two senior Genrō, Itō and Yamagata, and obtained their unequivocal support for embarking on necessary military preparations for the approaching war.[149] The situation compelled the Genrō to comply with the second-generation leaders.

Consequently on December 28, a special cabinet council was called to discuss final preparations for war. It established a Supreme War Council, amended the regulations concerning the Imperial Headquarters, and decided on the necessity to complete the Seoul-Pusan railway and on other military matters.[150] On December 30, another Genrō conference was held to determine policies toward China and Korea in case of a rupture of negotiations with Russia. The government's increased military concern was indicated by the fact that, for the first time, Chief of the Navy General Staff Itō Sukeyuki, Vice-Chief Ijūin Gorō, and Army Vice-Chief Kodama attended a cabinet-level conference.[151] It was decided that China must remain neutral throughout the war, while Korea would be placed under Japanese military domination.[152] The change in the attitude of the Genrō is shown by the fact that Genrō Yamagata urged that troops be sent immediately to Seoul in order to secure the region for later Japanese action. His proposal was turned down primarily because of the opposition of Navy Minister Yamamoto, who argued that the navy was not yet ready to engage in troop transportation and that sending troops to Korea at that moment might produce international repercussions harmful to Japan.[153]

Given this attitude among the Japanese decision-makers, the Russian counterproposals of January 6, 1904, which returned to the original plan for a neutral zone in Korea and an agreement not to use Korean territory for strategic purposes, merely confirmed the futility of further negotiations.[154] At an imperial conference on January 12, all agreed that the negotiations were entirely hopeless. Since more time was required before the collection of troopships at Sasebo was completed, the conference decided to present a final set of proposals to Russia.[155] The proposals of January 13 demanded the elimination of restrictions on the use of Korean territory for strategic purposes; exclusion of the subject of a neutral zone altogether; mutual recognition of the territorial integrity of both China and Korea; Russian admission that Korea was outside its sphere of interest in return for Japan's recognition that Manchuria was outside its sphere of interest; and recognition of Japanese treaty rights and privileges in Manchuria. Japan's rigid stand indicated clearly that it did not expect Russia to accept these final proposals. While stating that they were proposed "entirely in a spirit of conciliation," Japan concluded on an ominous note: "The Imperial Government further hopes for an early reply from the Imperial Russian Government, since additional delay in the solution of this question will be extremely disadvantageous to the two countries."[156]

On January 24, Katsura had an audience with the Emperor and reported to him that: (1) should Russia accept the Japanese proposals completely, Japan need not start a war; (2) should Russia reject the Japanese proposals, Japan would have no choice but to commence hostilities against Russia immediately; (3) should Russia accept some of the Japanese proposals and make concessions acceptable to Japan, Japan would then have to further consider what policy it should follow.[157] Meanwhile, Komura repeatedly instructed Minister Kurino to urge the Russian government to reply to the final Japanese proposals, but the end of January came without a Russian reply. Reports from Kurino convinced the Japanese decision-makers that Russia was stalling merely to gain time to strengthen its military position. Having by then practically completed its own military preparations, Japan believed that further delay could only be to Russia's advantage. On January 30, Itō, Yamagata, Katsura, Komura, and Yamamoto met at the prime minister's official residence, where they agreed unanimously to a memorandum drafted by Genrō Itō stating that the time had come for Japan to reach a resolute decision (*ittō ryōdan no ketsu*). It is significant that by now Itō had concluded that, in view of overall Russian policy, even if Russia should concede on the two points of a neutral zone and the strategic use of Korea, any diplomatic solution of the Manchuria-Korea problem would bring about only a temporary peace. Japan, he concluded, must therefore decide whether, in view of its present weakness, it would be content with a temporary peace or would risk the nation to halt Russian ambitions at once.[158]

Two days later, Chief of the Army General Staff Ōyama advised the Emperor that it was essential for Japan to strike first.[159] On February 4, following a Genrō conference on the third, an imperial conference was held. The Emperor's most trusted advisers expressed no confidence as to the outcome of a war but revealed only Japan's desperate military and financial position. Nevertheless, the protracted negotiations, which had officially begun in August 1903, had clearly shown that no satisfactory agreement could be reached. The oligarchic decision-makers therefore decided unanimously that Japan, however poorly prepared, should go to war at once, because further delay could only be detrimental to Japan.[160]

The Japanese decision-makers were fully aware of the risk involved in war. The army calculated that Japan had a fifty-fifty chance to win a war.[161] The navy expected that half its forces would be lost, but it hoped the enemy's naval forces could be annihilated with the remaining half.[162] Vice-Chief of the Army General Staff Kodama anticipated that, if Japan could carry on the war advantageously for any length of time, a third power would offer its good offices.[163] Genrō Itō regarded Theodore Roosevelt as the only person in a position to offer his good offices to belligerents. On the day of the fatal imperial conference, Genrō Itō asked Harvard-educated Kaneko Kentarō, an old acquaintance of Roosevelt, to go to the United States to promote good relations between Japan and America.[164] Somewhat later, in July 1904, on his departure for Manchuria as General Commander of the Manchurian Army, Field Marshal Ōyama reportedly said in his strong Satsuma accent to his fellow provincial, Navy Minister Yamamoto, "I will take care of the fighting in Manchuria, but I am counting on you as the man to decide when to stop."[165] Thus the Japanese oligarchic decision-makers were "thinking of ending the war at the time of beginning it."[166]

What finally brought about unity among the decision-makers in their decision for war was the proven futility of negotiations with Russia. Consensus was gradually reached only during, not prior to, the negotiations, as the Russian counterproposals discredited the validity of the moderates' stand. Consequently, we cannot accept what Malozemoff calls "Galperin's thesis that the Japanese entered into negotiations with Russia only to acquire a semblance of legality and justification for their attack on Russia."[167] The oligarchic decision-makers decided to go to war not because they had been hard pressed by the political activists, but because they regarded Russian activities in Manchuria as a serious threat to Korea and, consequently, to the security of Japan. Also, no satisfactory negotiated settlement appeared to be forthcoming.

The demands for a strong policy voiced by the political activists may have strengthened the position of the hard-liners within the decision-making circle, but they could not have forced the Genrō to make the final decision. What the political activists accomplished was to mobilize sufficient public support for war, so that when the oligarchs at last decided on war, there was little need to persuade the populace to fight. Popular enthusiasm was such that some observers have even termed the Russo-Japanese War a "popular war."[168] As Kiyosawa states, the Japanese public's cooperation with the government commenced with the start of the war. The celebrated *kyokoku itchi* (national unity) of the war, however, was largely an outward phenomenon. From the very inception of the war, a large gap existed between the war aims of the oligarchic decision-makers and those of the political activists. The gap was to grow as the war progressed.

CHAPTER FOUR

THE OLIGARCHS IN WAR
AND PEACEMAKING

The Decision-Makers and the War

THE WAR progressed "unexpectedly well"[1] for Japan. Japanese forces conquered Liaoyang in September 1904 and, in October, took control of Shaho. In January 1905, they occupied Port Arthur and, in March, won the Battle of Mukden.

The basic reason for the Japanese victories lay in the difference between the two belligerents' attitudes toward the war. "Russia is fighting for its dinner and Japan for its life."[2] Japan had been preparing for this war since the Triple Intervention of 1895. Russia seems to have miscalculated Japanese determination and thought that it would be able to compel Japan to succumb to its will by threat alone.

Russia also apparently underestimated Japan's military power. When the war broke out, Russia sent only reservists to the Manchurian front and second reservists long past the prime of manhood. Regarding Europe as the area most vital to its interests, and in order to be prepared against internal revolution, Russia kept its elite soldiers in Europe. Thus, the Russian forces in Manchuria at the beginning of the war were not only few in number but were mostly uneducated peasants who were useless in modern warfare.[3] These peasant soldiers were not aware of the purpose of the war and therefore detested fighting. Moreover, the Russian forces then were poorly equipped.[4]

The military situation on the Manchurian front, however, gradually changed as Russia realized that successive defeats in Manchuria were stimulating revolutionary movements at home. It started a full-scale strengthening of its military forces in Manchuria, transferring its elite troops from Europe. The balance between the two belligerents began to shift markedly to Japan's disadvantage in early September 1904, after the Battle of Liaoyang. Although the battle had ended in Japanese victory, the Japanese forces suffered unexpectedly great losses in the battle and, most important, were faced with a severe lack of munitions.[5] They therefore were unable to pursue the retreating enemy and missed the opportunity to deal the enemy a fatal blow.[6]

After the Battle of Liaoyang, while Russia continued to strengthen its forces, Japan's lack of soldiers and munitions grew increasingly serious. Although it could still replenish its supply of ordinary soldiers, it already faced great difficulty in supplying officers, horses, and munitions.[7] The production capacity of the munitions factories in Japan could not meet the needs of expanded operations; quality quickly deteriorated and duds became common on the front.[8] Japan managed to meet military demands only by purchasing munitions from such foreign manufacturers as the Krupps in Germany.[9] As for the fighting forces, Imperial Headquarters organized four new field divisions and 48 second reserve battalions by extending the term of service of the second reserves. The number of officers, however, was insufficient.

Under these conditions, the Battle of Shaho was fought in mid-October 1904. Here Japan's military supply system reached the limit of its capacity and was on the verge of total collapse. For the battle the Japanese army mobilized 120,800 men and suffered 20,500 casualties. The Russian army fought with 220,000 men and had 41,000 casualties.[10] The following exchange of telegrams shows how severely the Japanese army suffered from the shortage of munitions:

Telegram dated October 19, 1904
From: Chief of Staff of the Manchurian Army Kodama
To: Chief of the Army General Staff Yamagata

The enemy forces have stopped at the left bank of the Hun River and completed reorganization of disarrayed ranks. Now they seen to be planning to take the offensive again. In view of our present superiority in numbers and morale, I consider it most advantageous to strike one more blow at the enemy at this moment. Alas, however, we cannot take this golden opportunity because of the lack of munitions. The distance between our forces and the enemy is small, ranging from only 300-400 meters to 2000-3000 meters. Even though we exchange small fire day and night and nightly repeat our attacks, we still fail to deal the enemy a fatal blow. It is indeed regrettable that we are compelled to wait for the supply of munitions as we hold the line firmly at Shaho.

Telegram dated October 19, 1904
From: Chief of the Army General Staff Yamagata
To: Chief of Staff of the Manchurian Army Kodama

Re the matter of munitions: In spite of ordering munitions from abroad and
our best efforts to increase productivity at home, our supply is still poor. This
is indeed a pity. The other day at the Prime Minister's residence, when I
stressed the fact that the government should not spare money in procuring
military supplies, no cabinet minister was opposed to my opinion. However,
alas, as a result of many years of conservative planning, we are today unable
to expand our munitions production quickly enough. It is regrettable that we
repeatedly miss chances of victory merely because of lack of munitions.[11]

The Battle of Shaho ended in an indecisive victory for the Japanese
army. The two forces then withdrew from the field but remained at
Shaho, engaging in trench warfare. The Russian forces now had an
opportunity to prepare fully before they assumed the offensive, while
the Japanese could only wait.

At the same time, the Japanese operation against Port Arthur was
making no progress whatever. In August 1904, when the full-scale attack
upon the fortress was launched, the Japanese expected its immediate fall,
remembering how easily it had been won during the Sino-Japanese War.
This time, Port Arthur proved to have an entirely different kind of
defense structure and, in addition, there was the ever-present problem of
lack of munitions.[12] Japanese losses in the Port Arthur operation far
exceeded what Imperial Headquarters had anticipated. Moreover, the
operation in northern Manchuria, which had relied on the participation
of the forces that were already to have taken Port Arthur, was greatly
affected by the delay and the great losses there.

At home, the people prepared lanterns and flags for a victory celebration and impatiently awaited the expected news of the fall of Port
Arthur. The German doctor Baelz recorded in his diary:

The way in which they count upon taking Port Arthur is almost uncanny.
In all the streets of Tokyo, scaffolding and wires are arranged along the
houses or across the streets for the fixing of lanterns and flags. My next-door
neighbor wanted recently to buy some Japanese lanterns, but at all the shops
to which he applied he got the same answer, that they could take no further
orders, since their entire stock had been preempted for the Port Arthur
festival. Things are even worse in Yokohama. A great many storehouses are
filled up to the roof with materials for the celebrations. Nobody seems to

dream for a moment that it can be anything but absolutely certain that Port Arthur will fall![13]

Several lantern marches of celebration were actually carried out as erroneous news of victory reached Japan, and impatience grew at the slow progress of the Port Arthur operation.[14] In October 1904, the Emperor issued an edict cautioning the people against excessive emotionalism and urging that their energies be devoted instead to increased efforts for the war.[15]

The staff of the Manchurian Army feared not only that stagnation on the northern Manchurian front would adversely affect Japan's military operations and the morale of the people at home, but also, more seriously, that it would invite the contempt of the world upon the Japanese military capacity. They strongly advocated, therefore, taking a full-scale offensive.[16] Imperial Headquarters agreed with them but refused to assume the offensive because of the lack of munitions. After engaging in some comparatively small skirmishes, the Japanese forces in Manchuria were forced to remain inactive throughout the winter.

The Japanese army, aware of the disadvantages of a prolonged confrontation, challenged the Russian forces to a decisive battle at Mukden in February 1905. Spring had just come. General Ōyama stirred up the morale of his troops, calling this encounter "the Battle of Sekigahara of the Russo-Japanese War."[17] "Anybody who could fight at all on the front," including elderly reserves and raw recruits, had been mobilized. All Japan's land forces were concentrated there, and its military capacity was strained to the limit.[18] Nevertheless, Japan was able to put into battle 120,000 fewer men than did its opponent (249,800 Japanese to 376,200 Russians), and when the battle started, further Russian reinforcements were on their way from Europe.

The battle was fierce, ending on March 10 in a Japanese victory. But it was an indecisive victory, with Japanese casualties soaring to 72,008. The Russian forces retreated to the north "in good order" and began preparations for attack as reinforcements continued to arrive.[19]

It was becoming clear to Imperial Headquarters that they had seriously underestimated the Russian fighting capacity, and that the northern Manchurian region could accommodate at least one million troops.[20] Russia's financial strength also far surpassed Japanese calculations. Imperial Headquarters had estimated that at most eight trains a day could run on the single-track Siberian Railway and concluded that the maximum transportation capacity of the railway would be 200,000 men. Russia, however, had made great improvements on the imperfect track and cars, completed the trans-Baikal line on September 26, 1904, and constructed double tracks and sidings at key points. As the war proceeded, Russia stopped using the sidings and instead sent newly constructed cars eastward, abandoning them at their destination, in this way using the single-track line of several thousand miles with the same efficiency as a double-track line. As a result, it was able to run as many as 14 trains a day on the track and to send half a million elite troops from Europe.[21]

After their "calculated retreat," the Russian forces replenished their fighting capacity at the Manchurian border. On March 12, 1905, the tsar replaced Commander Kuropatkin with General Linievitch. The new commander was watching for an opportunity to turn the tide in Manchuria with a decisive battle.[22] By then, the Russian army was three times the size of the Japanese, and the Manchurian Army estimated that to defeat its powerful enemy decisively, Japan would have to increase its forces by six more divisions and obtain one billion additional yen for war expenses.[23]

The actual situation was such that to sufficiently reinforce the field troops on the extended front line would have required at least a year. Moreover, the weapons and munitions needed to accompany such an increase in field divisions could have been obtained only by imports. It was clear that Japan could not adequately prepare itself for another major battle.[24]

It was the Japanese military authorities who first recognized how critical the situation was. On March 8, 1905, War Minister Terauchi was already requesting Lloyd C. Griscom, the American minister in Tokyo, "quite seriously to convey to the President his opinion that the time had come when the war should cease and that he was quite ready to stop fighting," while stating "that this was his opinion, not as a minister of war, but as Seiki Terauchi, a private individual."[25]

On March 10, having received the report of victory in the Battle of Mukden, Yamagata "had an audience with the Emperor and advised him that now the adroit handling of national [foreign] policy was most urgent." On the same day Yamagata "discussed this matter fully with the authorities concerned" and demanded that "they, with careful planning and deliberation, not miss the opportunity when it presented itself."[26]

As mentioned above, Ōyama, the cautious and far-sighted commander of the Manchurian Army, on his departure for the Manchurian front had requested Yamamoto to "decide when to stop." He immediately realized what Yamagata had in mind; on March 13 he sent the following message to Imperial Headquarters urging the government to make a quick and appropriate diplomatic move:

Our military operations following the Battle of Mukden should be particularly in harmony with our national [foreign] policy. In other words, whether we decide to advance further in pursuit of the enemy or to take a course of positional warfare, unless our military operations are in accord with the national [foreign] policy, the struggle, perhaps costing several tens of thousands of lives, will be in vain.

If our national [foreign] policy were decided on the basis of military success, our army would suffer meaningless losses. This is not a trifling matter. The duty of our Manchurian Army is to push the enemy far out of Manchuria. In order to fulfill this great duty, we must conquer Tiehling, Changchun, and Harbin and still keep pursuing the enemy. If our national [foreign] policy were not in harmony with the activities of the Manchurian Army, the long march of full forces would be nothing but a movement in vain.

If our national [foreign] policy is in harmony with their activities, the Manchurian Army will not hesitate to march on, even to the banks of the Amur River. In short, whether we pursue the enemy further or resort to positional warfare, we must be fully prepared in advance. In particular, in order to move a great army across the mountainous areas from Mukden to east of Tiehling, we need war supplies. Therefore, at this juncture, when we have so damaged the enemy that it will be almost impossible for it to restore its forces soon, we desire to have our future military operations and our national [foreign] policy in complete accord. Your careful consideration would be appreciated.[27]

The following day Yamagata presented Ōyama's letter to the Emperor[28] and, on March 23, after obtaining the war minister's agreement,[29] outlined his views on "the combined tactics of war and diplomacy" to Prime Minister Katsura, Finance Minister Sone, and Foreign Minister Komura.

In a long memorandum expressing his opinion, Yamagata observed with calm realism that, in view of the fact that the enemy would never sue for peace, the war would continue for several more years and stated:

Before starting our operations for the third period of the war, there is something on which I am urged to request your careful deliberation, for the planning of great operations should always be in harmony with national [foreign] policy. If there were any discrepancy between them, victories on the battlefield would not promote the national interest. . . . Moreover, even after we have conquered Harbin and Vladivostok, we will not be able to say that we have injured the enemy fatally. Even at that juncture, the recalcitrant enemy will not readily request peace. Nay, judging from the situation up to today, the enemy will never request peace unless we have invaded Moscow and St. Petersburg. . . . Whether we take the offensive or the defensive, we are still a long way from peace. There are certain things to which we must give our most careful consideration. First, while the enemy still has powerful forces in its home country, we have already exhausted ours. Second, while the enemy still does not run short of officers, we have lost a great number since the opening of the war and cannot easily replace them. . . . There are other items that require our careful consideration: constructing a double-track railway for a distance of more than 100 *ri* between Mukden and Harbin to replenish military supplies; increasing the number of guards to correspond to the supply line extension; and creating as many new troops as quickly as possible. . . . In order to carry out the above, we must naturally expend a huge amount of money. The burden on the people will become much greater. . . . In short, our military operations in the third period of the war are of greatest significance, and should we make a mistake, our glorious victory thus far would be nullified. We must now be prudent.[30]

Yamagata's opinion was in fact nothing other than a request that the government make a quick diplomatic move for peace.

On March 28, Chief of Staff of the Manchurian Army Kodama was secretly summoned to Tokyo by Imperial order to report the details of the Battle of Mukden to the Emperor.[31] The main objective of his trip, however, was to urge that the Japanese government make moves toward peace. Upon seeing Vice-Chief of the Army General Staff Nagaoka Gaishi at Shimbashi Station, Kodama is said to have reprimanded him saying, "Nagaoka, don't be so stupid. If one has started a fire, he must put it out. Have you forgotten this?"[32]

After reporting to the Emperor on March 31,[33] Kodama remained to talk with cabinet members, the Genrō, and military leaders at Imperial Headquarters. He argued that the country that starts a war should know how to stop it, and that a poor country such as Japan had nothing to gain from a protracted war. He stressed the fact that the army had done its best and urged that Japan grasp the opportunity provided by the Mukden victory to terminate the fighting. He wondered if no measures could be taken to promote peace.[34]

The Japanese government was also aware of the necessity for a speedy termination of the war, but its attitude toward peace moves was not as favorable as that of the military leaders. Ōyama and Kodama of the Manchurian Army in particular viewed the action of governmental authorities as being disturbingly slow.[35] The enraged Kodama is said to have shouted, "Isn't there any Foreign Office in Japan?"[36]

The Official Terms of Peace

The Japanese oligarchic decision-makers, who could not even dream of subduing Russia completely, hoped for an early termination of hostilities. In fact, the question of a peace settlement had been a topic of diplomatic discussions since the beginning of the war. Reasons for this lay in the state of affairs in the two belligerent countries. For Japan, insufficient financial and military resources made a protracted war impossible; Russia, on its side, was threatened by internal revolutionary movements. Moreover, the Russo-Japanese War was a concentrated expression of the complex interests of the Powers, who showed great interest in the progress of the war and attempted to use it to their own advantage.[37] Because of this situation, in July 1904, Foreign Minister Komura told Japanese representatives in Europe that, as diplomatic policy, Japan wished to avoid an international conference for the settlement of the war and would accept no mediation by a third power unless such mediation were the only means to bring about direct negotiations with Russia.[38]

At the same time Komura recognized the necessity of defining the government's policy toward a peace settlement. Therefore, in July 1904, he presented to Prime Minister Katsura his opinion concerning the terms of peace, stating:

The terms of peace should, of course, be adjusted to the progress of the war. Nevertheless, in principle these terms must fulfill the following four major objectives:

1. To achieve Japan's war objectives; that is, to maintain the independence of Korea and the integrity of Manchuria and to establish eternal peace in the Far East.
2. To promote the development of Japan's national strength through the expansion of our rights and interests in Manchuria, Korea, and the Maritime Provinces.
3. To advance Japan's policy concerning the future of China.
4. To expand Japan's sphere of influence in Manchuria and Korea in accordance with the postwar situation.

Komura then enumerated Japan's major peace terms, based on the assumption that peace negotiations would be started immediately following the fall of Port Arthur and the Battle of Liaoyang.

Japan's Demands to Russia
1. To pay a war indemnity.
2. To recognize Japan's complete right of freedom of action in Korea and to promise not to interfere directly or indirectly with Japanese interests in that region.
3. To recognize the validity of all declarations made by the Korean government during the Russo-Japanese War.
4. To withdraw Russian troops from Manchuria within a period to be specified and to return to China administrative rights over the areas Russia had occupied.
5. To promise that the trans-Manchurian railway would not be used for the purpose of military or territorial expansion but exclusively for commercial purposes.
6. To cede to Japan the railway between Harbin and Port Arthur and all its branches together with all privileges and properties appertaining thereto.
7. To transfer to Japan the leased area of the Liaotung Peninsula together with all privileges and properties appertaining thereto.
8. To recognize the principle of equal opportunity for all nations in commerce and industry in Manchuria.
9. To cede Sakhalin and all islands appertaining thereto to Japan.
10. To grant to Japan full fishing rights along the coasts and rivers of the Maritime Provinces.
11. To grant Japanese ships the right of free navigation from the estuary of the Amur River to Blagovyeshchensk.
12. To open Nikolaevsk, Khabarovsk, and Blagovyeshchensk as trading ports and to permit the stationing of Japanese consuls at the three ports as well as at Vladivostok.

Japan's Demands to China

1. To promise not to cede any part of Manchuria to a foreign country.
2. To promise to carry out fully its responsibility for the maintenance of order and safety in Manchuria.
3. To promise to carry out the administrative, military, and police reforms necessary to fulfill this responsibility.
4. To recognize the transfer from Russia to Japan of the railway between Harbin and Port Arthur and its branches together with all privileges appertaining thereto.
5. To grant to Japan rights to construct railways from a certain point along the Yalu River to Liaoyang and from a certain point along the railway between Harbin and Port Arthur to Kirin.
6. To recognize the transfer from Russia to Japan of the leased area of the Liaotung Peninsula together with all privileges appertaining thereto.
7. To promise to open the following cities to foreign nations for commercial activities: Feng-huang-cheng, Liaoyang, Tiehling, and Tung-chiang-tzu in Shengching province; Kwan-cheng-tzu, Harbin, Kirin, Hunchun, and San-hsing in Kirin province; and Tsitsihar, Hailar, and Aigun in Heilungkiang province.
8. To grant Japanese ships the right of navigation on the Liao, Sungari, and Amur rivers and their tributary waters.
9. To grant Japan lumbering and mining rights along the Amur and Hun rivers.
10. To grant Japan full fishing rights along the coast of Shenching province.

Komura concluded his memorandum with the following statement:

The scope of these terms will not jeopardize the interests of the Powers. In view of our war objectives and the great sacrifices we have made for the war, our demands as set out above are not excessive. Since we will not be able to win a complete victory in this war, it is extremely unlikely that Russia will accept even such reasonable demands as these. However, keeping in mind the objectives for which we have risked the fate of our nation, and in view of the fact that the nature of the coming peace will have grave consequences for the security and future policy of our Imperial nation, we should make the utmost effort with full determination to achieve our war objectives.[39]

Prime Minister Katsura also formulated his private terms for peace in August 1904, before the Battle of Liaoyang. On the basis of four major objectives almost identical with those of Komura, Katsura listed his peace terms as follows:

1. To have Russia recognize Japan's freedom of action in Korea and thus eliminate any cause of future conflict.
2. In order to eliminate any future Russian threat to the northern boundary of Korea, to have Russia withdraw its troops from Manchuria, promise to use the trans-Manchurian railway exclusively for commercial purposes, and cede to Japan the railway between Harbin and Port Arthur and the leased area of the Liaotung Peninsula.
3. As terms that are not absolutely indispensable but should be secured as far as circumstances permit:
   (a) To have Russia pay a war indemnity.
   (b) To have Russia transfer Sakhalin to Japan.
   (c) To have Russia grant Japan full fishing rights along the coast of the Maritime Provinces.[40]

It is apparent that Katsura was more realistic and restrained than Komura in his demands. For example, the payment of a war indemnity is at the top of Komura's list of peace terms, whereas it is one of the accessory terms of peace on Katsura's list. However, in commenting on the second of the four major objectives—the expansion of Japan's rights and interests—both Katsura and Komura stressed that "since we cannot expect to obtain a satisfactory indemity, we must place a great deal of emphasis upon the expansion of our rights and interests."[41]

Katsura and Komura looked forward to negotiating a peace based on these terms. Russia, however, would not easily succumb. In March 1905, Komura presented to Katsura another memorandum on peace terms, this one based on the assumption that peace negotiations would be started immediately after the Battle of Mukden. It was more or less identical with his opinion of July 1904, except for the following modifications: First, the advancement of Japan's policy concerning the future of China was omitted from the list of major objectives. Second, payment of a war indemnity was made the seventh rather than the first demand to Russia and items eight (equal opportunity in commerce in Manchuria), eleven (right of navigation on the Amur River), and twelve (opening of the trading ports and the stationing of Japanese consuls) were all omitted. Third, of the demands to China, "the opening of Manchuria" was to be demanded instead of the opening of various cities.[42]

Kodama then began to make active moves toward peace. Through his forceful persuasion of government authorities, the Genrō, and Imperial Headquarters a cabinet conference was held on April 8, 1905, at which a decision was reached on the basis of Komura's memorandum of March 1905,[43] concluding that, since a cessation of hostilities was not in sight, Japan should prepare for a protracted war. At the same time the cabinet decided:

1. As to military operations, Japan should firmly hold the advantageous position it has been steadily gaining and should strive to obtain a more advantageous position as far as possible.

2. Diplomatically, Japan at this juncture should take appropriate measures to achieve a satisfactory peace as quickly as circumstances permit, while at the same time making an effort to achieve its ultimate objectives in the war. Japan should create closer relations and understandings with the Powers, particularly those friendly to Japan, to prevent an alliance of the Powers from working against it and even to gain their assistance in achieving our ultimate objectives in the war.[44]

The cabinet decision also listed as "matters under consideration":

1. To restrict Russian naval forces in the Far East.
2. To disarm Vladivostok and make it a trading port.
3. To demand that all Russian war vessels that had found refuge from battle in neutral ports be turned over to Japan.
4. To make a mutual agreement to set up a demilitarized zone along the Russo-Korean border at the lower Tumen River.

Meanwhile, on March 30, Yamagata, Kodama, Terauchi, and Nagaoka discussed the future operations of the Manchurian Army and decided on the following action: (1) The Manchurian Army was to conquer Harbin; (2) the army in north Korea was to march north as swiftly as possible and eradicate enemy elements in Korea, and (3) Sakhalin was to be conquered immediately.[45] On April 13, Imperial Headquarters gave these orders to Ōyama, with the instruction: "Henceforth military operations should be closely related to diplomatic policy. The Manchurian Army therefore should act in accordance with the progress of diplomacy."[46]

The implications of the cabinet decision of April 8 were twofold: Japan's military operations were to be carefully coordinated with its foreign policy; and Japan would welcome the attempts of a third power to mediate between the two belligerents for direct negotiations.[47] Nevertheless, the tone of the decision was one of "wait and see," for it included no positive and concrete recommendations for the start of peace negotiations. Kodama indicated in a letter dated April 21 to Ōyama[48] that the basic cause of this indecision lay in the "lack of agreement between Itō and Yamagata, on the one hand, and Katsura and Komura on the other, concerning diplomatic measures to promote peace." Kodama's letter does not make clear the exact nature of the disagreement between the Genrō and the cabinet ministers. We know that, on March 29, Itō had already told the Emperor that a victor might propose peace,[49] and it would therefore appear that the Genrō advocated that Japan formally request a third country to mediate, while the cabinet ministers continued to insist that the first peace moves must be made by the defeated nation and, consequently, that it would be improper for Japan to make the first move.[50]

In any event, as a result of Kodama's almost week-long mediation between the Genrō and the cabinet members, a Genrō conference was held on April 17. The conference decided that "Japan, using the United States as a mediator, would initiate a diplomatic move." Needless to say, the scheme of starting peace negotiations with President Roosevelt as mediator was what Itō had had in mind at the outbreak of the war. After this decision was made, the Japanese government began more actively to move for peace talks. On April 21, a cabinet conference decided several concrete terms for peace, to which the Emperor gave his sanction:

Absolutely Indispensable Items:
1. To have Russia acknowledge Japan's complete right of freedom of action in Korea, which has been the greatest obstacle to peace in the Far East.
2. To have Russia withdraw its troops from Manchuria within a period to be specified, in accordance with the doctrines on the security of Manchuria which our Imperial nation has been advocating. Japan will, needless to say, withdraw its troops from the region at the same time as Russia.
3. The control of Port Arthur and Dairen and the Harbin branch of the Chinese Eastern Railway has served as a tool of Russian aggression, enabling it to exercise great influence over southern Manchuria and further threaten the Korean border. Consequently, to eliminate future causes of trouble, Japan should secure the leased area of the Liaotung Peninsula and the above-mentioned branch railway.

Items Not Absolutely Indispensable but to Be Secured Insofar as Possible:
1. To have Russia pay Japanese war expenses.
2. To have turned over to Japan all Russian war vessels that had found refuge from battle in neutral harbors.
3. To have Russia cede Sakhalin and all islands appertaining thereto to Japan.
4. To have Russia grant Japan fishing rights along the coast of the Maritime Provinces.[51]

The payment of an indemnity, which stood first on Komura's July 1904 list and was vigorously demanded by the Japanese public,[52] was finally removed from the roster of absolutely indispensable items. The conclusion of the decision shows that the cabinet had little confidence that even these moderate demands could be achieved: "Since we have not dealt the final blow to Russia in spite of our repeated victories, we must expect to encounter extreme difficulty before we succeed in having Russia accept even these terms for peace."[53]

The Genrō agreed completely with the cabinet that Japan's military and financial situation made it impossible to demand more than modest peace terms. For instance, prior to the Battle of the Japan Sea, Itō had concluded after careful study of information from various quarters that "the war will expand more and more and will not be terminated in the near future." Pointing to the factional struggle within the Russian government, he stated that the terms for peace would have a great effect upon the activities of both the peace and war factions in Russia; therefore, in view of the fact that a protracted war was definitely disadvantageous to Japan, the latter should not make the mistake of prolonging it by making excessive demands and thereby strengthening the position of the war faction.[54]

The military leaders, who ardently desired peace, of course had no objection to the mild terms for peace. On the contrary, the cabinet decision seemed to them too optimistic. Upon finding among the peace terms the demand for the payment of war expenses, Kodama is said to have exclaimed, "The fool Katsura is still running after an indemnity!"[55] As noted earlier, although Katsura seriously doubted that Japan would get any indemnity from Russia,[56] it was impossible for Japan not to demand it at all.

After reaching a general agreement on peace terms, the Japanese decision-makers decided to approach President Roosevelt, who, as part of his policy of maintaining a balance between Russia and Japan in the Far East, had earlier indicated his willingness to mediate at an appropriate time.[57] At this time, however, the Russian Baltic fleet was on its way to the Far East, passing Singapore in April 1905, its movements watched by the entire world. The tsar, confident of Russian naval superiority over the Japanese, expected the activities of the massive fleet to bring about a complete change in the war situation and therefore would not listen to proposals for peace talks. Consequently, Roosevelt's mediation was postponed until the results of the Battle of the Japan Sea became clear. The Japanese naval victory of May 27 and 28 provided the awaited opportunity for peacemaking. News of total Russian defeat gave rise to renewed worldwide demands for the restoration of peace.[58] The tsar, who was greatly shocked by the defeat, was now inclined to consider peace talks.[59]

President Roosevelt's reaction to the Japanese victory was expressed in his words to Kaneko Kentarō immediately after the battle:

My heartfelt congratulations on the outstanding victory of the Japanese navy. This is the greatest phenomenon the world has ever seen. Even the Battle of Trafalgar could not match this. I could not believe it myself, when the first report reached me. As the second and third reports came, however, I grew so excited that I myself became almost like a Japanese, and I could not attend to official duties. I spent the whole day talking with visitors about the Battle of the Japan Sea, for I believed that this naval battle decided the fate of the Japanese Empire.[60]

The Japanese government, impatiently waiting for a chance to begin negotiations for peace, could not miss this opportunity.

On May 30, Prime Minister Katsura called on Itō and obtained his consent to request that President Roosevelt act directly as a mediator.[61] The following day, Katsura instructed the Japanese minister in Washington, Takahira Kogorō, to make a formal request to the president that "he see his way directly and entirely of his own motion and initiative to invite the two belligerents to come together for the purpose of direct negotiation." Takahira was further instructed to say that "if the President is disposed to undertake the service, the Japanese government will leave it to him to determine the course of procedure and which other power or powers, if any, should be consulted in the matter of suggested invitation."[62] Katsura also sent a letter to Yamagata informing him of the "direct action" the government had taken.[63]

Takahira met with President Roosevelt on June 1 and transmitted the request. The President willingly gave his consent[64] and immediately set out, with his characteristic straightforwardness, to persuade the tsar to agree to peace negotiations.[65] Having received the tsar's agreement, Roosevelt formally offered his good offices to the two belligerents. On June 9, 1905, he sent identical notes to both countries urging them, "not only for their own sakes, but in the interest of the whole civilized world, to open direct negotiations for peace with one another."[66]

On June 8 and 9, Prime Minister Katsura, War Minister Terauchi, and several high treasury officials considered the possibility of increasing revenues to support an extended war. The cabinet and the Genrō met on June 9 to discuss Roosevelt's invitation, and the views of the army were reported to the Emperor on June 9 and 10.[67] The Japanese government sent its acceptance on June 10,[68] and Russia did the same on June 12.[69]

Thus the way to peace negotiations was opened. After two months of discussions, Portsmouth, New Hampshire, was selected as the conference site. Foreign Minister Komura and Minister Takahira were appointed the Japanese plenipotentiaries, and Russia appointed Witte and Rosen.[70]

The Selection of the Plenipotentiary

In view of the responsibility and difficulty of the mission, the selection of its representative proved an arduous task for the Japanese government. When the Genrō conference was convened to decide this matter, Prime Minister Katsura stressed that, because of the magnitude of the mission, "the chief plenipotentiary should be a leading statesman who enjoys the fullest trust of the Emperor above and of the whole nation below. In other words, he must be a Genrō."[71] Katsura even intimated privately to the Emperor that the president of the Privy Council, Itō, and Foreign Minister Komura should be appointed.[72]

The Emperor, who had relied on Itō as his constant adviser throughout the war, did not want him to be absent from Tokyo.[73] Itō himself, for political reasons, did not want to go to Portsmouth. He is reported to have said, "One must harvest the result of what one has sown. I started the Sino-Japanese War, and therefore I naturally concluded it. I consider it in order that the present war be concluded by Katsura himself."[74] Itō instead recommended to Katsura the appointment of Foreign Minister Komura.[75] In all probability, Itō was most reluctant to go on the mission under Katsura, whose status was considerably lower than his own and who was Yamagata's protégé.[76] The basic reason for his unwillingness, however, is likely to have stemmed from the thankless nature of the mission. Itō was well aware of how difficult it would be for a Japanese plenipotentiary to conclude a satisfactory peace at Portsmouth; he also knew that he would then be doomed to bear complete responsibility for the diplomatic failure and to face alone the resulting popular indignation.

Itō's close followers were more worried than Itō himself about his future. When the rumor spread that the vainglorious Itō was falling easy prey to Katsura's skillful flattery and had privately expressed his willingness to become the plenipotentiary, Itō Miyoji, the Genrō's able protégé, forced himself, although critically weakened from a recent illness, to call on Itō and tell him, "It would not be the way of a wise man to bear the criticism that will arise among the people from the coming peace negotiations while glory and honor for the victory will be accorded solely to Katsura." Having convinced the Genrō of the folly of going on an obviously thankless mission, Itō Miyoji immediately telephoned Katsura and told him flatly to stop his manipulations.[77]

Tani Kanjō, Itō's close associate who, for a professional soldier, had unusual understanding of the realities of the war and of world events, had presented to Itō, even before the announcement of Roosevelt's mediation, a draft containing extremely moderate peace terms. He regarded the coming peace negotiations not as "the result of the victory of one side, but the result of mutual exhaustion in a protracted war," and he asserted that Japan should not even demand Sakhalin, much less a war indemnity.[78] When the choice of Japan's plenipotentiary was to be made, Tani dissuaded Itō from accepting the task, saying:

> The newspapers have been expressing their desire to trouble you again to accept the task of peace negotiations. This time you should have Katsura and Komura go. The matter does not require your toil. If you were plied by flattery and went, you should certainly find yourself in trouble and should fall into the trap a certain person has set. In any event, I would regret it if some people succeeded in making a fool out of you!
>
> If you are ordered by His Majesty to go and find no way to avoid the task, be sure to collect signatures of agreement from Marquis Yamagata and

every one of the cabinet ministers, so that they will later be unable to leave you to face the blame alone. You should make public the agreement with their signatures at an appropriate time; if not, you will certainly be regarded as a traitor by the people. You are able, learned, and wise, but you, I am afraid, tend to be easily taken advantage of. I find this very regrettable. The present war is totally different from the war against China in 1894–1895. It is more than obvious that the postwar situation of our nation will indeed be miserable. Whoever goes on this mission of peace negotiations will have no way to gain satisfactory results. Katsura and Komura are, therefore, good enough for the task. It is most unwise to invite needlessly the indignation of the ignorant. Don't become prey to Katsura's or Komura's manipulation![79]

Persuaded by such arguments, Itō backed out of the difficult task.[80] When the Genrō conference inquiry was directed to Komura, he reportedly stated with determination, "As foreign minister, I shall not shrug off the responsibility, even though I fear I am not equal to the task. I am therefore willing to accept the task, if His Majesty wishes to entrust it to me."[81]

Komura, as we know, was intimately connected with the prowar activists. Although known as a deliberate and prudent foreign minister, he was basically a believer in a strong foreign policy. In addition, as a Harvard-educated career diplomat who had risen in the foreign office hierarchy step by step without any clan support, it is possible that he viewed the impending conference as an opportunity—a gamble to be sure—to attain even greater eminence.[82] Lancelot Lawton, the *Daily Telegraph* correspondent in Japan during the war, observed:

It was evident that the position of the Japanese plenipotentiary was to be compared to that of a poker-player possessing an extremely doubtful hand. It is little wonder, therefore, that Itō, whose conception of duty and standard of patriotism could not be gainsaid, declined the offer of a tremendous task which came to him when, after an active career devoted wholly to the interests of the State, he was beginning to feel the burden of declining years. . . . The fact cannot be overlooked that Baron Komura was a young and ambitious man to whom the post of peace plenipotentiary in connection with one of the greatest wars ever fought in history must under any circumstances have seemed attractive.[83]

Indeed, by appointing Komura plenipotentiary, the Japanese decision-makers, as we shall see, invited a crisis in the coming negotiations.

Some of the Genrō were from the first suspicious of the headstrong, ambitious Komura. They were afraid that he might make harsh demands that would break up the negotiations. Navy Minister Yamamoto, the cabinet minister most eager to conclude peace, went so far as to say to Komura in the Genrō conference, "It is our understanding that, if the negotiations come to the point of rupture, you will make the final decision only after you have obtained governmental instructions. We would like to obtain your assurance on this point for the sake of our peace of mind." The conference made the final decision to appoint Komura only after he had replied, "Of course!"[84] Katsura immediately reported Komura's decision to the Emperor, and in an imperial conference the Emperor gave his sanction to the decision of the Genrō conference.

Factional considerations tenaciously alive behind the facade of national unity and the near impossibility of achieving a satisfactory peace thus freed Itō from bearing the responsibility of a thankless mission. It fell instead upon Komura, the career diplomat who was not from a major clan.

Katsura was deeply grateful for Komura's willingness to go on a mission so obviously difficult that the reputation-conscious Genrō were more than eager to avoid it. He realized with the greatest sympathy that Komura would have to negotiate with Witte of Russia under the scrutinizing eyes of the Powers, and that Russia, although badly beaten, had never recognized defeat and would still enjoy the friendly assistance of several of the Powers. Count Inoue Kaoru reportedly told Komura, "You are indeed in a most difficult position. Your past honors and achievements may be completely lost at the approaching Portsmouth Conference." The Genrō Itō Hirobumi is said to have expressed his sympathy by affirming, "Even if no one else is there, I shall be at the pier to receive you back to Japan after the Conference."[85]

Kampō (Official Gazette) announced the appointment of Komura and Takahira as plenipotentiaries on July 3, 1905.[86] On July 6, Komura had an audience with the Emperor, who gave him a tobacco case that he had long had for his personal use and encouraged him with these words:[87]

It was contrary to Our expectation to be compelled to resort to arms in spite of Our constant and abiding wish for peace. If, in consequence of the conciliatory spirit of Our opponent, the hostilities could be brought to an end, nothing would be more satisfactory than such consummation. . . . You should devote yourselves with all your power to the discharge of your mission and make every effort to secure the reestablishment of peace on a durable basis.[88]

After numerous conferences and meetings of the Genrō, the cabinet ministers, and high military and naval authorities, the Japanese government had formulated at a cabinet meeting on June 30 its final conditions for peace.[89] On July 5 imperial sanction was conferred upon the final decision, and the government's instructions for the peace negotiations were handed to Komura the following day.[90]

Instructions to the Plenipotentiaries to the
Peace Negotiations between Japan and Russia
Cabinet decision   June 30, 1905
Imperial sanction   July 5, 1905

We have decided to send you as our Imperial nation's plenipotentiaries to the coming peace negotiations with Russia. You are hereby instructed to conduct negotiations with the Russian plenipotentiaries in accordance with the following:

A. *Absolutely Indispensable Items:*
  1. That Russia acknowledge Japan's complete right of freedom of action in Korea.
  2. That Russia withdraw its troops from Manchuria within a period to be specified and at the same time that Japan withdraws its troops from the region.
  3. That Russia cede to Japan the leased area of the Liaotung Peninsula and the railway between Harbin and Port Arthur.

The above items are absolutely indispensable to achieving our war aims and guaranteeing the security of our Imperial nation forever. You are therefore instructed to do your utmost for their attainment.

B. *Relatively Important Items:*
  1. That Russia pay our war expenses. You are instructed to decide the appropriate amount in accordance with the progress of the negotiations, to the maximum amount of .... hundred million yen.
  2. That Russia transfer to Japan all Russian war vessels that have found refuge from battle in neutral harbors.
  3. That Russia cede to Japan Sakhalin and all islands appertaining thereto.
  4. That Russia grant Japan fishing rights along the coast of the Maritime Provinces.

The above items are not absolutely indispensable. You are, however, instructed to secure them insofar as circumstances permit.

C. *Additional Items:*

1. To limit Russian naval strength in the Far East.
2. To convert Vladivostok into a purely commercial port by leveling all fortifications there.

The above items may be demanded as bargaining points. Their use and adoption are left entirely to your discretion.

These are the major demands to be presented by the Imperial government. As to the details of these items, you are instructed to reach an appropriate agreement with the Russian representative in light of the progress of the negotiations.

It will of course be extremely difficult in the coming negotiations to secure the aims of our Imperial nation as listed above. Our Imperial government, however, places great trust in your ability and wishes you to exert your utmost efforts in the negotiations, keeping the interest of our government in mind, to bring about the restoration of an honorable peace as swiftly as possible.

Needless to say, you are instructed to report the progress of the negotiations in detail from time to time. If you should face the unfortunate possibility of the termination of negotiations, you are instructed to report the situation to your home government by telegram and to take appropriate measures only after you have received instructions in response to your report.[91]

These instructions were intended to serve as a guide for the plenipotentiary rather than as a rigid set of demands, and Komura made full use of the freedom of action thus given him. At the conference, he rearranged the Japanese demands to conform to his own hard-line convictions.[92]

CHAPTER FIVE

THE PEOPLE AND THE WAR

THE proceedings among the decision-makers we have thus far described had been kept strictly secret. Apart from the small group of participants in the oligarchic decision-making process, few people in Japan at that time even dreamed of what was actually happening.[1] Tokutomi Sohō, president of the semiofficial organ *Kokumin Shimbun*, recalled in his autobiography the attitude of the government during the Russo-Japanese War:

The Japanese authorities were more afraid of their own people than of the enemy. Only the officials in the government knew of the various internal weaknesses and overall vulnerability of the nation. They kept their knowledge strictly secret lest it have an adverse effect upon the morale of the people. One may criticize the government's attitude for its lack of sincerity toward the people, but the actual situation was such that nobody could tell what might happen if the whole truth were revealed. The government, therefore, chose to keep whatever it could strictly confidential, even if later, when the truth came to be known, it had to contend with the people's indignation.[2]

The Japanese government resorted to every means possible to maintain such secrecy. Both the army and navy strictly limited the number of Japanese war correspondents and the scope of their activities and reporting, setting up rigid "codes for war correspondents" that stipulated strict censorship of all news from the front and made it impossible for uncensored news to reach Japan. Consequently, articles about the war in the domestic newspapers were generally written by the "soft writers" at desks in the home country and were filled with sensational and incomplete descriptions of battles or details of the heroic actions of individual soldiers. Thus the public was not given an overall picture of the war. Exaggerated reports of victories, of the weakness of the Russian soldiers, and on revolutionary movements inside Russia all led the Japanese people to make light of the Russians and to become readily intoxicated by Japan's victories.[3]

The Japanese government also tightly restricted the activities of foreign correspondents.[4] The American minister in Tokyo, Lloyd C. Griscom, wrote: "They [foreign correspondents] could go nowhere without escort, everything they wrote had to be passed by a censor. Such restrictions had never been heard of."[5] Besides fearing the spread abroad of unfavorable news of the war, the Japanese authorities were apprehensive lest bad news reach the people in Japan through foreign dispatches.

Such rigid control of war news and the strict secrecy surrounding the activities of the decision-makers succeeded in keeping the people totally ignorant of reality. How, then, did the majority of Japanese view the progress of the war? What was the people's experience during the war?

The Domestic Front

The Russo-Japanese War cost Japan a total of 1,730,050,000 yen, an expenditure 8.5 times greater than for the Sino-Japanese War.[6] This was 6.6 times ordinary revenues for the year 1903 (260,220,000 yen) and 11.7 times the government's income from taxation (146,160,000 yen).[7]

In spite of rapid progress after the Sino-Japanese War, the Japanese national economy, with its still shallow foundation, naturally could not bear alone the cost of the war. More than 80 percent of the huge war expenditure was therefore supplied by loans, either domestic or foreign, more than half of which were floated at four different times in London, New York, and to a very limited extent in Berlin. These loans were guaranteed by customs receipts and the tobacco monopoly and were obtained at high rates of interest. Out of a total of 800,570,000 yen in loans floated abroad, Japan actually received 689,590,000 yen.[8]

Six domestic loans were issued, making a total of 783,460,000 yen, of which the government actually received 729,137,000 yen.[9] This was more than six times the total raised through domestic loans during the Sino-Japanese War and was equivalent to about 84 percent of the total paid-up capital of all the banks and companies in Japan at that time.[10]

Despite successful government attempts to increase its revenues from taxation by more than 100 million yen during the war, tax revenues provided less than one-fifth of total war expenditures. They supplied 146,160,000 yen in 1903, increasing to 194,360,000 yen in 1904 and to 251,280,000 yen in 1905. The main sources for the increase in 1905 were the land tax (about 43,000,000 yen and 32 percent of the increase) and various excise taxes (about 63,000,000 yen and 46 percent of the increase). Indirect taxes also rose. Income from government monopolies and property holdings grew from 55,700,000 yen in 1903 to 76,400,000 yen in 1904 and to 99,880,000 yen in 1905.[11]

The government's declaration of war was a long overdue response to the people's demands, and the government could expect maximum unity and cooperation in its execution of the war. Although the main burden of the increased excise taxes rested on laborers and small farmers, the people submitted to the heavy taxation and responded eagerly to every issue of war bonds.[12] Out of a total male working population of about ten million, the economic backbone of the nation, approximately two million men were mobilized for some form of war service. More than half of this number were in the army, and no fewer than 999,868 went to the front. Casualties were 60,083 killed in battle, 21,879 victims of disease, and 29,438 dismissed for ill health or other disabilities.[13]

The Japanese people endured these financial and human losses with stoic heroism. No murmur was heard among the people by outsiders. A foreign observer who traveled extensively in wartime Japan wrote:

. . . the whole country is sending its best flesh and blood without a whimper or a murmur to feed the war . . . the country may bleed to death internally without the world knowing it. Oh Japanese! You are a wonderful people, and mighty fighters.[14]

Beneath the stoic mask, however, many signs of suffering and misery began to emerge. There were many cases of shops and factories closing and many cases, too, of taxes in arrears.[15] In 1906 the Ministry of Agriculture and Commerce published the following figures on wages and prices, using 1903 as the base year:[16]

Year	Wages	Prices	Daily Necessities[a]
1903	100.0	100	100
1904	98.2	107[b]	111
1905	102.3	115[c]	121

[a]Average price indices of foodstuff and clothing only.
[b]Foodstuff 113, clothing 109, raw materials 102.
[c]Foodstuff 123, clothing 119, raw materials 108.

This means that in 1904, while average wages were 1.8 percent lower than in 1903, the prices of daily necessities had risen by 11 per cent. In 1905 the average wage was 2.3 percent higher than in 1903, but the prices of daily necessities went up as much as 21 percent. The relatively small increase in wages in 1905 could not match the sudden and much greater rise in the cost of daily necessities. The middle and upper classes suffered to some extent from high wartime taxes and other financial obligations; but the lower classes, as this statistical analysis shows, were hit much harder. The condition of the families of soldiers and sailors was still more miserable, since in most cases such families were deprived of their main breadwinner and many of them had no means of living without outside help. Through the aid of relief organizations, some barely escaped starvation; but despite the great need, relief work was very limited in scope. It could do no more than save from starvation those families in extreme distress. On the whole, the relief of the peasants' families, who produced the bulk of the soldiers, was left to their relatives and friends.[17] While the families of soldiers suffered most greatly, as in the Sino-Japanese War those directly or indirectly connected with munitions supplies and transportation profited enormously from the war.[18]

What supported the high public morale despite extreme hardship? In part it was the loyalty of the people to the Emperor and the state. But more than anything else it was the glorious news of the progress of the war and the numerous promises about the outcome of the war that the press was making with convincing unanimity. Moreover, in contrast to the news of unbroken victories on the front and the high morale and unity displayed by the Japanese people, the turmoil within Russia was reported to be increasingly grave, leading the masses to expect that the Russian government, pressed from both inside and out, would request peace at any moment.

The reports of successive victories must have had an intoxicating effect upon the Japanese, who had long lived in constant fear of Russia. They now saw the Russian giant toppling before the heroic assaults of Japanese soldiers. Their morale was further boosted by the nation-wide, lantern-march celebrations on the occasion of each major victory on land and sea. With the jubilation over victories, the illusion emerged of the ever-imminent approach of the day of complete victory. Thus the public continued its support of the war.

The Opinion Leaders

With the outbreak of the war, the Tairo Dōshikai was dissolved, for it had achieved its basic objective. Individual members in various places and capacities continued their efforts to maintain the nation's enthusiasm for the war. Some of them took part in military intelligence activities in Manchuria, and their accomplishments and sometimes heroic deaths were often printed in the wartime newspapers.[19]

Professors Tomizu and Nakamura continued their vigorous activities to encourage and unite national sentiment in favor of the war. At the opening of the Diet session in March 1904, the Japanese government made public diplomatic papers on the prewar negotiations with Russia, intending to demonstrate publicly to the Japanese people and the world how justly Japan had conducted the negotiations. But Tomizu and Naka-mura were angered upon reading the papers because of their knowledge of what had actually happened during the negotiations and the realiza-tion of how close the government had come to making vital concessions to Russia. Now, more than ever, they were convinced of the weakness of Japanese diplomacy. If Russia had been a little cleverer, they thought, it could have taken great advantage of Japan. At the same time, the two professors were enormously pleased, for they attributed Japan's decision to go to war to their efforts and influence. Exhilarated by this presumed success, they became even more deeply convinced of the need to arouse strong public opinion to ensure that the government would conduct its wartime diplomacy effectively.[20] Busily engaged in making speeches and writing articles for newspapers and journals, they constantly demanded that a strong diplomatic policy accompany the progress of the military situation in Manchuria.

Their writings reveal not only that they were completely ignorant of the actual military and diplomatic situation during the war but, in-deed, that this aspect of the war did not even particularly concern them. Rather, as the war continued to progress seemingly in Japan's favor, Tomizu and Nakamura began to concentrate their arguments on the fact that Manchuria was vital to Japan's national defense and future prosperity.

Professor Tomizu's speech, "Hegemony over East Asia," at Tokyo Im-perial University on September 25, 1904, was so flagrant in its disregard for Chinese sovereignty and the interests of the Powers in Manchuria that the government, through the president of the university, was com-pelled to admonish Tomizu not to make other similar speeches. When the speech was made public, it drew much protest from Chinese and Korean sources. The Japanese government, which was trying to persuade the Powers that Japan was fighting Russia for their interests as well as for its own, was understandably perturbed by Tomizu's activities.[21] As the war continued, the Japanese government's limited objectives in the war became increasingly divergent from the aims of wartime opinion leaders such as Tomizu and others like him.

Meanwhile, the press and the entire literary world had erupted into cutthroat competition for news, publications vying with each other in the glorification of fighting and heroism both at the front and at home. Newspaper circulation mounted, and a large number of new magazines appeared, all pressing for national unity in the war effort.[22]

The Wartime Diet

The attitude of the political parties was no exception to this surge of support for the government. Before the war the parties had been bent on revenge for the government's sudden dissolution of the nineteenth Diet session, which had been thrown into unprecedented turmoil at its inception by Speaker Kōno Hironaka's unusual reply to the Emperor's opening message. When hostilities with Russia commenced, however, the parties suddenly dropped their belligerent attitudes and, as did the chauvinistic groups and the press, joined hands with the government.[23]

On March 1, 1904, almost one month after the commencement of the war, the ninth general election was held. It was carried out with unusual orderliness, for the declaration of war and subsequent developments seemed to work to suppress all partisan disturbances. In fact, the election was hardly noticed by the people, who were completely absorbed in the war,[24] and it made no change in the existing political balance in the Diet.

The twentieth Diet session was convened soon after the election. Before its opening, both parties issued resolutions pledging to support all appropriations necessary for the prosecution of the war.[25] During the session, every bill was passed and the enormous war expenditures requested by the government were approved almost intact and practically without discussion.[26] This situation continued through the twenty-first Diet session, convened in late November 1904, during which the slightly hardened posture of the Kenseihontō toward the government was more than compensated for by the increasingly cooperative attitude of the

Seiyūkai. The period between these two sessions was marked, at least outwardly, by a high degree of harmony and unity among the parties in support of the government. The slogan *kyokoku itchi* (national unity) seemed to serve as a panacea.[27] With this attitude, the Diet readily lost even its right of indirect supervision over government conduct of the war and diplomacy.[28]

For its part, the government followed a policy of keeping the Diet ignorant of the progress of the war and diplomatic measures. Some Diet members complained, asserting that the war against Russia was not a private war of the cabinet but the people's war. When the foreign minister even failed to deliver the traditional address on foreign relations at the beginning of the twenty-first session, members demanded that "the foreign minister be more earnest in informing the public of the diplomatic progress of the war and solicit the more intelligent support of the people."[29] They failed, however, to change the attitude of the government, which enjoyed the constitutional right to remain above Diet "interference" in matters of war and diplomacy. The government's policy was to inform the political parties on the progress of the war within such limits, at such times, and through such means as it deemed "advisable."[30] In short, in the atmosphere of enthusiasm for national unity and support of the war, the Diet seemed to exist in name only.

This is not, however, a completely accurate picture of the wartime Diet, for behind the facade of national unity, political deals between parties and the government continued. Even during the war the major weapon of the political parties was the budget power of the Diet. In spite of the general spirit of cooperation, the necessity and desire to pass huge expenditure bills as smoothly as possible made the government's position vulnerable to the power-hungry political parties. Thus, taking advantage of the government's wish to maintain a facade of national unity, the political parties sought concessions from the government that would enhance their own interests.[31]

As we have already seen, the Sino-Japanese War created a new collaborative arrangement between the government and the political parties. Thereafter, this relationship became increasingly apparent, and in 1900 the birth of the Seiyūkai added a further dimension to this collaboration.

With Itō Hirobumi, a Genrō and the prime minister, as the founder and president of the Seiyūkai, wide avenues to political power were opened up to members of the party. After the Seiyūkai cabinet was compelled to resign in May 1901 because of an intraparty struggle over the budgetary question, however, the party's fortunes fell considerably. Itō relinquished the premiership at the same time, and the presidential absolutism (*sōsai sensei*) that he had enjoyed was thereby weakened markedly.[32] Itō's compromise with the government on the budget during the eighteenth Diet session in May 1903 caused further turmoil within the party, and its influence declined again when an Imperial order made Itō president of the Privy Council, compelling him to leave the party. Party leadership did not then fall to the former Liberal Party faction. This faction had been competing for leadership with the bureaucratic faction, which had controlled the party since its inception.[33] Itō instead selected Saionji Kimmochi, then president of the Privy Council, as his successor.

Before accepting the presidency, Saionji insisted upon three conditions. First, his power as party president was to be equal to Itō's (*sōsai sensei*); second, he was not to be responsible for fund-raising; finally, the membership was to understand that Saionji's role would be limited because of his poor health.[34] Saionji was a member of a Kyoto court family. He was Itō's personal friend and protégé and a bureaucrat. As the new president of the Seiyūkai, he had two able lieutenants, Matsuda Masahisa (1854–1914) and Hara Takashi (1856–1921).

Matsuda and Saionji had been close friends since they were students in Paris in the 1870s. In 1881, when Saionji started the *Tōyō Jiyū Shimbun* (Liberalist News of the Orient), Matsuda joined him. In 1890 he became a Liberal Party Diet member from Saga, Kyushu. He was appointed minister of finance in the Ōkuma Cabinet and minister of education in the fourth Itō Cabinet in 1900.[35]

The more important of Saionji's two lieutenants, however, was Hara Takashi. A grandson of the chief retainer of the Nambu clan in northern Japan, Hara was a boy of twelve when the tide of the Meiji Restoration swept away the seven-hundred-year-old dominion of the clan. His experience when government forces under Sat-Chō leadership subjugated his homeland was said to have fostered his political ambitions. Hara spent about 15 years in the Foreign Ministry, during which time he became well acquainted with Inoue Kaoru and Mutsu Munemitsu, who was foreign minister at the time of the Sino-Japanese War. This was a

turning point in Hara's career. In 1897, when Mutsu died, Hara resigned his post as minister to Korea and joined the *Osaka Mainichi Shimbun*. By the time Itō was preparing for the establishment of the Seiyūkai, Hara was editor and president of the newspaper. In 1900 Hara
joined the Seiyūkai as Itō's most trusted aide and later became minister
of communications in Itō's Cabinet.[36] He was elected a member of the
House of Representatives from his native Morioka in the seventh general
election in August 1902.[37]

Led by the Saionji-Matsuda-Hara triumvirate, the Seiyūkai thus faced
the Katsura Cabinet, whose prestige had been considerably enhanced by
its successful conclusion of the first Anglo-Japanese Alliance in 1902.

As the nineteenth Diet session approached, the Seiyūkai and the
Kenseihontō reached an agreement to put up a united front against the
government in the coming session. They planned a frontal attack upon
the government for its alleged mismanagement of diplomatic negotiations
with Russia and for its policy of administrative retrenchment. This
agreement was concluded despite serious opposition from the rank and
file of both parties. Dissension was particularly rife within the Kenseihontō, which was split into two groups: a minority, led by Hiraoka
Kōtaro and Kōmuchi Tomotsune, proposed to support the Katsura Cabinet in its conduct of the difficult diplomatic negotiations with Russia,
while the majority claimed the cabinet was not capable of leading the
country during the present national crisis. The majority was further
divided into two camps. One was opposed to collaboration with the
Seiyūkai, asserting that past experience clearly showed that such collaboration was harmful to the Kenseihontō; they therefore demanded that
the party oppose the government independently. The other group, led
by such high-ranking party officials as Ōishi Masami and Inukai Tsuyoshi, stressed the need for collaboration with the Seiyūkai and, in the end,
succeeded in skillfully overriding all opposition.[38] The two-party united
front, however, was foiled by Speaker Kōno's bombshell and the con-
sequent sudden dissolution of the nineteenth Diet session.

When Japan declared war against Russia on February 10, 1904, a
new political situation emerged. On March 1 the ninth election was
quietly held. The Seiyūkai increased its majority, winning 130 seats in
the Diet.[39] Its position *vis-à-vis* the government was much improved, for
the government needed the party's cooperation in the Diet for the smooth
execution of the war.

Hara Takashi now began his maneuverings. A brilliant political strategist, Hara spent his life in a slow but steady search for the method and timing with which to grasp the reins of power. In his endeavor to expand his party's strength in order eventually to overthrow the power of the oligarchs, Hara did not hesitate to compromise with the clan (*hanbatsu*) government.[40] The outbreak of the war did not stop his activities.[41]

Before the outbreak of the war, Hara had been bitterly critical of the government's policy of secret diplomacy.[42] When the war broke out, he accused the government of bringing on the war by playing upon chauvinistic public opinion concerning Russia.[43] When, at Itō Hirobumi's request, Kaneko and Suematsu were sent to America and England, respectively, Hara saw in the move a government scheme to weaken the strength of the party.[44] He was highly suspicious and critical of the government-sponsored consultation committee on economic affairs (*Kanmin Konwa Kai*), on which both the government and the political parties were represented.[45]

The Seiyūkai's attitude gradually softened as the twenty-first Diet session approached. Both the Seiyūkai and the Kenseihontō had cooperated with the government during the twentieth Diet session, and both had accepted the government's request for wartime finances. Thereafter the attitude of the Kenseihontō gradually hardened.

The twenty-first Diet session was to be convened on November 28, 1904. As it had done before the previous session, the government consulted the executive members of the two parties to request their cooperation in drafting a compromise budget plan before submitting its budget for the coming year to the Diet.[46]

Before an agreement was reached, the Seiyūkai and the Kenseihontō held party meetings. On November 26, each issued a resolution on the coming Diet session. These resolutions showed a clear difference between the attitudes of the two parties toward the government. The Seiyūkai made clear that it would cooperate with the government, stating: ". . . we shall not spare ourselves in providing necessary war expenses."[47] At the same party meeting, Saionji told his followers that he had readily given his promise of cooperation when Katsura requested the party's support for the government's financial policy in the coming Diet session. He urged party members "to bear the unbearable for the sake of the nation" and to pass the budget bill in the coming session.[48]

In contrast, the resolution of the Kenseihontō was sharply critical of the budgetary policy proposed by the government. On the key question of replenishing war funds, its resolution read: ". . . we shall make due amendments to the government's increase plan. We shall economize on government expenses through administrative reorganization and provide for the balance by the issuance of public bonds. . . ."[49] In a speech at the party meeting, party president Ōkuma attacked government diplomacy as "clumsy and slow," particularly in matters concerning China and Korea. Ōkuma asserted that government diplomacy was not sufficiently abreast of military action. In criticizing government financial policy, he warned that careless tax increases would soon exhaust the nation's vitality and thus work to destroy important sources of funds. He urged the government to retrench its administrative organization for a greater economy in national expenditures.[50]

On November 28, Katsura discussed the situation in a letter to Itō Hirobumi:

Concerning Count Ōkuma's speech at the general meeting of the Kenseihontō Diet members, I obtained information about it the night before last, and I have read carefully the reports of it that were in yesterday's morning newspapers. The Count's concern for our country is too frivolous. Although his speech may have been just another product of his usual pedantry, it was an act in which no one with a proper concern for the present situation would ever have engaged. I therefore had the editor of the *Kokumin Shimbun* criticize the speech in this morning's issue. In contrast, the speech of the president of the Seiyūkai seemed to be most appropriate to the present situation, and therefore I have expressed my heartfelt approval of the speech. . . . You must be aware of the situation in the Diet. In regard to the Seiyūkai, I have already had a chance to talk with Marquis Saionji. We talked without concealing anything from each other, and, no doubt thanks to your advice to the Marquis, the situation seems to be largely satisfactory. The Kenseihontō, however, as we can see in Count Ōkuma's speech, is playing to the gallery. . . . As I have already told you, at this juncture the government will act on the principle of sincerity, and without any manipulation it will take the initiative in achieving "national unity"![51]

The differences in the attitudes of the two parties seem to have arisen for two reasons. First, the Seiyūkai was relatively more unified under the Saionji-Matsuda-Hara triumvirate. Doubtless there were anti-triumvirate factions, but these elements, in the main, seem to have been vying with one another to gain more advantageous conditions of collaboration from the government and thus to grasp the leadership of the party. No Seiyūkai faction, therefore, was in essential conflict with the position of support for the government taken by the party leadership. Moreover, the leadership position of the triumvirate was quite secure.

The Kenseihontō, on the other hand, was critically divided. Although the party in general was opposed to the government, strong differences developed as to the method of opposition. Those under Ōishi and Inukai sought to oppose the government through an alliance with the Seiyūkai. Others, including party president Ōkuma, demanded outright opposition to the Katsura Cabinet. This split naturally weakened the position of the party and, as we shall see, gave Hara his desired opportunity to manipulate the Kenseihontō.

The second, and probably more decisive, reason lay in the channels of information available to the two parties and, ultimately, in the different quality of information each party received. The Seiyūkai had a great advantage over its rival, for it was in close communication with the decision-makers throughout the war. Its former president, Itō, became the foremost adviser to the cabinet as well as to the throne. Another Genrō, Inoue, with whom Hara was in close communication, was Katsura's financial adviser, along with Genrō Matsukata.[52] Hara's diary gives ample evidence of the great extent to which the leaders of the Seiyūkai were informed of the actual financial, military, and diplomatic situation.

The Kenseihontō lacked such channels of information and therefore tended to demand a harder wartime diplomatic policy, particularly toward Korea and China. Moreover, Ōkuma's alienation from other top party leaders who did have some contact with the Seiyūkai, as well as with the government, caused him to be largely uninformed in political and military matters.[53] Ōkuma, whose relations with the Genrō were cold at best, thus remained isolated and uninformed and made grand and sweeping speeches that only annoyed those in positions of real responsibility.[54]

In any event, Katsura, who had been discreetly feeling out the Seiyūkai as early as the preceding March, decided to approach the party more openly. When the Kenseihontō resolved on budget cuts that more than tripled those proposed by the Seiyūkai, Katsura proposed to collaborate only with the Seiyūkai.[55]

On December 6, 1904, Katsura informed Hara that the government found the Seiyūkai resolution agreeable, while the resolution of the Kenseihontō diverged too far from government policy. He stated that the government was therefore determined to act on the basis of the Seiyūkai plan and that, if the two parties should fail to come to an agreement, the government would follow the Seiyūkai resolution. Katsura then asked Hara to advise the government on the steps it should take in the budget negotiations, for he thought it inadvisable to side outright with the Seiyūkai. Hara answered that he regarded a split between the Seiyūkai and the Kenseihontō as extremely undesirable and added that a compromise must somehow be found between the divergent resolutions of the two parties.[56]

The following day Hara told Matsuda Masahisa, "If the cabinet relies on our party and acts in accordance with our party's resolution, it will inevitably alienate us from the Kenseihontō. Since this is a serious matter for our party, we need to ascertain Katsura's real intentions." They immediately consulted Saionji. The three suspected that Katsura's approach might be an attempt to use the party for his own immediate ends and feared that it could only harm the position of the Seiyūkai. They therefore decided to use Itō Hirobumi as an intermediary.[57] On December 8, Itō had a private talk with Katsura, who "declared that he was determined to place heavy trust upon the Seiyūkai." Upon hearing this, Hara and Matsuda immediately called on Saionji and told him the details of the story. That same day, Hara visited Katsura at his private residence, where they exchanged frank opinions from 10:30 p.m. until 1:30 a.m. They reached a secret agreement that (1) the Seiyūkai would support the Katsura Cabinet during the war even if it meant the party's alienation from the Kenseihontō, and (2) when Kastura resigned after the war, he would recommend Saionji for the position of prime minister, and Katsura would support the Saionji Cabinet.

Thus began the "Katsura-Saionji era" (Kei-En jidai), during which the reins of power were passed back and forth between the two men until the time of the Taishō change.

Hara also expressed his basic policy toward the Kenseihontō in the future, stating: "As long as you have determined to rely on us, we will assist you, even if it means separation from the Kenseihontō. However, I consider it to our advantage to keep the cooperation of the Kenseihontō as long as possible. Therefore, as we try to maintain good relations with the Kenseihontō, do not suspect that we are still in close alliance with them." This agreement was to be known only to Katsura, Finance Minister Sone Arasuke, and Navy Minister Yamamoto Gonnohyōe in the government and to Hara, Saionji, and Matsuda in the Seiyūkai. Hara wrote in his diary of his talks with Katsura: "Whatever may happen in the future, my visit with Premier Katsura tonight is, I believe, an event of great significance for both the cabinet and the Seiyūkai."[58]

The next day, December 9, a compromise budget plan was concluded between the government and the two parties.[59] Erwin Baelz recorded in his entry for December 15:

Today the Aoki-Hatzfeld wedding took place, the envoy officiating as registrar. Count Katsura, the Premier, was one of the witnesses to the marriage. After the wedding breakfast I congratulated him on looking well and cheerful in spite of his anxieties and overwhelming labours, and expressed my regret that the political parties were giving him so much trouble. "Oh, that's all right now," he said with a smile, tapping his breast. "Here in my pocket I have an agreement with the parties. They have dropped almost all their objections to our budget. I am going from here straight on to Parliament, where everything will run smoothly."

It was as he said. The two chief parties, which at first had been fiercely opposed, have given way at every point along the line.

Still, the taxes are extremely heavy. The tax on building land doubled, the tax on agricultural land increased by 50 percent. Salt monopoly, increased import duties, business tax, increased taxation on beer and spirits, income tax, death duties, and actually a tax on the means of communication, which in the case of the electric trams is to amount to not less than 35 percent of the gross receipts![60]

Behind the apparent rubber-stamping of government budget bills by the wartime Diet lay this deal between the government and the Seiyūkai. It was not simply a "period of submission and unanimity within the Diet," as Scalapino and others contend.[61] Appeals to "national unity" alone did not suffice to secure for the government the full cooperation of the Diet and political parties.

The Anti-War Activists

The forces opposed to the war, centering around the *Heimin Shimbun*, continued their activities in defiance of increasing government hostility.

They tried to convince the people that the war was merely bringing more misery to the general public and that only those who were in high positions in government and industry could benefit from the war.

The publisher of the *Heimin Shimbun*, Sakai Toshihiko, was imprisoned for two months because the twentieth edition of his paper, on March 27, 1904, bore the headline, "Ah! Tax Increase!"[62] The fifty-third issue, published on November 13, 1904, printed a complete translation of the *Communist Manifesto*, as a result of which Kōtoku Shūsui, the paper's leading writer, was sentenced to a five-month jail term, the paper was fined, and its printing presses were confiscated.[63] The *Heimin Shimbun* was thus forced by the government's restrictions to terminate publication on January 29, 1905. With the use of the facilities of the *Chokugen*, another socialist newspaper, however, publication was soon resumed.[64]

The anti-war elements consisted largely of intellectuals. As such, they were more interested in propagating their usually academic ideals than in cultivating the support of the people. In the face of the torrent of popular enthusiasm for the war, their valiant efforts were ineffective. They were, after all, another type of *shishi*, "people of exalted mind," possessed by a strong elite-consciousness.[65]

It was perhaps only through their emotional appeals that the anti-war advocates reached the Japanese people. In the September 1904, issue of *Myōjō*, the poetess Yosano Akiko published a poem entitled "Kimi shinitamō koto nakare" (Do not offer your life).[66] Dwelling upon the human losses inflicted by war, the poem acutely described the sorrow brought by war to the common people. Another poetess, Ōtsuka Naoko, published "Ohyakudo mōde" (Prayer to the gods), in which she said: "If I were asked which is more important to me, the state or my husband, I would just look down and not answer." But although such poets and the anti-war forces in general exerted a strong emotional appeal, they were unable to have any real influence on public opinion at this time.[67]

In spite of the nearly unanimous cries for war, Japanese public opinion seems to have been divided on the prospects for the war. One group expected and advocated a protracted war that would in the end have decisive results. The other eagerly anticipated an early termination of the war, as long as it would mean a Japanese victory, even if it was not a decisive one.[68]

Those demanding a protracted war believed with much chauvinistic conviction in Japan's indomitable military strength. Primarily ultra-nationalists like Tomizu, they replaced with fervor what they lacked in accurate information. At the beginning of the war, they seemed to be in the minority, but as Japan won repeated victories on the battlefield, their numbers increased. Continually wider acceptance was gained for the belief that the more decisive a victory Japan could win, the greater advantage it could obtain, and more and more people began to advocate expansion of the war in order to subdue the enemy completely. Their belief was strengthened and their demands for the fruits of victory grew as the war progressed unexpectedly well for Japan.

At first those who expected an early termination of the war were in the majority. A long-standing fear of Russia was probably paramount in most minds. Then too, there were those like Baron Shibusawa, members of the business community, who were aware of the limitations of Japan's fighting capability and the disadvantages Japan would suffer in a protracted war, and who were therefore eager to see the war's early, successful termination. This desire led them to anticipate a Russian request for peace on the occasion of every major Japanese victory in Manchuria. They waited expectantly when Port Arthur fell in January 1905, and again when Japan won the Battle of Mukden in March.

When these victories failed to elicit a peace request from Russia, and as confidence in Japan's army rose, disappointment gradually began to give way to chauvinism. Those who had hoped for an early end to the war now began to advocate its continuation and even its expansion.[69] This gradual change in the attitude of the majority of the Japanese public reached its zenith by the end of May 1905, when it became clear that even the navy's overwhelming victory over the Russian Baltic fleet in the Sea of Japan had failed to compel Russia to request peace. Thus, having given up hope for an early termination of the war and encouraged by favorable developments on the front, public opinion in Japan by late May of 1905, as expressed in the mass media, began unanimously to advocate a more positive and expanded campaign, in the belief that only a decisive victory could produce decisive results.

The Japanese public could not conceive of Japan's proposing peace to Russia. Neither could it imagine Japan's requesting mediation by a third country. Therefore, the only course possible for Japan, in the minds of its people, was to keep fighting, despite the great burden the war placed upon them, until Japan gained a decisive victory over Russia. In their desperate determination, a large segment of the Japanese public grew increasingly unrealistic and irrational.

Responses to Roosevelt's Good Offices

Under the circumstances, Japan's acceptance of Roosevelt's offer to mediate, announced in the Kampō on June 12, was a bolt out of the blue to the Japanese public.[70] The newspapers, except for the *Tokyo Nichi-nichi Shimbun*[71] and the government organ *Kokumin Shimbun*, quickly agreed that they opposed a truce before the conclusion of peace and that the offer of Roosevelt's good offices was premature. Ignorant of the background to the offer, the press judged that, as long as Japan had not gained a decisive victory over Russia despite the favorable progress of the war, Japan would be unable to obtain by negotiation a peace treaty that would adequately guarantee its war objectives.[72] Public opinion eventually accepted the government's decision to consent to Roosevelt's mediation. After all, there was really no other choice.

Concern gradually shifted to the prospects for the approaching negotiations, about which both optimism and pessimism were expressed. Optimism was represented by the *Kokumin Shimbun* and the *Tokyo Nichi-nichi Shimbun*, which accepted at its face value the good will Roosevelt expressed in offering to mediate and placed on it their hopes for the future of the peace negotiations.[73] Judging from the personality of the American president, they asserted that he had decided to offer his good offices only when he was confident of concluding a peace treaty to Japan's advantage. They were also certain that the coming peace negotiations had been arranged at Russia's request. Rumor had it that Roosevelt had been informed of the Russian terms for peace; after concluding that they would be acceptable to Japan, he had in turn informed the Japanese government of the Russian terms. The Japanese government had agreed to start peace negotiations only after it had approved these terms. So went statements in "optimistic" newspapers.

Pessimism was expressed by the *Tōyō Keizai Shimpō*, the *Tokyo Keizai Zasshi*, the *Jiji Shimpō*, and the *Asahi Shimbun*. Denying the optimists' speculations, they asserted that the coming peace negotiations were being held, not at Russian request, but on Roosevelt's initiative, and that Japan and Russia would be on an equal footing with each other. They therefore concluded that the actual war situation would not guarantee Japan an honorable peace. The newspaper *Nihon*, pointing out the weakness of Japanese diplomacy since Japan's return of the Liaotung Peninsula, expressed pessimism about the outcome of the negotiations because of Japan's lack of diplomatic skill.[74]

Professor Tomizu was particularly vehement in his opposition to Japan's acceptance of Roosevelt's offer to mediate. In the July 10 issue of the *Gaikō Jihō*, he published an article entitled "Has the Occasion for Peace Really Arrived?" in which he criticized the Japanese government for having readily accepted Roosevelt's offer and for having conceded the place for the negotiations to America. For this article Tomizu was suspended from his position at Tokyo Imperial University.[75]

The pessimists as well as the optimists thus were far from having an awareness of reality. They clearly revealed the narrow limits of their understanding of the progress of the war.

As the question of peace negotiations became a *fait accompli*, public discussion turned to the selection of plenipotentiaries and the terms for peace. Public opinion, which in general was anxious about the outcome of the negotiations, naturally demanded that the best man be sent to Portsmouth, and its choice was Itō Hirobumi. As we have seen, however, Itō, apart from his personal and political reasons, declined to go on the grounds that it was contrary to the Imperial wish. Anxiety about the future of the negotiations deepened when Komura, rather than Itō, was appointed Japan's chief plenipotentiary.[76]

The Popular Demands

Once the peace negotiations had become a reality, various individuals, organizations, and the press began to express their views on the terms of peace. Their demands varied greatly in details, but were more or less in agreement on two points: first, that the primary objective of the war was the security of Japanese control over Manchuria and Korea, and second, that Japan should obtain a war indemnity from Russia. Various figures were mentioned for the size of the indemnity. Such an indemnity, it was argued, was the right of the victor. The war was a just war for Japan, and Russia, since it was totally responsible for the outbreak of hostilities, should at least repay Japan's war expenses and the economic losses caused by the war. There was no doubt that the large indemnity Japan had gained after the Sino-Japanese War led the Japanese people to believe that an indemnity should always be awarded to the victor.[77] Another justification for claiming compensation was the enormous difficulty Japan would face in the repayment of foreign loans and in general postwar economic reconstruction. If the peace were concluded without an indemnity, the general public feared that high wartime taxes would continue; and business circles feared that their economic activities, which had started showing a comeback after the middle of the war, might decline because of lack of capital. Furthermore, an indemnity was thought to be indispensable for the future national defense and economic expansion in Korea and Manchuria.[78]

The business community, therefore, placed the highest priority upon an indemnity. Sonoda Kōkichi, former president of the Yokohama Specie Bank and now president of the Jūgo Ginkō, asserted that Russia should pay an indemnity of fifteen hundred million yen or more. Although Russian surrender of territory would be very satisfactory for Japan, Sonoda stated, a sufficient indemnity must be gained first, even if it entailed the sacrifice of territorial benefits.[79] Ikeda Kenzō, president of the Dai Hyaku Ginkō, concurring with Sonoda on the primary importance of an indemnity, proposed a figure of two billion seven hundred million yen.[80] Business circles in general strongly favored a large indemnity without territorial gains over a smaller indemnity with some territorial acquisitions. Basing their arguments on the future needs of Japan's postwar economy, they warned of the consequences of a treaty concluded without an adequate indemnity.

The Tairo Dōshikai (Anti-Russia Comrades' Society) formulated its peace terms as follows:

1. That the Ussuri coast district (the right bank of the Amur) and Sakhalin be ceded to Japan.
2. That the Chinese Eastern Railway and the lands leased to Russia in Manchuria be transferred to Japan.

3. That Russian troops be withdrawn from Manchuria and all other rights hitherto enjoyed by Russia in those provinces be annulled.
4. That three billion yen be demanded as an indemnity.
5. That all Russian war vessels interned in neutral ports be handed over to Japan, and that Blagovyeshchensk and Sretensk be opened to foreign trade.

Supplementary Terms:
1. That the negotiations be conducted within the Empire of Japan.
2. That no armistice be granted until a preliminary agreement has been signed.[81]

The demands of the "Seven Professors" were in the same spirit as those of the Tairo Dōshikai, but their demands—for example, that Russia be deprived of all her Asiatic territory east of Lake Baikal—were too outrageous to be influential. Confident of Japan's military supremacy, eager to resume a prematurely ended war, and totally ignorant of the actual diplomatic and military situation, the Tairo Dōshikai and the "Seven Professors" formulated demands that far exceeded realistic goals.[82]

Neither of the two major political parties, the Seiyūkai and the Kenseihontō, outlined any concrete terms for peace, but characteristically adopted very general attitudes.[83] On June 28, 1905, however, both parties issued declarations enumerating an adequate indemity, cession of territory, and solution of the Manchurian question as constituting the essential conditions for the conclusion of a peace treaty. The Seiyūkai declared:

Yet the acquisition of territory, the receipt of an indemnity, and the definite solution of all questions regarding Korea and Manchuria that relate to the future security of the rights and interests of our Empire and the preservation of the permanent peace of the Far East must, in compliance with the Imperial Rescript declaring war, be effected.[84]

The Kenseihontō was more specific and less moderate in its demands:

If, therefore, peace is now to be reestablished, we must demand an indemnity sufficient to cover the losses that we have sustained, the cession of territory important enough to guarantee the peace of the Far East, and the prohibition of all military enterprises at points that menace our national safety. Korea is already under our protection, and our actual power in Manchuria is recognized by the powers. It is therefore reasonable to demand that Russia abandon her privileges in Korea and Manchuria and that it be prevented from interfering in our enterprises there. As China's inability to defend herself has often been the cause of trouble for her neighbors, Russia must at this juncture be required to abstain from any undertaking likely to menace the Chinese frontiers, thus removing the possibility of international complications in this connection.[85]

Thus, although Japanese public opinion in general tended to be pessimistic as to the future of the peace negotiations, it belied with strong demands its anxiety about the cession of territory and receipt of an indemnity. These unofficial demands can be listed as including:

1. No armistice without a signed peace treaty.
2. The peace conference to be held in Japan.
3. War indemnity of about three billion yen.[86]
4. The cession of the whole of Sakhalin and the Maritime Provinces.[87]
5. The transfer of the entire Chinese Eastern Railway.
6. The transfer of the Russian leasehold in Manchuria, evacuation of Russian troops, and renunciation of Russian rights and interests there.
7. Surrender of all Russian vessels then in neutral ports.
8. Limitations upon the Russian navy in the Pacific and the Japan Sea.
9. No cession or lease of Chinese territory without the consent of Japan.[88]

In the midst of this clamor, the *Kokumin Shimbun* denounced the public formulation of demands as mere empty theorizing. It criticized the public discussion of peace terms, saying that such discussion only exposed internal disunity and tended recklessly to increase the demands. The people, the *Kokumin Shimbun* argued, should be prudent in their behavior, placing their complete trust in the authorities concerned.[89] This view, however, was shared only by the semiofficial organs and a small number of people who had close contacts with the decision-makers.[90]

Komura's Departure

Led by Chief Plenipotentiary Komura, the Japanese peace delegation left Shimbashi Station on July 8, 1905, amid shouts of "Banzai!" The next day the *Tokyo Asahi Shimbun* reported the tremendous bon voyage scene and printed a photograph of a confident-looking Komura. The article seems to reflect succinctly the anxiety and expectations the Japanese people felt about the peace negotiations.

The Glorious Victor's Plenipotentiary Departs
Our Sacrifices in the War of National Survival Are Now to Be Redeemed by Diplomatic Negotiations.

Peace Plenipotentiary Baron Komura Jutarō and his suite—Minister Resident Satō, Chief of the Political Affairs Bureau of the Foreign Office Yamaza, First Secretary of Legation Adachi, Secretary of the Foreign Office Honda, Diplomatic Probationer Konishi, Foreign Office Adviser Denison, and Military Attaché to the Japanese Legation in the United States Infantry Colonel Tachibana—departed by train from Shimbashi Station at 1:50 p.m. yesterday.

More than 5000 people gathered at the station to give the delegation a splendid send-off. The crowd included: Prince Fushimi's representative, Military Attaché Mihara; Prince Kan'in's representative, Military Attaché Nakajima; Prince Yamashina's representative, Military Attaché Maruhashi; Prince Nashimoto's representative, Steward Hidaka; Genrō Itō, Yamagata, Matsukata, and Inoue; cabinet members from Prime Minister Katsura down; members of the Privy Council; Generals Sakuma, Okazawa, and Itō; Vice-Ministers of the Cabinet Ishimoto, Saitō, Chinda, and others; Princes Tokugawa, Shimazu, Kujō, and others; Counts Ōkuma and Itagaki; members of both Houses; Imperial Headquarters staff from the Army and Navy; chiefs of bureaus and sections of ministries and other higher government officials; ministers of foreign delegations; Governor of Tokyo Senke and Mayor of the City of Tokyo Ozaki; business leaders; and representatives of various organizations.

The first- and second-class cars of the train were reserved for the delegation. Except for Prince Itō, Counts Inoue and Matsukata, Prime Minister Katsura, and the two service ministers, many people, including cabinet members, higher officials of the Foreign Office, and the families of the delegates, rode with the delegation as far as Yokohama to see it off there.

To welcome and send off the delegation, the people of Yokohama hoisted national flags from early morning on. At the station several hundred people were waiting for the arrival of the delegation. These included: Governor of Kanagawa Prefecture Shufu; Mayor of the City of Yokohama Ichihara and other honorary officers of the city; and representatives of various organizations.

The delegation's train arrived at the station at 3 p.m. Plenipotentiary Komura alighted from the train, preceded by the governor. He then rode in a coach that had been sent from the prefectural office for his use, giving a slight bow of recognition to the multitude that came out to welcome him. At that moment a firecracker, prepared well in advance for this occasion, exploded, and the brass bands of the city and other organizations started playing all at once. Now the several thousand people who had come to see the plenipotentiary shouted "Banzai!" The excitement of the people was indeed beyond description. It was the most splendid welcome we have ever seen.

Thus the delegates proceeded to the western pier, bathing in cries of "banzai" all the way. They left the pier on a small boat, prepared by the prefectural office, for the S.S. Minnesota. At this time several scores of firecrackers exploded. The Minnesota, fully dressed, hoisted the flag of the Rising Sun to the top of her mast out of respect to our delegation. The ship left for Seattle at 4 p.m., as scheduled.[91]

Of all those present on the occasion of his departure, perhaps Komura was the least sanguine.[92] He is reported to have turned to Katsura and said with a smile, "The people's reaction will have changed completely when I return."[93] Yamaza Enjirō, a member of the delegation, added, "When we return, we will be very lucky if the 'banzai' has only turned into 'bakayarō [you fool]'!" Katsura remained silent.[94] Well aware that the result of the peace negotiations would be totally disappointing to the people,[95] the decision-makers knew the Portsmouth Conference was indeed "the time to reap the harvest" of their previous secrecy in war and peace making.[96] Their state of mind was clearly revealed in the words of Prime Minister Katsura:

An old saying goes, "To start is easy, but to finish is difficult." "A hundred battles and a hundred victories" indeed tend to make the people puffed up. The Japanese people, who at the beginning of the war were anxious about the nation's fate, now, as a result of our successive victories, are puffed up with pride and regard the great Russian army as no more than a paper bear. Now we hear them cry that, with our ever-victorious forces, it would not be difficult at all to march on even to Moscow, not to speak of the Baikal. Their voice shouts, "How could a protracted war be disadvantageous to ever-victorious Japan?" We have already conquered the areas we had planned to occupy at the beginning of the war. If we march further into enemy territory, we must keep in mind the limitations of our military capacity. A further expansion of the battle lines would require a great deal of preparation, and to arrange the necessary expenses for this purpose is now of the utmost difficulty. Under these circumstances, those who bear the responsibility for the fate of the nation must contrive the restoration of peace at an opportune time with the most careful deliberations. And yet, they should never let their deliberations be known to the populace. When the great clash between the leaders and the people comes, the authorities, and I for one, should be ready to take the whole responsibility.[97]

CHAPTER SIX

THE PORTSMOUTH CONFERENCE

"Neither Victor nor Vanquished"

THE peace conference at Portsmouth started with a preliminary meeting on August 9, 1905. Altogether 12 sessions were held, in addition to which several private conferences between Komura and Witte took place.[1]

Witte attended the conference with the attitude that "there are no victors here and therefore no vanquished."[2] He agreed to eight of the twelve Japanese demands, but flatly rejected as dishonorable to Russia the demands for the cession of Sakhalin, the repayment of Japan's war expenses, the transfer to Japan of Russian warships in neutral ports, and the limitation of Russian naval forces in the Far East.[3] The tsar was adamant and held firmly to his words of instruction to Witte: "Russia will not pay even a kopeck. It will not cede one inch of its territory." Neither Japan's successive concessions nor Roosevelt's earnest pleas were sufficient to change the tsar's mind.[4] Komura, on the other hand, insisted on the demands for an indemnity and the cession of territory, despite the fact that these had only been among the "relatively important items" and thus were not to be considered as absolutely necessary for a peace agreement.

Finally, on August 26, Komura, judging that the peace negotiations had "reached a complete deadlock," reported to the home government his firm resolution to terminate negotiations at the next session. He then secretly ordered his men to prepare themselves to be able to leave Portsmouth directly upon receiving Tokyo's instructions. He made out a check for $20,000 to donate to the charity fund of the city of Portsmouth as a sign of his appreciation of the citizens' hospitality to the Japanese delegation.[5] His report read:

Report on the Crisis in the Peace Negotiations

Komura to Katsura
Telegram No. 105, August 26, 1905, New Castle
August 27, 1905, Tokyo

Our peace negotiations, as you may have judged from the last several telegrams, have today reached complete deadlock. Because of our sincere desire for the successful conclusion of negotiations and the restoration of peace, we have not only been most considerate in the presentation of our demands and made as many concessions as possible during the course of the piecemeal discussion of our terms, but we have also declared that in due course we would withdraw the two demands for the transfer of interned Russian warships and restriction of Russian naval power. Moreover, we have tried our best to bring the negotiations to a satisfactory conclusion by presenting a compromise plan on the two difficult questions of Sakhalin and the indemnity. Russia, however, has persisted in its stand on these two points and has never shown any sign of conceding. Throughout this time, as you are aware, the President has tried his best in various ways to bring about a successful conclusion of the peace negotiations. Despite his efforts, however, Russia will not reconsider its stand, and it now seems that Russian determination has grown even firmer. Since the tsar's reaction, of which you are aware, to the President's first telegram, it is clear that a second attempt by the President will be similarly fruitless. From what Witte told me in today's secret meeting, I cannot help but conclude that there is no hope at all that the tsar will change his mind. He seems to believe, on the basis of such information as Linievitch's reports, that his Manchurian Army is now superior to ours and that there is a good chance that Russia can bring about a drastic change in the military situation in Manchuria. Thus, we must conclude that at this time he has no intention of concluding peace.

However, since these two points have attracted the attention of the entire world since the beginning of the conference, and since in the last several sessions we have discussed them exclusively, it would greatly affect the honor of our Imperial nation if we should decide to withdraw them now. Therefore, unless we succeed in concluding our talks in accordance with our compromise plan, I consider that there is no longer any alternative but to cut off the negotiations.

Consequently, in the coming session, after receiving Russia's official reply to our compromise plan, we will terminate the negotiations with the following statement, in order to make clear the position of our Imperial nation:

From the beginning of the conference, we, the Japanese plenipotentiaries, have attended the negotiations in a spirit of mutual concession and reconciliation. After having made repeated concessions, we even presented a compromise plan on the questions of Sakhalin and the repayment of war expenses and thus tried our best for the sake of humanity and peace to conclude the negotiations successfully. Russia has stubbornly refused our compromise plan and now forces us to terminate the negotiations. Consequently, total responsibility for the continuation of the war should be borne by Russia.

As there is no reason to prolong the negotiations further, we, the Japanese delegates, will leave this place immediately upon termination of the negotiations. Since our swift action may bring about a change in the situation, we will watch its development from New York.

In conclusion, we greatly regret that the negotiations have reached this point despite our utmost efforts in accordance with the objectives of our Imperial nation at this conference. We have, however, decided to resort to this final measure, for we can find no solution to the present situation. We inform you in advance of what we are going to do and request your understanding of our decision.

A summary of today's secret conference has been privately given to the President through Baron Kaneko.[6]

This report reached Tokyo at about 8 p.m. on August 27. Alarmed by the seriousness of the situation, the Japanese government immediately instructed Komura to postpone the next session for a day[7] and called a joint conference of the Genrō and cabinet members at the home of Genrō Itō. Itō, Yamagata, and Inoue, Prime Minister and Acting Foreign Minister Katsura, War Minister Terauchi, Navy Minister Yamamoto, and Vice-Minister of Foreign Affairs Chinda attended the conference,[8] which lasted until midnight and, after a few hours recess, reconvened early the next morning.

The Japanese leaders who attended these extraordinary meetings to decide between peace by concession or war in fact had no choice. At the time of his departure for Portsmouth, Komura had stated four essential conditions for strengthening Japan's military situation and placing Japan in an advantageous diplomatic position: (1) to strike a blow against the newly arrived Russian troops led by Commander Linievitch; (2) to float new foreign loans in the amount of 300 million yen to cover war expenses; (3) to eliminate the Russian forces in north Korea;

and (4) to occupy the whole of Sakhalin. With considerable difficulty, Japan had managed to achieve the second and fourth conditions, but the peace negotiations had begun before it could attempt to attain the remaining two. For this reason alone, the decision-makers were well aware of the vulnerability of Japan's diplomatic position and of the fact that the course of peace negotiations did not warrant any optimism.[9]

Immediately after Komura's departure, Chief of Staff Yamagata had left for Manchuria.[10] He arrived at Mukden on July 21 and was briefed on the military situation by Commander Ōyama. The following day he personally inspected the military situation at the front line and on July 25 held a conference attended by Ōyama, Chief of Staff Kodama, and Commanders Kuroki, Oku, Nogi, Nozu, and Kawamura.[11]

It was clear that the military outlook for Japan was bleak. By that time the Russian forces were three times as strong as the Japanese. Furthermore, while the Japanese army was largely led by reserve officers, most of the regular officers having been killed or wounded, the Russian army consisted mainly of crack forces newly arrived from Europe. As far as morale was concerned, it was evident that the positions of the two belligerents had been reversed. Commander Linievitch had telegraphed an earnest plea to the tsar that Russia not make peace while the military situation in Manchuria was definitely advantageous to Russia.[12] Kuropatkin recalled: "Never in the whole of her military history has Russia put such a mighty army in the field as that formed by the concentration of the 1st, 2nd, and 3rd Manchurian Armies in August 1905."[13] Meanwhile, the pro-war faction around the tsar was growing larger daily and demanding the immediate termination of peace negotiations.[14]

On the Japanese side, Chief of Staff of the Manchurian Army Kodama, irked by the slow progress of the negotiations, repeatedly telegraphed the home government to urge an early conclusion of peace.[15] Navy Minister Yamamoto desperately pushed for concessions to bring about peace.[16]

The conference therefore decided that Japan must conclude a peace before the military situation in Manchuria deteriorated completely.[17] Under these circumstances, on August 28, at 2 p.m., a joint conference of the Genrō, the cabinet, and high military authorities was held in the

Emperor's presence.[18] The conference first sought the opinions of those members who would normally hesitate to speak.[19] Army Minister Terauchi stated that, because of the lack of officers the war could not continue any longer, and that the fighting could not be carried beyond the line of Changchun because communications there were completely cut. Finance Minister Sone said it would be impossible to find additional funds to continue the war. His opinion was supported by Matsukata and Inoue.[20] Yamagata likewise agreed that there was no way except to stop the war.[21] The conference informed the Emperor that militarily and financially Japan had no choice but to conclude peace.[22]

The Japanese government thereupon sent the following instruction to Komura:

The Cabinet Decision

Acting Foreign Minister Katsura to Komura
Telegram No. 69, August 28, 1905, 8:35 p.m.

Concerning your telegrams Nos. 104 and 105, our Imperial Government, after careful deliberation in cabinet meetings and an Imperial Conference, requested His Majesty's sanction to our decision, which is as follows:

Our government is well aware of the difficulty of continuing the negotiations now that Russia has flatly rejected our compromise plan. However, after carefully considering our military and economic situation and in view of the fact that through your negotiations we have already solved the more important questions of Manchuria and Korea, which were our objectives in this war, we have decided to reach an agreement in the negotiations at this time even if it means abandoning the two demands for indemnity and territory.

Because we consider it an appropriate step to take at this juncture and in light of the attitude we have held throughout the negotiations, to give up first the demand for an indemnity while maintaining the territorial demands, we hereby instruct you to propose the following in the coming session:

The Japanese government finds it extremely regrettable that the Russian government has failed to accept the compromise plan suggested by the plenipotentiaries of both countries. However, our Imperial government, out of its respect for humanity and civilization and for the sake of the true interests of both Japan and Russia, will as its last concession withdraw completely the demand for repayment of war expenses on the condition that Russia recognize the Japanese occupation of Sakhalin as a fait accompli.

You are instructed to make the above proposal, keeping in mind the true intent of our Imperial government; and even if the Russian plenipotentiaries should persist in their stand, you should not immediately break off negotiations.

In that case, you will attempt to persuade the President to recommend to us, as his last effort for peace, that we withdraw the territorial demand and accept his recommendation for the sake of humanity and peace. If the President should refuse to take this role of mediator, you are instructed to withdraw, as a last resort and our Imperial government's final concession, the territorial demand. In short, our Imperial government is determined to conclude peace by any means necessary during the present negotiations.

You are instructed to make the utmost efforts for the fulfillment of our government's objective in light of the intentions of our Imperial government.[23]

When the Japanese government obtained information that the tsar was prepared to cede the southern half of Sakhalin to Japan,[24] the instruction was immediately amended to read: "The Imperial government has decided, as a token of its earnest desire for peace, to relinquish its demand for the cession of the whole of Sakhalin Island and, as a final concession, to be satisfied instead with half of the island."[25]

Upon receiving the final instruction, Komura muttered, "This is what I thought they would tell me." Greatly disappointed, Komura unwillingly obeyed the instructions of his government. His trusted subordinates at Portsmouth, Yamaza Enjirō and Honda Kumatarō, both former Kogetsukai members, were extremely dejected.[26]

On August 29, 1905, Witte accepted the new Japanese terms. It is indeed ironic that the issues of indemnity and territory, which were secondary in the official Japanese demands, had so quickly become the central issue in the negotiations and that Komura, the most adamant of the Japanese oligarchic decision-makers in his demands, was later to be attacked for his "weak diplomacy."

Japanese Public Opinion and the Conference

The reaction of the Japanese public to the outcome of the conference was mixed. It had been expected that the peace terms Japan had demanded would be achieved. All the information available to the public had led to the belief that the war was proceeding favorably for Japan, and there was little doubt about Japan's military supremacy on the

Manchurian front. But the convening of the peace conference caused some apprehension. While the fighting in Manchuria had been successful for Japan, the people knew that Japan had not yet won a decisive victory over Russia, a victory that would guarantee the peace on the terms they desired. Regarding a permanent peace in the Far East as the ultimate war objective, the spokesmen for public opinion in Japan felt that the existing battle line in Manchuria was not then conclusive enough to bring this about. Furthermore, the cession, or at least the demilitarization, of Vladivostok, the "Lord of the East," was considered of paramount importance to a lasting peace. How could this be realized when Japan had not even occupied the harbor? Surely it was too early to negotiate, since Japanese forces had not yet set foot on Russian territory; Japan's position in making territorial demands would not be strong.

Thus, from the first, the Japanese public felt the peace overtures to be inopportunely timed and was sensitive to the ill omens that seemed to surround the opening of negotiations. The fact that Japan had accepted President Roosevelt's mediation offer two days before Russia had and that Russia had not publicly proposed peace, the equal status of Russia and Japan at the conference, the selection of Komura rather than Itō as the plenipotentiary, and Japan's ready agreement to hold the conference in the United States rather than in Japan, all tended to arouse disquiet among the people.

The mass media in Japan, therefore, anxiously and expectantly concentrated their full attention on the proceedings of the negotiations. A furious outburst of public opinion was touched off when the *Tokyo Asahi Shimbun* reported Witte's mid-ocean declaration that Russia would not pay one penny in the form of indemnity nor cede one inch of territory.[27] The *Tokyo Asahi Shimbun* was only expressing the general reaction when it wrote: "Only swords settle that which neither speech nor reason can arrange. Oh, for war! Oh, for a continuation of war! Let us not trouble about this emissary! There ought to be a Konishi Yukinaga in Japan today. Russia may misunderstand Japan, but Japan should never misunderstand Russia."[28]

Since there was no radio at the time, newspapers were the only means of reporting the news. The Japanese newspapers, in fierce competition with one another ever since the beginning of the war, sent special correspondents to Portsmouth.[29] Because of language difficulties and lack of foreign experience, however, these correspondents were not capable of mingling freely among the foreigners to gather news. They barely managed to obtain the proceedings of the negotiations from the suite of the Japanese plenipotentiaries, who attempted to keep most information confidential. The Japanese newspapers were, therefore, totally dependent upon the dispatches of American news agencies.[30] Before the Portsmouth Conference the *Osaka Mainichi Shimbun* had enjoyed a monopoly of news dispatches from America,[31] but as soon as the peace negotiations began, the *Osaka Asahi Shimbun*, the *Tokyo Asahi Shimbun*, and the *Jiji Shimpō* made special agreements with American news agencies to receive their dispatches.[32] Other Japanese newspapers, which could obtain the foreign dispatches only second hand, freely copied the special dispatches published in the four other papers and, using foreign dispatches gathered by stealth, often issued special editions.[33]

The reports based on these foreign dispatches were usually dull and lacking in depth, for all the dispatches came from basically the same limited sources, the major one being the Associated Press.[34] Furthermore, their contents were greatly affected by the attitudes of the plenipotentiaries, for whereas Komura honored his agreement with Witte to keep the negotiations secret and make public only such information as both had agreed to release, Witte paid great attention to the press and utilized it fully to influence American public opinion to Russia's advantage, completely ignoring his agreement with Komura. Some believed that, because of Witte's skillful use of the American press, the initially overwhelmingly pro-Japanese public opinion in America gradually became pro-Russian.[35] It is a fact that American newspapers and news agencies eventually came to report mainly the information and opinion provided by the Russian plenipotentiary. Consequently, the Japanese newspapers, which received their information from American news agencies, also came to publish news slanted toward Russia.[36]

In this closed situation, only the *Osaka Mainichi Shimbun* and the *Kokumin Shimbun* published comparatively vivid dispatches from America and attracted any exceptional public interest. Earlier the *Osaka Mainichi Shimbun* had astonished other newspapers with a special dispatch from Washington reporting President Roosevelt's willingness to undertake the role of mediator between the two belligerents. Its correspondent was Cal O'Laughlin, a Washington-based newspaperman who had been the special correspondent of the *Osaka Mainichi Shimbun* since the end of the Sino-Japanese War. He was intimate with influential figures in American politics, including Roosevelt, and was also a close acquaintance of Witte. The *Osaka Mainichi Shimbun*, therefore, was expected to show special insight in reporting the Portsmouth Conference.[37]

The *Kokumin Shimbun,* the unofficial organ of the Katsura Cabinet, naturally enjoyed the special favor of the government during the peace negotiations.[38] The advantageous position of the *Osaka Mainichi Shimbun* and the *Kokumin Shimbun* led the two papers to cooperate in sending an additional special correspondent to Portsmouth. Thus the *Osaka Mainichi Shimbun* obtained choice information, utilizing the special position of the *Kokumin Shimbun,* and the latter received information on the Russian and American attitudes through O'Laughlin.[39] This arrangement between the two papers, however, was purely one of convenience. Although it took advantage of the situation, the *Osaka Mainichi Shimbun* remained opposed to the Katsura Cabinet and continued to take a hard line toward the peace negotiations.

Other newspapers grew extremely jealous of these two papers. Their indignation was further inflamed by Komura's secretive attitude toward the Japanese as well as the foreign press and his open favoritism toward the *Kokumin Shimbun* correspondent at Portsmouth. The antigovernment position of the majority of Japanese newspapers was not a little intensified by these facts.[40]

Aside from their great difficulties in gathering news of the conference, the Japanese newspapers had a second big obstacle to contend with. Throughout the period of the negotiations, government control of the press grew increasingly severe.[41] Facing such strict controls, the newspapers contrived all sorts of ways to prevent dispatches from their correspondents at Portsmouth from being seized by the government, but to little avail.[42] This was one reason for the newspapers' fierce attacks at the conclusion of the conference upon the government's secret diplomacy and for their unsympathetic attitude toward the delicate position in which the government was placed.

The first reports of the conference to reach Japan indicated that great difficulty lay ahead and confirmed the pessimistic views held by the majority of Japanese. The headline of the August 12 issue of the *Tokyo Asahi Shimbun,* reporting the first meeting on August 9, read: "Russo-Japanese Peace Negotiations Underway. Unexpectedly Strong Attitude of the Russians Augurs a Storm in the Negotiations." It was accompanied by a photograph of the plenipotentiaries facing each other across a table and an article stating: "Russia will not agree to cede Sakhalin Island and to pay a war indemnity for military and industrial reasons and for the sake of national honor. They think the cession of Sakhalin to Japan will mean that Japan will then have the power to keep Russian fleets out of the Far East."[43]

The *Kokumin Shimbun,* as the unofficial government organ, was careful to respond with its own, more optimistic appraisal of the situation. On August 8, amid the critical clamor in the Japanese press, it presented the opinion that Russia's outward attitude did not indicate its real state of mind. Rather, the current state of affairs in Russia dictated that peace be made, and therefore Russian declarations were mere bombast in the face of overwhelming facts.[44]

On August 13 the *Tokyo Asahi Shimbun* and other papers published "Japanese Demands," a special dispatch dated August 11 from Washington. It created a great sensation among the Japanese people, for at the same time the public learned that the terms of peace demanded by Japan were revealed to the press by the Russian plenipotentiary, who sought to make his position advantageous in world public opinion by thus ignoring the agreement not to divulge such information. The Japanese public quickly concluded that a nation that would resort to such measures was not sincerely desirous of peace.

In addition, the Japanese terms as revealed by Witte seemed extremely modest to the Japanese, and his claim that the terms were "unreasonable" therefore intensified the hostility of the press toward Russia and the conference. The *Jiji Shimpō* on August 14 declared that Japan should require a simple "yes" or "no" to her demands within a fixed time, so as to end the conference quickly.[45] The *Tokyo Nichi-nichi Shimbun* of the same day stated: "Russia must pay something for peace if she wants it. What Japan asks her to pay is the very smallest price; it is a price remarkable for its moderation and conciliatory spirit." And the *Tokyo Asahi Shimbun* commented: "Japan has asked for less than the world would have endorsed its demanding. It has even endeavored to find terms that will make things easy for the enemy. If Russia does not accept these proposals, let it feel the consequences."[46] The *Tokyo Asahi Shimbun* and other papers foresaw an early rupture of peace negotiations and advocated that Japan, rather than conclude an unsatisfactory peace, insure eternal peace by fighting for two or three more years and completely defeating the enemy.[47] Some papers, however, while they stated that the Japanese terms for peace were too tolerant, did not oppose a peace concluded on this basis. At the same time, these papers all stated that a peace that conceded more than the announced demands would be totally unacceptable. The *Osaka Mainichi Shimbun* declared that Komura would not be welcomed back by the public if he made even the slightest concession.[48]

The reports from Portsmouth continued, with news of the difficulties of the negotiations and the pressuring of the Japanese delegates by Witte's skillful maneuvering.[49] The August 30 issue of the *Tokyo Asahi Shimbun*, reporting a dispatch dated August 26 from Portsmouth, concluded that the conference would almost certainly be ruptured.[50]

The opinion expressed by the *Tokyo Asahi Shimbun*, the *Nihon*, the *Jiji Shimpō*, and the *Nihonjin*, that the rupture of negotiations and continued fighting would be to Japan's advantage, represented the majority opinion in the press. What was behind their advocacy of continuing the war? Basically it was that the press estimated Japan's fighting capacity very highly and thought that by continuing the war Japan could win total victory. The English-language *Japan Daily Herald* stated on August 15: "All the facts go to show that Japan is prepared to renew the conflict, that she is even now making efforts to strike a still stronger blow at her enemy, and that the process of negotiations has in no way impeded her activity. . . . She is ready, if not anxious, to continue the war, but the next negotiations will not be conducted in the United States."[51] At present, they felt, the strong stand taken by Russia and the lack of skill of the Japanese delegates at the conference would prevent realization of important Japanese demands.

At the same time, they judged that Japan's international position was more advantageous than that of Russia.[52] Russia reportedly had failed to float new loans in the Paris market, so it was concluded that Russia's international position had so deteriorated that it could no longer obtain assistance even from its ally. The *Nihonjin,* which had made especially strong initial demands, stated that the Powers were displeased by Russia's advance into Manchuria because it threatened their own interests there; Japan's advance, on the other hand, would go unprotested, even though it might cause some anxiety, as long as Japan did not violate the Powers' rights and interests in the region. The journal therefore advocated that Japan work to attain its demands without being intimidated by such vague considerations as where the sympathies of the Powers lay.[53] After the Japanese demands were made public, the *Nihonjin* stated that, if the negotiations should break down because of Russian intransigence, Japan would only gain more support from the third powers and therefore be in a more advantageous position.[54]

The *Tōyō Keizai Shimpō,* which conjectured that the peace negotiations had not initially been sought by Russia, was extremely pessimistic about the conference. It stated that, even if peace came, it would be extremely disadvantageous to Japan, since Japan would be able to gain neither territory nor indemnity. The resulting peace would leave intact the Russian threat in Manchuria, and Japan would be compelled to strengthen its forces in Manchuria and Korea, necessitating a continuation of the enormous burden upon the Japanese people. Should the negotiations fail, the situation would actually be the same armed peace, since Japan would maintain its belligerent position at the line of Tiehling and, in this case, would have the opportunity to occupy Vladivostok. The journal concluded that, in the final analysis, the breakdown of negotiations would be more beneficial to Japan than the conclusion of a peace with concessions.[55]

A few newspapers and magazines did entertain some hope and optimism for the conclusion of a peace under conditions that would guarantee Japan's war objectives. The *Tokyo Keizai Zasshi* thought that the outcome was dependent upon Japan's diplomatic skill. This journal and the *Tokyo Nichi-nichi Shimbun* both stated that the attitude and resolution of the Japanese people would have a great effect upon the results of the negotiations. These optimistic newspapers and magazines, while regarding the reported Japanese demands as "tolerant, moderate, and considerate"[56] and declaring that they would never permit the conclusion of peace with lesser demands, asserted that, in the light of its seriously troubled domestic situation, Russia's strong attitude was a mere bluff, and they claimed that the key to success or failure lay in proof of Japan's determination.

On August 15, with the arrival of news of Russia's rejection of the demands for an indemnity and cession of territory,[57] the pessimistic press started to demand an immediate termination of the negotiations and continuation of the war. The *Jiji Shimpō* declared that, if Japan could not obtain reimbursement, it must indemnify itself by seizing territory on the mainland.[58] The optimistic press urged the government with increasingly strong arguments to take a firmer attitude. Katō Takaaki's *Tokyo Nichi-nichi Shimbun*, a leader among the optimistic press, repeatedly published editorials designed to stir up public opinion. It advised the government to fulfill the people's hopes by accepting the strong opinion of the public instead of controlling it.[59] On August 16 the newspaper published an editorial entitled "Don't Be Unduly Pessimistic. Don't Be Unduly Optimistic." Pointing out the trickery in Russian diplomacy, it demanded that the Japanese plenipotentiaries always keep the upper hand.[60]

When the Portsmouth Conference decided to discuss the other Japanese demands before taking up the demands for territory and indemnity, the *Tokyo Nichi-nichi Shimbun* of August 17 demanded that the government "first achieve the important items" of indemnity and territory. The newspaper stressed that, unless these demands were satisfied, agreement on other items would be useless and unacceptable to the Japanese people. On subsequent days the newspaper published the following editorials: "No Room for Compromise" (on the demands for indemnity and territory), August 20; "We Demand That the Government Make a Final Drive," August 21; "We Should Not Concede the Indemnity and Territory Questions" (even if we risk continuation of the war), August 25; "We Will Never Permit an Indecisive Peace," August 27; "Division of Sakhalin—No!" August 28. The newspaper attacked the weak attitude of the Genrō and the cabinet ministers and urged them to "take an ultimate stand" for "the fulfillment of our demands of indemnity and territory," August 29.[61]

Thus Japanese newspapers and magazines urged the government to take a strong stand and at the same time showed strong opposition to a peace agreement that conceded any of Japan's demands. As rumors of Japanese concessions reached Tokyo, ridicule of the government increased in intensity. When on August 28 the *Kokumin Shimbun* published telegrams confirming the news of a probable compromise, the *Hōchi Shimbun* headlined one article, "The Head of a Dragon, the Tail of a Worm." The *Yomiuri Shimbun* declared, "Let us have ministers who know how to safeguard the country's interests." The unbelieving *Niroku Shimpō* issued a special edition that said:

The Japanese plenipotentiaries have never departed in the least from their demands for the cession of the whole of Sakhalin and reimbursement to the extent of 1200 million yen. Therefore, unless success attends the efforts of the President and the Kaiser, there will be nothing for it but for the Japanese plenipotentiaries to abandon the conference and return home. We are persuaded that our plenipotentiaries never proposed anything such as the partition of Sakhalin.[62]

The confusion of rumors was compounded by an intensifying pessimism on the part of the press that served only to make more insistent the voices clamoring for an end to negotiations. In the midst of these vociferous demands by the press and the public, the *Kokumin Shimbun* alone continued to urge the Japanese people to watch the proceedings of the negotiations with absolute trust in their plenipotentiaries.

As the peace negotiations were prolonged, the Japanese public increasingly lost hope of success, and their demands for continuation of the war and immediate termination of negotiations grew stronger. The *Osaka Asahi Shimbun* viewed the situation thus:

But what has happened? The Japanese demands, framed on the basis of a so-called "irreducible minimum," are being whittled away little by little, contrary to the general expectation of the people, while Russia, by astute manipulation of the situation, is recovering by diplomacy what she lost in war. . . . Japan's gains from the peace conference . . . would seem not to be in the same proportion to what it has achieved in the field of arms. . . . The war, once undertaken, should rather be pushed to the bitter end than that peace be made on such unsatisfactory terms. The arrogant attitude maintained by Russia goes to show that the time is not yet ripe for the negotiation of peace.[63]

By August 28, when the Imperial conference was held, many people rejoiced, believing that it would decide to terminate the peace negotiations.[64]

PART FOUR

Domestic Repercussions

CHAPTER SEVEN

THE ANTI-PEACE TREATY
MOVEMENT

Press Agitation

AN EXTRA issued on the afternoon of August 30 stunned the Japanese people. The first story was carried only by the *Kokumin Shimbun* in Tokyo and the *Osaka Mainichi Shimbun* in the Kansai area, but the news spread quickly throughout the country.[1] According to a foreign news dispatch, Japan had withdrawn its demand for indemnity and had agreed to peace on the condition that it obtain the southern half of Sakhalin only. The general astonishment was so great that the newspapers simply announced the news in sensational headlines, with no editorial comment.[2] Many of their offices hung out flags with mourning crepe.[3]

The American minister Griscom reported to his home government:

A large section of the press demanded, and confidently expected, the cession of Vladivostok and the Russian Maritime provinces (*sic*), as well as the island of Sakhalin, and the payment of a thousand million dollars indemnity. Even the more reasonable and conservative classes expected the cession of Sakhalin and five hundred million dollars indemnity. It may be truthfully said that outside of the government nobody in the Empire expected that Japan would be obliged to accept the terms which it is now understood are contained in the Treaty of Peace.[4]

The following day the *Yorozu Chōhō* published a telegram from its correspondent Kawakami Kiyoshi concerning the coming of peace, under the heading, "Ah! Great Humiliation! Great Humiliation!"[5] Its lead article appealed to the people:

In the past many patriots have willingly sacrificed heart and blood for their country. This was so when the constitutional government was being established. When our people saw the humiliation and submission of the revised treaty system agreed upon by our nation and the Powers, didn't they dare to attack the person responsible for the treaty revision and even take away one leg?

When we are faced with a grave national question, we need a nationwide movement. . . . Rise, rise, rise! Endeavor to solve this great question. Rise, Rise, our people![6]

On this day also, the government for the first time made public an outline of the contents of the peace agreement, but only through its own press organ. The other papers could only copy the news verbatim as it was reported in the *Kokumin Shimbun*. This, on top of all the government's past acts of secrecy and press prejudice, only served to heighten the nationwide cry against the peace that had been agreed upon.[7]

The Japanese press could find in the information released to them on the war no reason why Japan had to make such a large concession in order to conclude peace. From the beginning of the war, the Japanese military forces were reported as being ever victorious on land and sea. Both the decisive victory of the Japan Sea in the end of May and the occupation of all of Sakhalin from the end of June to early August had been enthusiastically reported.[8] These facts convinced the press of Japan's military superiority, and they had no doubt that Japan would be ultimately victorious. From the way Japanese loans were being accepted on foreign markets, they judged that not only Japan's military position but also its financial position was superior to Russia's. In fact, after the commencement of peace negotiations, Japan had succeeded in floating foreign loans for three hundred million yen, and it was believed that the Japanese government still had sufficient war funds.[9] In international relations as well, the situation looked bright. The Anglo-Japanese alliance was renewed on August 12, 1905, and Japan was enjoying the sympathy of neutral countries.[10]

With such a conception of Japan's situation, the overwhelming majority of newspapers did not react calmly to the contents of the peace agreement. They charged that the agreement did not meet even the minimum conditions necessary to attain Japan's primary war objective, that is, the eradication of the Russian threat in Manchuria and Korea. They were also convinced that a peace without indemnity would throw a dark shadow over the postwar economic activities, for Japan would need great sums of money to repay the foreign loans and to expand its arms supply, thus adding to the heavy burden already carried by the people. The press judged that the "humiliating peace" was completely attributable to diplomatic failure on the part of the government and demanded unanimously a government explanation for the "unbelievable concession." The earlier tone of discontent suddenly crescendoed into a violent attack upon the government. Convinced that Japan would be able to conclude a more advantageous peace if fighting were continued, the newspapers requested the Emperor to reject the peace settlement; they also urged the Manchurian Army to continue the battle. Newspapers throughout the nation aroused public opinion against the peace and, making use of the popular rage, pressured the government to cancel the peace agreement. When they realized that the Katsura Cabinet, despite the violent opposition of the press, only kept silent and took no concrete action, the press began to call for the resignation of the cabinet. Some went so far as to propose openly the assassination of the Genrō and the cabinet ministers.[11]

The *Yorozu Chōhō* of September 1 published an article entitled "Receive Them with Flags of Mourning," that scorchingly criticized the Japanese plenipotentiary. The article stated:

The glory of our Imperial nation, demonstrated to all the world by our military triumphs, has been completely erased by none other than our plenipotentiary. It is our plenipotentiary who has smeared the face of the ever-victorious nation. It is our plenipotentiary who has acted miserably on the international stage and put himself to shame. On the day of his return he should be met with flags of mourning. Every person in the city should shut the door of his house and turn away from him. Any who welcome this soft fellow, who has invited unprecedented humiliation upon our nation, are wretched people with no blood, no public mind, no sense of righteousness.[12]

The *Osaka Asahi Shimbun* printed the terms of peace in a black frame and stated: "We are ashamed to report this. We here list the terms of negotiated peace, nay, the terms of pleaded peace, exactly as reported in the official organ, the *Kokumin Shimbun*."[13] With a large picture of a weeping skeleton,[14] an entire page was devoted to two long articles, "We Humbly Request His Majesty to Order the Peace Agreement Cancelled" and "We Appeal to the People to Inquire into the Responsibility of the Genrō and the Cabinet Ministers." The first article quoted part of the Imperial Declaration of War and said that the military and the people, obedient to the Imperial edict through their loyalty and heroic actions, had won an absolute victory. It continued:

With this humiliating peace agreement, how can we hope for the eternal peace which His Majesty and His subjects, too, desire? His Majesty's ministers have acted contrary to His will. They have violated the Imperial Declaration of War and smeared the glory of Our Imperial Nation which His Majesty and His subjects, loyal to him, have upheld. They are disrupting eternal peace. We, His loyal subjects, are at the extremity of tears, blood, and indignation. We, His loyal subjects . . . earnestly desire cancellation of the peace and continuation of the war. We are willing to fight to the last man, even if Japan must become a scorched land. . . . His Cabinet members, however, have slackened their efforts, by their error have forfeited our nation's objectives, and are now about to accept this humiliation. We, the people, know that in the light of His Majesty's Declaration of War, this is contrary to His Will. . . . The declaration of war and the making of peace are His Majesty's prerogatives. His Majesty has ordered the ministers to negotiate peace and entrusted the work to our plenipotentiary. But whether the agreed peace be ratified or rejected is the prerogative of His Majesty. We, His subjects, humbly request His Majesty to order cancellation of the peace agreement, which is contrary to His Will, before it is signed, to order wise men to form a new cabinet, and to command the military men to march on.[15]

The second article attributed the failure of the peace negotiations to weakness on the part of the Genrō and the ministers of state and to the clumsiness of Komura's diplomatic negotiations. It stated: "The Russo-Japanese War is not the battle of a few Genrō and cabinet ministers. It is a battle of the people. . . . The people are still not at all weary of fighting. The weary ones are the Genrō and the cabinet ministers. . . . Ah! The people have been betrayed by the Genrō and the cabinet ministers."[16]

Beside these, the most influential newspapers in Japan—including the *Tokyo Asahi Shimbun,* the *Jiji Shimpō,* the *Tokyo Nichi-nichi Shimbun,* the *Osaka Mainichi Shimbun,* the *Tokyo Mainichi Shimbun,* the *Hōchi Shimbun,* the *Miyako Shimbun,* the *Nihon,* the *Niiroku Shimpō,* and the *Yomiuri Shimbun*—all vociferously expressed their dissatisfaction with the peace terms, called for rejection of the peace and continuation of the war, and demanded that the government take full responsibility for the failure.[17] From September 2 on, the tone of the press became more and more violent. The titles of some lead articles from representative newspapers clearly show this tendency:[18]

September 2

"Explanation Is Necessary" (*Tokyo Asahi Shimbun*)

"The People Should Rise as One Body and Urge the Government to Cancel the Peace" (*Osaka Asahi Shimbun*)

"If We Don't Reject It, Russia Will" (*Osaka Asahi Shimbun*)

"The Start of a Coup d'Etat" (*Yorozu Chōhō*)

September 3

"The Unpardonable Crime" (*Hōchi Shimbun*)

"On the Patriot's Solution" (*Osaka Asahi Shimbun*)

"Reject the Peace, Manchurian Army. Keep on Fighting" (*Osaka Asahi Shimbun*)

"Continue the War" (*Osaka Asahi Shimbun*)

"Publish the Terms of the Peace Agreement Immediately!" (*Tokyo Nichi-nichi Shimbun*)

September 4

"The Authorities Should Resign" (*Jiji Shimpō*)

"Should We Acquiesce?" (*Yorozu Chōhō*)

"Itō and Katsura, Running Dogs" (*Yorozu Chōhō*)

"Disloyal and Disobedient Ministers" (*Yorozu Chōhō*)

"Botchy, Botchy, Botchy" (*Yorozu Chōhō*)

"Big Talkers, but Cowards" (*Yorozu Chōhō*)

"Forced Reading of the Official Organ" (*Yorozu Chōhō*)

"We Shall Shake the World with Our Public Opinion" (*Osaka Asahi Shimbun*)

"Actual Examples of Treaty Rejections and the Methods Employed" (*Osaka Asahi Shimbun*)

"The Peace and World Opinion" (*Tokyo Nichi-nichi Shimbun*)[19]

September 5

"Reject It, Reject It, Reject It" (*Yorozu Chōhō*)

"Join Us, Join Us, Join Us" (*Yorozu Chōhō*)

"We Are More and More Enraged" (*Yorozu Chōhō*)

This opinion, expressed by the large majority of newspapers and journals, was opposed by only a feeble minority, which merely served to enrage the majority further. The *Kokumin Shimbun* stated: "As the 'results of victory' we have achieved our war objectives. We have achieved every one of them. We have achieved all of them. Not only that, we have gained more than we had aimed for." The *Kokumin Shimbun* criticized those who demanded the acquisition of all of Sakhalin and an indemnity of three billion yen, stating that "these were only visions which our extraordinary victories on land and sea ushered forth."[20] The *Chūō Shimbun*,[21] which was regarded as an official organ of the Seiyūkai, the *Nihon*,[22] the *Chūgai Shōgyō Shimpō*,[23] and the *Osaka Shimpō*, whose president was Hara Takashi of the *Seiyūkai*,[24] published lead articles supporting the agreed-upon peace.[25] The English newspapers based in Yokohama and Kobe, papers such as the *Japan Daily Herald*, the *Japan Chronicle,* and the *Japan Daily Advertiser,* better informed of conditions outside Japan than the domestic papers, unanimously stated that the terms of peace had achieved Japan's war objectives and praised highly the insight of the Genrō and cabinet ministers for bringing an end to the war through "Japan's magnanimity."[26]

This minority stressed several points: The terms of peace had already fulfilled the basic war objectives of Japan. Indemnity and the other half of Sakhalin were, after all, of secondary importance. It would therefore be foolish to continue the war, not knowing what the outcome might be. Continuing the war would not only make it harder to get indemnity from Russia but would also demand enormous sacrifices from the Japanese people in terms of life and property. From the point of view of world peace and civilization, and of a possible rapprochement between Japan and Russia in the future, it was wisest to conclude peace at that juncture. Even Japan's postwar economic problems could be advantageously solved, since Japan could utilize its international prestige and credit, which would be considerably heightened by this victory.

But such minority opinion could not convince the outraged majority. The press agitation created a national climate of opinion that was decidedly hostile to the peace treaty. In fact, the day-after-day deluge of sensational lead articles and political cartoons was so effective that even those most ignorant of, and indifferent to, the peace question were caught up in the tornado of outrage.[27]

Confronted with this newspaper attack, the government made no announcements concerning the peace agreement except to leak the outline of its contents to the *Kokumin Shimbun*. The public judged the situation solely on the basis of the strong and partial opinions of the newspapers.

The People's Indignation

The common people seem to have been quickly inflamed by the reported peace terms and the violent reactions expressed in the newspapers. They had sacrificed their lives and paid the high prices and taxes of wartime, hoping only for Japan's victory. Now they were told that through the unsatisfactory peace they would not only gain nothing but would also have to continue to bear the financial burden they had endured during the war. On top of this, since the middle of August reports had anticipated a bad rice harvest for the year, so they foresaw an imminent rise in the price of rice, their daily staple.[28] They were even more upset by the report that the Genrō and cabinet members throughout the war had continued to live in luxury and pleasure, ignoring the sufferings of the common people. Some of the leaders allegedly had even taken advantage of their confidential knowledge of the coming peace to make great fortunes in stock market speculation.[29]

The common people's "sense of helpless indignation" was reflected in some of the letters to the editor published in the *Tokyo Asahi Shimbun* and the *Osaka Asahi Shimbun*.[30]

We Demand Compensation for the Losses We Have Suffered.

I couldn't believe it when I first heard about the peace. I didn't take it seriously because I just couldn't. But I hear it is true. I don't know the details, but what I know tells me that it is nothing more than a rehash about the war, and our spending as much as two billion yen, and our suffering deaths and casualties of one hundred thousand, this is all we get! This is nonsense! We people should demand that our government pay us for our losses.

Disgusting!

Not only the plenipotentiary but also the secretaries and interpreters, altogether seven or eight people, have gone as far as Portsmouth; and now who do you think has paid for their transportation and hotel expenses? This is disgusting!

Agreement of the Villagers [From a certain village in Kanagawa prefecture]

We, volunteers of this village, together have resolved that in the event of future war we shall not respond to drafts or to the issuance of national bonds. If anybody should say of our action that we are Russian spies, we are ready to retort, who has shown the best example of being Russian spies? If people are not satisfied with this answer, we will escape to the place of that peace-lover Mr. Tolstoi.

Clumsy, clumsy, clumsy, clumsy!

What a failure! What a mistake! They have made a victorious nation, unequaled by any in the world, suffer the greatest humiliation the world has ever known. The Genrō have sold the country down the river. The cabinet ministers have put His Majesty to shame. Who can be called traitors, if not *they*?

Russia's Distribution of Citations

The Russian citation list is arranged in the following order: First place goes to the Chief of General Staff of the Japanese Manchurian Army Kodama Gentarō; second place to Japanese Chief of Staff Yamagata Aritomo; third place to Japanese Prime Minister Katsura Tarō; and fourth place to Japanese Foreign Minister Komura Jutarō. These four men are of more value to Russia than even Linievitch.

Alas, Plenipotentiary Komura!

In the end, Komura would do better to become a citizen of Russia than to come home. If he should come home, what excuse for his great failure could he offer to His Majesty and to Field Marshal Ōyama and Admiral Tōgō and to us, fifty million of his countrymen?

Conclusion of Peace? What's This?

From a veteran: We have so much to fight bravely for, to march on for, to win and to gain. What on earth are the authorities doing? We have Tōgō on sea and Ōyama on land. Our strategy has been set. Have the Genrō and the cabinet ministers lost their courage?

From a factory worker: We are told that we should endure the war. Our wages, which were supposed to be raised at the end of last year, were not raised. I was looking forward to peace so I would be able to drink a cup of sake. But this peace, with bad terms, won't make any difference in our lives. We have only to keep on suffering.

From a farmer: We have somehow managed to pass through the typhoon season, but we are extremely worried because this year's harvest of rice is going to be very bad. We expected some change would come when the war ended. We are betrayed! Bad rice harvest, depression everywhere, farmers only suffer.

From a merchant: It's no good. A recovery of business activities has relieved us temporarily, but now comes a bad harvest. We expected that peace would bring something different. But now, with the peace concluded, business won't improve. Orders will be few. Payments will be slow. Stores will be deserted. We can't make it.

From a tenant: For what on earth did we endure the bitter life, buying salt at an outrageous price? This is no joke. If they don't care about us after having made a lot of money in stock market speculation, I won't forgive them. No, I won't forgive them.

Thus the voice of the common people, as expressed in the newspapers, was overwhelming in its attack on the government. The people had placed their hopes on the results of the peace negotiations, believing their hard-pressed lives would be improved. Now they felt that they had been betrayed by their government.[31]

Not only the common people were indignant. Some business leaders, hoping an indemnity would provide capital for postwar economic expansion and a pillar upon which to sustain the economy, which had shown improvement since the middle of the war, were also much upset when they heard there would be no indemnity.

The *Tokyō Nichi-nichi Shimbun*, in an article entitled "How Can We Overcome the Postwar Financial Difficulties?" wrote that "Since we have given up the only means to cure the economic ills of the people and to secure capital funds for postwar economic activity, it is inevitable that we shall now face the fate of bankruptcy." Watanabe Sentarō, an executive director of the Mitsui Bussan Company, stated that without indemnity Japan would be unable to plan any postwar economic measures.[32] Ikeda Kenzō of the Daihyaku Ginkō (Daihyaku Bank), referring to the terms of the peace, stated, "When I think of the finances and economy of the future, a chill goes up my spine." He felt that the large indemnity following the Sino-Japanese War was what had supplied the capital funds for postwar economic development. If Japan was not to get any indemnity from the Russo-Japanese War, in which Japan had invested ten times as much as it had in the Sino-Japanese War, then Japan's ". . . financial circles will be in great trouble, and the expansion of business enterprises will come to a standstill. As for overseas advancement, in view of the extreme difficulty of supplying the funds necessary for domestic economic activities, it is unthinkable for us to expand overseas after this exhausting war."[33] An important economics journal of the time, the *Taiheiyō*, pessimistically calculated the amount of capital that would be needed after the war in an article entitled "How Will the Postwar Economy Be?"

Since the outbreak of the Russo-Japanese War, the total for domestic and foreign loans has reached as much as one billion three hundred million yen. Even though of that amount we still have fifty million yen in unpaid domestic loans and two hundred fifty million yen in foreign loans recently floated in the London market, these together would be insufficient even to bring our army home from Manchuria. By the time we see the complete withdrawal of our expeditionary forces from the battlefield, war expenses will amount to 1.7 to 1.8 billion yen. Moreover, the interest on these loans is as high as 100 million yen. How can our country repay both the interest and the principal? Is the government going to attempt to repay these through an increase in taxes? Taxes have been extremely heavy since the beginning of the war under the pretext of wartime emergency. We are certain that however high the taxes are, the amount of revenue will not exceed 400 million yen.[34]

Another leading economics journal of the time, the *Tokyo Keizai Zasshi*, asserted that Russia would easily recover from the war, since no indemnity was demanded of it and that, holding its mighty naval base at Vladivostok and retaining its naval forces in the Far East, it would still pose a great threat to Japan. Japan, on the other hand, would face great financial difficulties, for, in addition to its burden of the war debts, it would have to maintain a military force sufficient to meet the continued Russian threat.[35]

Such pessimism in business circles invited a serious drop in the stock market. The *Tōkyō Asahi Shimbun* of September 2 reported the stock market activities of the previous day as follows:

Because of the humiliating peace, general transactions were extremely slow. The banks are increasingly cautious in making loans for stocks and bonds. Yesterday's stock market activities showed real signs of depression. The peace had wiped out the buyers and at the same time produced desperate sellers, and therefore stock quotations dropped abruptly. It was a devastating market. Moreover, we fear that when those who still entertain hopes for the outcome of the peace negotiations and who do not believe that there will be peace without indemnity are awakened from their illusions, there will be another further drop in stock market activity.[36]

Activity on the commodities market was also very low. It was reported that "the commodities market is just like a light which has been switched off. It is a miserable scene—more miserable than at any previous time."[37]

Some commercial leaders, while dissatisfied, expressed their doubts more quietly. Baron Shibusawa, president of the First National Bank and chairman of the Tokyo Chamber of Commerce, who was generally optimistic about the future, felt that the partition of Sakhalin was "particularly regrettable" and that the diplomacy of the government "could hardly be regarded as a success."[38]

It is worthy of note that the organizers of the first large-scale demonstration against the treaty[39]—in Osaka on September 3—consisted in large part of businessmen. But even though the initial reaction of the business community was generally one of dissatisfaction, as mass protest began to develop into violence, this attitude quickly changed to one of support for the treaty. Businessmen began to emphasize the gains won in the war and the importance of concentrating on postwar economic management. Here again, as during the prowar agitation before the war, business leaders can be seen to have been in basic agreement with the government.

Many well-known intellectuals of the time also expressed strong dissatisfaction with the peace. We have already seen that the novelist Futabatei Shimei showed his enthusiasm for the war with the cry that the war would make the common people of Japan the masters of the nation. He expressed his strong dissatisfaction with the peace in the same way as did the man in the street.[40] The young poet Ishikawa Takuboku, a hot-blooded patriot who had earlier instigated the villagers to clamor for war, wrote when the peace negotiations began: "Don't worry about what the powers may think! Don't hesitate! Don't be mild! The right and the power are in the hands of the victor. . . . The victor must only show boldly, openly, and sufficiently his heaven-bestowed right and power." Upon hearing news of the peace, he recorded his intense dissatisfaction in his diary.[41]

The philosopher Nishida Kitarō, one of the leading intellectuals of modern Japan, then thirty-five years old, documented the nationwide excitement in his diary, *Sunshin Nikki:*

August 28: Japan has made great concessions at the peace conference. *No good! No good!*
August 29: I read only Spinoza. . . . An extra was issued stating that

after an Imperial conference the government sent a telegram instructing
Komura to withdraw.

August 30: It seems that yesterday's extra was false. Last night another
extra was issued telling of a peace agreement.

August 31: I examined the agreed terms of peace. They are utterly
humiliating. How can the Genrō and the cabinet ministers face the people?
It is indeed *miserable* that we gain no indemnity, only half of Sakhalin,
and the railroad only as far as Changchun. Ah! This is the end of everything.[42]

It is clear that the views on the war expressed by intellectuals of the
time were after all no different from the simple-minded patriotism of
the common people. The intellectuals, too, could judge and criticize
the actual situation only on the basis of the extremely limited information given in the newspapers and magazines.

In this general wave of dissatisfaction, the voice of the minority, expressing reserved but approving opinion about the peace, was quickly
drowned out. Some of the minority held basically anti-war views; for
example, the socialists Sakai Toshihiko and Arahata Kanson[43] or Uchimura Kanzō, who had opposed the war from a Christian standpoint and
felt that it had brought only calamity to Japan.[44] General Tani Kanjō,
who had opposed the war up to the very moment of its outbreak and
who, as we have observed, proposed extremely reasonable terms for
peace, considered that, in view of the hardship that continuing the war
would mean for Japan, the only thing for Japan to do was to terminate
hostilities under the agreed-upon terms. He chided the dissenters and
stated that it was time for Japan to appraise calmly the international
power balance and to take its place among the other great nations.[45]

Not unexpectedly, "the Professors" who had led the movement for a
strong policy toward Russia before the war and demanded excessive
peace terms were unhappy about the peace. They all joined in the
chorus of disapproval.[46]

The newspapers reported that soldiers stationed at camps in Japan
were strongly opposed to the peace and that troops in the Manchurian
Army shouted that "they would not go home."[47] It was generally understood that the only reason for the apparently calm reaction on the part
of soldiers was strong military discipline.[48] In the navy, it was reported,
the officers held their tongues, but the sailors below deck grumbled
indignantly about what was regarded as a diplomatic surrender.[49]

Organized Opposition to the Peace Treaty

Opposition to the peace treaty was expressed by all strata of the people throughout the nation. In Tokyo, there was no rejoicing. Although every house was prepared to celebrate a victory, not a flag was hoisted nor a lantern hung out.[50] People exchanged no congratulations when they met. The men who gathered at the bulletin boards read the news in gloomy silence and turned away with an air of sullen discontent. There were no demonstrations and no signs of unusual excitement, but the whole population of the city seemed abnormally sober and dejected. From the people's demeanor, no one would have imagined for a moment that Japan, after an unbroken series of victories, had finally successfully terminated a gigantic war with one of the greatest powers in Europe. On the contrary, one would have assumed that the nation had suffered defeat, humiliation, and disgrace.[51]

This sullen dissatisfaction immediately following the arrival of news of the peace began gradually to be expressed outwardly as the press and leaders of various classes took a strong opposing stand and as the government kept silent. Both the *Osaka Asahi Shimbun* and the *Tokyo Asahi Shimbun* reported nationwide dissatisfaction, disappointment, and indignation. For example:[52]

Yokohama: Of all the people in the city, only two expressed their joy at the peace, hoisting national flags. But both were Frenchmen.

Kuwana: One family hurriedly hoisted a flag upon hearing the news of peace. Townsmen got angry and tore it down. These townsmen are sensible adults. Nobody expresses congratulations on the peace. People are dejected, business is slow. Whenever people get together they worriedly talk about the future of the postwar economy. For them a peace celebration is unthinkable.

Nagoya: Nobody is happy here. Everybody is angry at the dishonorable peace.

Gifu: The people are all indignant. Business is bad. Nobody celebrated peace.

Yamada: The townsmen, who went in a group to the Grand Shrine of Ise to thank the deity for each war victory, are angry and will not attend the shrine.

Osaka: "Miserable. Disgusting. Regrettable." This is the one cry of the people of this city.

Kobe: In barber shops, at rickshawmen's pools, and on the docks, the lower class people are lamenting. Some public bathhouses have closed their doors as an expression of anger. The steam of their anger is higher than the steam of the bath.

Onomichi: The people are all angry and depressed.

Kure: Some say that if the news of the peace is true, people should hoist flags of mourning.

Moji: We hear one voice—that of dissatisfaction and grumbling—from the soldiers, merchants, and craftsmen.

Maizuru: The people are extremely angry and are making violent statements. The newspapers of the city published news of peace in black frames, and people are planning to hoist flags of mourning and to hold a funeral lantern march.

Kanazawa: At the news of the peace, people put up national flags and lanterns and expressed their joy with drums. But upon hearing the contents of the peace agreement, suddenly the whole city grew silent.

There were a few exceptions to these reports of dissatisfaction. For example, the governor of Nagasaki prefecture, in his report to Acting Foreign Minister Katsura on the condition of the people in his prefecture stated:

There are some people who are indignant at the peace. But because of the business depression and the extremely bad harvest this year, it is no longer possible for the people to bear the burden of continued war. Some state that to hope for indemnity and territory is contradictory to the spirit of a so-called righteous war. Many, from an economic point of view or out of their desire for the soldiers' return, are hoping for immediate peace, regardless of the terms.[53]

Several days later, on September 8, a village head in Tokushima prefecture reportedly gathered at the village elementary school the soldiers' families, village councilmen, people in charge of military duties, and the "committeemen on current affairs" and told them:

No matter what public opinion says, the agreed peace is not humiliating to us. Our government concluded the peace out of its judgment of the current situation of our country and their respect for humanity. If we should continue the war, we wouldn't be able to subdue Russia easily and, moreover, we wouldn't be able to bear for very long the burden of war expenses.

It was reported that the people listened to the speech attentively and were deeply impressed. No opposition was expressed.[54]

But such rational and realistic opinions were usually lost in the rising tide of opposition. Many people who apparently realized that verbal protests were not sufficient to move the government began to mobilize for demonstrations. The *Osaka Asahi Shimbun* of September 3 reported:

The voice of dissatisfaction and indignation is growing louder day by day. It is now swirling all over Japan, with the intent of solving the problem in a united effort. What effect is this voice going to produce? What result will it bring about? "There is no use in mere lamenting. There is no way now to crush with one blow this unfair peace agreement. Turn from despair to action in rejecting the peace!" This is what the people are now shouting. . . . As evidence, the letters to the editor we received between yesterday and noon today number 569. Their wording differs but their intent is the same. "Reject the peace agreed upon." . . . We even observe in the atmosphere of the streets that because of their great disappointment people are ready to act. How are they going to act? Needless to say, they are going to march on until the peace is rejected.[55]

The first large-scale demonstration of the anti-peace movement was held in Osaka. The main body of this city's businessmen were textile manufacturers, whose products occupied the prime place in Japan's China and Korea trade. They were uneasy about the future of continental trade, for they believed that, because of the humiliating peace and the weak attitude of the Japanese government, Japanese business activities "would be held in contempt by the Chinese and Koreans."[56] They were joined in their attacks on the government by journalists of such newspapers as the *Osaka Asahi Shimbun* and the *Osaka Mainichi Shimbun*; together both groups resolved to stage a demonstration.

At the Osaka Hotel on the night of August 30, they held a dinner attended by fellow activists to discuss the peace question. The *Osaka Asahi Shimbun* of September 1 reported that people who had never shown any interest in political activities attended in large numbers.[57] Five members were selected for an executive committee, which met at the Osaka Chamber of Commerce on September 1 and decided to hold a citizens' assembly at the Nakanoshima City Hall at 5 p.m. on the third. Local politicians and lawyers as well as several leading Osaka businessmen were among the 24 organizers of this citizens' assembly.[58]

The citizens' assembly was held on September 3 as scheduled. Five thousand people, representing all strata of society, participated. The chairman of the Osaka Prefectural Assembly Mitani Kishū was its chairman and the chairman of the Osaka City Assembly Hino Kuniaki read the statement and declaration of the meeting.[59] This charged that the peace nullified the results of the successful war and would not serve at all to guarantee peace in the future. Therefore, it was a violation of the spirit of the Imperial Declaration of War and a betrayal of the people. In order to achieve the objective of the Imperial Declaration, the statement continued, Japan should reject the humiliating peace and continue the war. It expressed the determination of the Osaka citizens: "For this purpose we should be willing to make the utmost sacrifice in lives and property. Even if the whole country becomes a scorched land, we would rather be the protectors of righteousness than live to accept this humiliation."

The assembly passed a resolution that read:

1. The elder statesmen and the cabinet ministers responsible for the failure of the negotiations should take the proper course and apologize to the Emperor and the nation.

2. The peace agreed upon must be annulled and the war continued.

The following telegram was sent to plenipotentiary Komura:

The peace agreement that you are now about to sign cannot be accepted by the nation. You are asked to rescind the agreement at once.

Another to Field Marshal Ōyama read:

The people of the Empire will strive to have the disgraceful peace agreement stopped, and it is hoped that Your Excellency will continue the war and crush the enemy.

Several newspapermen continued with fervent speeches against the peace agreement. Then the political speeches started. Hino Kuniaki spoke of Kurushima Tsuneyoshi, who had attacked Ōkuma Shigenobu at the time of the treaty revision, and declared: "Assassination is not a Russian monopoly." Several policemen attempted to stop him, but he continued his speech and concluded, "We shall fight to the death with you people to achieve our objective."[60]

The atmosphere of the assembly is vividly shown in an elegy sung by the participants.[61]

ELEGY

I   Those great victories on land and sea
Which seemed like full-blown flowers,
They are now gone like dreams.
What can be done in this reality?
The chilly autumn wind, blowing,
     comes through the broken paper screen,
     broken at the Portsmouth Conference.
How can we mend it, this blunder?

II   The ghostly, lonely wilderness of Manchuria,
The white-turned bones lying there now,
For whom did they die like dogs?
What a pity, this reality.
On the wild sea, rough with waves,
The sailors fought to their death.
Their death for loyalty is now mere foam.
What a pity, this blunder.

III   The air is filled with a spirit of death,
The one heart of fifty million is flooded with indignation.
Should we just swallow our tears?
The spirit of swordsmanship is urging us to lead Japan into action.
Teeth grinding, arms rubbing,
The flickering between the clouds,
    Is that lightning or a sword?

Following the Osaka citizens' assembly, many large people's assemblies were held on the third and fourth of September throughout Japan from Yamagata City in the north to Tsushima in the south. Resolutions passed at these meetings, unanimously against the peace agreement, demanded that the Genrō and cabinet ministers take responsibility for the failure. At many places, people made agreements that in the future they would not respond to bond issues or requests for contributions for military purposes.[62]

Even when September 5 came, the government had not yet made public the details of the peace agreement. Supporting opinions by some of the Genrō, cabinet members, and military leaders were published in the form of interviews with newspapermen, but they lacked the detail and sincerity that might have satisfied the enraged people and so only resulted in pouring oil on the fire.[63]

Meanwhile the government did little to allay the growing opposition to the treaty. Prime Minister Katsura consulted such business leaders as Shibusawa Eiichi and Fujita Denzaburō about the idea of holding victory celebrations at various places, as had been done when the Liao-tung Peninsula was returned ten years before, to recover the government's popularity. But this attempt was foiled when the business leaders answered, "The people's indignation is like a raging fire. There will be no way to subdue it."[64] The government also urged the executives of the three streetcar companies in Tokyo to run celebration cars decked with flowers and flags, but this failed when a united streetcar workers' association threatened to destroy the streetcars if even one flag were hoisted.[65] The government distributed free the issue of the *Kokumin Shimbun* that carried the outline of the peace terms, but the paper was boycotted by the people. The government's attempt only resulted in intensifying other newspapers' grudges against the *Kokumin Shimbun*.[66]

The public resentment could not be controlled by such half-hearted measures. Starting on September 2, the *Tokyo Asahi Shimbun* carried a series of editorials entitled "Explanation Is Necessary," pressing the government in a comparatively mild tone. It concluded the series with the following statement:

We now positively declare that our authorities have made a mistake in their business of government. If they have any explanation for this, we will listen. The government newspaper states that the government could not talk with us without disclosing national secrets. We therefore assume that the authorities will present the same argument. And yet, what is the secret? What secret do they have to keep? We can never believe it. They only say that it is secret because they cannot explain it. So long as they do not present us with a satisfactory explanation, we people will never go along with them —the Marquis, the Count, the Viscount, and the Baron.[67]

The Response of the Government

The government, on its side, considered the Portsmouth Conference an unexpected success. It had not only achieved all of the "absolutely indispensable articles" but also attained some of the "relatively important articles" that were to have been fulfilled "as far as circumstances permit": acquisition of the southern half of Sakhalin and fishing rights along the coast of the Maritime Province. Therefore, true to its nickname, "Katsura's Silent Cabinet"[68] took no steps, other than the vain and feeble ones described above, to stave off the increasingly fervent, nationwide movement against the peace treaty. Its basic attitude was that "the masses would never understand the complex problems of the times";[69] therefore it was the duty of the government to execute its policy, ignoring any public opposition.[70] This attitude is succinctly revealed in a letter, dated September 2, from Katsura to Yamagata:

I have read your letter with appreciation. As you mention therein, people have been making quite a bit of noise about the peace agreement. We need not worry too much about the activities of *sōshi* [strong-arm men][71] and politicians. However, petty commercial newspapers and members of the Kōwa Mondai Dōshi Rengōkai [Joint Council of Fellow Activists on the Peace Question], which is a revival of the old Tai-Ro Dōshikai [Anti-Russia Comrades' Society], the journalists closely associated with the Shimpotō [Kenseihontō], and various organizations including the group of Watanabe Kunitake[72]—all these, using all sorts of methods, have been inciting the minds of the lower classes. Now the lower-class people have mixed up social problems with politics, and people like ricksha men and petty merchants are making noise without understanding the pros and cons of the problems, just because indemnity is not coming. I am a little worried about this point. I think it is urgent to separate this from social and economic questions and make it exclusively a question of politics. I am exhausting all possible means for this purpose. As I have already told you, I am well aware that the solution of this great problem is of course not easy. I have concluded that there is no better method than to assume as prudent an attitude as possible and to let the matter gradually take its own course. You sound as though you have been considerably disturbed by this noise, but I request your forbearance for awhile, since there is no other means. Also, the matter about which I consulted you the other day has already been transmitted to Vice-Minister of Foreign Affairs Chinda [Sutemi]. But since I have not received any reply from him yet, I am going to urge him to answer as soon as possible. Of this I would like to inform you now. In reply to your letter.

Sincerely,

Katsura Tarō[73]

Thus the people, alienated from the government by a dichotomized political system, were mobilized by political activists and a chauvinistic press. Katsura's specific concern was that the public might begin to make a distinction between state and individual interests. He was afraid that through the excitement growing out of the peace question, the common people would come to realize the costs of the war, which had caused their economic and social condition to deteriorate. He wanted to confine the issue to a political question, the solution to which was to be left to the decision-making elite alone. Katsura was apparently confident that he would succeed.

Political Parties and the Peace

Despite the nationwide excitement over the events at Portsmouth, the political parties remained silent. Their inactivity, particularly during the closing days of the negotiations, was disappointing to many, and after news of the peace agreement reached Japan, a great deal of criticism was voiced. Comments from readers published in the *Tokyo Asahi Shimbun* and the *Osaka Asahi Shimbun* reflect what seems to have been the general public reaction:

At this time of national crisis, what are our political party members doing? If they are working for these traitors, I will never tolerate them. [A swordsman]

In this, our nation's greatest crisis, why don't the political parties act? Have you been bribed by the cabinet members? Have you become running dogs for Russia? If you betray the people, we know what to do. Answer within three days. [A volunteer group in Ōsaka]

Do the people have no alternative in this great national humiliation but to swallow their tears quietly? Apparently we don't need political parties or the Diet. In the future we should not respond to taxes, the draft, or national loans. [An indignant man][74]

The political parties could have played a significant role at this time in spite of the constitutional limitations upon the power of the Diet and consequently upon the political parties. Through resolutions and in public assemblies, the parties could have attacked the government publicly and demanded that it explain its policies. In other words, they could have taken the initiative in leading a protest movement and mobilized the indignation of the public. It might also have been possible for the government to have used the political parties as a channel to inform the public of Japan's actual military and economic situation, and thus gradually to allay the public anger aroused by the Portsmouth agreement and avoid its further alienation from the people.[75] The political parties, however, were in no position to perform either of these functions. To find out the reason for their inactivity, we must return to where our discussion of the wartime Diet ended.

At the end of the twenty-first Diet session in December 1904, a political agreement was being made between Prime Minister Katsura and Hara Takashi of the Seiyūkai. Thereafter, Hara frequently visited Genrō Itō and Inoue to discuss with them the need to conclude peace at an early date.[76] On April 16, 1905, about a month after the Battle of Mukden, Katsura asked Hara's opinion on the question of peace. Hara stated:

I, for one, see no benefit in continuing this war and consider it better to terminate hostilities now if possible. . . . From the point of view of the Seiyūkai, however, we have to think further. The majority of the people will not be happy with whatever conditions you may make to terminate the war. At that point, unless the Seiyūkai is connected with the government in some way, such as in a coalition government, the party will have no choice but to join the people. To create such a situation would be harmful to our nation.

Pointing out how fiercely opposed the "voice of the people" would be after the conclusion of peace, Hara thus demanded that Katsura take the Seiyūkai into the government. Katsura agreed with Hara and reaffirmed their December agreement, stating: "When peace comes, the people will certainly be dissatisfied with the terms. I am ready to sacrifice myself. . . . I shall recommend to the Emperor that Saionji be my successor." He added that he would like to resign over the issue of postwar policy (*sengo keiei*) and proposed to prearrange with the Seiyūkai some issue on which the party would take an opposing stand, in order to give the cabinet a pretext for resigning.

Although Katsura obtained the Seiyūkai's cooperation by promising to transfer the premiership to its president, he was nevertheless opposed to a party cabinet, declaring that Saionji should recruit his cabinet from outside the party. He added, "I have already expressed privately to Itō and Inoue my intention to recommend Saionji. I have not told Yamagata yet, but I am certain that he will have no objections when the time comes."[77] Katsura thus indicated his independence from his patron, Yamagata.

Katsura's independence from Yamagata was to grow in succeeding years. Yamagata seems inadvertently to have made it possible for

Katsura to go his own way when they acted in collusion to transfer Itō Hirobumi to the Privy Council in July 1903. Until then, Yamagata's support was indispensable, for Katsura alone was no match for Itō. When Katsura and Yamagata succeeded in pushing Itō into the Privy Council, Katsura realized that he was capable of dealing directly with such persons as Saionji and Hara, and Yamagata's support became less vital to his manipulations.[78]

One suspects that in addition to wishing to gain support in the difficulties he was facing in the Diet and on the question, as yet in the future, of terminating the war, Katsura might have had another, hidden motive to seek an agreement with Saionji and the Seiyūkai. By dealing directly with the Seiyūkai leaders, Katsura might have hoped to gain independence from the Genrō, particularly from Yamagata. Behind his manipulations, perhaps, were plans for a new political future. While Hara shared Katsura's desire to reduce the power of the Genrō, his underlying concern was to expand the power of his party.

Of course, the Genrō could not be completely ignored, and it was fortunate that, in choosing Saionji for the premiership, Katsura and Hara chose a partner agreeable to their plans who also enjoyed great favor among the Genrō. After the fall of the fourth Itō Cabinet, he had been one of the first choices of the Genrō to form a new cabinet[79] and was thus a prime minister of whom the Genrō would unquestionably approve. That the choice of Saionji was initiated by Katsura for Genrō approval, however, signals the beginnings of a gradual shift of power and a decline in the influence of the Genrō.

Hara was unhappy with the timing Katsura proposed for the cabinet's resignation. He pressured Katsura with the threat that the Kensei-hontō was certain to oppose the government's peace terms as soon as they were announced, in which event the Seiyūkai would be forced to do the same. Further consideration clearly would have to be given to the position of the Seiyūkai. Katsura agreed that a smooth transfer of leadership would have to be possible before any postwar policy could be initiated. Promising to give further thought to the problem, Katsura and Hara agreed to keep the discussion to themselves. After deciding that Katsura in the near future would tell Saionji the results of their talk, they parted.[80]

Through subsequent meetings with Itō, Inoue, and Katsura, Hara became familiar with the military and financial problems Japan was facing. He was also kept informed of the government's moves for a peace conference.[81] Following the announcement of President Roosevelt's mediation, Hara consulted Saionji about the Seiyūkai's resolution on peace terms. On June 14 it had been decided to draw up an unspecific resolution demanding that the government conclude peace on terms that would ensure the rights and interests of the nation and guarantee eternal peace in the Far East. Immediately thereafter, Hara met with Ōishi Masami and Inukai Tsuyoshi, leaders of the Kenseihontō, who were hoping to form a coalition cabinet with the Seiyūkai. At this meeting Hara persuaded the two Kenseihontō leaders not to demand "extravagant terms for peace" and prompted an agreement that the Seiyūkai and the Kenseihontō would draft more or less similar resolutions to be made public on June 28, when the Diet members of each party were to meet.[82]

In endorsing the party resolution before the Kenseihontō Diet members on June 29, Ōkuma revealed his complete ignorance of the actual circumstances surrounding the coming peace conference when he declared:

Russia is extraordinarily fortunate that, although the actual situation will sooner or later require it to request peace, through American goodwill it has somehow managed to get an opportunity to negotiate with Japan on an equal footing. Our government has been too much concerned with diplomatic courtesy and has already made a great concession in allowing Washington to be chosen the site of the negotiations. In short, this coming peace conference will be an extremely simple matter. All that is necessary is that Russia admit its defeat and that we state our demands to the Russian delegates. For this purpose no diplomatic courtesy is necessary. I do not believe it is even necessary for us to send a plenipotentiary. If Russia should fail to recognize its defeat and refuse to seek peace sincerely, war will continue forever. And the longer the war continues, the greater our demands will become.[83]

In contrast, Saionji stated at the meeting of the Seiyūkai Diet members:

I realize that some people want to spell out their terms for peace. Whether these terms are mild or harsh, I think it unwise to do such a thing when under the gaze of our enemy. I even think it unnecessary. . . . As peace negotiations approach, I fear that rash and impatient opinions may be put forth in some quarters. You, the members of the Seiyūkai, ought not to be moved by these opinions. . . .[84]

Katsura was "quite satisfied with the resolution of the Seiyūkai and through Itō requested Saionji to distribute the party's resolution to its provincial members," but it is probable that this request was never carried out.[85]

The Portsmouth Conference opened in early August. On July 25 Ōishi Masami of the Kenseihontō proposed to Hara: "To maintain national unity after the war, it will be necessary for the government to cooperate with the political parties. Our two parties should now propose a coalition cabinet. If the government accepts our proposal, fine. If it rejects our proposal, it will give our two parties legitimate reason to oppose the government."[86] Hara did not give a definite answer but decided first to make certain that no change had occurred in Katsura's attitude toward the Seiyūkai. After consulting with Saionji, on August 14 he spent three hours with Katsura, who "firmly stated that there had been no change whatsoever in his intention to transfer the premiership to Saionji." Hara, on his part, promised that "the Seiyūkai will voluntarily express its approval of a peace agreement on whatever terms the agreement may be concluded," and he suggested that this might be done by having Saionji make a speech in support of the peace agreement. Katsura expressed appreciation for Hara's good will and said that he would resign whenever it suited Saionji, but only on the condition that Saionji not form a party cabinet or a coalition cabinet with any other party nor appoint to a cabinet position anyone "who represents behind-the-scenes political bosses."[87]

Stating that "an opposition party is good for the nation," Hara agreed and promised that the Saionji Cabinet would cooperate with the Katsura group. On his part Katsura promised to "use his influence with the Genrō and the House of Peers on behalf of the Saionji Cabinet." Itō had already consented to a Saionji Cabinet, Katsura said, and although Yamagata had not yet been told, he would see to it that Yamagata did not raise any objections. After Katsura informed Hara on the progress of the peace negotiations, they parted with the agreement that no one but Saionji would be told of their talk.[88]

Hara's goal of gaining control of the reins of power drew closer as the end of the Portsmouth Conference approached. On August 22 he told Katsura, "It is Saionji's intention to accept your recommendation that he succeed you, so long as he can enjoy the trust of His Majesty and the consent of the Genrō. He is very anxious to have sufficient assistance from you." Saionji, he said, thought the cabinet change would best take place before the coming ordinary session of the Diet, and Katsura replied that he would resign immediately before the session. He assured Hara that Itō, Inoue, and Matsukata would support a Saionji Cabinet, and even though he had not specifically informed Yamagata of his intention, Yamagata would not oppose the idea. "Should Yamagata oppose it," Katsura said, "I would tell him to form a cabinet. He would then have to consent to my plan. So I assure you that Yamagata will comply." Katsura then repeated his objection to Saionji's forming a party cabinet or selecting "the Genrō's representative" as a cabinet member. He stated his hope that there would be a smooth transfer of power that would keep intact "basic state objectives" in spite of the change in the cabinet.[89]

By the time the peace treaty was concluded, therefore, Hara's plans were nearly complete. The only problems that remained were, within his party, to keep strictly secret the succession of power that had been arranged and, outside the party, to keep the Kenseihontō ignorant, while maintaining outwardly close relations with it, by postponing any clear answer to the plan for a coalition cabinet proposed by Ōishi and Inukai.

Upon hearing the news of the peace on September 1, Ōishi and Inukai told Hara and Matsuda, "The situation in the Kenseihontō forces us to pass a resolution condemning the government for its failure." They urged the Seiyūkai to do the same. Hara replied, "I cannot promise anything until the situation is discussed at the consultative committee meeting tomorrow." Ōishi and Inukai repeated their proposal to form a coalition cabinet by uniting the strength of the two political parties, but Hara again declined to give a clear-cut answer, stating, "The matter requires careful consideration." He recorded in his diary, "From now on it will be totally impossible for our party to cooperate with the Kenseihontō. Such cooperation would be extremely harmful to us, and I have therefore avoided such an entanglement."[90]

On September 2, in the midst of strong public opposition to the peace, the Seiyūkai leaders' sudden support of the government came as a great surprise to the overwhelming majority of party members.[91] As planned, this support was declared in a speech made by party president Saionji at the consultative committee meeting:

I cannot help congratulating the government, which for the sake of civilization and humanity has restored peace. . . . After all, the Portsmouth Conference was an attempt to bring about peace between Japan and Russia on an equal footing, for the sake of "humanity" and in accordance with the earnest desires of the powers for international peace. It differs greatly from a peace conference in which the defeated requests peace of the victor.

He asked what kind of impression the powers would have if Japan shouted for continuation of the war merely because certain desired terms for peace were not fulfilled.

From the point of view of Japan's national interest, the war has already achieved the objective "of chastising Russia for its aggressive actions in Manchuria and Korea and driving Russia out of these areas." . . . Now, after the victory, is the time for us to work for political and economic development and thus to solidify the foundation of our great Empire.[92]

The speech may have expressed what Saionji understood and believed, but more likely was delivered primarily out of his desire to become premier, as agreed upon by Katsura and Hara.

In accordance with the by-laws of the Seiyūkai consultative committee, adopted at a general meeting of the party on December 3, 1903, the committee was to consist of 30 members, 20 Diet members and 10 appointed by the president. This method of selection reflected a general trend within the party toward centering power in those party members who were also Diet members, and a concomitant decline in the influence of party members with no seat in the Diet. In the consultative committee they were decidedly under-represented.[93]

The Diet members in the party, meanwhile, aspired to gain real power in the government. As their influence within the party grew, it became increasingly apparent to them that real power lay neither in the parties nor in the Diet but, rather, at the center. It was clear, too, that the only way to reach this center was to make deals and compromises with the government, through exchanging service for patronage. It was thus a natural consequence that a party whose power lay largely in the hands of its Diet members would be inclined to compromise with the government.[94]

Both Hara and Matsuda were members of the consultative committee. Hara, a presidential appointee, had been chairman of the committee since November 27, 1904;[95] the Hara-Matsuda leadership of the committee was quite secure. Their past compromises with the government in such matters as the budget and peace terms had encountered no difficulties in the committee, and after Saionji's speech, while characterizing the terms of peace as "unsatisfactory," the consultative committee merely drafted a resolution and avoided further positive action. The resolution stated:

This committee, after deliberation on the peace terms, considers it appropriate to turn the question over to be decided by the general assembly of the Diet members of the party, which will be held before the opening of the extraordinary Diet session that should be held immediately. We consider it urgent to give positive consideration to the future management of our nation in accordance with the points enumerated in President Saionji's speech.[96]

The speech was distributed "with some modifications" to local party branches.[97] It was so unexpected that, instead of calming the people, it served to make them more indignant. It also caused great dissatisfaction among the non-Diet members of the party. As early as December 1, 1903, the *Rikken Seiyūkai Ingaidan* (a group of non-Diet members of the Seiyūkai) was formed, but it was only a feeble counterweight to the trend toward the concentration of power in the hands of the Diet members in the party.

The Rikken Seiyūkai Ingaidan expressed strong dissatisfaction with the government's foreign policy and, before the opening of the nineteenth Diet session, it denounced the government for diplomatic blundering in negotiations with Russia. The members called for censure of the cabinet in the coming Diet session and supported Speaker Kōno's impeachment memorial as an expression of the will of the people.[98]

During the peace negotiations, the non-Diet members of the Seiyūkai and the Kenseihontō held a joint meeting at which they denounced the cabinet; first, for agreeing to a peace conference without previously ascertaining whether or not Russia was in earnest and, second, for postponing discussion of the more crucial demands until the close of the negotiations.[99]

On the day of Saionji's speech, a general meeting of the non-Diet members of the Seiyūkai adopted a resolution quite contrary in tone. They declared: "We oppose the terms of peace as being dishonorable and calculated to work lasting evil against Japan. The government should apologize to those above and below and resign quickly."[100] Saionji and Hara turned deaf ears to this resolution. Hara, who had ordered the

Osaka Shimpō to support the peace and the government, left Ueno Station at 7:40 p.m. on September 4, announcing that he was going to inspect mines in the northeastern region.[101]

Meanwhile, the Kenseihontō leaders were considering two courses of action: participation in the government through cooperation with the Seiyūkai and direct opposition to the government. After waiting in vain for Hara's answer to their proposal for a coalition government, they became aware for the first time of the folly of trying to take joint action and began to act independently. On September 2, the political affairs investigation committee issued the following resolution: "We believe that the terms of peace to which our plenipotentiary has agreed ignore the objectives of the war, go against the people's will, and are eternally humiliating."[102]

Although Count Ōkuma was highly critical of the peace terms, he was not primarily concerned with the issues of indemnity and the partition of Sakhalin, which had met with the opposition of the majority of his party. What drew his strongest condemnation was the failure of the negotiators to guarantee a permanent peace in the Far East. He contended that the terms entirely ignored the objective of the war, which had been to secure such a peace, and that within ten years there would be another war with Russia. Ōkuma further stated that Japanese diplomacy was doomed to failure from the moment Japan had accepted President Roosevelt's offer of mediation, for the Japanese plenipotentiaries had in reality been the President's prisoners of war.[103] This was in sharp contrast to the remarks he had made only two months earlier concerning the Kenseihontō's resolution on the peace terms, when he had said: "The American President, the mediator, is the friend of our nation. He represents a nation that has enormous sympathy for us. The President's sincerity in undertaking this task of mediation for the sake of the peace of mankind moves me more than anything else. The timing of his mediation, I am certain, is also appropriate."[104]

But it was too late for the Kenseihontō. With its leaders dreaming of a coalition government until just the day before Saionji's speech, the Kenseihontō was unable to formulate a policy to oppose the government. Hampered by their desire to participate in the government, they lacked the will to spearhead a movement against the treaty and the government that had negotiated it.[105] On September 4, the Kenseihontō's regular Diet members from the Tokyo district issued a resolution that was clearly influenced by those leaders who opposed the demands of the party rank and file for rejection of the peace. Their lukewarm statement merely said: "We have decided to announce to the world that the terms of peace do not correspond to the will of the Japanese people."[106]

Because of the secret manipulations of a small number of their leaders to gain power, the two major political parties lost both their independence and their power of united action. Other minor political parties took no position on the treaty. The only exception was the non-Diet group within the *Teikokutō*, which condemned it as a "humiliating agreement, one which contradicted the Imperial will expressed in the Declaration of War and nullified the results of Japan's victories."[107]

With the political parties rendered impotent, on the day of Saionji's speech, Katsura wrote to Yamagata: "We need not worry too much about the activities of *sōshi* (strong-arm men) and politicians."

On September 4, the *Osaka Asahi Shimbun* wrote with a flourish:

The cry "Reject the Peace" has spread swiftly from village to country, from town to city. It has now reached the point where there is nobody in this country who does not shout it. . . . There are some passive people who, hoping to reap without sowing, say that the Diet will soon be opened and that Diet members who represent us will with strong arguments press the government to repent. If this does not work, they say they will present memorials to the Emperor for His Majesty's decision. But how can we trust these Diet members? Look at the Seiyūkai. They are all duped and are praising the peace as if the government had achieved the impossible. . . . Now the people have decided to act. With that great spirit expressed against Russia at the outbreak of the war, they are determined to fight until the peace is rejected. They are about to push the government like a tidal wave, sending representatives from each village, each town, each city in Japan. "Even an ant's prayer reaches heaven." This is the energetic force of fifty million people. However stupid the government may be, how can it resist this force?[108]

When an enraged public turned to reject the peace with "that great spirit expressed against Russia at the outbreak of the war," those who led them were, just as it had been at the beginning of the war, neither the government nor the political parties but an indignant press and a few nationalistic agitators.

CHAPTER EIGHT

THE HIBIYA "ANTI-PEACE TREATY" RIOT

The Kōwa Mondai Dōshi Rengōkai

THE *Tairo Dōshikai*, which had spoken for Japanese pro-war public opinion before the outbreak of the Russo-Japanese War, was disbanded after the war started. But with peace negotiations imminent, the members of the defunct association called in other nationalists and, on July 7, a day before Plenipotentiary Komura's departure, held a general meeting at the Matsumoto Hotel, Hibiya, Tokyo.[1] Kōmuchi Tomotsune, the former chairman of the Tairo Dōshikai,[2] had died on June 21, 1905, so Kōno Hironaka, the "hero" of the nineteenth Diet session, was elected to be chairman of the meeting. While not actually a member, Kōno had been in close touch with the Tairo Dōshikai.

The opening speech was delivered by Kuroiwa Shūroku, publisher of the *Yorozu Chōhō*. He expressed his full confidence that complete military victory would be won and his distrust of the government's diplomatic ability.[3] As a farewell presentation to Komura, the group then drew up the following resolution:

Whether or not we have achieved military victory and are able to fulfill the objectives of this war depend solely upon the peace negotiations. His Majesty's will is evident. The people's opinion is united. We are willing to continue the war if our demands are not met in the coming negotiations. We desire that our plenipotentiary not conclude a precarious peace, leaving the causes of trouble still unsolved.[4]

Kōno then stressed the need for arousing strong public opinion about the coming peace negotiations and the meeting was adjourned with shouts of "banzai!" for the Emperor and the Empress and for the army and the navy. Out of this meeting the Kōwa Mondai Dōshi Rengōkai (Joint Council of Fellow Activists on the Peace Question) was to emerge.[5]

On July 8, Plenipotentiary Komura left for America. Eleven days after his departure, on July 19, representatives of eight nationalist groups met at the Kaikatei Restaurant in Kyōbashi, Tokyo, and formally set up the Rengōkai. These eight groups were: the former Tairo Dōshikai (Anti-Russia Comrades' Society), the Kokuryūkai (Amur River Society), the Seinen Kokumintō (Young Nationalist Party), the Kōko Kurabu (Kōko Club, primarily for lawyers), the Sakurada Kurabu (Sakurada Club), the Dōshi Kisha Kurabu (Fellow Newspapermen's Club), the Nitto Kurabu (Nitto Club) and the Nansa Sō (Nansa Villa Group). The Nansa Sō, set up in April 1903 by Matsuura Atsushi and Konoe Atsumaro, two nationalist members of the nobility, and former Finance Minister Watanabe Kunitake was closely connected with the "Seven Professors."

Central headquarters for the newly organized Rengōkai were set up in the former Tairo Dōshikai building.[6] The exact membership is not known. In his letter to Yamagata on September 2, 1905, Katsura had described the Rengōkai as "a revival of the old Tairo Dōshikai, the journalists closely associated with the Shimpotō, and various organizations including the group of Watanabe Kunitake." Available materials give the names of 51 individuals who were in some way directly connected with it.[7] Analysis of the backgrounds of these 51 individuals, whom, for lack of better information, we shall regard as the "active membership" of the Rengōkai, reveals the following facts:[8]

1. The average age of 41 of the 51 was 41 years (the oldest was 57 and the youngest 30).

2. The geographical distribution of the birthplaces of 38 members was as follows:

Chiba	1	Ibaragi	1	Osaka	1
Ehime	5	Kōchi	2	Saga	1
Fukuoka	3	Kumamoto	1	Saitama	1
Fukushima	3	Nagano	2	Tokyo	3
Gifu	1	Nara	1	Tottori	1
Gunma	2	Niigata	3	Yamagata	1
Hiroshima	1	Okayama	1	Yamanashi	1
Hyōgo	1	Ōita	1		

Thus none of these members came from either Chōshu (Yamaguchi) or Satsuma (Kagoshima).

3. Of the known occupations of 42 members, 19 were lawyers and 11 newspapermen.

4. Twelve of the 51 were or had been Diet members (seven former members and five incumbents).

An examination of their party affiliations shows that:[9]

1. All six elected in the sixth election (August 10, 1898) ran as members of the Kenseihontō, then the leading party in the Diet.

2. In the seventh election (August 10, 1902), two were elected on Kenseihontō tickets (with 93 seats in the Diet, the Kenseihontō was now second to the Seiyūkai, which held 191 seats), one on the *Jin'in kai* ticket (a minor party with 28 seats in the Diet), and one on the Dōshi Kurabu ticket (another minor party with 13 seats).

3. In the eighth election (March 1, 1903), six members were elected: two on the Kenseihontō ticket (85 seats), one on the Seiyūkai ticket (175 seats), one on the Dōshi Kurabu ticket (8 seats), and two as independents.

4. Six Rengōkai members participated in the nineteenth Diet session (December 10–11, 1903): two (Kōno Hironaka and Hiraoka Kōtarō) as members of the Kenseihontō (85 seats), two as members of the *Kōyū Kurabu* (25 seats), one from the *Dōshi Kenkyūkai* (19 seats), and one as an independent.

5. In the ninth election (March 1, 1904), five members won seats in the twentieth Diet session (March 20–30, 1904): one (Hiraoka Kōtarō) from the Kenseihontō (90 seats), two (Kōno Hironaka and Ogawa Heikichi) from the *Teikokutō* (19 seats), and two as independents. (The major party in this session was the Seiyūkai, with 130 seats.)

6. Five members held seats in the twenty-first Diet session (November 28, 1904 to February 27, 1905): three (Kase Kiitsu, Kōno Hironaka, and Ogawa Heikichi) with the *Dōkōkai* (28 seats), one (Hiraoka Kōtarō) with the Kenseihontō (95 seats), one (Ōtake Kan'ichi) as an independent. (The Seiyūkai held 139 seats.)

7. Again during the twenty-second Diet session (December 28, 1905 to March 28, 1906), five members held seats: four (Kase, Kōno, Ogawa, Ōtake) with the *Seikō Kurabu* (36 seats), and one (Hiraoka) with the Kenseihontō (98 seats). (The Seiyūkai held 149 seats.)

On the basis of these facts, the "active membership" of the Rengōkai may be described as follows:

1. They were a relatively young group, considerably younger than the decision-makers, whose average age was 59.

2. None of those whose birthplaces are known were from the Satchō area, in contrast to the preponderant representation of those prefectures in the decision-making group.

3. Lawyers and newspapermen predominated.

4. Those serving in the Diet left a major party, the Kenseihontō, for much more minor parties and thus were not in positions of influence in terms of their party affiliations. The only exception, Hiraoka Kōtarō, was far less active than were the other members.

The day the Rengōkai was set up, 19 members were also selected for an executive committee. Its exact membership, unfortunately, is not known, but it probably included Kōno Hironaka, Enjōji Kiyoshi (newspaperman of the *Yorozu Chōhō*, a member of the Kokumin Dōmeikai and the Tairo Dōshikai), Hosono Jirō (former Diet member from Gunma, Tokyo University graduate), Kunitomo Shigeaki (newspaperman of the *Nihon*, an old China activist), Matsumura Kōichirō (newspaperman of the *Tokyo Asahi Shimbun*), Nakajima Kijō (newspaperman of the *Nihon*, member of the Tairo Dōshikai), Nakamura Tasuku (newspaperman of the *Niroku Shimpō*, elder brother of Dr. Nakamura Shingo, one of the "Seven Professors"), Ogawa Heikichi (lawyer, member of the Tairo Dōshikai, Tokyo University graduate), Ōtake Kan'ichi (Diet member from Niigata), Ōtani Masao (newspaperman of the *Miyako Shimbun*), Sakurai Kumatarō (former official in the Home Ministry, lawyer, Kōko Kurabu member, contributor to the *Niroku Shimpō*, Tokyo University graduate), Suzuki Shigetō (former Diet member from Ehime, Tairo Dōshikai member), Takahashi Hideomi (journalist, Tokyo City Councilor, Seinen Kokumintō member), Tsuneya Seifuku (old Korea activist, Kokumin Dōmeikai and Tairo Dōshikai member), Uchida Ryōhei (founder of the Kokuryūkai, old China activist), and Yamada Kinosuke (judge, lawyer, former Diet member from Osaka, and Tokyo University graduate).[10]

On July 20, the Rengōkai decided to appeal to fellow-thinkers all over the nation through speaking tours and letters of appeal distributed in the provinces, as well as by making speeches at meetings in Tokyo.[11] Their first step was to publish a long letter of appeal, dated July 25 and apparently written by Kunitomo and Ōtake in accordance with the July 20 decision. Approximately 2500 copies were distributed to Diet members, prefectural assembly members, and newspapers throughout Japan. Ten copies were sent to the Manchurian army general headquarters and three copies each to Commanders Nogi, Kuroki, and Nozu, as well as to General Hasegawa in Korea.[12] The letter indicates the Rengōkai members' thinking about and understanding of the war situation:

For one and a half years, since the beginning of the war against Russia, wherever the flag of the Rising Sun has gone, Japan has been victorious. That the enemy has already succumbed to our military might is unanimously recognized by the powers. Now the annihilation of the Baltic fleet has shaken the minds and hearts of the people of the world and has unexpectedly motivated peace negotiations. The plenipotentiaries of both belligerents will meet within ten days. Will our plenipotentiaries' negotiation fulfill the objectives of the war? As our plenipotentiaries left the seat of His Majesty, the Commander-in-Chief, His Majesty gave them a special edict. It stated: "You should devote yourselves with all your power to the discharge of your mission and make every effort to secure the reestablishment of peace on a durable basis." How profound is his will! How could we dare to add even one word?

Throughout history Russia has been untrustworthy. . . . It snatched away the fruit of our victory, the Liaotung Peninsula, and took advantage of the Boxer Rebellion to occupy Manchuria, thus disturbing the tranquillity of the East. These actions compelled us to accuse it, and we, the Japanese people, shall never forget this. It is as clear as crystal that Russia is going to try to escape the obligations of the defeated. Although it secretly covets peace, by diplomatic conniving and underhanded methods it will skillfully cover up its own calamities and exhaustion in the war and its inner turmoil. Our plenipotentiary should guard against being deceived by this façade. We see no signs of sincere repentance in the historically arrogant and violent Russia. We feel strongly that peace negotiations are premature. However, in appreciation of His Majesty's will, which is utterly benevolent and desirous of peace, and of the progress of humanity, at this juncture we have no choice but to dedicate our small means to the cause of his nation. What Russia today most desires, however, is a truce. If the negotiations should start with discussions of a truce, and if our plenipotentiary should concede without gaining adequate concessions, Japan will have been trapped by Russian deceit at the very beginning of the negotiations. Our Manchurian armies have already come close to Kirin and Changchun, and Harbin is within a stone's throw. Once our army in north Korea crosses the Tumen River, the position of Vladivostok will be extremely precarious. Our northern expeditionary forces in one stroke have already conquered Sakhalin and are about to step onto the Maritime Province. With no hope of victory, Russia fears more than anything else that the war may continue. A truce will benefit Russia, but not us. We should continue our great operations, with the army and navy in close cooperation.

It is of course the duty of the plenipotentiaries to make efforts to restore peace. If we desire eternal peace, we must remove the teeth and claws of the enemy, thus guaranteeing that he can never again move against us. Are our plenipotentiaries capable of fulfilling this great task? We are indeed concerned about this matter. In the past our diplomats have often missed opportunities and have disappointed the people greatly. An example is not far in the past—the return of the Liaotung Peninsula. Now is the time for the people to rise and encourage our leaders. For what reason have we sacrificed our lives and fortunes and risked the fate of the nation? We shall never be satisfied with an indecisive peace. If we cannot attain the objectives of the war, all the people are prepared to keep on fighting, regardless of how much longer it takes. We wish to proclaim to the world where our public opinion lies and at the same time to urge our forces on land and sea to continue their mighty activities. Rise and join us, patriots of our nation. The success or failure of our nation is in your hands![13]

A forum was held on July 30 at the Kabuki Theatre in Tokyo. Nineteen members of the Rengōkai spoke on such topics as: "Diplomacy That Lags behind Military Victory"—Nakajima Kijō, "Peace terms"—Ogawa Heikichi, "Restoration of Eternal Peace"—Sakurai Kumatarō, "The Decisive Five Minutes"—Hosono Jirō, "War Objectives and the Peace Conference"—Ōtake Kan'ichi, and "An Absurd Opinion on the Peace Conference"—Takahashi Hideomi.[14]

The Metropolitan Police Board recorded: "The atmosphere of the meeting was not violent. We warned only Nakajima Kijō [a newspaperman of the *Nihon*] and Takahashi Hideomi, who were going too far in their criticism of the foreign policy of the present cabinet. The audience numbered approximately 2000. No incidents occurred."[15] The activities of the Rengōkai were not yet of such a nature as to invite especially rigid surveilance by the authorities.

In August two groups of Rengōkai members made trips in the northeast and central provinces, speaking at Maebashi, Mito, Nagaoka, Niigata, Sendai, Sanjō, Aomori, Hirosaki, Nagano, Matsumoto, Suwa, Fukushima, and Utsunomiya. They returned to Tokyo on August 15. According to the police reports sent to the Metropolitan Police Board, the meetings were held peacefuly, even though there were some police warnings and intervention, and they made "a considerable impression on the people." A speaking tour to the Osaka area was canceled because development in the peace negotiations at Portsmouth necessitated the presence in Tokyo of the Rengōkai committee members.[16]

By August 13, news of the terms for peace presented by the Japanese plenipotentiaries had already reached Japan, and protest that these demands were too modest was growing. The Rengōkai executive committee met on August 16 and decided to hold a meeting of the Council, to be followed by a forum with 16 speakers.[17] On August 17 at 3 p.m., the Council meeting was held at the Meiji Theatre in Nihombashi, with 35 members attending. Following an opening statement by Chairman Kōno Hironaka, Suzuki Shigetō took over the chair; Ōtake Kan'ichi and Yamada Kinosuke reported on the speaking tours. Three resolutions were unanimously approved:

Resolution 1: We regard the terms of peace presented by our plenipotentiary as being excessively modest and insufficient to guarantee eternal peace in the East. If our government should make any further concession, we believe it would lose the fruits of military victory and must be held responsible for our nation's troubles long into the future.

Resolution 2: We can hope for successful negotiations at the peace conference only when they are backed up by vigorous military activity. We therefore greatly regret that while, on the one hand, we see the peace negotiations approaching their high point, on the other, we see a truce on the military side. While we are convinced of the masterful strategy of our Imperial headquarters, we earnestly desire that our forces on the battlefield continue their heroic activities.

Resolution 3: [a telegram sent to Komura] Our entire nation is indignant at Russia's impudence. We desire that Your Excellency take decisive measures to refuse negotiations that would lead to an indecisive peace.

At Suzuki's initiative, three *banzai* were shouted for the Emperor and Empress, and the speeches began immediately afterward.[18] The audience at this forum numbered about 1400. It was conducted peacefully, with only one speaker being suspended by the police.[19]

The Rengōkai watched developments in the peace negotiations closely. Several times the negotiations faced rupture over the questions of indemnity and territory, and as successive Japanese concessions were reported to Japan, public opinion, as we have described, grew more heated. On August 24, the Rengōkai sent 60 to 70 telegrams to various provincial political organizations, stating: "We are very anxious about the outcome of the peace negotiations. We request you to warn the authorities by telegram against further concession."[20] On August 26, the executive committee members drafted the following resolutions:

Resolution 1. We send the following telegram to Plenipotentiary Komura: Russia's procrastination is evidence of its insincerity. We request Your Excellency to cut off negotiations decisively now.

Resolution 2: We send the following resolution to Prime Minister Katsura: Russia's procrastination is evidence of its insincerity. We are already convinced that the terms for peace presented by our delegation are not sufficient to guarantee eternal peace in the East, and request our government to terminate the negotiations immediately.[21]

When the news reached Japan that a peace agreement had been concluded in which Japan had gained only the southern half of Sakhalin and had completely abandoned its demand for an indemnity, public opinion rose against the government. The Rengōkai stood at the forefront of a national movement to censure the government and reject the peace agreement. On August 31, its executive committee adopted another resolution:

We believe that the peace agreement reached by our plenipotentiaries nullifies our military victory and fails to deal with the important affairs of His Majesty's nation. We are determined to have the present cabinet members and the plenipotentiaries reject the peace agreement and apologize for their crimes to the Emperor above and the people below.

They also sent the following telegram to Komura:

We believe that the peace agreement you have reached fails to deal with the important affairs of His Majesty's nation. Apologize immediately for your crime to the Emperor above and to the people below and resign.[22]

To carry out their resolution, they decided to hold a national assembly in Tokyo, to distribute letters of appeal throughout Japan, to send a memorial to the Emperor, to organize speeches and tours, and to take any additional measures that might seem useful. Six members of the executive committee were selected to organize the rally: Ōtake Kan'ichi, Sakurai Kumatarō, Ogawa Heikichi, Tsuneya Seifuku, Hosono Jirō, and Takahashi Hideomi.[23] Kōno Hironaka was chairman of the Rengō-kai, but its planning and activities were actually carried out by Ogawa, Ōtake, and Takahashi.[24]

On September 2, the Rengōkai distributed 30,000 copies of the following letter, which greatly appealed to the people:[25]

Well! A peace agreement has been reached. What have we gained? Only eternal humiliation. Only the contempt of the powers. The loyal sacrifices of a hundred thousand soldiers are now in vain. A burden of 200 million yen is now placed upon the living. For what have we Japanese people endured the unendurable for ten long years? For what have we sacrificed our lives and property and achieved great military victories that have shaken the world? If this is what we get, who will sacrifice himself for our nation in future crises? The foundation of our nation, nourished for the last 3000 years, is to be suddenly shaken. We are afraid that the unprecedented military victory may have paved the way to national ruin. You authorities, how can you face the spirits of our ancestors? Your crime will never be forgiven. His Majesty some time ago gave our plenipotentiary the mission to restore eternal peace. The agreed terms, however, not only fail to guarantee eternal peace but also open the way to national ruin. We people, how can we acquiesce to this? Anybody who understands His Majesty's will should determinedly refuse it. The Emperor, who decided on war, after listening to public opinion, will, we believe, perceive the trend of national opinion on the matter of peace also. In the past, when the nation rose in opposition, the Emperor refused to ratify the treaty agreed upon by Foreign Minister Ōkuma. Now in this crisis, whether or not we succeed in rejecting the peace is solely dependent upon the determination of the nation's people. Rise! Patriots, don't miss this opportunity!

Kōwa Mondai Dōshi Rengōkai[26]

The statement that the Emperor had "decided on war after listening to public opinion" clearly indicates the Rengōkai's belief that the Emperor had overruled the Katsura Cabinet and had declared war in response to public pressure. They therefore hoped that strong public opinion would lead the Emperor to refuse to ratify the peace agreement.[27]

On September 4, another of the measures they decided to adopt was carried out when at 11 a.m. Kōno Hironaka, representing the Rengōkai, presented himself at the Imperial Household Ministry bearing a memorial to the Emperor signed by 28 people. The memorial attributed the people's dissatisfaction to the failure of the cabinet ministers and requested the Emperor to reject the peace.[28]

Two days earlier, on the afternoon of September 2, more than ten Rengōkai executive committee members had held what the Metropolitan Police Board called a "secret meeting" to draw up a concrete plan for the national assembly in Tokyo:[29]

1. The national assembly would be held at Hibiya Park at 1 p.m. on September 5.
2. Speeches opposing the peace treaty would begin at 2 p.m. at the Shintomi Theater, followed by a get-acquainted meeting at which a box lunch and a bottle of sake would be sold for 20 sen.
3. At 6 p.m. a joint discussion would be held among the provincial participants at Kōyōkan Hall in Shiba Park.
4. Visits should be paid to the Privy Councilors and attempts should be made to persuade the Seiyūkai and the Kenseihontō to join the anti-peace movement.
5. The national assembly at Hibiya Park would be conducted as follows: (a) gathering at 1 p.m.; (b) assembly opened with a firecracker; (c) selection of the chairman; (d) resolutions; (e) banzai for the Emperor; (f) banzai for the army and navy; (g) closing firecracker.
6. Details of the assembly:
   (a) In anticipation of inadequate preparations for the meeting: to maintain order, participants were to follow the huge flag of the National Assembly Against the Peace.
   (b) If the assembly at Hibiya Park were prohibited, it was to be held at Mitsubishi-ga-Hara, (the area near the western entrance to present-day Tokyo station).
   (c) During the speeches at Shintomi Theater, five-minute, unscheduled speeches would be permitted so that everyone would have an opportunity to express his indignation.

The Rengōkai sent telegrams all over Japan urging local volunteers to participate in the national assembly.[30] On the morning of September 4, through Takada Sanroku,[31] a request was made to the Tokyo City Office for permission to use Hibiya Park for the assembly. The written application stated: "I request official permission to use this property to shoot off two firecrackers in the bushes near the Matsumoto Hotel in Hibiya Park."[32] After filing his request, Takada went to play *go* and stayed overnight at Uchida Ryōhei's home. The police later interpreted this as an attempt on Takada's part to avoid official response to his request for fear that it would be rejected.[33] The preparations at Shintomi Theater were conducted by Hosono Jirō, who was in charge of the speech meeting.

The Rengōkai had made a contract with the theater on September 2, but the following morning the manager had requested that the contract be canceled. The Rengōkai was enraged, suspecting that the police had intervened, and refused to cancel the contract.[34]

The materials necessary for the national assembly were ordered from Hiromeya, a store in the Ginza, on September 3. The major items were two firecrackers, seven balloons, one large flag about fifteen feet long, ten long flags about eight feet long, and five thousand small flags. A band was also hired. Black cloth and crepe paper for mourning were attached to the flags and captions were written on the long flags and balloons:[35] (on the long flags)—"The Whole Nation, One Heart," "Cut Down Traitors," "Woe! The Greatest Humiliation," "Reject! Reject!" "Small Men Wrong the Nation," "A Historical Truth," "Sincerity Shakes Heaven and Earth"; (on the balloons)—"We Approach His Majesty with Tears," "We Have Swords To Cut Down Traitors," "How Shall We Meet the Spirits of Our Ancestors?" "The Life-and-Death Crisis of Our Nation."

To maintain order among the crowds and to perform other miscellaneous tasks, Hosono Jirō employed about 20 day-workers as flag-bearers. In consultation with Tsukuda Nobuo,[36] Ogawa Heikichi hired several *sōshi*, including Yoshizawa Fujio.[37]

After preparations were completed, 30,000 invitations were distributed in the city of Tokyo and its vicinity:

Come, You Patriots!
The results of military victory, for which we sacrificed one hundred thousand loyal soldiers and two hundred million yen, are eternal, ineradicable humiliation and the contempt of the powers. Ah! Who is responsible for this? The time has come to make a great resolution in accordance with His Majesty's will for eternal peace. We therefore convene a national assembly at 1 p.m. this coming September 5 at Hibiya Park so that together with fellow-patriots of our nation we may express our will and show our absolute determination. Regardless of age or station, anyone who is patriotic should come and join us.
September 4, 1905

The Promoters of the National Assembly[38]

The Kōwa Mondai Dōshi Rengōkai was typical of political activist groups in Japan. Blinded by chauvinism and ignorant of the actual military and diplomatic situation, they were incapable of viewing Japan's predicament realistically. Consequently, the terms for achieving their war objective—the maintenance of eternal peace in the Far East—were far more extensive than those of the decision-makers and formulated without regard to how they were to be achieved. In short, they were victims of their ideals.

They justified their activities by the conviction that the government's diplomacy was traditionally weak and clumsy and therefore required their supervision and encouragement. They had no part in the oligarchic decision making, and as our analysis of their party affiliations reveals, were not even members of the influential political parties.

When they realized that a "humiliating peace" had been concluded, they mobilized for action. They harked back to the triumph they thought they had achieved at the outbreak of the war. Convinced that at that time they had led public opinion and that the Emperor had heeded them in ordering the Katsura Cabinet to terminate negotiations with Russia and go to war, they readily adopted the same tactics to press their cause. They believed that by arousing strong public opposition to the treaty and by memorializing the Emperor, the Emperor would refuse to ratify the treaty.

The Hibiya Riot[39]

On Tuesday, September 5, 1905, the peace treaty was signed in Portsmouth, New Hampshire. In Tokyo the thermometer stood at 96 degrees. In spite of the heat, great crowds gathered at Hibiya Park in response to the leaflets distributed by the Kōwa Mondai Dōshi Rengōkai and the encouragement of many Tokyo newspapers.[40] The *Yorozu Chōhō* on that day wrote:

Come! Come! Come! A national assembly to protest the treaty is going to be held today at Hibiya. Come, those who have blood. Come, those who have tears. Come, those who have backbones. Come, those who have strong wills. Come, those who know justice. Come, those who know shame. Come, and all together raise a voice of opposition to the humiliating and shameful peace. His Majesty will surely appreciate the sincerity of his subjects.[41]

In contrast to the situation before the war, when it could utilize the actions of pro-war activists, the government could not tolerate a massive demonstration and therefore decided to prevent it by police force. The

Metropolitan Police Board was ordered to inform the Rengōkai that the assembly would be prohibited in accordance with Article Eight of the Peace Police Law (*Chian Keisatsuhō*) and to arrest several of the Rengōkai leaders.[42] The Police Board mobilized 350 policemen to guard the six gates to Hibiya Park beginning at 8 a.m. on September 5. They erected solid wood barricades to close these gates. Skirmishes soon broke out between the crowd and the police. After a two-hour struggle, the people, numbering about 30,000[43] broke into the park shouting "banzai! The Rengōkai leaders, including Kōno Hironaka, Ōtake Kan'ichi, and Ogawa Heikichi, proceeded to the park from their headquarters, protected by *sōshi*. They entered the park, carrying the huge flag of the national assembly and several long flags inscribed with captions, and distributed small national flags hung with mourning crepe to the multitude. It was then about 1 p.m.[44]

A firecracker exploded, balloons rose into the air, the brass band played a sad tune, and the assembly began. Yamada Kinosuke read the opening statement and recommended that Kōno Hironake be named chairman of the assembly.[45] Ōtake Kan'ichi took the platform, stated why the treaty should be rejected, and said that there was no course left except to appeal to His Majesty and persuade him by the united sincerity of his subjects. Chairman Kōno then read three resolutions, which were overwhelmingly approved by the applauding and cheering crowd. The first resolution was identical to the Rengōkai's first resolution of August 31 calling for rejection of the peace treaty.[46]

Resolution 2 (telegram to the Manchurian Army): We are determined to reject the humiliating treaty with national unity. We earnestly desire our Manchurian Army to carry on the brave fight to crush the enemy.

Resolution 3 (to the Privy Councilors): Today's issue we cannot even bear to mention again. We earnestly desire that the Privy Councilors advise His Majesty to refuse to ratify the peace treaty and thus save our nation in this great crisis.

The brass band played the national anthem, "Kimi ga Yo," and everyone took off his hat and shouted "banzai" three times for the Emperor, the army, and the navy. The meeting closed with the explosion of another firecracker. The entire assembly had lasted only about 30 minutes.[47]

After the assembly the people had been expected to attend the speech meeting at the Shintomi Theater, scheduled to begin at two o'clock, but the Rengōkai leaders suddenly changed the schedule. Instead, a crowd of about 2000 persons, led by Kōno Hironaka and Ōtake Kan'ichi, proceeded through the Sakuradamon[48] to the Imperial Palace, with the national assembly flag in front and the brass band behind. This action was a great surprise to the police and threw them into consternation, fearing that the crowd was bent on making a direct appeal to the Emperor by breaking into the palace grounds.[49]

Kōno and Ōtake assembled the crowd in front of the *Nijūbashi*, the double bridge at the entrance to the palace. Standing before the crowd, they made a most respectful obeisance toward the palace, then led the "banzai" for the Emperor three times and had the brass band play the national anthem.

Police troops dashing to the spot allegedly did not realize that the band was playing the national anthem and started confiscating the musical instruments and the flags with mourning crepe. Kōno and Ōtake scolded the police, declaring, "It is *lèse majesté* to interfere with the playing of the national anthem." Skirmishing began between the police and the crowd, and there were casualties on both sides[50] before the fighting subsided around 2:30 p.m. Kōno left the palace grounds, leading the crowd through the Babasakimon gate in the direction of the Shintomi Theater in Kyōbashi. Several scuffles with the police occurred on the way to the Shintomi Theater where, at 2 p.m., according to the Rengōkai program, several short speeches were to be followed by a get-acquainted meeting with box lunches.

By eleven o'clock that morning, the Kyōbashi police headquarters had stationed about 200 uniformed policemen and plainclothesmen inside as well as outside the theater. At noon the theater was filled with more than 2000 people, and more kept coming, until by 1:30 p.m., the street was filled for several blocks. The audience inside the theater, in response to the tumult outside, was making riotous noise. Around 1:40 p.m., before the program had actually started, the chief of the Kyōbashi police headquarters ordered the crowd dispersed. Angered by this order, some of the crowd started fighting with policemen. The fighting quickly spread. It was finally brought under control around 5 p.m. when the police started arresting the most belligerent individuals.[51] Some of the people then started moving toward other possible targets.

The *Kokumin Shimbun* was located at Hiyoshichō, Kyōbashi. Owned

by Tokutomi Sohō, its support of the peace treaty had aroused great
public animosity and was looked on as the official organ of the government and even as traitorous by some. The staff of the newspaper, ex-
pecting the attacks, had armed themselves with clubs and swords, and
with tempura lunches personally supplied by Tokutomi. When the
attack came, in spite of their frantic defense, the building and its printing machines were seriously damaged by a stone-throwing mob of
about 1000 persons.[52]

The official residence of the minister of home affairs was also near
Hibiya Park, and soon after 1:30 p.m., when the national assembly was
over, people quickly gathered around the residence. The home minister,
Viscount Yoshikawa Akimasa, as the official most responsible for the
prohibition of the national assembly, was the focus of the crowd's attack. About two o'clock someone stuck a poster on the fence near the
back gate of the official residence. Under the words "The Justice of
Heaven," the heads of Komura, Takahira, and Roosevelt were painted,
running with "blood" drawn in red ink. Those in the crowd who saw
the paper applauded, and threw stones at policemen who tried to take
it down, starting a skirmish. At that point, those who had left the
Kokumin Shimbun building arrived, swelling the gathering to about
30,000.[53] Soon someone set fire to the guard's house next to the front
gate. A rumor spread that Prime Minister Katsura was inside the residence; this report further enraged the crowd, and they charged the
front gate with angry shouts of "Burn them up!" The police, swords in
hand, held back the crowd. Now large-scale skirmishes began, the policemen fighting with swords, the people with sword canes, clubs, and
stones. Around 5:45 p.m., someone set fire to a building inside the
grounds, and a ghastly scene unfolded as the flames illuminated the
forms of people throwing slates from the burning roof, people charging
with bared swords, and the crowd cheering them on.

The government requested that army troops be sent to rescue the
residence. Three companies of soldiers from the Imperial Guard Division
and the First Division rushed to the spot, to be welcomed with shouts
of "Army banzai!" from the crowd,[54] which gradually began to draw
away from the residence of the home minister and to move toward
Kyōbashi, Shiba, and Kanda. Its anger, spurred by police intervention
and violence, was now directed against the police and the police sta-

tions. The anti-peace treaty movement seemed all but forgotten. All night long groups of hundreds and thousands attacked police stations and police boxes throughout Tokyo and its environs, their attacks continuing until the night of September 6. Altogether, 219 police boxes were destroyed by fire and 45 were broken up—more than 70 percent of the total number of police boxes in Tokyo and vicinity. Almost all of the police boxes in the Asakusa, Shitaya, Kanda, Kyōbashi, Nihonbashi, Ushigome, Hongō, and Shinjuku police districts were burned down.[55]

Meanwhile, where were the Rengōkai leaders? Following the skirmishes at the Nijūbashi, Kōno, who "felt extremely tired because of the heat and activities of the morning," left the crowd and went to the Buddhist Life Insurance Company, of which he was president, to take a nap.[56] When he arose two hours later and went to Shintomi Theater, the meeting had already been dispersed by the police. Thereupon, a little after five o'clock, he went to Kōyōkan Hall, Shiba, where the joint discussions among provincial participants in the assembly had been scheduled. He recalled later: "It was such a hot day, and since I was running all over the place, I got sweaty and dirty. While I was taking a bath, I heard thunderous applause at the meeting place. There were even shouts of 'banzai!' I got out of the bath, dashed to the meeting place, and found that the official residence of the minister of home affairs had been set afire and was burning vigorously. Streetcars were also burning. I thought it was ridiculous to shout 'banzai' at this unfortunate incident, and I warned the people not to lose their senses."[57] Uchida Ryōhei had gone to the Mitsui Club, which was located near Hibiya Park, to rehearse for a judo exhibition scheduled to be given the following day at a party in honor of Edward H. Harriman.[58]

About 200 persons, including the Rengōkai leaders and representatives from the provinces, gathered at the Kōyōkan. After Kōno was selected to chair the meeting, Enjōji Kiyoshi of the *Yorozu Chōhō* spoke on behalf of the Rengōkai. He declared:

Diplomatic blundering in 1873 resulted in the war against China in 1894. Diplomatic blundering in the conclusion of that war was inevitable. The humiliating peace on this occasion will no doubt bring about war on an even larger scale within five or six years. Who has inflicted this great pain upon the nation and the people?[59]

Ōtake Kan'ichi declared, "We have no choice but to reject the treaty," and the Rengōkai members agreed on the following programs to implement their determination:

Agreement: We shall urge public and private organizations in prefectures, towns, and villages and individuals all over Japan to send memorials to the Emperor and to present their views to the Privy Councilors and to members of both Houses.

Resolution: We resolve to strive to fulfill our objective of bringing about the rejection of the peace treaty through close cooperation with all who agree with us throughout Japan.

Program: We shall visit Privy Councilors and members of both Houses and plan speech meetings and speaking tours in the prefectures. These and any other feasible means will be used to fulfill our objective.

They then held a party and parted around eleven o'clock.[60]

It is said that the rioting in Hibiya Park was clearly heard by the Emperor, whose palace was separated from the park by only one moat. Deeply concerned, he is reported to have gone frequently into the corridor to listen to the noise. When he heard gunfire, a weary look came over his face and he exclaimed, "The military police have fired on the people!" Prime Minister Katsura hurriedly requested an audience with the Emperor and "earnestly begged the Emperor's forgiveness for what was happening." But the riot grew more and more vociferous and throughout the night, it is said, the Emperor listened from the hallway to the noise outside.[61]

The rioting continued the following day, but the attacks were now concentrated on churches and streetcars. It is not clear why the churches were attacked, but the main reasons seem to have been the suspicion of some that Christians were Russian spies, the fact that some clergymen had supported the peace treaty in their sermons, and the fact that certain individuals who had resented the Christians' purification movement took this opportunity for revenge. Altogether, 13 churches were destroyed.[62]

On the night of the sixth, 15 streetcars were destroyed by fire. The immediate cause of these attacks can be attributed to anger at streetcar interference with the mass actions of the previous day, and to ricksha men, who had been deprived of their work by streetcars and saw this as an opportunity to destroy the competition.[63] The rumor that street-cars would be decorated with flowers in celebration of the peace agreement further enraged the mob.

Crowds also gathered at the Metropolitan Police Board, the Ministry of Foreign Affairs, the official and private residences of the prime minister, the official residence of the foreign minister, the official residence of Itō, President of the Privy Council, and the residences of Yamagata and Matsukata. The crowds were violent but were dispersed by the police and the army without causing much damage. Fifty-three houses of private citizens were destroyed by fire.[64]

On the night of the 5th, a crowd of about 1000 persons gathered around the American Legation, but no serious incidents occurred. Because of the riot, American Minister Griscom and Edward H. Harriman, who were attending a party at the finance minister's residence, interrupted their dinner and quickly returned to the legation. On the way, Harriman's personal physician, Doctor Lyle, received a slight wound from a thrown stone.[65]

On September 6, the government proclaimed martial law in Tokyo and vicinity. This was the first time martial law was ever used to suppress rioters in Japan. At the same time, an emergency Imperial Edict was issued to control newspapers and magazines, by which the government stopped publication of those periodicals that were carrying reports sympathetic to the rioters.[66]

A heavy rain began to fall the next morning and continued throughout the day. By evening the rioting that had engulfed the whole city of Tokyo for three days had ended.[67] The police authorities recorded that 500 were wounded on the government side, including 6 police superintendents, 26 police inspectors, 422 policemen, and about 40 firemen and soldiers. It can be seen that most of the casualties were regular policemen, wounded by stones, swords, or clubs. In many cases plain-clothesmen were reported to have unknowingly fought with one another.[68]

The casualties among the rioters were reported to be between one and two thousand, but since many of the wounded hid to escape arrest, the actual number is unknown. Recorded casualties numbered 528, including 17 deaths. Most were due to cuts by police swords, particularly in the back. This fact led to widespread accusations of police brutality, a complaint that later developed into a large-scale movement for the abolition of the Metropolitan Police Board.[69]

Because the riot had spread so rapidly, the police made arrests and conducted their investigations in the belief that it had been carefully planned. Among the conspiracy theories they considered were:[70] (1) that the riot was planned by a group within the Kenseihontō, which had been out of power for a long time, as a desperate attempt to seize control; (2) that the riot was planned by Kōno Hironaka and his faction; (3) that the riot was planned by Akiyama Teisuke, a former Diet member who had been forced to resign because he was suspected of collaborating with the Russians; (4) that the riot was planned by Watanabe Kunitake, an ultranationalist politician who had resigned from the Seiyūkai because of a disagreement with the party leaders (Katsura mentioned him in his September 2 letter to Yamagata); and (5) that the riot was planned by socialists or anarchists.

The police arrested about 2000 persons, of whom 308 were indicted and tried and 87 were convicted. Eighteen of these were fined, 29 received suspended sentences, and 40 received prison terms of varying lengths. The following is a breakdown by occupation and age of those indicted:

Occupation

Craftsmen and factory workers	109
Rickshamen and draymen	55
Small store owners	47
Shop clerks and employees	20
Students	8
Others	47
No occupation	22
Total	308

Age

Below 20	68
21–25	90
26–30	51
Over 31	95
Unknown	4
Total	308

As these tables indicate, most of the rioters were overwhelmingly those "lower-class people" that Katsura had referred to in his letter to Yamagata. They were not organized and had a low degree of political consciousness. These were people who would sing the national anthem and shout "banzai" for the Emperor and the Imperial army whenever the occasion arose. Certainly not the leaders of a "revolutionary movement"![71]

The leaders of the Rengōkai were among those indicted. The prosecution, with the personal encouragement of Prime Minister Katsura, who was eager to restore his honor, sought to find among them the ringleaders of the conspiracy. Despite their desperate efforts, in the end all of the Rengōkai leaders were released for lack of evidence. The riot had gone far beyond what the Rengōkai had planned and was to them "indeed a surprising consequence . . . something that is extremely regrettable."[72] The group that had planned the national assembly and the mob that had participated in the riot were clearly two different bodies.[73]

As news of the rioting in Tokyo spread, mass meetings were held all over Japan. By September 30, as many as 230 resolutions opposing the peace treaty and urging the cabinet ministers to resign had emanated from these assemblies.[74] On September 21, six Tokyo Imperial University professors—Tomizu, Terao, Kanai, Nakamura, Tatebe Tongo, and Okada Asatarō—intensely dissatisfied with the treaty, presented a memorial to the Emperor. This long memorial stated, first, that the treaty nullified Japan's unquestioned victory and failed to achieve the objectives of the war. It stated that, according to international law, a head of state has the absolute right to refuse to ratify a treaty concluded by his representatives. Pointing out that the Japanese economy was sufficiently strong to continue the war, the memorialists beseeched the Emperor to order a resumption of the war. The acceptance of this "humiliating peace," they said, would invite the contempt of the Powers and create a national depression not only in the economy but in the spirit of the people as well.[75]

Forums opposing the peace developed into riots in Kobe on September 7, and in Yokohama on September 12. In Kobe some police boxes were burned down and a statue of Itō Hirobumi on the premises of the Minatogawa Shrine, where Kusunoki Masashige was enshrined, was toppled by rioters who considered Itō's presence there blasphemy.[76]

Not until September 8 did Prime Minister Katsura invite the important members of both Houses to his official residence and explain the proceedings of the peace negotiations and the contents of the treaty. His explanations, however, added nothing to what his guests already knew through foreign dispatches. Many of the visitors were not satisfied with his explanation.[77]

After the riot, some members of the Seiyūkai and the Kenseihontō presented to the party leaders resolutions attacking the government, but the leaders paid no attention to them.[78] The party members, while dissatisfied with the treaty, gradually assumed the attitude that rejection of the treaty at such a late date would harm Japan's position in the eyes of the world.

The Rengōkai quickly became inactive. Chairman Kōno refused to make speaking tours of the provinces on the pretext that "we have already presented our memorial to the Emperor and indicated his subjects' sincerity. It is time for us to wait obediently for His Majesty's decision." In fact, on September 6, Kōno was called upon by Katsura's younger brother, Katsura Jirō, to convey the prime minister's request that Kōno cooperate with Katsura to keep the people under control. Kōno willingly accepted and told Katsura that he would distribute hand bills appealing for public calm, if Katsura would guarantee that he would be guarded by military police.[79]

The Imperial Edict on the control of newspapers and magazines, meanwhile, effectively restricted and supervised the press. Newspapers and magazines gradually lessened their attacks on the government, and some even began to criticize the rioters.[80] Attention was increasingly concentrated on soldiers and sailors returning from the war and on news of the festive preparations being made to welcome the British fleet, which visited Tokyo Harbor in October 1905. Businessmen also began to contend that it was not the time to argue about a peace that had already been decided upon, but rather that it was time to concentrate on postwar economic activities.[81]

Katsura, who was greatly upset by the unexpected rioting, soon recovered his composure and wrote as follows to Yamagata on September 18:

Against my will I have waited this long to write to you, being preoccupied with the recent affairs. I congratulate you on feeling better and better and passing splendid days. The riot in the capital was indeed beyond what I had expected. I am terribly sorry for this; it happened because our advance information was faulty. However, now that it has happened, I think it necessary to take extraordinary measures to calm the people's minds as quickly as possible. We first resorted to such instruments as the proclamation of martial law and the press control edict. After all, the riot was caused by bad elements in our society who took the opportunity to agitate the good elements. As the people's excitement dies down, their reason is also being restored day by day. Meanwhile, if the government operates with complete sincerity, its original purpose will not be too difficult to fulfill. Nay, I believe that we must reach our objective at any cost. I have many things to talk over with you not only about the present situation, but also about the future. However, because of my present preoccupation, I am unable to do so right now. I will call on you in the near future, but meanwhile I inquire about your health with this short letter.

Yours sincerely,

Katsura Tarō[82]

On September 20, Yamagata, who was deliberate in everything he did, wrote Commander Ōyama requesting him to exercise tighter control over his troops:

I am certain you are very happy that the peace treaty has at last been signed. However, this peace treaty did not satisfy the people's desires. As a result of our victories, they expected to gain the absolute rights of a victor. Newspapers both in Tokyo and in the provinces have criticized the government authorities and myself. As a result, the lower class people grew excited and unexpectedly rioted. In the end, we were compelled to proclaim martial law in the capital. It was most regrettable. This situation is still going on in the provinces, and our local officials have been doing their best to suppress the movement. I am particularly anxious about what will happen on the day we exchange ratifications. If this excitement should extend to our one million soldiers, both within the country and in foreign lands, it would be a serious matter indeed. As to preventive methods, I have been consulting with the minister of war and hereby request you to take appropriate measures to ensure that this wave of excitement will not affect the army in Manchuria.[83]

On October 5, the peace treaty was unanimously approved by the Privy Council.[84] The Emperor ratified it on October 14, and two days later the Kōwa Mondai Dōshi Rengōkai was disbanded.[85] The same day, October 16, the government for the first time published the peace treaty, together with an Imperial Edict taking note of the restoration of peace. Drafted by Katsura, the Imperial Edict stated that the Emperor was pleased with every aspect of the treaty and concluded: "We strongly caution our subjects against manifestations of vainglorious pride and command them to attend to their lawful vocations and to do all that is in their power to strengthen the Empire."[86]

Finally, on November 29, the government rescinded martial law.[87] On January 7, 1906, the Katsura Cabinet resigned after four years and seven months in power, and the Saionji Cabinet was formed. Saionji, Hara, and Matsuda were the only members from the Seiyūkai, in fulfillment of the promise to Hara that Katsura had made long before.[88]

Thus ended the Hibiya Riot.

The Hibiya Riot has been widely regarded as an anti-American riot. For example, Robert J. C. Butow states: "Japanese public opinion placed the blame on Theodore Roosevelt, and the Japanese government—relieved at being provided with a scapegoat—did nothing to set the record straight or apprise the people of the truth. Anti-American riots raged throughout Japan and in Tokyo surged so violently that martial law was proclaimed."[89] The reports and recollections of eyewitnesses present two diametrically opposed views. American Minister Griscom wrote in his memoirs, published in 1940: "The demonstrations had taken on a particularly anti-American tone. President Roosevelt's picture, which adorned many Japanese houses, was turned to the wall. I had quite a number of anonymous letters saying that the mob would shortly again visit the Legation to express appreciation of the part we had played in depriving Japan of the fruits of victory."[90] F. M. Huntington Wilson, first secretary under Griscom, concurred with his superior in his memoirs, published in 1945.[91]

George Kennan, special Far Eastern correspondent for *Outlook*, however, wrote from Tokyo on September 17, 1905:

[The] violence was directed against the civil authorities and the police, and not at all against foreigners. Telegrams sent from Tokyo with regard to the burning of Christian churches and an attack on the party of Mr. Harriman may have given an impression in the United States that the riot was the work of Japanese "Boxers," or that it was a manifestation of hatred for Americans on account of the part taken by President Roosevelt in bringing about an unwelcome peace. Such an impression, however, would be wholly erroneous. It is true that a few native Christian churches were burned, but investigation seems to indicate that, in some cases at least, Japanese members of these churches had given offense by supporting the Government and publicly approving the terms of peace. Be this, however, as it may, there certainly was no concerted movement against Christian churches in general. It is true also that Dr. Lyle, of the Harriman party, was struck by a stone in the street; but this might have happened to any one who attempted to force his way, in a jinrikisha, through a howling mob. If the rioters had been inspired with a feeling of hatred for foreigners, they would have made hostile demonstrations in front of the legations, or would have attacked the Imperial Hotel. The latter was full of Englishmen and Americans, and it was only a hundred yards distant from the scene of the wildest disorder. In the later stages of the rioting I went in a jinrikisha to various parts of the city, but I was neither molested nor insulted. On the contrary, I was treated by the common people in several cases, with unnecessary and conspicuous courtesy.[92]

The Belgian Minister, Albert d'Anethan, then Dean of the Diplomatic Corps in Tokyo, telegraphed his home government, on September 10, 1905: "At no time did the movement have an anti-foreign character. . . . There will be neither a conspiracy, nor an organized attack, nor any hostile demonstration against foreigners." In his October 19 telegram, d'Anethan stated, "It is against the [Japanese] Ministry alone, that the general dissatisfaction is directed. The press does not attack the President of the United States and no one doubts the loftiness of his views and the disinterestedness of his policy."[93] The *Japan Chronicle*, on September 8, 1905, reported:

A foreign resident of Tokyo who arrived by train at Kobe yesterday morning . . . in going out to see what had happened was agreeably surprised that, despite the anger of the crowd, no anti-foreign feeling prevailed, evidenced by the fact that although an attempt was made to destroy the residence of the Home Minister, not so much as a pane of glass was broken at the Imperial Hotel nearby.[94]

It is always difficult to determine the basic character of such an essentially amorphous event as a riot. Eyewitness accounts can be greatly affected by the individual background of each reporter; therefore equal weight cannot be given to them. An official representative of the United States would naturally view the event quite differently than would a magazine correspondent from America. The Belgian Minister's stake in the event was not the same as that of his American colleague. It would clearly be an overstatement to say that there was no element of anti-foreign or anti-American feeling in the riot at all. We will recall from the Japanese police record on September 5, 1905, that the crowd behind the home minister's official residence cheered the sight of a picture of heads of Komura, Takahira, and President Roosevelt running with "blood," and that on the same night a crowd of about a thousand persons gathered around the American Legation, although they caused no serious incident. In addition, several Americans staying at the Imperial Hotel were attacked by a mob and forced to flee to the American Legation.[95]

Although it would be an exaggeration to call the Hibiya Riot an anti-American riot, Japanese-American relations seem to have entered a new, less friendly phase after the Russo-Japanese War. The immediate causes for this shift seem to have derived from Japan's new position in the world, particularly in the Far East, and the ensuing rivalries among the Powers concerning Manchuria. Tension between the two nations must first have been felt at the policy-makers' level, not among the rioters in the Tokyo streets. Surveying the contemporary newspapers, trial documents, and other pertinent materials on the riot, one finds no evidence that the Rengōkai members, much less the rioters, had considered lodging a protest against President Roosevelt for his role in the peace conference.

Recently it has been revealed that the American Minister Griscom himself dispatched a long report to Secretary of State Root, dated September 15, 1905, "making it clear that the riots were directed primarily against the police, secondarily against the Japanese government officials, and only incidentally against foreigners." Furthermore, Secretary of War Taft, who was in Japan at the time of the riot with Alice Roosevelt, the President's daughter, sent Roosevelt a telegram on September 17, 1905, stating: "Any effort to create the impression that there is anti-foreign demonstration or anti-American sentiment in the great body of the people of Japan is unjust."[96]

Further evidence refuting the view that the Hibiya Riot was anti-American may be found in a recent Kokuryūkurabu publication which states that, on September 6, Uchida Ryōhei was at the Mitsui Club, located at the corner of Hibiya junction, entertaining with his almost superhuman skill in judo the eminent American E. H. Harriman and his daughter.[97] Had the riot raging in the street outside indeed been anti-American, how could the *oyabun* of the Kokuryūkai have been doing such a thing? We accept the version of Griscom's September 15 telegram as the most accurate description of the actual nature of the riot.

The leaders of the Kōwa Mondai Dōshi Rengōkai neither planned nor anticipated the riot. Their initial objective was to arouse a strong public opinion in Japan in order to strengthen Japan's position at the conference table. As far as their initial objective was concerned, it must have been one to which the oligarchs would give at least tacit acquiescence.[98] The Rengōkai leaders' encouragement and support of the government changed to opposition only when they learned that a peace treaty far short of their expectations was going to be concluded. Even then their objective was to arouse the public against the peace treaty by making speeches and convening a national rally to pass resolutions to petition the Emperor and other key members of the government. The anti-government activities of these political activists, who upheld the doctrine of *kokutai* and demanded strong foreign policies to strengthen Japan's national power, would not have gone beyond a certain limit. To lead a mass movement that might produce a change in the existing political structure was something they would not even have dreamed of.[99]

The immediate cause of the riot was police intervention with the mass demonstrations against the peace treaty. Had the government, as Katsura had written to Yamagata on September 2, 1905, "let the matter gradually take its own course," the riot could most likely have been avoided. Contemporary opinions almost unanimously support this view.[100] It is particularly regrettable, therefore, that we have yet to find materials which reveal exactly how the government authorities reached the decision to intervene. After the incident, a protest movement was led by lawyers, professors, and others to demand that the government assume responsibility for the allegedly improper administration of the police.[101] Prime Minister Katsura himself seemed quite amenable to this demand and compelled Minister of Home Affairs Yoshikawa to resign in an apparent attempt to localize the government's responsibility for the riot.[102] The commissioner of the Metropolitan Police Board also resigned.

The riot was thus triggered by unwise action on the part of the police. It was what Neil J. Smelser terms a "hostile outburst."[103] In view of the oligarchic decision-making system created by the Meiji constitution and of the officially propagated public image of the Emperor as the father and ever-benevolent ruler of his people, the participants in the anti-treaty demonstration must have regarded their appeal to the Emperor as a last, but rightful resort. When this was interfered with by the police, their frustration suddenly reached the point of explosion. Firm in the belief that the government's diplomatic blundering was about to nullify all the desperate efforts of the nation both on the battlefield and on the home front, the demonstrators must have been convinced that theirs were acts of loyalty and patriotism. Why should they be stopped by the police? In "righteous indignation," therefore, they reacted to intervention with violence. It is clear that officials of the Metropolitan Police Board had greatly underestimated the intensity of dissatisfaction among the general public and failed to take any precautionary measures to deal with the possible consequences of police intervention. In the ensuing violence, however, the mob had no leadership, organization, ideology, or clear objective. Their violence was directed mainly against the immediate object of their hatred—the police. In addition, some found in the riot an opportunity to settle private grievances or to engage in looting. The public protest against the peace treaty, the original objective of the demonstration, was practically forgotten in the process. It would be a gross mistake to state, as have Inoue Kiyoshi and other "progressive" historians who seem to be under the peculiar spell of those magic words "the masses" or "the people" (*jinmin, taishū, minshū*), that the Hibiya Riot was, in the final analysis, an "anti-establishment struggle" of "the people," initiated by right-wing nationalists but in the end transcending the limited objectives of its "reactionary leadership."[104]

The Hibiya Riot has been viewed by some as the earliest precursor of urban mass movement and the beginning of a "trend toward the masses playing a role in Japanese politics," a trend that eventually culminated in the political movement of the Taishō era.[105] It is true that an impressive number of city dwellers were successfully mobilized by the political activists and that an increasing number of urban strikes and demonstrations occurred in Japan following the Russo-Japanese

War. It is dubious, however, if a direct connection can be made between the Hibiya Riot and the Taishō political movement. Suffice it to say here that the nature of the riot as shown by the present study makes the view that it was the earliest precursor of urban mass movements appear overly sanguine.[106]

In any event, we must note that the underlying cause of public frustration, which exploded into a riot with police intervention, was the oligarchs' failure to prevent the political activists from misleading the masses in their conclusion that the government had committed a diplomatic blunder at Portsmouth.

PART FIVE
Conclusion

CHAPTER NINE

CAPABILITIES OF OLIGARCHIC FOREIGN POLICY MAKING AND MODERN JAPAN'S DILEMMA

AT THE TIME of the Russo-Japanese War, Japan's foreign policy was controlled by a decision-making oligarchy. This small group of 14 men consisted of the Emperor, the five Genrō, five cabinet ministers, and three top military leaders. The group was not monolithic. On the contrary, it contained elements conducive to both unity and disunity. Unity among its members was strengthened by their sense of national mission, an overall similarity in domains of origin, personal backgrounds, and experience in state affairs, the fact that they were few in number and shielded by the constitution from outside pressures. Factors making for disunity included differences in age and point of view between the senior and junior members and potential rivalries between the civilian and military members as well as the two armed services. The group was under the declining but still effective leadership of the Genrō.

The public had no control, direct or indirect, over these decision-makers. Their appointment and removal were vested exclusively in the Imperial prerogative and they were finally accountable only to the throne. The Diet had no direct part in, or effective power of, supervision over the making of foreign policy. Public opinion on foreign policy issues, however, was anything but feeble and acquiescent. Its strongly nationalistic quality reflected national aspirations and fear of Western encroachment, and the official indoctrination of the masses in a state-centered ideology reinforced this basic tendency. Public opinion at the time of the Russo-Japanese War was promoted and led by those individuals whom we have called political activists. Among them were journalists, lawyers, university professors, not too successful party politicians, and members of nationalist societies. They did not seek office. They were largely uninformed, unrealistic enthusiasts of nationalistic causes. While they lacked the direct legal means to exert pressure on the decision-makers, the political activists created a vociferous public opinion and persistently demanded that the oligarchs take a forceful stand in foreign policy.

Strengths and Weaknesses

In deciding to go to war, the oligarchs were not swayed by the clamor of chauvinistic public opinion. They arrived at the final decision independently, only when they themselves were convinced that no compromise could be reached with Russia on the terms the oligarchs believed to be the irreducible minimum for Japan's national security. Before opening hostilities, the oligarchs had adopted every possible measure to assure as wide international support for the war as Japan could receive. Aware of Japan's limited war potential, the oligarchs made preparations for an early peace settlement even before the war began. Neither victories on land and sea nor vociferous domestic opinion could dislodge them from this basic position of realism and caution. They never lost sight of Japan's primary war objectives. With good coordination between military strategy and diplomatic maneuvering, the oligarchs created the possibility of a peace settlement and successfully concluded the peace treaty on realistic terms that sufficed to elevate Japan to the position of a new world power. In short, the Japanese oligarchs, as the decision-making group, showed these outstanding capabilities in the war against Russia: realism and flexibility in the formulation and execution of policy, the ability to maintain, on the whole, good coordination between the civilian government and the military authorities, and the ability to resist public pressure.

Paradoxically, however, the present study has shown that the weaknesses of oligarchic control of foreign policy arose from the very sources that produced its strengths. The oligarchs showed their strength in resisting the pressure of public opinion. We commented in the Introduction on the fact that competent foreign policy leadership should lead public opinion, not follow it. Japan's oligarchs did not follow public opinion. They did not, however, lead it. Rather, they virtually disregarded it. As a result, the leadership of public opinion was left to the political activists. Led by the political activists, the Japanese public demanded an immediate war against Russia. As long as Japan's relations with Russia steadily deteriorated in the direction of an ever-imminent war, a strong chauvinistic public opinion was an asset for Japan. It could impress Russia with Japanese determination. The situation, however, became critical when the oligarchs decided to seek peace on terms unacceptable to the public. Having no effective means and apparently little inclination to communicate with the public even as much as circumstances would have allowed the government to do, the oligarchs did nothing. They virtually let the political activists lead the masses to anticipate far more than Japan could objectively expect to gain from the war. The oligarchs failed to prevent the political activists from leading the masses to the misinformed belief that the Portsmouth Treaty was a "national humiliation."

The resulting mass demonstrations against the government for its alleged diplomatic blunder were the underlying, though not direct, cause of the greatest riot in the annals of the city of Tokyo. It is possible that, if the police had not interfered with the public demonstration, the riot could have been avoided. One might, however, say, that the police action, together with the government's under-estimation of the intensity of public dissatisfaction with the treaty, simply reflected the oligarchic decision-makers' attitude toward the populace. In any event, in failing to lead public opinion, they alienated themselves from the public and let the political activists misguide the masses into the anti-government movement. It seems extremely difficult for an oligarchy also to succeed in cultivating informed public support of its policies.

The anti-government movement was quickly quelled. The episode, nevertheless, points to the inherent weakness and potential danger in oligarchic decision making. Fortunately for Japan, no national crisis immediately followed the war against Russia, for had such a crisis arisen soon after the war, forcing the oligarchs to seek public support of wartime intensity, they would have had a great deal of difficulty in getting it. A credibility gap between the government and the people affects even oligarchic leadership. Unfortunately, the Hibiya Riot seems to have taught the oligarchic decision-makers nothing. They seem to have regarded the whole affair as purely a police question. Extensive efforts to create a well-informed public capable of independent judgment on foreign policy issues never seem to have been made by the Japanese authorities. Nevertheless, in spite of the domestic repercussions and their harmful consequences, we must still conclude that in the Russo-Japanese War, Japan's oligarchic leadership showed a high level of competence and served the state well.

What were the sources of its strengths? Being shielded by the constitution from direct public interference in policy making, the oligarchs were able to resist public pressure. The fact that they were few in number facilitated effective coordination among them. Structure alone, however, could not have guaranteed the high quality of leadership they displayed. The present study has revealed that the Genrō provided the pillar of unity and realism in Japan's oligarchic decision making. It was essentially the five Genrō, with their prestige, experience, and concurrent appointments in key military and civilian positions, who collectively provided the system with the capabilities shown in this study.

That the oligarchic system depended so vitally upon the Genrō points to the more fundamental and, in the long run, fatal weakness of oligarchic control of Japan's foreign policy. Could the Genrō system be perpetuated? The answer was no. The Genrō were the products of peculiar historical circumstances, and only their prestige and the unique personal experiences, world outlook, and cohesive geographical backgrounds, which that particular period of Japan's modern century inculcated in these few select men, made them the Genrō as we know them. No legal procedure or imperial edict could produce or reproduce them. None of their successors could fully supplant them. Herein lay the fatal weakness of the oligarchic system. It was a system that could not perpetuate its original high level of leadership.

The Dilemma of Foreign Policy Making in Modern Japan

Returning to our free rearrangement of Ward's proposition in the Introduction, we must agree that the oligarchic form of government and the ideology of a strong Japan worked well for Japan on the road to rapid modernization. The deaths of the older leaders and the rise of second-generation political leaders gradually weakened the power of the Genrō, who constituted the core of the oligarchy. "Significant liberalization tendencies" set in in the governmental system. With the diminishing power of the Genrō and their eventual elimination as a dominant political force, the central unifying power vital to the multi-elite ruling system created by the Meiji Constitution also disappeared. The second-generation political leaders and their successors could not replace the lost power at the core of Japan's political system. Increasingly the products of a more confident and powerful Japan, they were not equipped with the hard-learned realism and caution of the Genrō. The erosion of Genrō power was definitely detrimental to Japan's foreign policy making.

The dilemma Japan soon faced was that, even after the high quality of leadership, the vital substance of an effective oligarchic foreign policy, had been lost, the form of the oligarchic control of foreign policy remained. Meanwhile, a viable democratic system of foreign policy making and a better-informed public opinion on foreign affairs were nowhere in sight. Thus, with a deteriorated and disunited leadership, Japan came to face increasingly complex international situations. Internally, Japan's deteriorated leadership became more and more susceptible to the clamor of public opinion, continuously led by successive political activists and persistently demanding a strong foreign policy. Voices calling for moderation and caution in foreign policy were feeble and sporadic. The dichotomy between the positions of the government and the public on foreign policy issues largely disappeared in later years, as the government leaders, who more often than not failed to differentiate slogan from program, came to share the viewpoint of the political activists. Thus, Japan's foreign policy was increasingly entrusted to those who shared the political activists' aspirations. Kōno Hironaka, the chairman of the Kōwa Mondai Dōshi Rengōkai, joined the Ōkuma (Twenty-One Demands) Cabinet in 1915. Ogawa Heikichi, a leading member of the Rengōkai, became famous as a xenophobic minister in the Tanaka Giichi Cabinet from 1927 to 1929. As premier, Tanaka, the former Kogetsukai activist, promoted his "positive" China policy. In 1903, Hirota Kōki, as a Tokyo University student, went on an "inspection tour" of Korea and Manchuria at the request of Komura's right-hand man, the Kogetsukai Yamaza Enjirō. From 1933 to 1938, as foreign minister and prime minister, Hirota was responsible for Japan's expansionist foreign policy. When the indecisive Konoe Fumimaro, the son of the nationalist prince who had led the Kokumin Dōmeikai and the Tairo Dōshikai, became once again prime minister of Japan in 1940, the dilemma of having, on the one hand, a deteriorated central leadership and, on the other, a vociferous, ill-informed, chauvinistic public opinion became a national tragedy. Japan tried desperately to regain the strength it had lost in the decision-making process with the decline and disappearance of the original Genrō power. A series of high-level coordination schemes—the Advisory Council on Foreign Relations, the Four Ministers' and Five Ministers' Conferences, the Imperial Head-quarters-Cabinet Liaison Conference, the Senior Statesmen's Conference, and the Supreme War Council—attests to this vain endeavor. None of them could rescue Japan from the dilemma of a basically outmoded oligarchic foreign policy-making system directed by a deteriorated, disunited leadership.

In the end, Japan's rapid modernization was betrayed by the very institution and ideology that had at first supported the process of political modernization. The roots of its dilemma could already be perceived in the heyday of the oligarchic decision-makers.

NOTES

Introduction

1. Recent studies include: Bernard C. Cohen, *The Political Process and Foreign Policy: The Making of the Japanese Peace Settlement* (Princeton University Press, 1957); R. Barry Farrell (ed.), *Approaches to Comparative and International Politics* (Evanston: Northwestern University Press, 1966); James N. Rosenau (ed.), *Domestic Sources of Foreign Policy* (New York: The Free Press, 1967); Kenneth N. Waltz, *Foreign Policy and Domestic Politics: The American and British Experience* (Boston: Little, Brown and Co., 1967).

2. "Foreign politics demand scarcely any of those qualities which are peculiar to a democracy; they require, on the contrary, the perfect use of almost all those in which it is deficient. . . . A democracy can only with great difficulty regulate the details of an important undertaking, persevere in a fixed design, and work out its execution in spite of serious obstacles. It cannot combine its measures with secrecy or await their consequences with patience." de Tocqueville, *Democracy in America*, Vol. 1, pp. 243–45. For some other views on democratic foreign policy making, see Lippmann, *The Public Philosophy*, Markel and Others, *Public Opinion and Foreign Policy*; Wright, *The Study of International Relations*, pp. 168–78; Huddleston, *Popular Diplomacy and War*; Bailey, "The Dilemma of Democracy," *American Perspective*, 2, No. 5 (a Symposium), *American Perspective*, (October 1948), 211–17; "Can Foreign Policy Be Democratic?" 2, No. 4 (September 1948) 1–33; Morgenthau, "Conduct of American Foreign Policy," *Parliamentary Affairs*, 3, No. 1 (Winter 1949) 147–61.

3. Almond, *The American People and Foreign Policy*; Bailey, *The Man in the Street*; Cohen, *The Press and Foreign Policy*; Cohen, *The Influence of Non-Governmental Groups on Foreign Policy-Making*; Rosenau, *Public Opinion and Foreign Policy*. For studies in crisis situations, see Hilsman, *To Move a Nation*; Paige, *The Korean Decision (June 24–30, 1950)*.

4. Brzezinski and Huntington, *Political Power: USA/USSR*; Armstrong, "The Domestic Roots of Soviet Foreign Policy," *International Affairs*, 41, No. 1 (January 1965) 37–47; Pipes, "Domestic Politics and Foreign Affairs," *Russian Foreign Policy*, edited by Ivo J. Lederer, pp. 145–69; Ulan,

"Nationalism, Panslavism, Communism," *Russian Foreign Policy*, pp. 39–67; Waltz, *Foreign Policy and Domestic Politics*, pp. 307–11; Vernon V. Aspaturian, "Internal Politics and Foreign Policy in the Soviet System," in Farrell, *Approaches to Comparative and International Politics*, pp. 212–87.

5. Farrell, "Foreign Policies of Open and Closed Political Societies," *Approaches to Comparative and International Politics*, pp. 207–208.

6. Friedrich, "International Politics and Foreign Policy in Developed (Western) System," in Farrell, *Approaches to Comparative and International Politics*, pp. 100 and 102. For his earlier view see his *Foreign Policy in the Making*.

7. Waltz, *Foreign Policy and Domestic Politics*, p. 16.

8. Morgenthau, *Politics among Nations: The Struggle for Power and Peace*, p. 142.

9. For example, Yamazaki Tanshō, *Tennōsei no Kenkyū*, pp. 238–42; Tsunoda Jun, "Nihon Gendaishi eno Ichi Shikaku (I): Seisen Ryōryaku no Kōsatsu," *Gaikō Jihō*, No. 1028 (May 1966) 81–91.

10. Robert E. Ward (ed.), *Political Development in Modern Japan*, pp. 577–92. To be fair to Professor Ward, we must add that he states: "These are all fairly simple and highly generalized propositions. Being based solely on the Japanese experience, they are also highly suppositious." He certainly did not anticipate our way of manipulating his propositions.

11. In selecting a date for the beginning of Imperial Japan, Marius B. Jansen states, with a convincing series of supportive events, that the "decade between Shimonoseki and Portsmouth marks the center of the process, and 1900 serves as a convenient milestone." Jansen (ed.), *Changing Japanese Attitudes toward Modernization*, pp. 76–77.

12. They include James William Morley, *The Japanese Thrust into Siberia, 1918* (New York: Columbia Universisty Press, 1957); Yale Candee Maxon, *Control of Japanese Foreign Policy: A Study of Civil-Military Rivalry, 1930–1945* (Berkeley: University of California Press, 1957); Richard Storry, *The Double Patriots: A Study of Japanese Nationalism* (Boston: Houghton Mifflin Co., 1957); Robert J. C. Butow, *Tojo and the Coming of the War* (Princeton: Princeton University Press, 1961); Sadako N. Ogata, *Defiance in Manchuria: The Making of Japanese Foreign Policy, 1931–1932* (Berkeley: University of California Press, 1964); James B. Crowley, *Japan's Quest for Autonomy: National Security and Foreign Policy, 1930–1938* (Princeton: Princeton University Press, 1966).

13. Studies of this incident in English include Robert A. Scalapino and Junnosuke Masumi, *Parties and Politics in Contemporary Japan* (Berkeley: University of California Press, 1962); George R. Packard, III, *Protest in*

Tokyo: The Security Treaty Crisis of 1960 (Princeton: Princeton University Press, 1966).

Chapter 1. The Oligarchic Structure of Japan's Foreign Policy Making

1. The drafting of the Meiji Constitution has been the subject of some penetrating studies. Earlier studies include: Ike, *The Beginnings of Political Democracy in Japan*; Beckmann, *The Making of the Meiji Constitution: The Oligarchs and the Constitutional Development of Japan, 1868–1891*. Recent studies take a somewhat revisionist view, recognizing more initiative and a more forward-looking attitude on the part of the Meiji oligarchy; for example, Akita, *Foundations of Constitutional Government in Modern Japan, 1868–1900*, particularly pp. 1–75; Pittau, S. J., *Political Thought in Early Meiji Japan, 1868–1889*. The most comprehensive Japanese study on this subject is Inada, *Meiji Kempō Seiritsushi*, 2 vols.

2. For detailed discussion of the imperial prerogatives, see Hozumi, *Kempō Teiyō*, pp. 354–69; and Uesugi Shinkichi, *Kempō Jutsugi*, pp. 620–45, for conservative interpretation. See Minobe, *Kempō Satsuyō*, pp. 221–84; Yamazaki, *Tennōsei no Kenkyū*, pp. 193–242; Nakano, *The Ordinance Power of the Japanese Emperor*, for the liberal view.

3. Itō Hirobumi, *Commentaries on the Constitution of the Empire of Japan*, translated by Itō Miyoji, pp. 29–31. The English text of the Meiji Constitution, including the Preamble, quoted here is taken from this book. In the Privy Council debates on the draft constitution, there were some mild arguments for Diet participation in foreign policy making, but they were easily overruled by Itō Hirobumi. Inada, *Meiji Kempō Seiritsushi*, Vol. 2, pp. 619–23. Popular opinion regarding Article 13 at the time of the promulgation of the constitution was generally optimistic, believing that the Diet, through its budgetary power, would be able to restrict the imperial prerogative based on this article. See Iyenaga, "Meiji Kempō Seitei Tōsho no Kempō Shisō," in Iyenaga (ed.), *Meiji Kokka no Hō to Shisō*, pp. 461–504.

4. Miyaoka Tsunejirō, "Treaty-Making Power under the Constitution of Japan," *International Conciliation*, No. 221 (June 1926) 1–17; Colegrove, "The Treaty-Making Power in Japan," *The American Journal of International Law*, 25 (April 1931) 270–97; Takeuchi, *War and Diplomacy in the Japanese Empire*, pp. 3–21, 425–60.

5. Colegrove, "The Treaty-Making Power in Japan," *The American Journal of International Law*, 25 (April 1931) 272.

6. Inada, "Taiheiyō Sensō Boppatsu to Tennō Genrō oyobi Jūshin no Chii," in Ueda (ed.), Taiheiyō Sensō Geninron, pp. 26–32.

7. Webb, The Japanese Imperial Institution in the Tokugawa Period, p. 260. The conclusion of this work presents a succinct discussion of changes and developments in the imperial institution during the Meiji period.

8. Rikugunshō (ed.), Meiji Tennō Godenki Shiryō: Meiji Gunjishi, Vol. 2, pp. 1309–1537; Watanabe, Meiji Tennō, Vol. 2, pp. 139–43.

9. Hackett, "Political Modernization and the Meiji Genrō," in Ward, (ed.), Political Development in Modern Japan, pp. 65–97; Silberman, "Bureaucratic Development and the Structure of Decision-Making in the Meiji Period: The Case of the Genrō," The Journal of Asian Studies, 27, No. 1 (November 1967) 81–94. No comprehensive study has been done of this subject.

10. Hackett, "Political Modernization and the Meiji Genrō," in Ward, Political Development in Modern Japan, p. 78.

11. Shumpōkō (ed.), Itō Hirobumi Den, 3 vols. See also Hiratsuka (ed.), Itō Hirobumi Hiroku.

12. Tokutomi (ed.), Kōshaku Yamagata Aritomo Den, 3 vols.

13. Tokutomi (ed.), Kōshaku Matsukata Masayoshi Den, 2 vols.

14. Sakatani (ed.), Segai Inoue Kō Den, 5 vols.

15. Ono Sanenobu (ed.), Gensui Kōshaku Ōyama Iwao.

16. See Scalapino, "The Foreign Policy of Modern Japan," in Macridis (ed.), Foreign Policy in World Politics, p. 284.

The Rev. William Elliot Griffis, author of "The Mikado's Empire," writes: "A half-dozen Genro, or Senators in the Privy Council, best incarnate the nation. Their mind has been one with the Mikado's, ever since New Japan, on the third of January, 1868, was born. Their prenatal political potency as well as public career has been one with his. One word of an 'Elder' weighs a milliard of tons. Compared with his judgment, that of a young man, however able or brilliant, avails little or nothing. The characters formed in the sevenfold-heated furnace of the pre-Restoration decade, from 1853 to 1868, and beaten, like a Muramasa sword, to finest temper on the anvil of the events which preceded the constitutional year of 1889, count supremely with nation and chief ruler. The giving of a written constitution magnified the Genro, while it reduced other men to a common calibre. Tested amid storm and stress with their protégé and comrade, the young Emperor, whose boyhood's baptism was one of exile, fire, war, and struggle between contending forces of reaction and advance, the Elder Statesmen enjoy the absolute confidence, both of sovereign and people." "The Elder Statesmen of Japan: The Power behind the Portsmouth Treaty," The North American Review, 182 (1906) 216.

17. Fairbank, Reischauer, and Craig, *East Asia: The Modern Transformation*, p. 305.

18. Article 76 says: "Existing legal enactments, such as laws, regulations, ordinances, or by whatever names they may be called, shall, so far as they do not conflict with the present Constitution, continue in force."

19. For a detailed discussion of the function of the cabinet, see Hozumi, *Kempō Teiyō*, pp. 301–17; Uesugi Shinkichi, *Kempō Jutsugi*, pp. 646–700; Minobe, *Kempō Satsuyō*, pp. 284–312.

20. Minobe, *Kempō Satsuyō* pp. 327–28; Matsushita, *Meiji Gunsei Shiron*, Vol. 2, pp. 187–89, 302–304. This important but highly ambiguous provision has been variously translated in Western writings; some translations are wrong. See, for example, McLaren (ed.), "Japanese Government Documents," *Transactions of the Asiatic Society of Japan*, 42, Part I (1914) 232–33; Quigley, *Japanese Government and Politics: An Introductory Study*, pp. 595–96.

21. Minobe, *Kempō Satsuyō*; Matsushita, *Meiji Gunsei Shiron*, Vol. 2, pp. 322–29.

22. Takeuchi, *War and Diplomacy in the Japanese Empire*, p. 28.

23. Matsushita, *Meiji Gunsei Shiron*, Vol. 2, p. 401.

24. Tōyama and Adachi, *Kindai Nihon Seijishi Hikkei*, p. 29.

25. Article 10 says: "The Emperor determines the organization of the different branches of the administration, and salaries of all civil and military officers, and appoints and dismisses the same."

26. Minobe, *Kempō Satsuyō*, pp. 306–11.

27. Itō Hirobumi, *Teikoku Kempō Kōshitsu Tempan Gikai*, pp. 102–103.

28. Katsura, "Jiden," *Meiji Shiryō*, No. 7 (June 1961) 1–48; Tokutomi, *Seijika to shite no Katsura Kō, pp.* 96–112; Shumpōkō, *Itō Hirobumi Den*, Vol. 3, pp. 503–509; Kudō, *Teikoku Gikaishi*, Vol. 2, pp. 366–76; Miyake, *Dōjidaishi*, Vol. 3, pp. 229–34.

Itō Miyoji, a shrewd but not disinterested political observer, long regarded as Itō Hirobumi's protégé, recorded in his diary the advice he had given to Katsura, as follows:

"Although the Genrō have controlled the reins of government since 1881, they have not surived thus far through their own strength alone. Nevertheless, the afterglow of their brilliant achievements in the past still lingers on, so that the Emperor immediately summons the Genrō whenever a problem arises. This practice was not questioned in the past, but now people are tired of these Genrō activities. Moreover, but for the aid of others, however much they might exert themselves, the Genrō would not know what to do. We must therefore be aware that the days left in the political life of the Genrō are numbered. Whenever they find themselves in trouble, they seek our assistance; but when things go well, they are arrogant and think nothing of those at the second level and below. Hasn't this been your personal experience for these many years?

"Now two or three Genrō urge you to form a cabinet. This is nothing but a last desperate attempt to whitewash their past blunders, and they are certainly not motivated by sincere concern for our imperial nation. Even when they realized that today's situation indeed demands some determined efforts on the part of the second level political leadership, they first recommended that the senile Count Inoue form a cabinet; and when he failed, they then for the first time turned their attention to the leaders at the second level. Now they attempt to conceal their embarrassment with the excuse that they had had the second level political leaders in mind right from the beginning. We can only pity them. Now you [Katsura] should wait patiently for a little while longer, until the right opportunity arrives, and then exert your utmost efforts for the sake of our nation. Until then, never let the Genrō think that you might be anxious to gain quick fame. . . . Today is truly the Sekigahara of both the Genrō and the younger men. Avoid revealing your sharp edge to the Genrō now. Continue upholding the Genrō and let them first exhaust every means they have. After they have revealed their incompetence to the nation, and when the populace, having completely deserted the Genrō, come around to demand the determined efforts of the second level political leaders, only then should you give serious consideration to forming a cabinet." Kurihara Hirota, *Hakushaku Itō Miyoji*, Vol. 1, pp. 354–55. See also Masumi, *Nihon Seitō Shiron*, Vol. 2, pp. 384–85.

29. Kaigun (ed.), *Yamamoto Gonnohyōe to Kaigun*, pp. 126–27.

30. Tokutomi (ed.), *Kōshaku Katsura Tarō Den*, 2 vols.

31. Ko Hakushaku Yamamoto (ed.), *Yamamoto Gonnohyōe Den*, 2 vols.

32. Hara (ed.), *Hara Kei Nikki*, Vol. 3, December 2, 1911 entry, pp. 190–91.

33. Shinobu Junpei, *Komura Jutarō*, p. 10.

34. Uchiyama Masakuma, "Komura Gaikō Hihan," *Hōgaku Kenkyū*, 41, No. 5 (May 1968) 123–50. See also Ishii, *Gaikō Yoroku*, pp. 363–64.

35. Gaimushō (ed.), *Komura Gaikōshi*, Vol. 2, p. 489.

36. Kuroda, *Gensui Terauchi Hakushaku Den*.

37. Shimonaka (ed.), *Shinsen Daijinmei Jiten*, Vol. 3, p. 595.

38. *Ibid.*, Vol. 6, pp. 450–51.

39. Inoue Masaaki (ed.), *Hakushaku Kiyoura Keigo Den*, 2 vols.

40. Shimonaka, *Shinsen Daijinmei Jiten*, Vol. 5, p. 126.

41. Ōurashi (ed.), *Ōura Kanetake Den*.

42. Shimonaka, *Shinsen Daijinmei Jiten*, Vol. 2, pp. 445–46.

43. Tokutomi, *Seijika to shite no Katsura Kō*, pp. 106–12; Kudō, *Teikoku Gikaishi*, Vol. II, pp. 374–76.

44. Mitani, *Nihon Seitōseiji no Keisei: Hara Takashi no Seiji Shidō no Tenkai*, pp. 11–12.

45. Itō Miyoji was one of those who refused to join the first Katsura Cabinet. See Kurihara Hirota, *Hakushaku Itō Miyoji*, Vol. I, pp. 358–62; Tokutomi, *Seijika to shite no Katsura Kō*, p. 108.

46. Honda, *Tamashii no Gaikō*, pp. 51–52; Gaimushō, *Komura Gaikōshi*, Vol. 1, pp. 199–200.

47. Article 11: "The Emperor has the supreme command of the Army and Navy." Article 12: "The Emperor determines the organization and peace standing of the Army and Navy."

48. Itō Hirobumi, *Teikoku Kempō Kōshitsu Tempan Gikai*, pp. 26–29.

49. Matsushita, *Meiji Gunsei Shiron*, Vol. 2, pp. 3–17, 285–329; Nakano, *Tōsuiken no Dokuritsu*; Itō Miyoji, *Suiusō Nikki*, edited by Kobayashi Tatsuo, pp. 823–932.

50. Minobe, *Kempō Satsuyō*, pp. 321–43.

51. *Ibid.*, pp. 330–33.

52. Matsushita, *Meiji Gunsei Shiron*, Vol. 2, pp. 531–35; Rikugunshō, *Meiji Tennō Godenki Shiryō: Meiji Gunjishi*, Vol. 2, pp. 1291–93.

53. Shimonaka, *Shinsen Daijinmei Jiten*, Vol. 1, p. 305.

54. Kodama Gentarō is often considered to be from Chōshū, but his native Tokuyama clan, which was from the Chōshū region, was merely a branch family of the Yamaguchi clan. See Shukuri, *Kodama Gentarō*. A British officer wrote of Kodama: "Japanese is his only language. . . . [An] Oriental of the Orientals." Hamilton, *A Staff Officer's Scrap-Book during the Russo-Japanese War*, Vol. 1, pp. 32–33.

55. Shimonaka, *Shinsen Daijinmei Jiten*, Vol. 1, pp. 236–37.

56. For the Gensuifu, see Rikugunshō, *Meiji Tennō Godenki Shiryō: Meiji Gunjishi*, Vol. 1, pp. 1023–24; Matsushita, *Meiji Gunsei Shiron*, Vol. 2, pp. 468–72; Inaba (ed.), *Daihon'ei*, pp. 77–78. At the time of the Russo-Japanese War the only two members of the Gensuifu were Yamagata Aritomo and Ōyama Iwao. See Kyoto (ed.), *Nihon Kindaishi Jiten*, p. 720.

For the Gunji Sangiin, see Rikugunshō, *Meiji Tennō Godenki Shiryō*, Vol. 2, pp. 1291–94; Matsushita, *Meiji Gunsei Shiron*, Vol. 2, pp. 535–39; Inaba, *Daihon'ei*, pp. 139–59. At the time of the Russo-Japanese War, there were seven members in the Supreme War Council. Appointed on Jan. 14, 1904 were: General Kuroki Tametomo (60 years old, Satsuma), General Nozu Michitsura (63, Satsuma), General Oku Yasutaka (58, Kokura), Admiral Inoue Yoshika (59, Satsuma). Appointed on Mar. 17, 1904:

Lieutenant-General Yamaguchi Motoomi (58, Chōshū; died Aug. 7, 1904). Appointed in January 1905: General Prince Sadanaru (46, imperial prince), Admiral Prince Takehito (42, imperial prince).

The council apparently was never convened during the war, for four of its members were in Manchuria, one was in Europe, and one died on Aug. 7, 1904. Shimonaka, *Shinsen Daijinmei Jiten*, Vol. 1, pp. 347, 650; Vol. 2, pp. 477–78; Vol. 3, pp. 130–31; Vol. 4, pp. 119–20; Vol. 5, p. 74; Vol. 6, pp. 332–33. Nihon Kokusei Jiten (ed.), *Nihon Kokusei Jiten*, Vol. 4, pp. 456, 486, 559.

57. Inaba, *Daihon'ei*, pp. 329–37; Matsushita, *Meiji Gunsei Shiron*, Vol. 2, pp. 557–69. Emperor Meiji seldom asked questions at Imperial Head-quarters conferences, allegedly because he did not wish to trouble his subordinates with questions. Imperial questions always required proper responses! Tani, *Kimitsu Nichiro Senshi*, pp. 139–40.

58. Article 56 provides: "The Privy Councilors shall, in accordance with the provisions for the organization of the Privy Council, deliberate upon important matters of state, when they have been consulted by the Emperor." Several important treaties were concluded without obtaining the formal advice of the Privy Council, an outstanding example being the Anglo-Japanese Alliance of 1902.

59. For detailed discussion of the Privy Council, see Minobe, *Kempō Satsuyō*, pp. 313–21; Hozumi, *Kempō Teiyō*, pp. 317–26; Uesugi Shinkichi, *Kempō Jutsugi*, pp. 701–704; Takeuchi, *War and Diplomacy in the Japanese Empire*, pp. 31–42. The Privy Council was to be composed of a president, a vice-president, and 24 councillors. The total number, however, often fluctuated.

60. Ijiri (ed.), *Rekidai Kenkan Roku*, pp. 20–23; Tōyama and Adachi, *Kindai Nihon Seijishi Hikkei*, pp. 106–109.

61. The post of secretary-general of the Privy Council was held at the time of the ratification of the Portsmouth Treaty by Tsuzuki Keiroku, a son-in-law of Genrō Inoue Kaoru. The secretary-general often exerted great influence upon the actions of the Council.

62. See Snyder and Furniss, *American Foreign Policy: Formulation, Principles, and Programs*, pp. 92–93.

63. There will be detailed discussion of these conferences in later chapters. For a general discussion of the imperial conferences, see Inada, "Taiheiyō Sensō Boppatsu to Tennō Genrō oyobi Jūshin no Chii" in Ueda, *Taiheiyō Sensō Geninron*, pp. 27–32; Burks, "The Government and Politics of Japan," in Linebarger, Chu, and Burks (eds.), *Far Eastern Governments and Politics: China and Japan*, pp. 378–79.

64. Vice-Minister of Foreign Affairs Chinda Sutemi was present at the Genrō conference of Aug. 27, 1905, and at the imperial conference the next day. He seems to have been merely a substitute for Komura, who was then at Portsmouth. Chinda acted as recording secretary for these conferences. He is therefore not included among the decision-makers in this study. Kikuchi (ed.), *Hakushaku Chinda Sutemi Den,* pp. 295–96; Shidehara Heiwa (ed.), *Shidehara Kijūrō,* p. 51; Takeuchi, *War and Diplomacy in the Japanese Empire,* p. 153.

65. "The opposition spoke only to vote military expenditure and to declare its patriotic ardors. No voices were raised against [the Sino-Japanese War], and the only note of dissent, if it may be so called, was a suspicion that the government would make peace too soon." Sansom, *The Western World and Japan,* p. 495.

"The years of the Russo-Japanese War were a period of submission and unanimity within the Diet, similar to the wartime period of 1894–1895." See Scalapino, *Democracy and the Party Movement in Prewar Japan: The Failure of the First Attempt,* p. 187.

Numerous writings in Japanese share the same view of the wartime Diets. Many of these writings praise such an attitude on the part of the Diets as a virtue of Japanese politics. Some are critical of these Diets for their "complete submission" to the government. For example, see Uehara, *Nihon Minken Hattatsushi Meiji Taishōshi,* Vol. 6, pp. 241–47.

Chapter 2. The Dichotomy in Attitudes on Foreign Relations

1. Kiyosawa, *Nihon Gaikōshi,* Vol. 1, pp. 5–7.

2. For example, Maruyama Masao states: "It is significant that, ever since the Meiji period, demands for a tough foreign policy have come from the common people, that is, from those who were at the receiving end of oppression at home." Maruyama, *Gendai Seiji no Shisō to Kōdō,* p. 26; English translation in Masao Maruyama, *Thought and Behaviour in Modern Japanese Politics,* edited by Ivan Morris (London: Oxford University Press, 1963) p. 19. See also Maruyama, "Meiji Kokka no Shisō," in Rekishigaku (ed.), *Nihon Shakai no Shiteki Kyūmei,* pp. 226–27; Jansen, *The Japanese and Sun Yat-sen,* particularly Chapter I, "The Ideology and Political Content of Meiji Expansionism," pp. 13–31; Conroy, *The Japanese Seizure of Korea: 1868–1910: A Study of Realism and Idealism in International Relations.*

3. Jansen characterizes foreign policy debates during the Meiji period as follows: "Foreign policy tended to be discussed in a setting of charge and

countercharge, with terms like 'positive' and 'fundamental' held up in opposition to 'weak' and 'irresolute.' " Jansen, "Modernization and Foreign Policy in Meiji Japan," in Ward (ed.), *Political Development in Modern Japan*, p. 187.

4. Terms such as "the policy and opinion elites" and "the opinion-makers" have been used to describe this segment of the public. They refer, however, to certain articulate groups of the public in a democratic political system and seem therefore to presuppose that these groups can have some degree of direct effect upon policy decision making. In order to avoid such a presupposition, we use the term "political activists" in this study. See Almond, *The American People and Foreign Policy*, Chapter 7, "The Elites and Foreign Policy," pp. 136–57; Rosenau, *Public Opinion and Foreign Policy*, Chapter 5, "The Opinion-Makers," pp. 42–73.

5. See Oka, "Kokuminteki Dokuritsu to Kokka Risei," in *Kindai Nihon Shisōshi Kōza* 8 (1961), 11–15; "Kindai Nihon Seiji no Tokuisei," in Oka and others, *Kindai Nihon no Tokuisei*, pp. 1–43; Maruyama, "Meiji Kokka no Shisō," in Rekishigaku (ed.) *Nihon Shakai no Shiteki Kyūmei*, pp. 183–236; Jansen, *Changing Japanese Attitudes toward Modernization*, p. 65; Scalapino, "Ideology and Modernization—The Japanese Case," Apter (ed.), *Ideology and Discontent*, p. 97.

6. We maintain this position despite Conroy's forceful argument against the hypothesis that a Japanese plot existed to annex Korea.

7. Stead (ed.), *Japan by the Japanese*, p. 1.

8. See Oka, *Reimeiki no Meiji Nihon*, pp. 5–133.

9. For a recent study of this episode, see Masumi, *Nihon Seitō Shiron*, Vol. 1, pp. 115–212. A good summary of the event in English is presented in Conroy, *The Japanese Seizure of Korea: 1868–1910*, pp. 17–77. Jansen states that the debate over Korea "was the first major turning point in national policy after the Restoration, and its resolution was achieved at the cost of a drastic narrowing of the base of political leadership. . . . Stability of leadership and purpose was well served by the narrowed base. After the oligarchic leadership was reduced in numbers it became far more united and effective." Jansen, "Modernization and Foreign Policy in Meiji Japan," in Ward (ed.), *Political Development in Modern Japan*, p. 168.

10. See Tsunoda and others, *Sources of Japanese Tradition*, pp. 657–62.

11. See Masumi, *Nihon Seitō Shiron*, Vol. 1, pp. 213–369.

12. Scalapino, for example, asserts: "[The] early party movement in Meiji Japan was a part of—not apart from—the nationalist tides and its leaders were fervent nationalists dedicated to the cause of a greater Japan." Scalapino, "Japan: Between Traditionalism and Democracy," in Neumann

(ed.), *Modern Political Parties*, p. 314. Jansen summarizes: "Political parties were perhaps the strangest fruit of the chauvinistic discontent of the samurai. . . . Whatever parties hoped to find popular support would have to criticize the government for its weak foreign policy. Chauvinism was the prerequisite of political success." Jansen, *The Japanese and Sun Yat-sen*, p. 28.

13. See Oka, "Meiji Shoki no Jiyū Minken Ronsha no Me ni Eijitaru Tōji no Kokusai Jōsei," in Meiji Shiryō Kenkyū Renrakukai (ed.), *Minken Ron Kara Nashionarizumu e*, pp. 33–83; and "Meiji Kokka, Sono Seikaku to Isan," *Kokka Gakkai Zasshi*, 80, Nos. 9–10, pp. 509–18.

14. Oka, "Jōyaku Kaisei Rongi ni Arawareta Tōji no Taigai Ishiki," *Kokka Gakkai Zasshi*, 67, Nos. 1–4 (August–September 1953), 1–24, 183–206; Rōyama, *Seijishi*, 234–36; Suzuki Torao, (ed.), *Katsunan Bunroku*, pp. 667–94; Jansen, *The Japanese and Sun Yat-sen*, p. 31.

15. Blacker, *The Japanese Enlightenment: A Study of the Writings of Fukuzawa Yukichi*, pp. 122–37; Ishida Takeshi, *Meiji Seiji Shisōshi Kenkyū*, pp. 292–334; Oka, "Nisshin Sensō to Tōji ni okeru Taigai Ishiki," *Kokka Gakkai Zasshi*, 68, Nos. 3–4 (December 1954) 223–54, and Nos. 5–6 (Feb. 1955) 101–29.

16. Oka, "Kokuminteki Dokuritsu to Kokka Risei," *Kindai Nihon Shisōshi Kōza*, 8 (1961), 23–37.

17. English translations of the "Imperial Rescript Relating to the Retrocession of the Peninsula of Liaotung (May 10, 1895)" and the "Imperial Address to the Soldiers and Sailors of the Empire (May 13, 1895)" may be found in Stead, (ed.), *Japan by the Japanese*, pp. 14–16.

18. Kimura, *Nihon Nashonarizumu no Kenkyū*, pp. 61–102, 383–410.

19. Tokutomi, *Sohō Jiden*, p. 310. Ōsugi Sakae, the leader of the anarchist movement in Japan during the Taishō period, like many Japanese schoolboys, was greatly enraged by the intervention. He memorized the imperial rescript on the retrocession of the Liaotung Peninsula and recited it every morning. Ōsugi, *Jijoden*, p. 62. See also Matsushita, *Ni-Sshin Sensō Zengo*, pp. 294-96. For a recent study in English, see Iklé, "The Triple Intervention: Japan's Lesson in the Diplomacy of Imperialism," *Monumenta Nipponica*, 22, Nos. 1–2, 122–30.

20. Matsushita, *Meiji Gunsei Shiron*, Vol. 1, pp. 114–15.

21. Fujimura Michio, "Gunbi Kakuchō to Kaikyū Mujun no Tenkai," in Shinobu Seizaburō and Nakayama Jiichi (eds.), *Nichiro Sensōshi no Kenkyū*, pp. 68–69.

22. Gaimushō, *Nihon Gaikō Nempyō narabini Shuyō Bunsho*, Vol. 1, pp. 174–76, 186–87.

23. Masumi, *Nihon Seitō Shiron*, Vol. 2.

24. For a history of the Genyōsha, see Genyōshashi (ed.), *Genyōsha shi;* Kokuryūkai (ed.), *Tōa Senkaku Shishi Kiden* and Kokuryūkurabu (ed.), *Kokushi Uchida Ryōhei Den.* See also Kimura, *Nihon Nashonarizumu no Kenkyū,* Chapter 7, "Genyōsha no seiritsu to sono igi," pp. 427–56; and Norman, "The Genyōsha: A Study in the Origins of Japanese Imperialism," *Pacific Affairs,* 17, No. 3 (September 1944) 261–81. The major difficulty confronting a serious student of the Genyōsha and other nationalist societies is that he has to rely on largely unreliable materials prepared by the societies themselves or by people who shared their aspirations. Such materials display narcissism to a disgusting (or if one is more broad-minded, humorous) degree. In their official biographies, the major figures in these societies appear as supermen. This type of biography might be called *"Banzai* (Hurrah!) biography." It is regrettable that biography-writing in Japan still remains largely at Garraty's "prematurity" level. See Garraty, *The Nature of Biography.*

25. Genyōshashi (ed.) *Genyōshashi,* p. 225.

26. *Ibid.,* pp. 408–409.

27. For a succinct discussion of the nature and role of Japanese nationalist societies before World War II, see Maruyama, "Senzen ni okeru Nihon no Uyoku Undō," in *Gendai Seiji no Shisō to Kodō,* pp. 187–99; an English translation is Morris, *Nationalism and the Right Wing in Japan,* pp. xvii–xxviii.

28. For largely unanalytic, factual information about the Japanese press during the Meiji period, see Nishida Taketoshi, *Meiji Jidai no Shimbun to Zasshi;* Ono Hideo, *Nihon Shimbun Hattatsushi;* Yamamoto Fumio, *Nihon Shimbunshi;* and Kawabe, *The Press and Politics in Japan.*

29. Toriyabe, "Shimbunshi Zasshi oyobi Shuppan Jigyō," in Soejima (ed.), *Kaikoku Gojūnenshi,* pp. 395–97.

30. Yamamoto Fumio, *Nihon Shimbunshi,* p. 192.

31. Masumi, *Nihon Seitō Shiron,* Vol. 4, p. 88.

32. Ward, "Japan: The Continuity of Modernization," in Pye and Verba (eds.), *Political Culture and Political Development,* pp. 39–51.

33. See Miyahara, *Kyōikushi,* pp. 1–211; and Passin, *Society and Education in Japan.*

34. See Ishida Takeshi, *Meiji Seiji Shisōshi Kenkyū,* pp. 1–215; Maruyama, "Chūsei to Hangyaku," in *Kindai Nihon Shisōshi Kōza,* Vol. 6, pp. 379–471.

In 1903, Uchimura Kanzō said, "Nothing is easier than to urge today's Japanese to start a war, for they have been taught that loyalty and patriotism merely mean fighting against a foreign country." Uchimura, *Uchimura Kanzō Zenshū*, Vol. 14, p. 304.

35. Herschel Webb, discussing the universalization of the emperor cult by means of the religious and educational apparatus of the Meiji state, writes: "Modern Japan has thereby agreed to run the risk that careers of righteous law-breaking might appeal to some ('Taishō Restorationists' and 'Shōwa Restorationists' of the twentieth-century, right-wing movement, for example) and that such a course of action would be argued by appeal to the imperial name. That risk was accepted for the sake of the advantages to a modernizing nation of mass acceptancee of and participation in the polity." Webb, *The Japanese Imperial Institution in the Tokugawa Period*, p. 264. See also Scalapino, "Ideology and Modernization—The Japanese Case," in Apter (ed.), *Ideology and Discontent*, p. 108; Uyehara, *The Political Development of Japan, 1867–1909*, p. 27; and Reischauer, *Japan: Government-Politics*, p. 82.

36. Shils, *Political Development in the New States*, p. 72.

Chapter 3. The Oligarchs and the Political Activists in the Coming of War with Russia

1. Several scholars have commented on the difficulty of measuring the influence of the political activists upon the Japanese government's decision for war against Russia. See, for example, Jansen, *Changing Japanese Attitudes toward Modernization*, p. 73; Conroy, *The Japanese Seizure of Korea: 1868–1910*, pp. 412–13. In addition to the works cited in the Introduction, useful general discussions on the role of public opinion in foreign policy making are found in Benson, "An Approach to the Scientific Study of Past Public Opinion," *Public Opinion Quarterly*, 31, No. 4, (Winter 1967–1968) 522–67; May, "An American Tradition in Foreign Policy: The Role of Public Opinion," in Nelson and Loewenheim (eds.), *Theory and Practice in American Politics*, pp. 100–21.

2. For Russian policy in the Far East during this period, see Malozemoff, *Russian Far Eastern Policy, 1881–1905, with Special Emphasis on the Causes of the Russo-Japanese War*; Romanov, *Russia in Manchuria, 1892–1906*; Dallin, *The Rise of Russia in Asia*, particularly pp. 62–77; essays by von Laue, Pipes, and Treadgold in Lederer (ed.), *Russian Foreign Policy: Essays in Historical Perspective*; White, *The Diplomacy of the Russo-Japanese War*, pp. 1–131.

3. Ōtsu Jun'ichirō, *Dai Nihon Kenseishi*, Vol. 5, pp. 354–55; Nakayama Yasuaki (ed.), *Shimbun Shūsei Meiji Hennenshi*, Vol. 11, pp. 128–29;

Nihon Kokusei Jiten (ed.), *Nihon Kokusei Jiten,* Vol. 3, pp. 302–03; Kawae Suihō (ed.), *Shiryō Kindai Nihonshi,* pp. 24–25 (section on the year 1900); Kudō, *Konoe Atsumaro Kō,* pp. 158–80. Prince Konoe Atsumaro's diary is now being published in five volumes and undoubtedly contains a great deal of information about the Kokumin Dōmeikai and the Tairo Dōshikai, which is discussed below. Unfortunately, the Konoe diary was not available at the time of this writing.

4. Kokuryūkai (ed.), *Tōa Senkaku Shishi Kiden,* Vol. 1, pp. 707–08; Nakayama Yasuaki, *Shimbun Shūsei Meiji Hennenshi,* Vol. 11, p. 128; Ōtsu, *Dai Nihon Kenseishi,* Vol. 5, p. 354.

5. Kudō, *Meiji Kenseishi,* pp. 739–40; Nihon Kokusei Jiten, (ed.), *Nihon Kokusei Jiten,* Vol. 4, pp. 9–10; Ōtsu, *Dai Nihon Kenseishi,* Vol. 5, p. 338.

6. Nakayama Yasuaki, *Shimbun Shūsei Meiji Hennenshi,* Vol. 11, p. 128; Ōtsu, *Dai Nihon Kenseishi,* Vol. 5, p. 359.

7. *Seiyū,* No. 1, Oct. 15, 1900, pp. 86–91; Ōtsu, *Dai Nihon Kenseishi,* Vol. 5, pp. 355–56; Kokuryūkai, *Tōa Senkaku Shishi Kiden,* Vol. 1, p. 708.

8. Nakayama Yasuaki, *Shimbun Shūsei Meiji Hennenshi,* Vol. 11, p. 199; and *Seiyū,* No. 5, Feb. 10, 1901, p. 83.

9. For details of the Kokumin Dōmeikai's activities, see *Seiyū,* No. 2, Nov. 10, 1900, pp. 75–84; No. 3, Dec. 10, 1900, pp. 87–90; No. 4, Jan. 10, 1901, pp. 83–87; No. 5, Feb. 10, 1901, pp. 81–83; No. 6, Mar. 10, 1901, pp. 74–75; No. 8, May 10, 1901, pp. 12–15. Also Ōtsu, *Dai Nihon Kenseishi,* Vol. 5, pp. 356–61; Kokuryūkai, *Tōa Senkaku Shishi Kiden,* Vol. 1, pp. 706–13; Nihon Kokusei Jiten (ed.), *Nihon Kokusei Jiten,* Vol. 4, pp. 12, 30; Nakayama Yasuaki, *Shimbun Shūsei Meiji Hennenshi,* Vol. 11, pp. 168–69, 185, 200, 224, 294.

10. Gaimushō, *Komura Gaikōshi,* Vol. 1, pp. 202–203. Hasegawa Yoshinosuke, who held a Ph.D. in engineering from Columbia, was a close friend of Komura from their college days and is said to have provided funds for the Kokumin Dōmeikai and its successor, the Tairo Dōshikai. Kokuryūkai, *Tōa Senkaku Shishi Kiden,* Vol. 1, p. 725; and Kokuryūkurabu (ed.), *Kokushi Uchida Ryōhei Den,* p. 273. Available sources, however, do not list Hasegawa among the founding members of the Kokumin Dōmeikai.

11. Nakayama Yasuaki, *Shimbun Shūsei Meiji Henneshi,* Vol. 11, p. 409; Ōtsu, *Dai Nihon Kenseishi,* Vol. 5, pp. 381–84.

12. Tomizu, *Kaikoroku,* pp. 1–2. This memoir seems to be the only primary source available on this early stage of the professors' activities. See also Kawai, *Meiji Shisōshi no Ichi Danmen,* Chapter 12. This is a biography of Kanai Noburu by his son-in-law.

13. Tomizu, *Kaikoroku*, p. 9.

14. *Ibid.*, pp. 6–8.

15. *Ibid.*, p. 10.

16. *Ibid.*, pp. 15–139; Kawai, *Meiji Shisōshi no Ichi Danmen*, p. 274.

17. Tomizu, *Kaikoroku*, pp. 141–272. For the writings during this period of Tomizu, the most vociferous of the professors, see *ibid*, pp. 333–577. Tomizu concedes that some of the many letters he received from the public were strongly critical of his opinions.

18. Kokuryūkurabu (ed.), *Kokushi Uchida Ryōhei Den*, pp. 1–170, 181–84; Kokuryūkai, *Tōa Senkaku Shishi Kiden*, Vol. 1, pp. 674–79.

19. Kokuryūkurabu (ed.), *Kokushi Uchida Ryōhei Den*, p. 245. Kuzū, *Nisshi Kōshō Gaishi*, Vol. 1, p. 520.

20. Yamaza Enjirō was from Fukuoka. When he married Kōmuchi Tomotsune's daughter, Hiraoka Kōtarō acted as their go-between. As an élève-consul at Pusan before the Sino-Japanese War, Yamaza assisted the Genyōsha activists in Korea. When Komura became foreign minister, he promoted Yamaza, then second secretary at Seoul, to chief of the Political Affairs Bureau of the Foreign Ministry. Thereafter Yamaza was Komura's right-hand man. See Hasegawa, *Tairiku Gaikō no Senku, Yamaza Kōshi*, pp. 49, 55; Kokuryūkai (ed.), *Tōa Senkaku Shishi Kiden*, Vol. 1, pp. 153–62, and Vol. 3, pp. 468–70.

21. Kokuryūkurabu, *Kokushi Uchida Ryōhei Den*, pp. 246–60. It is significant to note that, in April 1901, Kōtoku Shūsui's *Nijisseiki no Kaibutsu Teikokushugi* (A Specter of the Twentieth Century: Imperialism), a socialist and anti-militarist work, was published and enjoyed great popularity.

22. Kokuryūkurabu, *Kokushi Uchida Ryōhei Den*, pp. 261–63.

23. Ōtsu, *Dai Nihon Kenseishi*, Vol. 5, pp. 641–42; Kokuryūkai (ed.), *Tōa Senkaku Shishi Kiden*, Vol. 1, pp. 714–15; Tomizu *Kaikoroku*, pp. 273–74.

24. *Japan Weekly Mail*, Apr. 18, 1903, p. 414.

25. Matsuura (ed.), *Matsuura Atsushi Haku Den Shibun Shō*, p. 28.

26. The Nansa Sō was a villa used for their nationalistic activities by Prince Konoe, Matsuura Atsushi, Cambridge-educated heir of the Matsuura family, the former lords of the Hirado-han, and Viscount Watanabe Kunitake who as finance minister had caused the fall of the fourth Itō cabinet. Matsuzaki Kuranosuke had earlier been appointed a college president and left the professors' group. Takahashi, who was very close to Prince Konoe, returned from Europe in 1901 and persuaded his intimate friend Onozuka

to join the group. Matsuura, *Matsuura Atsushi Haku Den Shibunshō*, pp. 28–29; Tomizu, *Kaikoroku*, pp. 276–77; Kawai, *Meiji Shisōshi no Ichi Danmen*, p. 275; Nambara and others, *Onozuka Kiheiji: Hito to Gyōseki*, pp. 126–29; Takahashi Sakue, *Manshū Mondai no Kaiketsu*, pp. 231–32.

27. Takahashi Sakue, *Manshū Mondai no Kaiketsu*, p. 233.

28. Tomizu, *Kaikoroku*, pp. 277–79; Takahashi Sakue, *Manshū Mondai no Kaiketsu*, pp. 233–35.

29. Takahashi Sakue, *Manshū Mondai no Kaiketsu*, pp. 235–52; Tomizu, *Kaikoroku*, pp. 279–89.

30. For the Takahashi draft and the final version of the statement, see Takahashi Sakue, *Manshū Mondai no Kaiketsu*, pp. 236–50; Tomizu, *Kaikoroku*, pp. 280–88.

31. On the *Niroku Shimpō*, see Muramatsu, *Akiyama Teisuke wa Kataru*, pp. 209–52; Nishida Taketoshi, *Meiji Jidai no Shimbun to Zasshi*. After it resumed publication in 1899, the circulation of the *Niroku Shimpō* is said to have once reached 157,000 (Akiyama claimed 180,000). Yamamoto Fumio, *Nihon Shimbunshi*, pp. 187–88.

32. Tomizu, *Kaikoroku*, p. 290; Takahashi Sakue, *Manshū Mondai no Kaiketsu*, pp. 252–53.

33. Tomizu, *Kaikoroku*, pp. 290–96; Takahashi Sakue, *Manshū Mondai no Kaiketsu*, pp. 253–55; *Japan Weekly Mail*, June 27, 1903, p. 697.

34. Nishida Taketoshi, *Meiji Jidai no Shimbun to Zasshi*, pp. 237–38. The circulation of the *Tokyo Nichi-nichi Shimbun* in 1904 was reportedly 35,000. Yamamoto Fumio, *Nihon Shimbunshi*, p. 221. Hara Takashi of the Seiyūkai wrote in his diary, "I hear that the *Tokyo Nichi-nichi Shimbun* is now just as if it were the private property of Itō Miyoji. . . . It seems to be receiving a great deal of money from the Katsura Cabinet." Hara (ed.), *Hara Kei Nikki*, Vol. 2, Oct. 21, 1902 entry, p. 31.

35. See, for instance, Uchiyama Shōzō (ed.), *Aizan Bunshū*, pp. 52–53; *Tōyō Keizai Shimpō*, No. 273 July 5, 1903, pp. 9–11, and No. 275, July 25, 1903, pp. 9–10; Takahashi Sakue, *Manshū Mondai no Kaiketsu*, pp. 255–67; *Japan Weekly Mail*, July 4, 1903, p. 6. Tomizu asserts that none of the many letters he received from the public on this occasion opposed his argument. Tomizu, *Kaikoroku*, pp. 312–19. As we shall see later, the first imperial conference to discuss the question of direct negotiations with Russia was held on June 23.

36. Tomizu, *Kaikoroku*, pp. 297–303; Takahashi Sakue, *Manshū Mondai no Kaiketsu*, p. 267; Nakamura Seiji (ed.), *Danshaku Yamakawa Sensei Den*, pp. 120–21.

37. Once the statement was published, Tomii became inactive. Onozuka

withdrew from the group, his place being taken by Dr. Tatebe Tongo, a professor of literature at Tokyo Imperial University. Prior to his joining the group, Tatebe had submitted his opinion on the Manchurian question to Prime Minister Katsura and five other cabinet ministers. See Tomizu, *Kaikoroku*, p. 303; Matsuura, *Matsuura Atsushi Haku Den Shibun Shō*, p. 29.

For writings illustrating the increasing urgency of the professors' demands for war, see Tomizu, *Kaikoroku*, pp. 320–33, 578–738; Takahashi Sakue, *Manshū Mondai no Kaiketsu*, pp. 145–227, 271–313; Kurahara, *Nichiro Kaisen Ronsan*. Kawai is critical of the quality of the essay by his father-in-law, Kanai Noburu, in Kurahara's book, saying that it must certainly have damaged the reputation of the "Seven Professors." Kawai, *Meiji Shisōshi no Ichi Danmen*, pp. 276–77. Many of the professors' writings appeared in the *Taiyō* and *Gaikō Jihō*.

38. The figures give circulation in thousands for the year 1904. Party names indicate the political parties the papers seem generally to have supported. This, of course, does not mean that they served as organs for these parties, for the great majority of papers carefully maintained their political independence, as discussed earlier. Ono Hideo, *Nihon Shimbun Hattatsushi*, p. 285; Yamamoto Fumio, *Nihon Shimbunshi*, pp. 206–07, 221–25; Nishida Taketoshi, *Meiji Jidai no Shimbun to Zasshi*, pp. 235–49.

39. Nishida Taketoshi, *Meiji Jidai no Shimbun to Zasshi*, p. 241; Yamamoto Fumio, *Nihon Shimbunshi*, p. 207. It is well known that Uchimura Kanzō had supported the war against China in 1894–1895.

40. Ishida Takeshi, *Meiji Seiji Shisōshi Kenkyū*, pp. 166–67.

41. Nishida Taketoshi, *Meiji Jidai no Shimbun to Zasshi*, p. 238.

42. See Chapter 2.

43. Tokutomi, *Sohō Jiden*, pp. 308–11, 379–83.

44. Shumpōkō, *Itō Hirobumi Den*, Vol. 3, pp. 582-84; Tokutomi, *Kōshaku Katsura Tarō Den*, Vol. 2, pp. 117–22; *Itō Hirobumi Den*, Vol. 3, p. 541; Gaimushō, *Komura Gaikōshi*, Vol. 1, pp. 304–306. It is not known exactly who initiated the Murin'an meeting. As is typical in Japanese biographies, each of the above sources gives this credit to its respective subject.

45. Shumpōkō, *Itō Hirobumi Den*, Vol. 3, pp. 579–80; Hiratsuka (ed.), *Itō Hirobumi Hiroku*, pp. 2–3.

46. Tokutomi, *Kōshaku Katsura Tarō Den*, Vol. 2, pp. 995–96.

47. For the great debate over the Anglo-Japanese Alliance, see *ibid.*, pp. 1045–1131; Shumpōkō, *Itō Hirobumi Den*, Vol. 3, pp. 515–58; Nish, *The Anglo-Japanese Alliance: The Diplomacy of Two Island Empires 1894–1907*.

48. Tokutomi, *Kōshaku Katsura Tarō Den*, Vol. 2, p. 119.

49. *Ibid.*, Vol. 1, p. 1071; Vol. 2, p. 161; Tsunoda Jun, *Manshū Mondai to Kokubō Hōshin*, pp. 154–57.

50. Tani, *Kimitsu Nichiro Senshi*, pp. 35–36. This is a confidential record of the Russo-Japanese War, prepared by the then Colonel Tani, an instructor at the Army War College. See also Rikugunshō, *Meiji Tennō Godenki Shiryō: Meiji Gunjishi*, Vol. 2, pp. 1243–44; Tsunoda Jun, *Manshū Mondai to Kokubō Hōshin*, p. 157.

51. Tsunoda Jun, *Manshū Mondai to Kokubō Hōshin*, p. 157; Tani, *Kimitsu Nichiro Senshi*, p. 82.

52. Tani, *Kimitsu Nichiro Senshi*, p. 42; Inaba (ed.), *Daihon'ei*, p. 329.

53. Inaba, *Daihon'ei*, p. 330; Tani, *Kimitsu Nichiro Senshi*, p. 82; Tokutomi, *Kōshaku Yamagata Aritomo Den*, Vol. 3, pp. 543–44.

54. Sources disagree on the date of the meeting, the earliest date being May 17 and the latest May 29. The membership of the group is from Tōyadate (ed.), *Sono Koro o Kataru*, pp. 204–209; Kuroita, *Fukuda Taishō Den*, pp. 72–80; Takakura (ed.), *Tanaka Giichi Denki*, Vol. 1, pp. 260–64; Matsuoka (ed.), *Kaigun Taishō Yamashita Gentarō Den*, pp. 143–51; Hasegawa, *Tairiku Gaikō no Senku, Yamaza Kōshi*, pp. 71–72; Kokuryū-kai, *Tōa Senkaku Shishi Kiden*, Vol. 1, pp. 726–27; Rikugunshō, *Meiji Tennō Godenki Shiryō: Meiji Gunjishi*, Vol. 2, p. 1263; Tani, *Kimitsu Nichiro Senshi*, p. 37; Tsunoda, *Manshū Mondai to Kokubō Hōshin*, pp. 158-59; Ōhata, "Nichiro Sensō to Mankan Mondai," *Kindai Nihonshi Kenkyū*, No. 6 (September 1958) p. 11.

55. For instance, Kamiizumi reportedly visited the Seven Professors at the Nansa Sō on at least one occasion. Yashiro as military attaché at St. Petersburg associated with Uchida Ryōhei. Sometime during 1903, Tōyama Mitsuru reportedly called upon Prime Minister Katsura, at Yashiro's request, and urged Katsura to make an immediate decision for war. Kokuryū kai, *Tōa Senkaku Shishi Kiden*, Vol. 1, pp. 729–30, 734–35; Kokuryū-kurabu, *Kokushi Uchida Ryōhei Den*, p. 155. On Sept. 28 and Oct. 21, 1903, Sakata of the Foreign Ministry requested Ikebe Kichitarō, editor-in-chief of the *Tokyo Asahi Shimbun*, to call upon government leaders and convince them of the inevitability of a war. Asahi Shimbun (ed.), *Murayama Ryūhei Den*, pp. 381–85.

56. Fukuda later recalled that the Kogetsukai members resolved that they would commit hara-kiri in the event that war should be averted and their secret pro-war alliance become known to the public. Kuroita, *Fukuda Taishō Den*, pp. 90–91.

57. Major General Fukushima Yasumasa, Chief of the Second Division

of the Army General Staff, is said to have stated his support of the Kogetsu-kai activities as follows: "There is no longer room for discussion. We must fight Russia even if it means defeat. Our struggle for arms expansion has had only one purpose: to fight Russia. If we do not fight now, all our efforts will have been in vain. If we should lose, Russia might take away Taiwan and impose a heavy indemnity upon us. This is the worst possible outcome. Russia would not take Hokkaido. In any event, even if we should lose, Japan will not disappear from the earth. But if we do not fight now, it is evident that Russia, which has been invading the Far East with full force, will soon replenish its strength in Manchuria and advance into Korea. In that case, an agreement between Japan and Russia will come to be only a piece of paper, and Japan will inevitably be shut out of the Continent. Russia will attempt to invade the Iki Islands, Tsushima Islands, and even Kyushu. Then, Japan will become another India, or Burma. When we think of this, there is no choice but to fight. Even if we should lose, we can avenge ourselves against Russia within a hundred years, if we work at it with tightened belts. This is no time for compromise." (Kokuryūkai, *Tōa Senkaku Shishi Kiden*, Vol. 1, pp. 733-34.)

58. Tōyadate, *Sono Koro o Kataru*, pp. 204, 206; Kuroita, *Fukuda Taishō Den*, p. 85. It is said that Tanaka Giichi, who was a military attaché at St. Petersburg when Genrō Itō visited Russia in 1901 to negotiate a Russo-Japanese entente, tried to convince Itō of the futility of the Man-churia-Korea exchange policy and of the need to fight Russia before it completed the Trans-Siberian Railway. Itō reportedly rejected Tanaka's argument as "the immature theory of a green youth." Takakura, *Tanaka Giichi Denki*, Vol. 1, p. 175.

It is charged that, in December 1903, Tanaka deliberately changed a report from an Army General Staff officer concerning the transportation capacity of the Trans-Siberian Railway by decreasing drastically the figure given. He feared that the government leaders would never go to war if they knew the truth. *Ibid.*, Vol. 1, pp. 229–42.

59. Kokuryūkai, *Tōa Senkaku Shishi Kiden*, Vol. 1, pp. 730–31.

60. Kuroita, *Fukuda Taishō Den*, p. 88; Ōhata, "Nichiro Sensō to Mankan Mondai: II," *Kindai Nihonshi Kenkyū*, No. 6, (September 1958), p. 11. It is said that when Genrō Itō heard that a drunken Yamaza remarked, "We must kill the pro-Russian Genrō Itō," he complained to Komura that he should restrict his subordinate's behavior. Hasegawa, *Tairiku Gaikō no Senku, Yamaza Kōshi*, pp. 75–78.

It is interesting to note that, during the summer of 1903, Yamaza sent Hirota Kōki, then a student at Tokyo Imperial University, to Korea and

Manchuria for a three-month inspection tour. Yamaza had been introduced by Tōyama to the Genyōsha-trained Hirota. Born in Fukuoka, Hirota had wanted to be a professional soldier, but he changed his mind at the time of the Triple Intervention and decided to become a diplomat. Hirota (ed.), *Hirota Kōki,* pp. 13, 27–35.

61. Shukuri, *Kodama Gentarō,* pp. 504–505.

62. Kuroita, *Fukuda Taishō Den,* p. 88.

63. Tani, *Kimitsu,* pp. 82–93; Rikugunshō, *Meiji Tennō Godenki Shiryō: Meiji Gunjishi,* Vol. 2, pp. 1256–61; and Tsunoda Jun, *Manshū Mondai to Kokubō Hōshin,* pp. 159–60. As will be discussed later, the war with Russia cost Japan 1,730,050,000 yen.

64. Tani, *Kimitsu,* p. 84; Rikugunshō, *Meiji Tennō Godenki Shiryō: Meiji Gunjishi,* Vol. 2, pp. 1261–63; Tsunoda Jun, *Manshū Mondai to Kokubō Hōshin,* pp. 160–62.

65. Gaimushō, *Komura Gaikōshi,* Vol. 1, pp. 322–34; Tokutomi, *Kōshaku Katsura Tarō Den,* Vol. 2, pp. 128-29; Gaimushō (ed.), *Nihon Gaikō Bunsho,* Vol. 35, No. 1, pp. 1–4; Tsunoda Jun, *Manshū Mondai to Kokubō Hōshin,* pp. 163–67.

Russian War Minister Aleksei N. Kuropatkin made an official visit to Tokyo on June 12, 1903. He exchanged views with Katsura, Komura, and Terauchi, but no significant results were achieved by his visit, as far as alleviating the tense relations between the two countries was concerned. On the contrary, Kuropatkin's visit probably created a greater sense of urgency among the Japanese decision-makers. Tokutomi, *Kōshaku Katsura Tarō Den,* Vol. 2, pp. 123–37; Gaimushō, *Komura Gaikōshi,* Vol. 1, pp. 311–13. See also Hara, *Hara Kei Nikki,* Vol. 2, June 12, 1903 entry, p. 67.

66. Kaigun, *Yamamoto Gonnohyōe to Kaigun,* pp. 134–36.

67. Tokutomi, *Kōshaku Katsura Tarō Den,* Vol. 2, pp. 130–39.

68. Shumpōkō, *Ito Hirobumi Den,* Vol. 3, pp. 590–605. Inoue, however, declined the appointment, reportedly because of extensive business dealings. Tokutomi, *Sohō Jiden,* p. 387.

69. Tokutomi, *Kōshaku Katsura Tarō Den,* Vol. 2, pp. 130–46.

70. Kurihara Hirota, *Hakushaku Itō Miyoji,* Vol. 1, pp. 326–41; Tokutomi, *Kōshaku Yamagata Aritomo Den,* Vol. 3, p. 552; Hara, *Hara Kei Nikki,* Vol. 2, July 7, 1903 entry, pp. 69–70.

71. Katsura's relations with members of the Seiyūkai will be discussed later.

72. Komura's note to the British government contained the following statement: "A settlement embodying those principles would, it is believed, be entirely fair to all parties. It is not necessary at this time to attempt to

say what the result of Russia's rejection of such proposals would be but the responsibility for whatever consequences might ensue would rest solely with her." Gaimushō, *Gaikō Bunsho*, Vol. 36, No. 1, pp. 4–6.

73. Japan, Foreign Office, *Correspondence Regarding the Negotiations between Japan and Russia (1903–1904)* (translation), presented to the Imperial Diet, March 1904, pp. 3–4. (Hereafter cited as *Correspondence.*)

It is said that Henry W. Denison, the American adviser to the Japanese Foreign Ministry who composed the Japanese proposals and instructions in English, was aware of Komura's determination to risk war. He therefore deliberately avoided high-handed and provocative expressions in the Japanese communications so that, when they were made public after the outbreak of war, they would serve to impress upon the reader Japan's sincerity and conciliatory attitude in the negotiations. Ōhata, "Nichiro Kaisen Gaikō," *Kokusai Seiji*, No. 3 (April 1962), p. 112.

74. *Japan Weekly Mail*, June 27, 1903, p. 697.

75. Prince Konoe was ill. He died on Jan. 1, 1904.

76. Nakayama Yasuaki, *Shimbun Shūsei Meiji Hennenshi*, Vol. 12, pp. 96–98; Nihon Kokusei Jiten (ed.), *Nihon Kokusei Jiten*, Vol. 4, pp. 191–92. Uchida Ryōhei apparently did not attend the August 9 meeting. He was in Korea from sometime in the fall of 1903 to early November of the same year. Kokuryūkurabu, *Kokushi Uchida Ryōhei Den*, pp. 268–69. Very little is known as to the Kokuryūkai's activities during the prewar negotiations.

77. *Japan Weekly Mail*, Oct. 10, 1903, p. 383.

78. Nakayama Yasuaki, *Shimbun Shūsei Meiji Hennenshi*, Vol. 12, p. 110; *Japan Weekly Mail*, No. 21. 1903, p. 546; Ōtsu, *Dai Nihon Kenseishi*, Vol. 5, pp. 658–59; Hara, *Hara Kei Nikki*, Vol. 2, Oct. 7 entry, 1903, p. 76, and Feb. 11 entry, 1904, p. 11.

79. *Japan Weekly Mail*, Oct. 3, 1903, p. 354, Oct. 10, 1903, p. 383, Nov. 28, 1903, p. 575; *Tōyō Keizai Shimpō*, No. 280, Sept. 15, 1903, pp. 17–18.

80. Ōtsu, *Dai Nihon Kenseishi*, Vol. 5, pp. 648–49.

81. Nihon Kokusei Jiten (ed.), *Nihon Kokusei Jiten*, Vol. 4, pp. 192-94; Ōtsu, *Dai Nihon Kenseishi*, Vol. 5, pp. 650–52; *Japan Weekly Mail*, Oct. 10, 1903, p. 383.

82. Nakayama Yasumaki, *Shimbun Shūsei Meiji Hennenshi*, Vol. 12, p. 116; Nihon Kokusei Jiten (ed.), *Nihon Kokusei Jiten*, Vol. 4, p. 194; *Japan Weekly Mail*, Oct. 17, 1903, p. 410. Details on this group are not known.

83. Nakayama Yasuaki, *Shimbun Shūsei Meiji Hennenshi*, Vol. 12,

pp. 132–33; Nihon Kokusei Jiten (ed.), *Nihon Kokusei Jiten*, Vol. 4, pp. 197–98; Shumpōkō, *Itō Hirobumi Den*, Vol. 3, pp. 617–18; Ōtsu, *Dai Nihon Kenseishi*, Vol. 5, pp. 653–54; *Taiyō*, Vol. 9, No. 14, Dec. 1903, pp. 7–11, 229–30; *Japan Weekly Mail*, Nov. 14, 1903, p. 518, Nov. 21, 1903, p. 546.

Uragami Masataka, Genyōsha member who had once been imprisoned as a suspected accomplice in Kurushima's attempt to assassinate the then Foreign Minister Ōkuma, is said to have been contemplating the assassination of Genrō Itō. Kokuryūkai, (ed.), *Tōa Senkaku Shishi Kiden*, Vol. 1, pp. 717–18; and Shumpōkō, *Itō Hirobumi Den*, Vol. 3, p. 629.

For a vivid description of Tōyama's confrontation with Genrō Itō, see Kokuryūkai, (ed.), *Tōa Senkaku Shishi Kiden*, Vol. 1, pp. 718–21; Fujimoto Naonori, *Kyojin Tōyama Mitsuru Ō*, pp. 484–88. The Kokuryūkai source claims, "This parley had a most significant bearing upon the decision for war with Russia. It is also said that Japan's Russian policy was virtually determined by the parley." Kokuryūkai (ed.), *Tōa Senkaku Shishi Kiden*. Vol. 1, p. 720.

84. Ōtsu, *Dai Nihon Kenseishi*, Vol. 5, pp. 659–60; *Taiyō*, Vol. 9, No. 14, Dec. 1903, pp. 11–12, 230–31; *Japan Weekly Mail*, Nov. 14, 1903, p. 519; Tokutomi, *Kōshaku Katsura Tarō Den*, Vol. 2, p. 182.

85. Ōtsu, *Dai Nihon Kenseishi*, Vol. 5, p. 662; Watanabe, *Nihon Kinsei Gaikōshi*, pp. 356–60. Watanabe claims that the Emperor personally read the memorial. See also Kokuryūkai, *Tōa Senkaku Shishi Kiden*, Vol. 1, pp. 721–24.

86. Ōtsu, *Dai Nihon Kenseishi*, Vol. 5, p. 662; Watanabe, *Nihon Kinsei Gaikōshi*, pp. 360–61.

87. Ōtsu, *Dai Nihon Kenseishi*, Vol. 5, pp. 662–64.

88. Fujimura Michio, "Kaisen Yoron no Kōzō," in Shinobu Seizaburō and Nakayama Jiichi (eds.), *Nichiro Sensōshi no Kenkyū*, pp. 207–208.

89. Nakayama Yasuaki (ed.), *Shimbun Shūsei Meiji Hennenshi*, Vol. 12, pp. 117–20.

90. Fujimura Michio, "Kaisen Yoron no Kōzō," in Shinobu Seizaburō and Nakayama Jiichi (eds.), *Nichiro Sensōshi no Kenkyū*, p. 208.

91. Ishida Takeshi, *Meiji Seiji Shisōshi Kenkyū*, p. 337.

92. *Japan Weekly Mail*, Oct. 17, 1903, p. 410.

93. Fujimura Michio, "Kaisen Yoron no Kōzō," in Shinobu Seizaburō and Nakayama Jiichi (eds.), *Nichiro Sensōshi no Kenkyū*, p. 208.

94. Yamamoto Fumio, *Nihon Shimbunshi*, p. 208; *Taiyō*, Vol. 9, No. 14, Dec. 1903, pp. 6–7; *Japan Weekly Mail*, Nov. 14, 1903, pp. 526–27.

95. Yamamoto Fumio, *Nihon Shimbunshi*, p. 208.

96. *Ibid.*

97. Ishida Takeshi, *Meiji Seiji Shisōshi Kenkyū*, p. 338.

98. Ono Hideo, *Nihon Shimbun Hattatsushi*, p. 286.

99. *Ibid.*, p. 287.

100. Ishida Takeshi, *Meiji Seiji Shisōshi Kenkyū*, p. 388. The *Tokyo Nichi-Nichi Shimbun* also changed its stand, however, as soon as the imperial conference decided in favor of war on Feb. 4, 1904. On Feb. 6, an editorial entitled "The Decision of Our Imperial Nation," vehemently supported the war. See Mainichi (ed.), *Mainichi Shimbun Shichijūnen*, p. 574.

101. For example, Hara Takashi, who as the top lieutenant of the Seiyūkai met almost daily with Genrō Itō and Inoue, had very little knowledge of the progress of the negotiations. Hara, *Hara Kei Nikki*, Vol. 2, June 25, 1903 entry, p. 69, and Oct. 17, 1903 entry, p. 76.

102. Dai Nihon (ed.), *Dai Nihon Teikoku Gikaishi*, Vol. 5, pp. 1869, 1902, 1913–24, and 1943–45.

103. Nihon Kokusei (ed.), *Nihon Kokusei Jiten*, Vol. 4, p. 196.

104. Kobayashi Yūgo, *Rikken Seiyūkaishi*, Vol. 2, pp. 11–12; Hara, *Hara Kei Nikki*, Vol. 2, Oct. 14, 1903 entry, p. 76.

105. Kobayashi Yūgo, *Rikken Seiyūkaishi*, Vol. 2, pp. 41–43; Nakayama Yasuaki, *Shimbun Shūsei Meiji Hennenshi*, Vol. 12, p. 139. We mentioned one *ingaidan* in Chapter 2. Details of the Seiyūkai Ingaidan are not known.

106. Nihon Kokusei (ed.), *Nihon Kokusei Jiten*, Vol. 4, pp. 198–99.

107. Tsukada (ed.), *Rikken Minseitōshi*, Vol. 1, p. 124; Hara, *Hara Kei Nikki*, Vol. 2, Nov. 19, 1903 entry, p. 79, and Dec. 1, 1903 entry, p. 83.

108. Tsukada, *Rikken Minseitōshi*, Vol. 1, p. 125.

109. Ōtsu, *Dai Nihon Kenseishi*, Vol. 5, p. 637.

110. Ishida Takeshi, *Meiji Seiji Shisōshi Kenkyū*, p. 350.

111. See Nakayama Gisuke, *Kōno Banshū Den*.

112. Dai Nihon, *Dai Nihon Teikoku Gikaishi*, Vol. 5, pp. 2007–12.

113. Nakayama Yasuaki, *Shimbun Shūsei Meiji Hennenshi*, Vol. 12, pp. 144–45. Translated in Kawabe, *The Press and Politics in Japan*, p. 130.

114. Nihon Kokusei (ed.), *Nihon Kokusei Jiten*, Vol. 4, p. 205; *Taiyō*, Vol. 10, No. 1, Jan. 1904, pp. 5–13.

115. It is reported that many people wrote letters of gratitude to Kōno. Nakayama Yasuaki, *Shimbun Shūsei Meiji Hennenshi*, Vol. 12, p. 147.

116. Takeuchi, *War and Diplomacy in the Japanese Empire*, p. 141.

117. For more detailed description of this incident, see Nakayama Gisuke, *Kōno Banshū Den*, Vol. 2, pp. 612–44; Muramatsu, *Akiyama Teisuke wa Kataru*, pp. 209–52; Hayashida, *Meiji Taishō Seikai Sokumenshi*, pp. 389–431; *Japan Weekly Mail*, Dec. 19, 1903, pp. 677–78; Hara, *Hara Kei Nikki*, Vol. 2, Dec. 2–15 1903 entry, pp. 83–86.

118. Fujimura Michio, "Kaisen Yoron no Kōzō," in Shinobu Seizaburō and Nakayama Jiichi (eds.), *Nichiro Sensōshi no Kenkyū*, pp. 193–94; Ishida Takeshi, *Meiji Seiji Shisōshi Kenkyū*, p. 344.

119. Fujimura Michio, "Kaisen Yoron no Kōzō," in Shinobu Seizaburō and Nakayama Jiichi (eds.), *Nichiro Sensōshi no Kenkyū*, pp. 185–86.

120. *Tōyō Keizai Shimpō*, No. 281 (Sept. 25, 1903), pp. 5–6.

121. Shibusawa Seien (ed.), *Shibusawa Eiichi Denki Shiryō*, Vol. 28, pp. 472–76, 510–11; *Japan Weekly Mail*, Nov. 7, 1903, p. 490; and Suehiro, *Danshaku Kondō Rempei Den*, pp. 193–97.

122. Shibusawa Seien, *Shibusawa Eiichi Denki Shiryō*, Vol. 28, p. 512.

123. *Tōyō Keizai Shimpō*, No. 279 (Sept. 5, 1903), pp. 8–10.

124. Fujimura Michio "Kaisen Yoron no Kōzo," in Shinobu Seizaburō and Nakayama Jiichi (eds.), *Nichiro Sensōshi no Kenkyū*, p. 196.

125. *Tōyō Keizai Shimpō*, No. 384 (Oct. 25, 1903), pp. 17–18.

126. Ishida Takeshi, *Meiji Seiji Shisōshi Kenkyū*, pp. 357–58.

127. *Ibid.*, p. 358.

128. Fujimura Michio, "Kaisen Yoron no Kōzō" in Shinobu Seizaburō and Nakayama Jiichi (eds.), *Nichiro Sensōshi no Kenkyū*, p. 209. The Belgian Minister in Tokyo, Albert d'Anethan, reported to his government on Jan. 22, 1904: "It would be natural to think that ideas of peace would prevail in the world of business and finance. It is unusual for bankers and capitalists to express warlike sentiment. Yet in Japan there is this surprising phenomenon." Baron d'Anethan, *The d'Anethan Dispatches from Japan, 1894–1910*, selected, translated, and edited with a historical introduction by Lensen, p. 176.

129. Hara, *Hara Kei Nikki*, Vol. 2, Feb. 11, 1904 entry, p. 91.

130. For complete editions of these two papers, see Rōdō Undōshi (ed.), *Shūkan Heimin Shimbun* and *Chōkugen*.

131. Rōdō Undōshi, *Shūkan Heimin Shimbun*, Vol. 1, p. 115.

132. For studies of the anti-war movement, see Matsushita, *Meiji Taishō Hansen Undōshi*, pp. 33–90 and *Sandai Hansen Undōshi*; Shinobu Seizaburō, Watabe, and Koyama (eds.), *Gendai Hantaisei Undōshi*, pp. 117–26; Nakamura Katsunori, *Meiji Shakaishugi Kenkyū*; Shimomura, "Nichiro Sensō zen Seron Keisei no Ichi Kyokumen: Kōtoku Shūsui o Chūshin ni

shite," *Kokushigaku*, No. 71 (Mar. 1959) 1–15; Nishida Taketoshi, "Heimin Shimbun to Sono Jidai: Hisenron o chūshin to shite," *Bungaku*, 21, No. 10 (1953) 976–82; Kublin, "The Japanese Socialists and the Russo-Japanese War," *Journal of Modern History*, 22, No. 4 (Dec. 1950) 322–39.

133. Toku Berutsu (ed.), *Berutsu no Nikki*, translated by Sugamura Ryūtarō, Part 2, Vol. 1, p. 131.

134. Ishikawa, *Takuboku Zenshū*, Vol. 8, p. 43; Vol. 2, pp. 47–48.

135. Futabatei, *Futabatei Shimei Zenshū*, Vol. 12, pp. 78, 80.

136. McKenzie, *From Tokyo to Tiflis: Uncensored Letters from the War*, pp. 3, 9–10.

137. D'Anethan, *The d'Anethan Dispatches from Japan: 1894–1910*, p. 167.

138. Treat, *Diplomatic Relations between the United States and Japan: 1895–1905*, p. 194.

139. The seat of negotiations had been transferred to Tokyo. For accounts of the negotiations from the Russian side, see Malozemoff, *Russian Far Eastern Policy, 1881–1905*, pp. 237–49; White, *The Diplomacy of the Russo-Japanese War*, pp. 95–131. David J. Dallin states, "Russian policy on the eve of the Russo-Japanese War appears as a series of zigzags, oscillations, and reversals, a model of confusion and indecision." Dallin, *The Rise of Russia in Asia*, p. 76.

140. *Correspondence*, pp. 12–13.

141. Tokutomi, *Kōshaku Katsura Tarō Den*, Vol. 2, pp. 188–92, and *Kōshaku Yamagata Aritomo Den*, Vol. 3, pp. 582–90; Shukuri, *Kodama Gentarō*, pp. 520–33.

142. Tani, *Kimitsu Nichiro Senshi*, pp. 38–39; Tōyadate, *Sono Koro o Kataru*, pp. 208–209; Takakura, *Tanaka Giichi Denki*, Vol. 1, pp. 224–27.

143. Gaimushō, *Komura Gaikōshi*, Vol. 1, pp. 335–40.

144. *Correspondence*, pp. 16–17.

145. *Ibid.*, pp. 24–25.

146. Watanabe, *Nihon Kinsei Gaikōshi*, pp. 364–65.

147. *Correspondence*, pp. 25–26; Shumpōkō, *Itō Hirobumi Den*, Vol. 3, pp. 620–21.

148. Ikebe Kichitarō, editor-in-chief of the *Tokyo Asahi Shimbun*, wrote in his diary on December 21, 1903, that Itō said that the Genrō should be mindful of the spirits of Kido and Ōkubo, and refrain from risking the nation as long as they lived. Asahi Shimbun, *Murayama Ryūhei Den*, p. 387; Watanabe, *Nihon Kinsei Gaikōshi*, p. 364.

149. Tani, *Kimitsu Nichiro Senshi*, p. 42. Griscom reported to Washing-

ton on January 11, 1904: "I think it may be fairly stated that until the middle of December the 'Elder Statesmen' had no intention of permitting Japan to take up a position which might bring it into conflict with Russia. . . . A complete and unforeseen metamorphosis came over the situation when it suddenly became known on December 30 that the 'Elder Statesmen' had met and counseled the Emperor to take a determined stand. . . . The unexpected withdrawal of the opposition of the 'Elder Statesmen' enabled the Cabinet to take this sudden war measure." Treat, *Diplomatic Relations between the United States and Japan: 1895–1905*, pp. 188–89.

150. Rikugunshō, *Meiji Tennō Godenki Shiryō: Meiji Gunjishi*, Vol. 2, pp. 1291–95.

151. Kaigun, *Yamamoto Gonnohyōe to Kaigun*, p. 145. Another source states that these military men attended cabinet-level meetings for the first time on January 7, 1904. Tani, *Kimitsu Nichiro Senshi*, p. 42.

152. Gaimushō, *Nihon Gaikō Bunsho*, Vol. 36, No. 1, pp. 41–45.

153. Kaigun, *Yamamoto Gonnohyōe to Kaigun*, pp. 145–50.

154. *Correspondence*, pp. 27–28.

155. Due to illness, Katsura did not attend the imperial conference, and Yamamoto acted in his stead. Finance Minister Sone Arasuke attended an imperial conference for the first time. Kaigun, *Yamamoto Gonnohyōe to Kaigun*, pp. 193–201.

156. *Correspondence*, pp. 28–29.

157. Tokutomi, *Kōshaku Katsura Tarō Den*, Vol. 2, pp. 197–98.

158. Shumpōkō, *Itō Hirobumi Den*, Vol. 3, pp. 625–27.

159. Rikugunshō, *Meiji Tennō Godenki Shiryō: Meiji Gunjishi*, Vol. 2, pp. 1305–1307.

160. Tokutomi, *Kōshaku Katsura Tarō Den*, Vol. 2, p. 199, and *Kōshaku Matsukata Masayoshi Den*, Vol. 2, pp. 884–85; Gaimushō, *Nihon Gaikō Bunsho*, Vol. 36, No. 1, pp. 1–49; Vol. 37, No. 1, pp. 1–101; Supplement 1 to Vols. 37 and 38, pp. 1–154; Tokutomi, *Sanjū Shichi-Hachinen Eki to Gaikō*, p. 107; Tachi, "Meiji Sanjū Shichi Hachinen Sen'eki to Yōroppa oyobi Amerika Kyōkoku no Gaikō," in Tachi (ed.), *Tachi Hakushi Gaikōshi Ronbunshū*, p. 507. One source states that the Emperor suggested in the conference that he personally telegraph the Tsar requesting that the latter reconsider. The Emperor gave up the idea when his advisers told him the situation no longer merited such action. Shumpōkō, *Itō Hirobumi Den*, Vol. 3, p. 629.

161. Kaneko, *Nichiro Sensō Hiroku*, p. 26.

162. *Ibid.*, pp. 28–29.

163. Ōtsu, *Dai Nihon Kenseishi*, Vol. 6, p. 22.

164. *Kaneko, Nichiro Sensō Hiroku,* pp. 17–19. Itō sent his son-in-law Suematsu Kenchō to England. Both Kaneko and Suematsu belonged to the Seiyūkai.

165. Ono Sanenobu, (ed.), *Gensui Koshaku Ōyama Iwao,* pp. 672–73; Kaigun, *Yamamoto Gonnohyōe to Kaigun,* pp. 216–18.

166. Storry, *The Double Patriots: A Study of Japanese Nationalism,* pp. 17–18 (particularly p. 18, footnote 1). For the decision-makers' anxieties about the future of the war, see Watanabe, *Meiji Tennō,* Vol. 2, p. 126; Ōtsu, *Dai Nihon Kenseishi,* Vol. 5, pp. 700–09; Tokutomi, *Kōshaku Yamagata Aritomo Den,* Vol. 3, pp. 601–602.

167. Malozemoff, *Russian Far Eastern Policy, 1881–1905,* p. 237.

168. Brown, *Nationalism in Japan: An Introductory Historical Analysis,* p. 142; Gulick, *The White Peril in the Far East: An Interpretation of the Significance of the Russo-Japanese War,* p. 135. Taguchi Ukichi said, "The people dragged the government into war by its hands and feet." Taguchi (comp.), *Teiken Taguchi Ukichi Zenshū,* Vol. 5, p. 534. Griscom reported, "It is the opinion of all fair-minded observers here that Japan has indeed exercised great moderation and patience. The pressure of public opinion for war has been strong from the very first, but the Japanese Government has kept the situation well in hand." Treat, *Diplomatic Relations between the United States and Japan: 1895–1905,* p. 191. Komura allegedly stated, "It is quite difficult to manage the Japanese people. Whatever you may try, you find yourself in trouble. But you will feel assured because they certainly follow you, once the first shot is heard." Gaimushō, *Komura Gaikōshi,* Vol. 1, p. 343.

Chapter 4. The Oligarchs in War and Peacemaking

1. Ōtsu, *Dai Nihon Kenseishi,* Vol. 6, p. 28.

2. The Times, *The War in the Far East: 1904–1905,* p. 32. For a comparison of military preparations for war between the two antagonists, see White, *The Diplomacy of the Russo-Japanese War,* pp. 135–54.

3. A Russian foreign service officer who was at St. Petersburg during the war recalls: "St. Petersburg had no idea of the real strength of Japan, and thought that tiny Japan would never dare to make war against mighty Russia. The reports of our military agents in Tokyo, like most reports, presented things not as they were, but as the central authorities wanted them to be, confirming the belief that the Japanese army was no match for a European army. . . . There was a complete lack of enthusiasm, half of the population not even knowing where Manchuria was located. The only people

who rejoiced were the revolutionists who had always seen their only chance for success in the demoralization of an unsuccessful war. The conflict found us unprepared, with an insufficient number of troops in the Far East." Abrikosow, *Revelations of a Russian Diplomat,* edited by Lensen, pp. 89–91.

"There is wide agreement among the sources, Russian as well as foreign, on the indifferences or outright hostility of public opinion in Russia to the Far Eastern ventures undertaken by the Tsar and his companions, and on the great unpopularity of the Russo-Japanese War. A perusal of contemporary journals confirms this estimate." Pipes, "Domestic Politics and Foreign Affairs," in Lederer (ed.), *Russian Foreign Policy: Essays in Historical Perspective,* p. 154.

Shinobu Seizaburō, *Kindai Nihon Gaikōshi,* pp. 159–60.

4. Tani, *Kimitsu Nichiro Senshi,* pp. 656–60; Fujimura Michio, "Sensō to Minshū," in Shinobu Seizaburō and Nakayama Jiichi (eds.), *Nichiro Sensōshi no Kenkyū,* p. 290.

Reuter's special correspondent in Manchuria, Lord Brooke, reported that "he [the private soldier] bears no enmity against the Japanese, nor does he understand for what the war is being waged." Lord Brooke, *An Eye-Witness in Manchuria,* p. 310.

5. Numata, *Nichiro Rikusen Shinshi,* p. 102. Tani, *Kimitsu Nichiro Senshi,* pp. 424–48.

6. Gaimushō, *Komura Gaikōshi,* Vol. 2, p. 110. Kiyosawa, *Nihon Gaikōshi,* Vol. I, p. 326. For details of the battles of Liaoyang and Shahō, see Tani, *Kimitsu Nichiro Senshi,* pp. 449–517. Oka, *Yamagata Aritomo,* p. 94. Yamagata seems to have had some confidence in the initial stages of the war; see Kinkidō (ed.), *The Russo-Japanese War,* No. 10, pp. 1414–16.

7. Numata. *Nichiro Rikusen Shinshi,* pp. 127–129.

8. Tani, *Kimitsu Nichiro Senshi,* pp. 485–517; Tsurumi, *Nihon no Hyakunen,* Vol. 7, p. 126.

9. Tokutomi, *Kōshaku Yamagata Aritomo Den,* Vol. 3, p. 655. Yamagata's letter to War Minister Terauchi, dated Oct. 12, 1904, *Terauchi Ke Bunsho,* reprinted in *Seiji Keizaishigaku,* No. 17 (June 1964) p. 35.

10. Tsurumi Shunsuke, *Nihon no Hyakunen,* Vol. 7, pp. 127–28.

11. Numata, *Nichiro Rikusen Shinshi,* pp, 128–29.

12. The Chief of Staff of the Third Army, which attacked Port Arthur, openly complained of the lack of munitions. He was severely reprimanded by Yamagata, who was afraid of the effect such complaints might have on the morale of the army. Tokutomi, *Kōshaku Yamagata Aritomo Den,* Vol. 3, pp. 659–61.

13. Baelz (ed.), *Awakening Japan: The Diary of a German Doctor: Erwin Baelz,* p. 288.

14. Nakayama Yasuaki, *Shimbun Shūsei Meiji Hennenshi,* Vol. 12, pp. 290–91.

15. Ōtsu, *Dai Nihon Kenseishi,* Vol. 6, p. 27.

16. Numata, *Nichiro Rikusen Shinshi,* pp. 138–39.

17. Ono Sanenobu, *Gensui Kōshaku Ōyama Iwao,* p. 715.

18. Gaimushō, *Komura Gaikōshi,* Vol. 2, p. 110.

19. Shukuri, *Kodama Gentarō,* pp. 623–29. For details of the Battle of Mukden, see Tani, *Kimitsu Nichiro Senshi,* pp. 528–54.

20. Ono Sanenobu, *Gensui Kōshaku Ōyama Iwao,* p. 736.

21. Gaimushō, *Komura Gaikōshi,* Vol. 2, p. 111. Tanaka reported, as noted in Chapter 3, a deliberately underestimated figure for Russian transportation capacity. Actually, Russian transportation capacity was even greater than the more correct figures, which Tanaka withheld.

22. Shinobu Seizaburō, *Kindai Nihon Gaikōshi,* p. 160.

23. Shukuri, *Kodama Gentarō,* p. 633.

24. Tokutomi, *Kōshaku Yamagata Aritomo Den,* Vol. 3, p. 687. Ishii, *Gaikō Yoroku,* p. 87; Hiratsuka, *Itō Hirobumi Hiroku,* pp. 238–39; Tokutomi (ed.), *Kōshaku Katsura Tarō Den,* Vol. 2, p. 245.

25. Treat, *Diplomatic Relations between the United States and Japan: 1885–1905,* pp. 238–41.

26. Ono Sanenobu, *Gensui Kōshaku Ōyama Iwao,* p. 735. About the same time Yamagata told a newspaperman, "It is unwise to keep fighting a recalcitrant enemy." Gurū Kikin (ed.), *Kabayama Aisuke Ō,* p. 333.

27. Ono Sanenobu, *Gensui Kōshaku Ōyama Iwao,* p. 735.

28. Rikugunshō, *Meiji Tennō Godenki Shiryō: Meiji Gunjishi,* Vol. 2, p. 1479; Watanabe, *Nihon Kinsei Gaikō,* p. 374.

29. Yoshimura Michio, "Nichiro Kōwa Mondai no Ichisokumen," *Kokusai Seiji,* No. 3 (1961) 126.

30. Tokutomi, *Kōshaku Yamagata Aritomo Den,* Vol. 3, pp. 678–80.

31. Takakura, *Tanaka Giichi Denki,* Vol. 1, pp. 331–33. Katsura's letter to Itō Hirobumi, dated Mar. 23, 1904, in "Itō (Hirobumi) ke Bunsho" (unpublished material in Kensei Shiryōshitsu, Kokuritsu Kokkai Toshokan.) On Apr. 2, 1905, Genrō Inoue told Hara Takashi of the Seiyūkai: "The Chief of Staff of the Manchurian Army has secretly returned to Tokyo and has informed the government that any further advance by the army is impossible." Hara, *Hari Kei Nikki,* Vol. 2, Apr. 2, 1905 entry, p. 130.

32. Shukuri, *Kodama Gentarō,* p. 630.

33. Rikugunshō, *Meiji Tennō Godenki Shiryō: Meiji Gunjishi,* Vol. 2, p. 1479.

34. Honda, *Tamashii no Gaikō,* p. 160; Yoshimura, "Nichiro Kōwa Mondai no Ichisokumen," *Kokusai Seiji,* No. 3 (1961), p. 126.

35. White, *The Diplomacy of the Russo-Japanese War*, p. 202.

36. Itō Jintarō, *Meiji Rimenshi*, Vol. 2, p. 561.

37. Yoshii Hiroshi, "Nichiro Sensō no Shinten to Kokusai Kankei no Hendō," in Shinobu Seizaburō and Nakayama Jiichi (eds.), *Nichiro Sensō-shi no Kenkyū*, pp. 292–329. Kogiso Teruyuki, "Pōtsumasu Kōwa Kaigi," *ibid.*, pp. 377–98; Tachi, "Meiji Sanjū Shichi Hachinen Sen'eki to Yōroppa oyobi Amerika Kyōkoku no Gaikō," in Tachi (ed.), *Tachi Hakushi Gaikō-shi Ronbunshū*, pp. 483–547; White, *The Diplomacy of the Russo-Japanese War*, pp. 135–206.

38. Gaimushō, *Komura Gaikōshi*, Vol. 2, p. 27.

39. Gaimushō, *Nihon Gaikō Bunsho*, supplementary volume to Vols. 37 and 38, *Nichiro Sensō* (hereafter referred to as *Gaikō Bunsho, Nichiro Sensō*), No. 5, pp. 59–63.

40. Tokutomi, *Kōshaku Katsura Tarō Den*, Vol. 2, pp. 265–67. Katsura's letter to Itō Hirobumi, dated Dec. 5, 1904, "Itō (Hirobumi) ke Bunsho" (unpublished material in Kensei Shiryōshitsu, Kokuritsu Kokkai Toshokan).

41. Ōtsu, *Dai Nihon Kenseishi*, Vol. 6, p. 50; Gaimushō, *Gaikō Bunsho, Nichiro Sensō*, No. 5, p. 60.

42. Gaimushō, *Gaikō Bunsho, Nichiro Sensō*, No. 5, pp. 69–72.

43. Honda, *Tamashii no Gaikō*, p. 141. Shinobu Junpei, *Nidai Gaikō no Shinsō*, p. 299.

44. Gaimushō, *Gaikō Bunsho, Nichiro Sensō*, No. 5, pp. 102–04.

45. Rikugunshō, *Meiji Tennō Godenki Shiryō: Meiji Gunjishi*, Vol. 2, pp. 1482–85.

46. Ono Sanenobu, *Gensui Kōshaku Ōyama Iwao*, p. 736; Rikugunshō, *Meiji Tennō Godenki Shiryō: Meiji Gunjishi*, Vol. 2, pp. 1490–91.

47. Shinobu Junpei, *Nidai Gaikō no Shinsō*, pp. 299–300.

48. Gaimushō, *Gaikō Bunsho, Nichiro Sensō*, No. 5, pp. 105–106. The same Kodama letter included in Ono Sanenobu, *Gensui Kōshaku Ōyama Iwao*, pp. 737–38, is incomplete.

49. Gaimushō, *Komura Gaikōshi*, Vol. 2, p. 29.

50. Yamazaki, *Tennōsei no Kenkyū*, p. 241.

51. Gaimushō, *Gaikō Bunsho, Nichiro Sensō*, No. 5, pp. 104–105.

52. Public demands will be discussed in Chapter 5.

53. Gaimushō, *Gaikō Bunsho, Nichiro Sensō*, No. 5, p. 105. Dennett states that Japanese terms for peace grew as the war continued, but he mistook the peace terms demanded by political parties and such people as Ōkuma for those of the government. See Dennett, *Roosevelt and the Russo-Japanese War*, p. 156, 203–207.

It has been asserted that the Japanese peace terms were greatly influenced by several Yale University professors, who allegedly presented their draft of peace terms to Kaneko Kentarō, and through him to the Japanese government and the Emperor. See Stokes, *Yale, the Portsmouth Treaty and Japan.*

54. Hiratsuka, *Itō Hirobumi Hiroku,* 285–86. As early as February 1905, Itō gave a pessimistic assessment of Japan's financial condition. On Feb. 2, 1905, Itō told naval officers at a party for Admiral Tōgō that the military should not be carried away by Japanese victories and demand severe peace terms. Itō's statement incurred criticism from some officers and newspapermen. Nakayama Yasuaki, *Shimbun Shūsei Meiji Hennenshi,* Vol. 12, p. 375. See also Takahashi Korekiyo, *Takahashi Korekiyo Jiden,* p. 704.

55. Gaimushō, *Komura Gaikōshi,* Vol. 2, p. 39; Tani, *Kimitsu Nichirō Senshi,* p. 645.

Commander of the Fourth Army Nozu, who had often disobeyed Ōyama, was not happy with the news of peace negotiations. He is reported to have said, however, that "since the matter has entered the diplomatic stage, a soldier has nothing to say about it." Gurū Kikin, *Kabayama Aisuke Ō,* pp. 335–37.

56. Gaimushō, *Komura Gaikōshi,* Vol. 2, pp. 39–40.

57. Beale, *Theodore Roosevelt and the Rise of America to World Power,* pp. 253–334.

58. Sakamoto, "Nichiro Sensō ni okeru Kōwa e no Michi," *Nihon Kindai Shigaku,* No. 1 (1958) 48; White, *The Diplomacy of the Russo-Japanese War,* pp. 208–209.

59. Witte, *The Memoirs of Count Witte,* translated and edited by Yarmolinsky, p. 132.

60. Gaimushō, *Gaikō Bunsho, Nichiro Sensō,* No. 5, p. 731.

61. Shumpōkō, *Ito Hirobumi Den,* Vol. 3, p. 647.

62. Gaimushō, *Gaikō Bunsho, Nichiro Sensō,* No. 5, pp. 231–32; Dennett, *Roosevelt and the Russo-Japanese War,* p. 215.

63. Katsura wrote: "This action was taken on the basis of our previous consultation. I hope you understand that this is the reason I did not consult you before taking the action." Tokutomi, *Kōshaku Yamagata Aritomo Den,* Vol. 3, p. 692.

64. President Roosevelt wrote to his close friend Henry Cabot Lodge: "I was amused by the way in which *they* asked me to invite the two belligerents together directly on my own motion and initiative. It reminded me of the request for contributions sent by campaign committees to officeholders wherein they are asked to make a voluntary contribution of ten per cent of their salaries. It showed a certain naïveté on the part of the Japanese." Dennett, *Roosevelt and the Russo-Japanese War,* p. 192.

65. Gaimushō, *Gaikō Bunsho, Nichiro Sensō,* No. 5, pp. 234–35.

66. *Ibid.,* pp. 235–38. For the latest works on Roosevelt's efforts to medi-

ate and his role during the Portsmouth Conference, see White, *The Diplomacy of the Russo-Japanese War*, pp. 227–329; Esthus, *Theodore Roosevelt and Japan*, pp. 1–96.

67. Takeuchi, *War and Diplomacy in the Japanese Empire*, p. 150.

68. Gaimushō, *Gaikō Bunsho, Nichiro Sensō*, No. 5, pp. 238–39.

69. Dennett, *Roosevelt and the Russo-Japanese War*, p. 150.

70. Gaimushō, *Gaikō Bunsho, Nichiro Sensō*, No. 5, pp. 240–62. Kamikawa (ed.), *Nichibei Bunka Kōshōshi*, Vol. 1, pp. 474–77.

71. Ko Hakushaku Yamamoto, *Yamamoto Gonnohyōe Den*, Vol. 1, pp. 736–37.

72. Kiyosawa, *Nihon Gaikōshi*, Vol. 1, p. 330; Gaimushō, *Gaikō Bunsho, Nichiro Sensō*, No. 5, p. 259.

73. Watanabe, *Nihon Kinsei Gaikōshi*, p. 389. Shumpōkō, *Itō Hirobumi Den*, Vol. 3, pp. 648–49. Some years later Itō explained to Hara Takashi why he did not go on the mission, saying that "he had expressed to the Emperor his willingness to go to America, so long as his absence would not cause any anxiety to His Majesty. When the Emperor asked Katsura if he would be able to handle matters without Itō at hand, Katsura revealed himself to be not too confident. The Emperor thereupon ordered Itō not to go to America." Hara, *Hara Kei Nikki*, Vol. 2, Mar. 7, 1909 entry, p. 344.

74. Gaimushō, *Komura Gaikōshi*, Vol. 2, p. 17; Takeuchi, *War and Diplomacy in the Japanese Empire*, p. 151.

75. Ko Hakushaku Yamamoto, *Yamamoto Gonnohyōe Den*, Vol. 1, p. 737. Shumpōkō, *Itō Hirobumi Den*, Vol. 3, p. 649.

76. Kiyosawa, *Nihon Gaikōshi*, Vol. 1, p. 330; Akagi, *Japan's Foreign Relations, 1542–1936: A Short History*, p. 251.

77. Itō Jintarō, *Meiji Rimenshi*, Vol. 2, pp. 463–65.

78. Shimanouchi (ed.), *Tani Kanjō Ikō*, Vol. 2, pp. 289, 670–71. For Tani Kanjō, see Hirao, *Shishaku Tani Tateki Den*.

79. Shimanouchi (ed.), *Tani Kanjō Ikō*, Vol. 2, pp. 670–71.

80. Ko Hakushaku Yamamoto, *Yamamoto Gonnohyōe Den*, Vol. 1, p. 738. On June 7, 1905, Itō had told Tani Kanjō that it would be impossible to force Russia to disarm Vladivostok. Hirao, *Shishaku Tani Tateki Den*, pp. 784–85.

On June 13, 1905, Inoue Kaoru told Hara Takashi of the Seiyūkai: "The question of peace has not been settled yet. From the financial point of view, however, we will need another half billion yen by next March, and should the war continue throughout the coming year, we will need one billion yen. If we look at the situation from the financial point of view, we see that we must conclude peace with reasonable demands." Hara,

Hara Kei Nikki, Vol. 2, June 13, 1905 entry, p. 138. See also Sakatani, *Segai Inoue Kō Den*, Vol. 5, p. 89.

81. Ko Hakushaku Yamamoto, *Yamamoto Gonnohyōe Den*, Vol. 1, p. 737.

82. In addition to sources cited in Chapter I above, there is a biography of Komura in Masumoto, *Shizen no Hito Komura Jutarō.*

83. Lawton, *Empires of the Far East*, Vol. 1, pp. 247–49.

84. Ko Hakushaku Yamamoto, *Yamamoto Gonnohyōe Den*, Vol. 1, p. 738; Tani, *Kimitsu Nichiro Senshi*, pp. 641–42. Kamikawa, *Nichibei Bunka Kōshōshi*, p. 474.

Prime Minister Katsura held a party for the Japanese delegation at his official residence. The four Genrō, Itō, Yamagata, Matsukata, and Inoue, and all the cabinet ministers were present. At the dinner table one of the Genrō started talking proudly of his diplomatic success. Suddenly the usually quiet Komura remarked teasingly, "But it seems to me that people from the major clans are not good at wartime diplomacy, for they always have somebody who is not from any of these clans handle it." The quick-witted Katsura barely managed to dispel the awkward atmosphere that swept the room by quickly changing the subject. Honda, *Tamashii no Gaikō*, pp. 169–70.

85. Watanabe, *Nihon Kinsei Gaikōshi*, p. 392; Gaimushō, *Komura Gaikōshi*, Vol. 2, p. 40. As he had promised, Itō met Komura at Yokohama on Oct. 16, 1905. *Ibid.*, p. 156.

86. Nakayama Yasuaki, *Shimbun Shūsei Meiji Hennenshi*, Vol. 12, p. 452.

87. Itō Masanori, *Gunbatsu Kōbōshi*, Vol. 1, p. 384. The Emperor also composed the following poem for the departing Japanese delegation:

Senbetsu	*Farewell*
Sakazuki o Agetezo Iwau	With a toast, I celebrate,
Totsukuni ni	That the people going abroad
Tabiyuku Hito no	Will stay in good health.
Tsutsu ga nakareto.	

Sasaki, *Meiji Tennō Gyoshū Kinkai*, p. 276.

88. Gaimushō, *Gaikō Bunsho, Nichiro Senso*, No. 5, pp. 240–41.

89. Nakayama Yasuaki, *Shimbun Shūsei Meiji Hennenshi*, Vol. 12, p. 435; *Takeuchi, War and Diplomacy in the Japanese Empire*, p. 151.

90. Gaimushō, *Komura Gaikōshi*, Vol. 2, pp. 33–34; Tani, *Kimitsu Nichiro Senshi*, pp. 643–46.

91. Gaimushō, *Gaikō Bunsho, Nichiro Senso*, No. 5, pp. 106–107.

92. White, *The Diplomacy of the Russo-Japanese War*, p. 249.

Chapter 5. The People and the War

1. Watanabe, *Nihon Kinsei Gaikōshi*, pp. 391–92. Some of those who were sufficiently informed to know of Kodama's secret trip to Tokyo on Mar. 28, 1905, believed that the real objective of the trip was to express the army's protest against the peace movement led by some politicians. (Hiratsuka, *Itō Hirobumi Hiroku*, p. 238.) The well-informed Tani Kanjō visited Itō on June 7, 1905, but he had no inkling of the coming Roosevelt mediation effort. (Shimanouchi, *Tani Kanjō Ikō*, Vol. 2, p. 289.) Vice-Chief of Staff Nagaoka, not quite certain who was the real initiator of the mediation, asked Itō for details about the events that had lead to the mediation. According to Nagaoka, Itō simply replied, "It is not important who initiated the mediation!" (Shukuri, *Kodama Gentarō*, p. 631.)

2. Tokutomi, *Sohō Jiden*, p. 396. Lancelot Lawton wrote: "The object of the government in endeavouring to observe secrecy in regard to certain matters was not, always, so much to deprive the Russians of information as to keep the truth back from the masses." Lawton, *Empires of the Far East*, Vol. 1, p. 348.

3. In a speech made at the Kenseihontō's general assembly on Nov. 26, 1904, party president Ōkuma Shigenobu warned the people against being unduly influenced by the wartime press: "The world is still wondering which country will be the final victor in this war. What will end that doubt is our people's endurance and spirit of self-denial. It is a historical truth that those who excessively belittle the enemy lose. When the people indulge themselves in slighting the enemy, unexpected calamities may come upon them. I am afraid that our newspapers, particularly the government organs, have not been prudent enough in this regard. The people should continue their efforts for the final victory, patiently and steadfastly, without being misled by the senseless national pride of the government newspapers." Ichijima (ed.), *Ōkumakō Hachijūgonen Shi*, Vol. 2, pp. 431–32.

Uchimura Kanzō also criticized the wartime newspapers: "No newspaper reported the truth. They all covered up any unfavorable news about Japan and reported small events unfavorable to the enemy in the most exaggerated way. . . . They only tried to fan the people's fighting spirit. Our wartime newspapers ignored the truth and sought only victory. I am convinced that during the 20 months of war, there was no newspaper worthy of the name in Japan. Not one reported the truth upon which we could fairly have based our judgment of the progress of the war." Uchimura, *Uchimura Kanzō Zenshū*, Vol. 14, pp. 387–88.

On government control of domestic newspapers, see Ono Hideo, *Nihon*

Shimbun Hattatsushi, p. 290; Yamamoto Fumio, *Nihon Shimbunshi,* pp. 210–11; Asahi Shimbun (ed.), *Murayama Ryūhei Den,* pp. 409–19; Treat, *Diplomatic Relations between the United States and Japan: 1895–1905,* p. 196; Baelz, *Awakening Japan: The Diary of a German Doctor: Erwin Baelz,* p. 241.

4. On control of foreign correspondents, see Treat, *Diplomatic Relations between the United States and Japan: 1895–1905,* pp. 212–13; and Baelz, *Awakening Japan: The Diary of a German Doctor: Erwin Baelz,* pp. 271, 281–83, 289–91. Government censorship of foreign correspondents was so strict that it created among them a strong animosity and led to adverse effects. At one point, the treatment of foreign correspondents by the Manchurian Army caused such a storm of worldwide criticism that Chief of General Staff Kodama was compelled to present a letter of resignation in spite of the critical military situation. He remained in his position by imperial order, however. Shukuri, *Kodama Gentarō,* pp. 581–83.

Thomas F. Millard presents a convincing argument that a pro-Japanese public opinion was fostered by the British and American press during the war, and that the news reaching the Japanese people from these countries accorded with the government's intentions. He goes so far as to state that Russian "censorship was more liberal than the Japanese." Millard, "The Fruits of Japan's Victory," *Scribner's Magazine,* No. 2 (August 1905), 240–51.

5. Griscom, *Diplomatically Speaking,* p. 249. See also Hohenberg, *Foreign Correspondence: The Great Reporters and Their Times,* pp. 178–85. Gaimushō (ed.), *Gaikō Bunsho, Nichiro Sensō,* No. 3, pp. 109–46.

6. Ogawa, *Expenditures of the Russo-Japanese War,* p. 107.

7. Shinobu Seizaburō, *Taishō Seijishi,* Vol. 1, p. 92.

8. Ogawa, *Expenditures of the Russo-Japanese War,* p. 69. Takahashi Korekiyo, the financial commissioner responsible for raising foreign loans during the war, gives in his memoirs details of Japanese efforts to obtain foreign loans; see Takahashi Korekiyo, *Takahashi Korekiyo Jiden,* pp. 641–793. Also, Gaimushō, *Nihon Gaikō Bunsho,* Vol. 37, No. 2, pp. 124–99; and Vol. 38, No. 2, pp. 46–101; Gamaike Satoshi, "Nichiro Sensō o Meguru Gaisai Mondai," in Shinobu Seizaburō and Nakayama Jiichi (eds.), *Nichiro Sensōshi no Kenkyū,* pp. 330–53.

9. Ogawa, *Expenditures of the Russo-Japanese War,* p. 69.

10. Koyama and Asada, *Nihon Teikokushugi Shi,* Vol. 1, p. 169.

11. Ōuchi Hyōe, "Keizai," in Yanaihara (ed.), *Gendai Nihon Shōshi,* Vol. 1, p. 187; Kobayashi, *War and Armament Taxes of Japan,* pp. 29–37; Ogawa, *Expenditures of the Russo-Japanese War,* pp. 51–101.

12. Suzuki Takeo, *Zaiseishi*, p. 91. In the first bond issue, for 100 million yen, on Feb. 19, 1904, the total subscription amounted to as much as 452.11 million yen. Fujimura Michio, "Sensō to Minshū," Shinobu Seizaburō and Nakayama Jiichi (eds.), *Nichiro Sensōshi no Kenkyū*, p. 277.

13. Ono Sanenobu, *Gensui Kōshaku Ōyama Iwao*, p. 752. Losses in the Russo-Japanese War were as follows:

Cause	Officers	Non-Commissioned Officers and Enlisted Men	Civilians in the Army and Navy	Total
Killed in battle	1926	58,105	52	60,083
Died from disease	278	21,197	404	21,879
Dismissed from service	71	29,367	——	29,438
Total	2275	108,669	456	111,400

See Ogawa, *Expenditures of the Russo-Japanese War*, pp. 29, 113–14.

14. Weale, *The Re-Shaping of the Far East*, Vol. 1, p. 423.

15. Fujimura Michio, "Sensō to Minshū," Shinobu Seizaburō and Nakayama Jiichi (eds.), *Nichiro Sensōshi no Kenkyū*, pp. 276–82; Lawton, *Empires of the Far East*, Vol. 1, p. 243.

16. Nōshōmushō, *Meiji Sanjū Hachinen no Chingin ni oyoboseshi Sensō no Eikyō*, pp. 4–7. For a detailed study of wage and price fluctuations during the war, see: Nōshōmushō, *Meiji Sanjū Shichinen no Chingin ni oyoboseshi Sensō no Eikyō*; *Meiji Sanjū Shichinen no Bukka ni oyoboseshi Sensō no Eikyō* and *Meiji Sanjū Hachinen no Bukka ni oyoboseshi Sensō no Eikyō*. All three are reprinted in Meiji Shiryō Sōsho Kankōkai (ed.), *Meiji Bunka Shiryō Sōsho*, Vol. 2, pp. 223–320.

On July 28, 1904, Baelz recorded in his diary: "In Tokyo foodstuffs, and especially fish, have risen in price from 20 to 60 per cent, because fishermen will no longer venture out to sea." Baelz, *Awakening Japan: The Diary of a German Doctor: Erwin Baelz*, p. 292.

17. Ogawa, *Expenditures of the Russo-Japanese War*, pp. 244–48; Fujimura Michio, "Sensō to Minshū," Shinobu Seizaburō and Nakayama Jiichi (eds.), *Nichiro Sensōshi no Kenkyū*, pp. 280–81.

18. Ogawa writes: "It is said that army and navy contractors did not profit as greatly in the war with Russia as in the war with China, but the Mitsui Bussan Kaisha, the Mitsubishi Gōshi Kaisha, the Fujita-Gumi, the Ōkura firm of canned-goods contractors, and the Takata Shokai (which supplied the navy with goods) were reported to head the list of those who made stupendous fortunes through the war. Those engaged in coal mining, shipping, and sea transportation also amassed large sums of money." Ogawa,

Expenditures of the Russo-Japanese War, p. 249. See also Fujimura Michio, "Sensō to Minshū," Shinobu Seizaburō and Nakayama Jiichi (eds.), *Nichiro Sensōshi no Kenkyū*, pp. 284–86.

19. Kokuryūkai, *Tōa Senkaku Shishi Kiden*, Vol. 1, pp. 739–859; Nakayama Yasuaki, *Shimbun Shūsei Meiji Hennenshi*, Vol. 12, pp. 235, 240, 250.

20. Tomizu, *Zoku Kaikoroku*, pp. 4–13. For Tomizu's wartime writings, see *ibid.*, pp. 443–851.

21. *Ibid.*, pp. 30–108. Also *Gaikō Jihō*, No. 83 (Sept. 19, 1904) 45–68. Because Tomizu urged that Japan extend her control as far as Lake Baikal, the Japanese press nicknamed him Baikal Hakase (Dr. Baikal).

Ariga Nagao, a well-known professor of international law at Tokyo Imperial University asserted that after the war Japan should at least obtain a mandate over part of Manchuria. Ariga Nagao, *Manshū Inin Tōchi Ron*.

22. A typical wartime picture magazine was Kunikida (ed.), *Senji Gahō*. For a discussion of wartime literature, see Homma, *Zoku Meiji Bungakushi*, Vol. 3, pp. 1–162; Furukawa, "Meiji Bungaku to Shakai I: Nichiro Sensō," *Kenkyū Ronshū*, No. 14, Part I (March 1965) 34–45.

Based on his well-known theories of social Darwinism, Katō Hiroyuki publicly predicted that Japan would win a complete victory. Katō Hiroyuki, *Shinkagaku yori Kansatsu shitaru Nichiro no Unmei*.

23. See Uehara Etsujirō, *Nihon Minken Hattatsushi*, Vol. 1, pp. 300–304; Miyake, *Dōjidaishi*, Vol. 3, pp. 327–28.

24. Kudō, *Meiji Kenseishi*, p. 779.

25. Ōtsu, *Dai Nihon Kenseishi*, Vol. 5, pp. 823–26.

26. Nakayama Yasuaki, *Shimbun Shūsei Meiji Hennenshi*, Vol. 12, pp. 217–18.

27. Ōtsu, *Dai Nihon Kenseishi*, Vol. 5, pp. 855–56.

28. Takeuchi, *War and Diplomacy in the Japanese Empire*, p. 49; Takahashi Seigo, *Seiji Kagaku Genron*, pp. 441–42.

29. Dai Nihon (ed.), *Dai Nihon Teikoku Gikaishi*, Vol. 6, pp. 185–86, 211–14 (the twenty-first Diet session); Takeuchi, *War and Diplomacy in the Japanese Empire*, p. 147.

30. Takeuchi, *War and Diplomacy in the Japanese Empire*, p. 148.

31. Before the twentieth Diet session, the government originally planned to obtain wartime appropriation through an imperial ordinance based on Article 70 of the constitution, which stipulated: "When the Imperial Diet cannot be convoked, owing to the external or internal condition of the country, in case of urgent need for the maintenance of public safety, the Government may take all necessary financial measures, by means of an Imperial Ordinance. . . ." This plan, however, was put aside, for the govern-

ment thought it desirable to maintain a show of unity in the war effort by obtaining the cooperation of the political parties. Sakatani, *Segai Inoue Kō Den*, Vol. 5, pp. 54–57.

32. Masumi, *Nihon Seitō Shiron*, Vol. 2, pp. 335–455.

According to the Seiyūkai by-laws of Sept. 15, 1900, the top level of the party structure was to consist of a president (*sōsai*) an unspecified number of general affairs directors (*sōmuiin*), a party secretary (*kanjichō*), and an unspecified number of executive secretaries (*kanji*). The president was to decide the number of general affairs directors and executive secretaries and to select the personnel for all posts. He was also empowered to set up *ad hoc* committees. Kobayashi Yūgo, *Rikken Seiyūkaishi*, Vol. 1, p. 37.

33. Maeda, *Hara Takashi Den*, Vol. 2, p. 50.

34. Hara, *Hara Kei Nikki*, Vol. 2, July 14, 1903 entry, pp. 71–72.

35. Maeda, *Hara Takashi*, p. 129. This is a shorter, revised edition of Maeda's biography of Hara, *Hara Takashi Den*. In writing this new edition, Maeda used Hara's diary, which was made public in 1950. The older edition, however, contains much valuable information that is not superseded by the new edition. See also Kyoto (ed.), *Nihon Kindaishi Jiten*, p. 570.

36. Maeda, *Hara Takashi*, p. 129. Although in later years Hara became a leading party politician, his diary records that, immediately after he joined the Seiyūkai, he requested Itō Hirobumi to recommend him for a seat in the House of Peers. Hara, *Hara Kei Nikki*, Vol. 1, Oct. 15, 1900 entry, p. 301.

37. Hara, *Hara Kei Nikki*, Vol. 2, Aug. 11, 1902 entry, p. 22.

38. The leaders of the Kenseihontō cajoled their opposition into a compromise with the following meaningless resolution: "Our party will cooperate not only with the Seiyūkai but with anyone, regardless of his party affiliation, who shares our party's view." Ōtsu, *Dai Nihon Kenseishi*, Vol. 5, pp. 610–17. See also Kudō, *Teikoku Gikaishi*, Vol. 3, pp. 222–23; Kobayashi Yūgo, *Rikken Seiyūkaishi*, Vol. 2, pp. 48–54.

39. The election results were as follows:

Parties	20th Diet Session	21st Diet Session
Rikken Seiyūkai	130	139
Kenseihontō	90	95
Teikokutō	19	19
Kōshin Kurabu	39	27
Jiyūto	18	19
Mumei Kurabu	24	—
Independents	58	35
Dōkō Kai	—	28
Yūshi Kai	—	17

Tōyama and Adachi, *Kindai Nihon Seijishi Hikkei*, p. 123.

40. Maeda, *Hara Takashi Den,* Vol. 1, pp. 257–58. On the difficulties Hara encountered as a "non-clan" political aspirant, see Mitani, *Nihon Seitō-seiji no Keisei: Hara Takashi no Seiji Shidō no Tenkai,* pp. 3–69. See also Imai Seiichi, "Seiji Shidōsha no Shisōteki Yakuwari," in Kuno and Sumiya (eds.), *Kindai Nihon Shishōshi Kōza,* Vol. 5, pp. 68–73.

Hattori, *Meiji no Seijika Tachi: Hara Takashi ni tsuranaru Hitobito,* Vols. 1 and 2. Hattori states, "Hara Takashi was greater than any of his political rivals or friends." *Ibid.,* Vol. 1, p. 31.

Oka, "Gaikenteki Rikkensei ni okeru Seitō: Seitō Seijika to shite no Hara Takashi," *Shisō,* No. 333 (March 1952) 32–37.

Hara's ardent desire for power is vividly revealed in an entry in his diary recording a conversation with Itō Hirobumi on June 6, 1903: "When Itō preached to me that one should not be too eager to grasp the reins of power, I told him, 'You may have no particular desire now, since you have already done many great things. But people like myself feel differently. Moreover, you are gradually entering into the last stage of your life. Unless you train your successor, some day it [the Seiyūkai] will fall apart. . . .' " Hara, *Hara Kei Nikki,* Vol. 2, June 16, 1903 entry, p. 68.

41. We have relied on Hara's diary for this description of Hara's political maneuverings, for it seems to be the only primary source on the subject. No information in biographies of people directly connected with this topic was found. The Katsura autobiography in the collection of the Japanese Diet Library (Kensei Shiryōshitsu) might shed some light. However, Professor Masumi Junnosuke, who recently discussed it in his *Nihon Seitō Shiron,* seems to have found no pertinent information in the Katsura material, although he has used it extensively in connection with other topics. The Hara diary is the only primary source Masumi used.

Recently a good study of this subject appeared in English: Najita, *Hara Kei in the Politics of Compromise, 1905–1915.* See especially the first two chapters.

42. Tanaka (ed.), *Hara Takashi Zenshū,* Vol. 1, pp. 1081–89.

43. Hara, *Hara Kei Nikki,* Vol. 2, Feb. 11, 1904 entry, p. 90.

44. *Ibid.,* Vol. 2, Feb. 26, 1904 entry, p. 92.

45. *Ibid.,* Vol. 2, July 26, 1904 entry, p. 106; Oct. 15, 1904 entry, p. 112. *Taiyō,* 10–14 (November 1904) 90. Also Nakayama Yasuaki, *Shimbun Shūsei Meiji Hennenshi,* Vol. 12, p. 322.

46. Hara, *Hara Kei Nikki,* Vol. 2, Nov. 11, 1904 entry, p. 114; Kudō, *Teikoku Gikaishi,* Vol. 3, pp. 280, 314–17; Tsukada, *Rikken Minseitōshi,* Vol. 1, p. 135; Kobayashi, *Rikken Seiyūkaishi,* Vol. 2, pp. 145–46.

47. Kobayashi, *Rikken Seiyūkaishi,* Vol. 2, pp. 158–98; Kudō, *Teikoku Gikaishi,* Vol. 3, pp. 302–304.

48. Kobayashi, *Rikken Seiyūkaishi*, Vol. 2, pp. 158–65, 178–91. Hara, *Hara Kei Nikki*, Vol. 2, Nov. 26, 1904 entry, p. 116.

49. Tsukada, *Rikken Minseitōshi*, Vol. 1, pp. 135–36. Kudō, *Teikoku Gikaishi*, Vol. 3, p. 304.

50. Ōtsu, *Dai Nihon Kenseishi*, Vol. 5, p. 824. Kudō, *Teikoku Gikaishi*, Vol. 3, p. 303.

51. "Itō (Hirobumi) ke Bunsho." (Unpublished material.)

52. Tokutomi, *Kōshaku Matsukata Masayoshi Den*, Vol. 2, pp. 884–85; Hara, *Hara Kei Nikki*, Vol. 2, entries for Feb. 25, 1904, p. 91; Mar. 6, 1904, p. 93; May 16, 1904, p. 99; Sept. 30, 1904, p. 110; Nov. 7, 1904, p. 113.

It is widely believed that Hara was close to Inoue because Mrs. Hara was the daughter of Inoue's wife from a previous marriage. (Masumi, *Nihon Seitō Shiron*, Vol. 2, p. 361.) This, however, contradicts the statement in Hara's diary: "I learned from the wife of Ijūin Kanetsune of Tokyo that my wife Sadako's [real] mother, who married a man named Imamura, an engineer in the government printing bureau, after her divorce from the Nakai family, died of some sickness." Hara, *Hara Kei Nikki*, Vol. 1, Dec. 5, 1887 entry, pp. 121–22.

53. It seems that Ōishi was once willing to promote a Kenseihontō alliance with the Seiyūkai, even if it meant forcing Ōkuma to retire as party president. Hara, *Hara Kei Nikki*, Vol. 2, July 16, 1903 entry, p. 72. During the war the Ōishi group planned to send Ōkuma as an adviser to Korea, as Japan's initial step toward making the country a Japanese protectorate. *Ibid.*, Nov. 16, 1904 entry, p. 115.

54. For Ōkuma's wartime speeches and the expansive terms of peace he demanded, see Takei, *Ōkuma Haku Jikyokudan*.

55. Hara, *Hara Kei Nikki*, Vol. 2, Dec. 9, 1904 entry, p. 119; Kudō, *Teikoku Gikaishi*, Vol. 3, p. 314.

56. Hara, *Hara Kei Nikki*, Vol. 2, Dec. 6, 1904 entry, p. 117.

57. *Ibid.*, Dec. 7, 1904 entry, p. 117.

58. *Ibid.*, Dec. 8, 1904 entry, pp. 117–19.

59. *Ibid.*, Dec. 9, 1904 entry, pp. 119–20. Kudō, *Teikoku Gikaishi*, Vol. 3, pp. 315–17.

60. Baelz, *Awakening Japan: The Diary of a German Doctor: Erwin Baelz*, p. 330.

61. Scalapino, *Democracy and the Party Movement in Prewar Japan: The Failure of the First Attempt*, p. 187. See also Ōtsu, *Dai Nihon Kenseishi*, Vol. 5, pp. 855–56; Uehara, *Nihon Minken Hattatsushi*, Vol. 1, pp. 301–304. The sequence and consequences of this Katsura-Hara deal will be further discussed in Chapter 7.

62. Rōdō (ed.), *Shūkan Heimin Shimbun*, Vol. 1, p. 163.

63. *Ibid.*, Vol. 2, p. 427.

64. Rōdō (ed.), *Chokugen;* Sumiya, "Heimin Shimbun to Sono Kōzo-kushi," *Shisō*, No. 461 (November 1962) 136–41; Nishida Taketoshi, "Heimin Shimbun to Sono Jidai," *Bungaku*, 21, No. 10 (1953) 976–82.

65. Maruyama, "Chūsei to Hangyaku," *Kindai Nihon Shisōshi Kōza*, Vol. 6, p. 445.

66. Myōjō (ed.), *Myōjō*, pp. 51–52. A complete translation of Yosano Akiko's poem can be found in Maruyama, *Thought and Behavior in Modern Japanese Politics*, edited by Ivan Morris, pp. 154–56.

67. Homma, *Zoku Meiji Bungakushi*, Vol. 3, p. 46. Ōtsuka Naoko, widely regarded as a heroine of the anti-war forces, composed the vehemently chauvinistic "Shingeki no uta" (A song for march). *Taiyō*, 10, No. 8 (June 1904).

68. Nakamura Sadako, "Pōtsumasu Kaigiki ni okeru Nihon Gaikō ni taisuru Yoron," *Seishin Joshidaigaku Ronsō*, 7 (December 1955) 2.

69. This trend was encouraged by the growing enthusiasm of business-men for the war as their economic activities started showing marked improvement in the middle stages of the war. See Ogawa, *Expenditures of the Russo-Japanese War*, pp. 249, 251; Fujimura Michio, "Sensō to Min-shū," Shinobu Seizaburō and Nakayama Jiichi (eds.), *Nichiro Sensōshi no Kenkyū*, p. 288.

70. Nakayama Yasuaki, *Shimbun Shūsei Meiji Hennenshi*, Vol. 12, p. 434.

71. The *Tokyo Nichi-nichi Shimbun* was established in 1872. It was a leading pro-government newspaper, being traditionally the mouthpiece of the Chōshū clan. In 1904, the president of the newspaper was Itō Miyoji, a protégé of Genrō Itō Hirobumi. The newspaper, as we observed earlier, took a noncommittal attitude toward the war until its outbreak, a reflection, of course, of the attitude of Itō Hirobumi, who was most disinclined toward the war. During the war, Katō Takaaki often met with Itō Miyoji for political discussions. They were soon united in a common animosity toward Katsura. Katō, who found that the *Tokyo Nichi-nichi Shimbun* was worth from 20 to 30 political followers, bought it from Itō Miyoji on Oct. 11, 1904, for 100,000 yen, paying for it with money from the Mitsubishi family of his wife. Thereafter Katō used the newspaper to promote his political cause. His position toward the government changed gradually from one of support or encouragement to one of opposition as he began to perceive that the days of the Katsura Cabinet were numbered. See Itō Masanori (ed.), *Katō Takaaki*, Vol. 1, pp. 517–20, 538–43.

72. Kudō, *Meiji Kenseishi*, p. 823. Takeuchi, *War and Diplomacy in*

the Japanese Empire, p. 150; Ōtsu, *Dai Nihon Kenseishi*, Vol. 6, p. 144. Nakamura Sadako, "Pōtsumasu Kaigiki ni okeru Nihon Gaikō ni taisuru Yoron," *Seishin Joshidaigaku Ronsō*, 7 (December 1955), 13.

73. *Japan Weekly Mail*, June 17, 1905, pp. 2, 3, 5, 6; Nakamura Sadako, "Pōtsumasu Kaigiki ni okeru Nihon Gaikō ni taisuru Yoron," *Seishin Joshidaigaku Ronsō*, 7 (December 1955) 13.

74. Nakamura Sadako, "Pōtsumasu Kaigiki ni okeru Nihon Gaikō ni taisuru Yoron," *Seishin Joshidaigaku Ronsō*, 7 (December 1955) 14. *Taiyō* Vol. 11, No. 11 (August 1905) 33–35.

75. Tomizu, *Zoku Kaikoroku*, pp. 262–72. Tomizu's suspension later developed into a major dispute between the government and university professors, who regarded the suspension as an interference with academic freedom. The latter finally won the battle when they forced the Minister of Education to resign over the resulting controversy. *Ibid.*, pp. 371–442. Ishida Takeshi, *Meiji Seiji Shisōshi Kenkyū*, pp. 250–72.

76. A majority of the people apparently were disappointed by the appointment of Komura as chief plenipotentiary. See Nakayama Gisuke, *Kōno Banshū Den*, Vol. 2, p. 660.

When Kōno Hironaka visited Itō to urge him to go on the mission, Itō said: "Nobody else in the government has such deep feelings on this matter as you. They have decided to send Komura, because they consider me a weak diplomatist." *Ibid.*, Vol. 2, pp 657–60. There were some who believed that the first peace negotiations would end in failure, so the government kept Itō at home in order to be able to use him for the second round of negotiations. Gaimushō, *Gaikō Bunsho, Nichiro Sensō*, No. 5, p. 785.

Ōtsu Jun'ichirō, one-time Diet member and author of the ten-volume study of Japanese constitutional political history, goes so far as to say: "If Itō had gone, the people would have been somewhat tolerant even if the results of the peace negotiations had turned out to be unsatisfactory to them. This was not the case with Komura." Ōtsu, *Dai Nihon Kenseishi*, Vol. 6, p. 64.

President Roosevelt reportedly expressed his satisfaction with Komura's appointment as the Japanese plenipotentiary, while regretting the fact that Itō had not come. Shinobu Junpei, *Nidai Gaikō no Shinsō*, p. 355; Kamikawa, *Nichibei Bunka Kōshōshi*, Vol. 1, p. 474. See also Ueda, "Nichiro Sensō to Rūzuberuto," *Kindai Nihon Gaikōshi no Kenkyū*, p. 150; *Tōyō Keizai Shimpō*, No. 345 (July 5, 1905) 2–4.

77. See Nakamura Sadako, "Pōtsumasu Kaigiki ni okeru Nihon Gaikō ni taisuru Yoron," *Seishin Joshidaigaku Ronsō*, 7 (December 1955), p. 17; *Tōyō Keizai Shimpō*, No. 344 (June 5, 1905) 2–4; No. 345 (July 5, 1905) 6–7; No. 346 (July 15, 1905) 2–4; No. 347 (July 25, 1905) 2–4.

"The more humble people upon whom the burden of taxation had fallen heavily, and many of whom had suffered bereavements as a result of the war, were inclined to be indifferent until told by bellicose agitators that the absence of an indemnity would inevitably lead to the perpetuation, if not the heavy increase, of special taxation and might conceivably threaten the nation with bankruptcy. The more ignorant among the masses seemed to imagine that an indemnity meant a general share out among the victorious people, and that they would not only receive back all that they had paid in the form of taxation, but in addition for their patriotic sacrifice." Lawton, *Empires of the Far East,* Vol. 1, p. 255.

78. Fujimura Michio, "Hikōwa Undō," Shinobu Seizaburō and Nakayama Jiichi (eds.), *Nichiro Sensōshi no Kenkyū,* p. 423.

79. Hagino (ed.), *Sonoda Kōkichi Den,* pp. 251–53; *Japan Weekly Mail,* June 17, 1905, p. 3.

80. *Japan Weekly Mail,* June 17, 1905, p. 14.

81. *Nihon Bengoshi Kyōkai Rokuji,* No. 88 (June 28, 1905) 2–11. The society was once disbanded, but it became active again with the opening of the negotiations.

82. Tomizu, *Zoku Kaikoroku,* pp. 254–56.

83. Ōtsu, *Dai Nihon Kenseishi,* Vol. 6, p. 146. For a detailed discussion, see Chapter 7 below.

84. Kobayashi, *Rikken Seiyūkaishi,* Vol. 2, pp. 242–43; Ōtsu, *Dai Nihon Kenseishi,* Vol. 6, p. 147. The purpose of the war was specified in the Imperial Declaration of War as being to ensure the security of Japanese interests by preserving the integrity of Korea and by driving Russia out of Manchuria. Gaimushō, *Gaikō Bunsho, Nichiro Sensō,* No. 5, pp. 142–45.

85. Tsukada, *Rikken Minseitōshi,* Vol. 1, p. 140; Ōtsu, *Dai Nihon Kenseishi,* Vol. 6, p. 147.

86. Some regarded one or one and a half billion yen as a sufficient indemnity, although most demanded such equivalents as commercial treaties in addition. Some demanded five billion yen, believing that a large indemnity would slow down Russian recovery and weaken the threat of the Russian naval base at Vladivostok. Nakamura Sadako, "Pōtsumasu Kaigiki ni okeru Nihon Gaikō ni taisuru Yoron," *Seishin Joshidaigaku Ronsō,* 7 (December 1955) 17. See also Gaimushō, *Gaikō Bunsho, Nichiro Sensō,* No. 5, pp. 796–97; Nakayama Jiichi, "Gaikō Kakumei ni okeru Furansu no Sekkyokuteki Yakuwari," *Nagoya Daigaku Bungakubu Kenkyū Ronshū,* 14 (History 5, 1956) 65.

87. Some demanded territory east of the Baikal and in Heilungkiang province. Ōtsu, *Dai Nihon Kenseishi,* Vol. 6, p. 146. For a representative

exposition of such sweeping demands, see Nishi, *Nichiro Senkyoku Kōwashigi*.

88. Ōtsu, *Dai Nihon Kenseishi*, Vol. 6. p. 146; Gaimushō, *Gaikō Bunsho, Nichiro Sensō*, No. 5, pp. 776–802. On Jan. 28, 1905, Baelz recorded the following in his diary: "The Lawyers' Society of Japan appointed a subcommittee to report on the Manchurian question from the outlook of international law. At the next general meeting of the society, the subcommittee will propose the following motion: 'In the interest of universal peace and for the greater safety of China proper, the Chinese empire should unconditionally cede the sovereignty of Manchuria to Japan.' " Baezl, *Awakening Japan: The Diary of a German Doctor: Erwin Baelz*, p. 341.

89. Nakamura Sadako, "Pōtsumasu Kaigiki ni okeru Nihon Gaikō ni taisuru Yoron," *Seishin Joshidaigaku Ronsō*, 7 (December 1955), p. 18.

90. An outstanding example was Shimanouchi (ed.), *Tani Kanjō Ikō*, Vol. 2, p. 671.

91. Nakayama Yasuaki, *Shimbun Shūsei Meiji Hennenshi*, Vol. 12, p. 457. Note that Komura was accompanied by four known members of the pro-war government officials' group, the Kogetsukai: Yamaza Enjirō, Honda Kumatarō, Tachibana Koichirō, and Ochiai Kentarō (who was not mentioned in the newspaper article).

92. Lawton, *Empires of the Far East*, Vol. 1, p. 248.

93. Gaimushō, *Komura Gaikōshi*, Vol. 2, p. 41.

94. Kiyosawa, *Nihon Gaikōshi*, Vol. 1, p. 331. Watanabe, *Nihon Kinsei Gaikōshi*, p. 392. Shidehara Kijūrō, then chief of the telegram section of the Ministry of Foreign Affairs, reported that the departing Komura whispered to him with a smile, "When I return, these people will turn into unruly mobs that will attack me with mud pies or pistols. So I had better enjoy their 'banzai' now." Shidehara, *Gaikō Gojūnen*, p. 21.

95. Hara, *Hara Kei Nikki*, Vol. 2, Apr. 16, 1905 entry, p. 131.

96. Tokutomi, *Sohō Jiden*, p. 396.

97. Tokutomi, *Kōshaku Katsura Tarō Den*, Vol. 2, p. 295, and *Kōshaku Yamagata Aritomo Den*, Vol. 3, p. 707. Of course, Japanese government leaders, under the Meiji Constitution, considered themselves accountable for their actions only to the throne.

Chapter 6. The Portsmouth Conference

1. For the official Japanese record of the proceedings of the peace negotiations, see Gaimushō, *Gaikō Bunsho, Nichiro Sensō*, No. 5, pp. 390–538. For details of the negotiations, see Esthus, *Theodore Roosevelt and Japan*,

pp. 76–86; White, *The Diplomacy of the Russo-Japanese War*, pp. 227–309; Long, "The Diplomacy of the Portsmouth Conference, 1905" (unpublished Master's essay, Columbia University, 1965).

2. Shinobu Junpei, *Nidai Gaikō no Shinsō*, p. 419; Akagi, *Japan's Foreign Relations, 1542–1936: A Short History*, p. 257.

3. The 12 Japanese demands were as follows:

1) Russia must acknowledge that Japan possesses paramount political, military, and economic interests in Korea and must engage not to obstruct or interfere with any measures of guidance, protection, or control that Japan finds it necessary to take in Korea.

2) Russia must evacuate Manchuria within a specified period and must relinquish all territorial advantages, all rights of occupation, and all preferential and exclusive concessions and franchises in the region that impair Chinese sovereignty or are inconsistent with the principle of equal opportunity.

3) Japan must restore Manchuria to China, with the exception of the leased territories subject to guarantees of reform and improved administration.

4) Japan and Russia must reciprocally engage not to obstruct any general measures taken by China and affecting all countries for the development of the commerce and industries of Manchuria.

5) Russia must cede to Japan Sakhalin and adjacent islands and all public works and properties thereon.

6) Russia must transfer and assign to Japan the leases on Port Arthur, Talien, and adjacent territory and territorial waters, together with all rights, privileges, and concessions connected with or forming part of such leases, as well as all public works and properties.

7) Russia must transfer and assign to Japan the railway between Harbin and Port Arthur and all its branches, together with all rights, privileges, and properties appertaining thereto, as well as coal mines belonging to, or worked for, the benefit of the railway.

8) Russia may retain and use the trans-Manchuria railway subject to the condition that the same be employed exclusively for commercial and industrial purposes.

9) Russia must reimburse to Japan the actual expenses of war, the time and method of payment and the amount to be mutually agreed upon. [Upon the advice of President Roosevelt, "indemnity" was changed to "reimbursement" of war expenses.]

10) Russia must surrender to Japan as lawful prizes all vessels of war that have sought asylum and were interned in neutral ports in consequence of injuries received in battle.

11) Russia must agree to limit her naval strength in the Far East.

12) Russia must grant to Japanese subjects full fishing rights along the coasts and the bays, harbors, inlets, and rivers of her possessions in the Japan, Okhotsk, and Bering seas.

Akagi, *Japan's Foreign Relations, 1542–1936: A Short History,* pp. 255–56.

4. Kogiso, "Pōtsumasu Kōwa Kaigi," Shinobu Seizaburō and Nakayama Jiichi (eds.), *Nichiro Sensōshi no Kenkyū,* pp. 396, 401.

5. Gaimushō, *Gaikō Bunsho, Nichiro Sensō,* No. 5, p. 305; and *Komura Gaikōshi,* Vol. 2, p. 109.

6. Gaimushō, *Gaikō Bunsho, Nichiro Sensō,* No. 5, pp. 297–98.

7. *Ibid.,* p. 299. Less than two hours after he had sent telegram No. 105, Komura sent another, even more determined message to his home government, in which he stated:

"Witte makes increasingly clear what Russia really wants. Russia refuses not only the payment of indemnity but also the concession of even a part of Sakhalin. Moreover, Russia is now inclined to retreat from the agreements already concluded between the two plenipotentiaries. In short, there is no doubt that Russia has no intention of seeking a conciliation.

"Witte himself seems to desire peace, but the situation in Russia has undergone a drastic change. Now the prowar faction is again in the ascendant and the tsar is completely swayed by their influence. Thus it is clear that, in spite of his personal wishes, Witte has already concluded that he can take no other course than to break off negotiations.

"This situation compels us to make a choice between the following alternatives: to give up both indemnity and Sakhalin or to continue fighting. There is no hope at all for a compromise on Sakhalin even if we give up the indemnity. Abandoning these two demands, however, simply means submission to Russia. Worse yet, even if we should reach a peace agreement with Russia under such conditions, the actual execution of the peace terms would be in serious doubt. For instance, to transfer the Liaotung leaseholds and the Chinese Eastern Railway would require the two belligerents first to obtain the consent of China. If Russia so wishes, it will be able to act freely to prevent Japan from obtaining such consent from China. If this happens, our agreement regarding the above two items will amount to nothing, and we will not be able to achieve our basic objective. Therefore I believe that Japan must continue fighting with full determination until another opportunity for peace arrives. Even if we decide to break off the negotiations now over the questions of indemnity and Sakhalin, we will have no difficulty in keeping the world's sympathy on our side. I have no doubt that the world will recognize the justice of Japan's position, particularly in view of the fact that we have tried to reach an agreement even at the sacrifice of a part of Sakhalin that has been totally under Japanese occupation." Gaimushō, *Komura Gaikōshi,* Vol. 2, pp. 108–109.

For some unknown reason this telegram apparently was not presented to the top-level conference. Kogiso, "Pōtsumasu Kōwa Kaigi," Shinobu Seizaburō and Nakayama Jiichi (eds.), *Nichiro Sensōshi no Kenkyū,* p. 411. It is not printed in Gaimushō, *Gaikō Bunsho, Nichiro Sensō,* No. 5.

8. Takeuchi, *War and Diplomacy in the Japanese Empire,* p. 153.

9. Gaimushō, *Komura Gaikōshi,* Vol. 2, pp. 34–39. Some on the Russian side interpreted the fact that Japan did not attack the defenseless island of Sakhalin until just before the opening of the peace negotiations as evidence of Japan's inability to continue full-scale fighting. *Ibid.,* p. 38. Rosen, *Forty Years of Diplomacy,* Vol. 1, p. 261.

10. Rikugunshō, *Meiji Tennō Godenki Shiryō, Meiji Gunjishi,* Vol. 2, pp. 1516–17.

11. Kuroda, *Gensui Terauchi Hakushaku Den,* p. 405.

12. His telegram, which was signed by the leading generals, read as follows: Immediately upon learning of the offer of President Roosevelt's good offices and your Majesty's consent to the opening of peace negotiations, I called a council of war of all the generals at present at the headquarters. I have the honour to inform your Majesty that all my comrades and myself, after fully discussing the arguments for peace and the respective positions of the opposing armies, unanimously and resolutely voted for the continuation of the war until such time as the Almighty shall crown the efforts of our brave troops with success.

It is no time to talk of peace after the battle of Mukden and of Tsushima. Flushed with success, the enemy cannot fail to exact dishonouring terms which there is absolutely no reason we should grant, for we are not quite reduced to such straits yet. The disaster of Tsushima is undoubtedly regrettable, but it in no way affects our brave army, which is in fine condition now and burns with desire to avenge itself upon the enemy by a success which I have every reason to hope is now close at hand.

We occupy an admirably fortified position. The wet weather has hitherto prevented me from taking the offensive, but now that our losses at Mukden have not only been made good, but that we have been reinforced by a fresh army corps from Europe, I feel myself able to more than hold my own against the enemy. Indeed, I hope before the month is out to take the offensive and change completely the complexion of affairs.

I beg to repeat, therefore, that your Majesty can have confidence in the force and strength of our troops. I again affirm that our position is in no way of such a critical nature as to necessitate the conclusion of peace on terms unfavorable for Russia. Signed: Linievitch, Commander-in-Chief; Kuropatkin, etc.

See McCormick, *The Tragedy of Russia in Pacific Asia*, Vol. 2, pp. 189–90. Also Tatsumi Kijirō, *Kyokutō Kinji Gaikōshi*, pp. 471–73.

Witte, however, presents a contradictory view of the strength of the Russian forces at the time: "We had exhausted all our means and had lost our credit abroad. There was not the slightest hope of floating either a domestic or a foreign loan. We could continue the war only by resorting to new issues of paper money, that is, by preparing the way for a complete financial and consequently economic collapse." Witte, *The Memoirs of Count Witte*, p. 135.

The Reuters special correspondent in Manchuria commented: "As long ago as last February [1905] the majority of the officers of the Russian army in the field were in favour of peace. . . . They had no belief in the prospects of recovering the ground lost. The private soldier in Manchuria . . . desires peace. . . ." He then concluded that the soldiers, the middle class, and peasants desired peace and that "only official Russia hoped for the one great victory which would have enabled Russia to escape from the mess with honour." Brooke, *An Eye-Witness in Manchuria*, pp. 308–12.

13. Kuropatkin, *The Russian Army and the Japanese War, Being Historical and Critical Comments on the Military Policy and Power of Russia and on the Campaign in the Far East*, Vol. 1, p. 23.

14. Gaimushō, *Gaikō Bunsho, Nichiro Sensō*, No. 5, p. 302.

15. Ōtsu, *Dai Nihon Kenseishi*, Vol. 6, p. 33. Takeuchi, *War and Diplomacy in the Japanese Empire*, p. 154; Watanabe, *Nihon Kinsei Gaikōshi*, p. 392; Ishii, *Gaikō Yoroku*, p. 86.

16. Watanabe, *Nihon Kinsei Gaikōshi*, p. 134. Takeuchi, *War and Diplomacy in the Japanese Empire*, p. 154. On August 26, Yamagata wrote Yamamoto requesting that he take great precautions against Komura's bringing the negotiations to the breaking point by making excessive demands. Kaigun, *Yamamoto Gonnohyōe to Kaigun*, p. 260.

17. Kuroda, *Gensui Terauchi Hakushaku Den*, p. 406.

18. Takeuchi, *War and Diplomacy in the Japanese Empire*, p. 153.

19. Hara, *Hara Kei Nikki*, Vol. 2, May 26, 1907 entry, p. 242.

20. Hara, *Hara Kei Nikki*, Vol. 2, May 26, 1907 entry, p. 344. Jacob Schiff, who had been a major subscriber to Japanese foreign bond issues, warned Takahira on Aug. 25, 1905, that the American, British, and German financial markets were no longer willing to support Japanese foreign bonds unless the end of the war was in sight. Gelber, *The Rise of Anglo-*

American Friendship, pp. 236–37. See also Adler, *Jacob H. Schiff: His Life and Letters,* Vol. 1, pp. 231–32.

21. Hara, *Hara Kei Nikki,* Vol. 2, May 26, 1907 entry, p. 242, March 7, 1909 entry, p. 344.

22. *Ibid.,* May 2, 1907 entry, p. 242. Yamagata soon afterward requested Katsura to state only the financial reasons, instead of both financial and military reasons. He was afraid that to cite military reasons for an early peace might harm his record as chief-of-staff. *Ibid.,* Vol. 2, pp. 242, 344. Oka, *Yamagata Aritomo,* p. 97. Takahashi Korekiyo, *Takahashi Korekiyo Jiden,* p. 698. Yamagata's later statements about the Japanese government's decision for peace gave without exception only financial reasons. He maintained that militarily Japan could have continued to fight. Kinkidō (ed.), *The Russo-Japanese War,* No. 10, pp. 1414–16. Gaimushō, *Gaikō Bunsho, Nichiro Sensō,* No. 5, pp. 301–02. This last is a part of the Katsura collection and contains the outline of the August 28 discussions. It should be noted, however, that it was written by Yamagata; hence financial difficulties alone were emphasized.

Hara Takashi wrote in his diary: "Saionji told me the following: Yamagata from the beginning was willing to make huge concessions in our demands and wanted to conclude peace under any conditions whatever. Itō interpreted this as a scheme by Yamagata to attribute the unsatisfactory outcome of the peace negotiations totally to diplomatic failure and not to military reasons at all. Relations between Itō and Yamagata have been like this for the last several years."

Hara, *Hara Kei Nikki,* Vol. 2, Aug. 28, 1905 entry, p. 147. See also Kikuchi, *Hakushaku Chinda Sutemi Den,* pp. 295–96. Katsura's mistress Okoi (Andō Teruko) was present for a scene that reveals something of the inner workings of the Meiji leadership in times of crisis. While the exact date of this event is not known, her account leaves no doubt that it took place immediately before August 28, 1905, possibly on the night of the 27th.

"On a certain night in August, Katsura came back to Okoi's Enokizaka home, walking all by himself. Overwork day after day had exhausted him, and his haggard face caused his personal physician to suspect a stomach cancer. It was a little after ten o'clock. [He must have left in the middle of the conference at Itō's home, when agreement was not yet in sight.] He looked unusually moody and said, 'I have been at Itō's. I don't want to eat anything. I am going to examine some documents.'

He asked that a white linen mosquito net be set up in a room upstairs. He took a desk inside the mosquito net and started reading documents.

Okoi, who was fanning him from the side, observed an expression of resoluteness on his face.

Shortly after midnight, somebody knocked loudly at the gate. When Okoi went out, she found Genrō Itō standing there with a policeman. She invited Itō in and reported his coming to Katsura. Katsura dashed downstairs, pulling the mosquito net down over the candle flame.

Okoi quenched the fire, went downstairs, and found 64-year-old Genrō Itō Hirobumi and 57-year-old Prime Minister Katsura Tarō weeping and embracing each other! She heard Itō say, 'Yes, that's right. The matter has been settled as you wished.' Katsura exclaimed, 'Is it true? Are you telling me that Matsukata, Inoue, Ōyama [*sic.*, although he must have been in Manchuria at the time], and all the others have accepted my proposal?'

A long silence ensued. Later, after toasting the occasion with a glass of wine, the two politicians went out together in the small hours of the morning."

Andō Teru, *Okoi Monogatari,* pp. 475–86; Koizumi, *Zuihitsu Saionji Kō,* pp. 247–50.

23. Gaimushō, *Gaikō Bunsho, Nichiro Senso,* No. 5, pp. 300–301.

24. Ishii, *Gaikō Yoroku,* p. 86. Shidehara implies that this important information was obtained only after he had urged the unwilling Ishii Kikujirō to go to the British legation and meet the official who gave Ishii the information. Shidehara, Kijūrō, *Gaikō Gojūnen,* pp. 16–21. Navy Minister Yamamoto, anxious lest the conference should fail, reprimanded Ishii for reporting this information. Ishii, *Gaikō Yoroku,* p. 86. Griswold, *The Far Eastern Policy of the United States,* p. 121.

25. Gaimushō, *Nihon Gaikō Nenpyō narabini Shuyō Bunsho,* Vol. 1, p. 159.

26. Gaimushō, *Gaikō Bunsho, Nichiro Senso,* No. 5, p. 305; Honda, *Tamashii no Gaikō,* pp. 21–22.

27. This news was transmitted to the *Tokyo Asahi Shimbun* by E. J. Dillon, the correspondent of the *London Daily Telegraph* who accompanied Witte. Lawton, *Empires of the Far East,* Vol. 1, p. 249.

28. *Japan Daily Herald,* Aug. 4, 1905, p. 1. Konishi Yukinaga, one of the generals in Toyotomi Hideyoshi's army that invaded Korea in 1592, failed in the ensuing peace negotiations with the Ming dynasty.

29. Yamamoto Fumio, *Nihon Shimbunshi,* pp. 211–12; Ono Hideo, *Nihon Shimbun Hattatsushi,* p. 297.

30. Ono Hideo, *Nihon Shimbun Hattatsushi,* pp. 297–98.

31. *Ibid.,* p. 297.

32. Asahi Shimbun, *Murayama Ryūhei Den,* p. 403.

33. *Ibid.*

34. Almost all the news reports were from the Associated Press. Okamoto Mitsuzō (ed.), *Nihon Shimbun Hyakunenshi*, p. 295.

35. Dennett, *Roosevelt and the Russo-Japanese War*, p. 264. The following works disagree with the view that American public opinion became pro-Russian during the course of the negotiations: Thorson, "American Public Opinion and the Portsmouth Peace Conference," *American Historical Review*, 53, No. 3 (April 1948) 439–64. Tupper and McReynolds, *Japan in American Public Opinion*, pp. 8–17.

36. Ono Hideo, *Nihon Shimbun Hattatsushi*, pp. 299–300.

37. *Ibid.*, p. 208; Yamamoto Fumio, *Nihon Shimbunshi*, p. 212.

38. Tokutomi, *Sohō Jiden*, p. 394.

39. Ono Hideo, *Nihon Shimbun Hattatsushi*, p. 299. Araki, *Kōhon Motoyama Hikoichi Ō Den*, p. 218.

40. Araki, *Kōhon Motoyama Hikoichi Ō Den*, p. 220.

41. Takahashi Yūsai, *Meiji Keisatsushi Kenkyū II: Meiji Sanjū Hachinen no Hibiya Sōjō Jiken*, p. 25.

42. Special correspondents sent coded telegrams to their home offices to prevent their seizure by the government, but even this did not work. Yamamoto Fumio, *Nihon Shimbunshi*, p. 212.

43. Nakayama Yasuaki, *Shimbun Shūsei Meiji Hennenshi*, p. 468.

44. *Japan Weekly Mail*, Aug. 12, 1905, p. 1.

45. *Japan Daily Herald*, Aug. 14, 1905, p. 1; Senki Meicho Kankōkai Henshūbu (ed.), *Kiji Sono Mama Nichiro Sensō Tōji no Naigai Shimbun Shō*, pp. 419–22.

46. *Japan Weekly Mail*, Aug. 19, 1905, p. 186.

47. *Gaimushō, Gaikō Bunsho, Nichiro Sensō*, No. 5, p. 791.

48. Gaimushō, *Nichiro Jiken Gaihyō Ippan: VIII* (Japanese Army and Navy Archives, 1868–1945, Reel No. 44, Film No. 58140). An outstanding exception was Gotō Shimpei, chief of the Civil Affairs Bureau of the Governor-General of Formosa, who told the government that territory and indemnity were not necessarily Japan's war objectives. Tsurumi Yūsuke, *Gotō Shimpei*, Vol. 2, pp. 607–608. It should be noted that he was the right-hand man of Governor-General Kodama, who was taking a leave of absence from his position to fight in Manchuria.

49. Nakayama Yasuaki, *Shimbun Shūsei Meiji Hennenshi*, Vol. 12, pp. 469–70.

50. *Ibid.*, p. 476.

51. *Japan Daily Herald*, Aug. 15, 1905, p. 4.

52. Nakamura Sadako, "Pōtsumasu Kaigiki ni okeru Nihon Gaikō ni taisuru Yoron," *Seishin Joshidaigaku Ronsō*, 7 (December 1955), p. 20.

53. *Ibid.*, pp. 20–21.

54. *Ibid.,* p. 21. Asahi Shimbun, *Murayama Ryūhei Den,* p. 403. Gai-musho, *Gaiko Bunsho, Nichiro Sensō,* No. 5, p. 805. The *Nihonjin* was published by such nationalist journalists as Shiga Shigetaka, Miyake Setsurei, and Sugiura Jūkō.

55. *Tōyō Keizai Shimpō,* No. 346, July 15, 1905; No. 349, Aug. 15, 1905; No. 350, Aug. 25, 1905.

56. Itō Masanori, *Katō Takaaki,* Vol. 1, p. 540.

57. Nakayama Yasuaki, *Shimbun Shūsei Meiji Hennenshi,* Vol. 12, p. 469.

58. *Japan Weekly Mail,* Aug. 26, 1905, p. 215.

59. Nakamura Sadako, "Pōtsumasu Kaigiki ni okeru Nihon Gaikō ni taisura Yoron," *Seishin Joshidaigaku Ronsō,* 7 (December 1955), p. 21.

60. Itō Masanori, *Katō Takaaki,* Vol. 1, p. 540.

61. Itō Masanori, *Katō Takaaki,* Vol. 1, pp. 540–41; Fujimura Michio, "Hikōwa Undō," Shinobu Seizaburō and Nakayama Jiichi (eds.) *Nichiro Sensōshi no Kenkyū,* p. 423; Maejima Shōzō, *Nihon Seitō Seiji no Shiteki Bunseki,* p. 162. Kawae (ed.), *Shiryō Kindai Nihonshi,* pp. 47–48.

62. *Japan Weekly Mail,* Sept. 2, 1905, pp. 239, 243.

63. *Japan Chronicle,* Aug. 30, 1905, in Japan Chronicle (ed.), *A Diary of the Russo-Japanese War,* Vol. II, p. 328. (Hereafter referred to as Japan Chronicle.)

64. Weale, *The Truce in the East and Its Aftermath,* pp. 7–8.

Chapter 7. The Anti-Peace Treaty Movement

1. Ono Hideo, *Nihon Shimbun Hattatsushi,* p. 300; Weale, *The Truce in the East and Its Aftermath,* p. 8.

2. Weale, *The Truce in the East and Its Aftermath,* p. 9.

3. Baroness d'Anethan, *Fourteen Years of Diplomatic Life in Japan,* p. 449.

4. Treat, *Diplomatic Relations between the United States and Japan: 1895–1905,* p. 248.

5. Takahashi Yūsai, *Meiji Keisatsushi Kenkyū II: Meiji Sanjū Hachinen no Hibiya Sōjō Jiken,* p. 27; Kawae, *Shiryō Kindai Nihonshi,* p. 48.

6. Takahashi Yūsai, *Meiji Keisatsushi Kenkyū II: Meiji Sanjū Hachinen no Hibiya Sōjō Jiken,* p. 27; Shinobu Seizaburō, "Meiji Makki no Minshū Undō," in Tozawa (ed.), *Burujoa Kakumei no Kenkyū* p. 351; Shira-yanagi, *Meiji Taishō Kokuminshi: Tairiku Shinshutsu,* p. 354.

7. Asahi Shimbun, *Murayama Ryūhei Den,* pp. 403–404; Ono Hideo, *Nihon Shimbun Hattatsushi,* p. 300.

8. Nakayama Yasuaki, *Shimbun Shūsei Meiji Hennenshi*, Vol. 12, pp. 437–41, 465–66.

9. *Ibid.*, p. 457.

10. Murajima Shigeru, "Nichiei Dōmei no Kaitei," in Shinobu Seizaburō and Nakayama Jiichi (eds.), *Nichiro Sensōshi no Kenkyū*, p. 371.

11. Weale, *The Truce in the East and Its Aftermath*, p. 11; McLaren, *A Political History of Japan during the Meiji Era, 1867–1912*, p. 299.

12. Matsumoto Takehiro, "Iwayuru Hibiya Yakiuchi Jiken no Kenkyū," *Shisō Kenkyū Shiryō*, Special Issue, No. 50, p. 37.

13. Takahashi Yūsai, *Meiji Keisatsushi Kenkyū II: Meiji Sanjū Hachinen no Hibiya Sōjō Jiken*, p. 28, Tsurumi Shunsuke, *Nihon no Hyakunen*, Vol. 7, p. 178.

14. Asahi Shimbun, *Murayama Ryūhei Den*, p. 404.

15. Nakayama Yasuaki, *Shimbun Shūsei Meiji Hennenshi*, Vol. 12, pp. 12, pp. 477–78.

16. *Ibid.*, pp. 478–79.

17. McLaren, *A Political History of Japan during the Meiji Era, 1867–1912*, p. 299; Ono Hideo, *Nihon Shimbun Hattatsushi*, pp. 301–03. Nakamura Sadako, "Pōtsumasu Kaigiki ni okeru Nihon Gaikō ni taisuru Yoron," *Seishin Joshidaigaku Ronsō*, 7 (December 1955), p. 23. The *Miyako Shimbun* had a circulation of 60,000 in 1904. Yamamoto Fumio, *Nihon Shimbunshi*, p. 221.

18. Ono Hideo, *Nihon Shimbun Hattatsushi*, pp. 300–03; Nakayama Yasuaki, *Shimbun Shūsei Meiji Hennenshi*, Vol. 12, pp. 480–84. Kawae, *Shiryō Kindai Nihonshi*, pp. 47–49. The *Osaka Mainichi Shimbun* on September 2 published a sketch of the battlefield after the battle for Port Arthur. When it was forwarded by the *Mainichi* correspondent during the war, the government had not permitted its publication. An editorial in this issue declared that the struggle of 18 months and the sacrifice of a hundred thousand lives had been made worthless by the diplomacy of a fortnight and warned that the indignation of patriots might endanger the peace of the Empire. *Japan Chronicle*, Sept. 3, 1905, Vol. 2, p. 332.

19. Katō Takaaki wrote that behind their outward praise the powers were laughing at Japan for its failure in the negotiations. Itō Masanori, *Katō Takaaki*, Vol. 1, p. 541.

20. Matsumoto Takehiro, "Iwayuru Hibiya Yakiuchi Jiken no Kenkyū," *Shisō Kenkyū Shiryō*, Special Issue, No. 50, 39–40; Shinobu Seizaburō, *Taishō Demokurashiishi*, Vol. 1, pp. 14–15.

21. The *Chūō Shimbun* was owned by Ōoka Ikuzō, one of the top leaders of the Seiyūkai. Nishida Taketoshi, *Meiji Jidai no Shimbun to Zasshi*,

p. 244. Its circulation in 1904 was 40,000. Yamamoto Fumio, *Nihon Shimbunshi*, p. 221.

22. The *Nihon's* sudden and brief changes of opinion are explained by Kojima Kazuo, one of its editorial writers. The editor-in-chief of the paper was Kuga Minoru, one of the leading journalists of the day and an enlightened nationalist. While Kuga approved of the treaty, his subordinates did not. Therefore the paper sometimes took a position in favor of the peace, and at other times in opposition to it. Kojima Kazuo, *Ichi Rōseijika no Kaisō*, p. 64. For additional information on Kuga Minoru, see Maruyama Masao, "Kuga Katsunan to Kokumin Shugi," in Meiji Shiryō (ed.), *Minkenron kara Nashionarizumu e*, pp. 192–209.

23. The *Chūgai Shōgyō Shimpō* was a commercial journal controlled by business tycoon Ōkura Kihachirō, which reflected the milder opinion of some business leaders. *Japan Chronicle*, Sept. 3, 1905, II, 333. See also Yamamoto Fumio, *Nihon Shimbunshi*, p. 214; Ono Hideo, *Nihon Shimbun Hattatsushi*, p. 303; Takeuchi, *War and Diplomacy in the Japanese Empire*, p. 155. (Circulation for the *Chūgai Shōgyō Shimpō* in 1904 was 10,000.)

24. See Hara, *Hara Kei Nikki*, Vol. 2, Feb. 20, 1905 entry, p. 126. (Circulation for the *Osaka Shimpō* in 1904 was 50,000.)

25. See Mainichi, *Mainichi Shimbun Shichijūnen*, p. 108; Shinobu Seizaburō, *Taishō Demokurashiishi*, Vol. 1, p. 35. Maeda Renzan, *Hara Takashi Den*, Vol. 2, pp. 62–63.

26. Gaimushō, *Nichiro Jiken Gaihyō Ippan VIII*, Reel No. 44, Film Nos. 58178-81, 58191-92, and 58207-216.

27. Lawton, *Empires of the Far East*, Vol. 1, p. 255.

28. Fujimura Michio, "Hikōwa Undō," Shinobu Seizaburō and Nakayama Jiichi (eds.), *Nichiro Sensōshi no Kenkyū*, pp. 426–27. Shinobu Seizaburō, *Taishō Demokurashiishi*, Vol. 1, pp. 20, 22; Takahashi Masao, "Meiji Sanjū Hachinen no Hi-Kōwa Undō," *Nihon Rekishi*, No. 55 (December 1953) 20.

29. Matsumoto Takehiro, "Iwayuru Hibiya Yakiuchi Jiken no Kenkyū," *Shisō Kenkyū Shiryō*, Special Issue, No. 50, p. 34; Shioda and Inumaru, "Hibiya no Yakiuchi," *Rekishi Hyōron*, No. 39 (October 1952), p. 8. Shinobu Seizaburō, *Taishō Demokurashiishi*, Vol. 1, pp. 23–24; Nakayama Yasuaki, *Shimbun Shūsei Meiji Hennenshi*, Vol. 12, pp. 419, 466, 473; Komuro, "Hibiya Yakiuchi Jiken no Saikentō," *Kindai Nihonshi Kenkyū*, No. 5 (April 1958), p. 11.

30. Nakayama Yasuaki, *Shimbun Shūsei Meiji Hennenshi*, Vol. 12, pp. 479–81; Shinobu Seizaburō, *Taishō Demokurashiishi*, Vol. 1, pp. 24–26.

31. *The Outlook*, 81 (September-December 1905) 94, 104–07.

32. Fujimura Michio, "Hikōwa Undō," Shinobu Seizaburō and Naka-yama Jiichi (eds.), *Nichiro Sensōshi no Kenkyū*, p. 425; *Tōyō Kenzai Shimpō*, No. 351, (Sept. 5, 1905) 10–11.

33. Shinobu Seizaburō, *Taishō Demokurashiishi*, Vol. 1, pp. 26–27.

34. Fujimura Michio, "Hikōwa Undō," Shinobu Seizaburō and Naka-yama Jiichi (eds.), *Nichiro Sensōshi no Kenkyū*, p. 425.

35. Nakamura Sadako, "Pōtsumasu Kaigiki ni okeru Nihon Gaikō ni taisuru Yoron," *Seishin Joshidaigaku Ronsō*, 7 (December 1955), p. 24.

36. Nakayama Yasuaki, *Shimbun Shūsei Meiji Hennenshi*, Vol. 12, p. 480; Weale, *The Truce in the East and Its Aftermath*, pp. 11–12.

37. Shinobu Seizaburō, *Taishō Demokurashiishi*, Vol. 1, p. 27.

38. Shibusawa's mild attitude invited attack. See *Nihon Keizai Shimbun*, June 19, 1964; Shibusawa Seien, *Shibusawa Eiichi Denki Shiryō*, Vol. 28, pp. 657–58. For businessmen's views on postwar economic management, see Tokyo Ginkō Shūkaijo, "Sengo Keizai ni kansuru sho Meirū Iken," in Meiji Bunka (ed.), *Meiji Bunka Shiryō Sōsho*, pp. 321–86; Kennan, "The Sword of Peace in Japan," *The Outlook*, No. 81 (Oct. 14, 1905) 359.

39. This demonstration is discussed later in this chapter.

40. Futabatei, *Futabatei Shimei Zenshū*, Vol. 12, pp. 165–66.

41. Ishikawa, *Takuboku Zenshū*, Vol. 8, pp. 47–48.

42. Nishida Kitarō, *Sunshin Nikki*, p. 152; Miyajima, *Meijiteki Shisō-kazō no Keisei*, pp. 127–30.

43. Komura, "Hibiya Yakiuchi Jiken no Saikentō," *Kindai Nihonshi Kenkyū*, No. 5 (April 1958), pp. 13–15; Arahata, *Kanson Jiden*, p. 112.

44. Uchimura, *Uchimura Kanzō Zenshū*, Vol. 14, p. 383.

45. Shimanouchi, *Tani Kanjō Ikō*, Vol. 2, pp. 673–77.

46. Kennan, "The Sword of Peace in Japan," *The Outlook*, No. 81 (Oct. 14, 1905), p. 360. Huntington-Wilson, *Memoirs of an Ex-Diplomat*, p. 117.

A remark on the Japanese people and foreign policy today is of special interest here: "In general Japan lacks [these] politically neutral forums for foreign policy discussion. As a result, one cannot speak of a relatively broad foreign policy attentive public in Japan." Almond, "Democracy and Foreign Policy Making: Some Comparative Observations on the U.S. and Japan," *Bulletin of the International House of Japan*, No. 11 (April 1963) 24. See Tomizu, *Zoku Kaikoroku*, pp. 226–371.

47. Shukuri, *Kodama Gentarō*, p. 641. Lawton, however, expressed a contradictory opinion: "Towards the end of the campaign the soldiers in Manchuria were showing unmistakable signs of home-sickness; and numerous letters received in Japan from the front told of their eager desire to see peace restored." Lawton, *Empires of the Far East*, Vol. 1, p. 244.

48. Kudō, *Meiji Kenseishi*, pp. 830–31.

49. "On September 10 [1905], the Japanese flagship in the Battle of the Japan Sea, *Mikasa*, took fire. It was widely believed that the *Mikasa* may have been sent to her doom as some demented sailor's perverted protest against the supposed betrayal at Portsmouth." Falk, *Tōgō and the Rise of Japanese Sea Power*, pp. 421–22. See Ishikawa, *Takuboku Zenshū*, Vol. 13, p. 105.

50. d'Anethan, *Fourteen Years of Diplomatic Life in Japan*, p. 450. Shinobu Seizaburō, "Meiji Makki no Minshū Undō," Tozawa (ed.), *Burujoa Kakumei no Kenkyū*, p. 346. See also Kennan, "The Sword of Peace in Japan," *The Outlook*, No. 81 (Oct. 14, 1905), p. 357.

51. Kennan, "The Sword of Peace in Japan," *The Outlook* No. 81 (Oct. 14, 1905), p. 357.

52. Shinobu Seizaburō, *Taishō Demokurashiishi*, Vol. 1, pp. 15–16; Gaimushō, *Gaikō Bunsho, Nichiro Sensō*, No. 5, p. 808.

53. Gaimushō, *Gaikō Bunsho, Nichiro Sensō*, No. 5, p. 811.

54. *Ibid.*, pp. 837–38.

55. Tsurumi Shunsuke, *Nihon no Hyakunen*, Vol. 7, p. 179.

56. Shinobu Seizaburō, *Taishō Demokurashiishi*, Vol. 1, pp. 28–29.

57. Fujimura Michio, "Hikōwa Undō," Shinobu Seizaburō and Naka-yama Jiichi (eds.), *Nichiro Sensōshi no Kenkyū*.

58. Shinobu Seizaburō, *Taishō Demokurashiishi*, Vol. 1, pp. 28–29.

59. *Ibid.*, p. 29; Kennan, "The Sword of Peace in Japan," *The Outlook*, No. 81 (Oct. 14, 1905), p. 360; Nakayama Yasuaki, *Shimbun Shūsei Meiji Hennenshi*, Vol. 12, p. 482.

60. Shinobu Seizaburō, *Taishō Demokurashiishi*, Vol. 1, pp. 30–31.

61. Nakayama Yasuaki, *Shimbun Shūsei Meiji Hennenshi*, Vol. 12, p. 482.

62. Shinobu Seizaburō, *Taishō Demokurashiishi*, Vol. 1, pp. 30–31; Gaimushō, *Gaikō Bunsho, Nichiro Sensō*, No. 5, pp. 807–19.

63. Nakayama Yasuaki, *Shimbun Shūsei Meiji Hennenshi*, Vol. 12, p. 479; Kinkidō (ed.), *The Russo-Japanese War*, Vol. 10, pp. 1414–16.

64. Fujimura Michio, "Hikōwa Undō," Shinobu Seizaburō and Naka-yama Jiichi (eds.), *Nichiro Senōshi no Kenkyū*, p. 428.

65. Takahashi Yūsai, *Meiji Keisatsushi Kenkyū II: Meiji Sanjū Hachi-nen no Hibiya Sōjō Jiken*, p. 132; Shinobu Seizaburō, "Meiji Makki no Minshū Undō," Tozawa (ed.), *Burujoa Kakumei no Kenkyū*, p. 347.

66. Tokutomi, *Soho Jiden*, pp. 401–402. Shinobu Seizaburō, *Taishō Demokurashiishi*, Vol. 1, p. 31. The *Osaka Asahi Shimbun* reported that the police in certain prefectures summoned the district newsagents and "ordered" them to exert themselves to obtain subscribers to the *Kokumin*

Shimbun, explaining that the contradictory reports published in other news-papers were apt to mislead the public, while the news published in the *Kokumin* was accurate. *Japan Chronicle,* Sept. 1, 1905, Vol. 2, p. 329.

67. Asahi Shimbun, *Murayama Ryūhei Den,* p. 407.

68. Ko Hakushaku Yamamoto, *Yamamoto Gonnohyōe Den,* Vol. 1, p. 498.

69. Kiyosawa, *Nihon Gaikōshi,* Vol. 1, p. 336.

70. Komura said to Yamaza, "The treaty should be ratified even if it requires martial law." Gaimushō, *Komura Gaikōshi,* Vol. 2, p. 155.

71. Scalapino defines *sōshi* as men "whose chief task was to act as body-guards for their employers and as 'rough men' toward the opposition." Scalapino, *Democracy and the Party Movement in Prewar Japan: The Fail-ure of the First Attempt,* p. 219.

72. Watanabe Kunitake, who as Minister of Finance had wrecked the fourth Itō Cabinet, together with "the Professors" formed the nationalistic club Nansa Shō. Tomizu, *Zoku Kaikoroku,* pp. 27–28. This point will be discussed more fully in the following chapters.

73. Tokutomi, *Kōshaku Katsura Tarō Den,* Vol. 2, pp. 296–97. Public anger was also directed against Katsura's mistress Okoi, and many threaten-ing letters were delivered to her home from all over Japan. On the morning of September 4, Okoi took all these letters to Katsura at his official residence. Katsura, with a smile, pointed to the piles of letters in the room. Not one was opened.

On Sept. 4, when Katsura was told that even ricksha men were refusing to take guests in the direction of Enokizaka (the place of Okoi's residence), he had some serious telephone conversations with such leading nationalists as Tōyama Mitsuru and Sugiyama Shigemaru. The contents of the conver-sations, however, are not known. Andō, *Okoi Monogatari,* pp. 491–94.

Sugiyama Shigemaru was a member of the Genyōsha. He also knew Katsura, Kodama, and Gotō intimately and therefore acted as an interme-diary between the Genyōsha and the government leaders. Kokuryūkai, *Tōa Senkaku Shishi Kiden,* Vol. 2, pp. 748–63. Interestingly enough, during the riot Sugiyama fought the mobs with drawn sword at the gate of Katsura's official residence. Andō Teru, *Okoi Monogatari,* p. 444.

Tōyama's activities during the war are not well known. As we shall see later, Tōyama did not participate in person in the rally in Hibiya Park. Whether Katsura's telephone call was directly connected with this rally is a matter of conjecture. However, the actions of both these leaders indicate to some extent the degree of closeness which existed between government officials and the nationalist groups through informal channels.

74. Shinobu Seizaburō, *Taishō Demokurashiishi,* I, 24–25. *Tokyo Asahi*

Shimbun, Sept. 6, 1905, in Asahi Shimbunsha, *Asahi Shimbun Shakaimen de miru Sesō Shichijūgonen, 1879–1954,* p. 38.

75. Miyake, *Dōjidaishi,* Vol. 3, p. 440.

76. Hara, *Hara Kei Nikki,* Vol. 2, Mar. 9, 1905 entry, p. 129; Apr. 2, 1905 entry, p. 130.

77. *Ibid.,* Apr. 16, 1905 entry, pp. 131–32.

78. Masumi, *Nihon Seitō Shiron,* Vol. 2, p. 452.

79. Tokutomi, *Kōshaku Matsukata Masayoshi Den,* Vol. 2, p. 804.

80. Hara, *Hara Kei Nikki,* Vol. 2, Apr. 16, 1905 entry, pp. 131–32; Apr. 17, 1905 entry, p. 133.

81. Hara, *Hara Kei Nikki,* Vol. 2, May 12, 1905 entry, pp. 134–35.

82. *Ibid.,* entries for June 14, 19, 22, and 24, 1905, p. 139.

83. *Seiyū,* No. 62, July 25, 1905, p. 39. Ōkuma seems to have agreed that it was advisable not to specify the Japanese demands because, he believed, Japan's terms of that day might have been quite different from its terms the following day should Russia have failed to take the opportunity to conclude peace. *Japan Weekly Mail,* July 8, 1905, p. 33.

The Foreign Affairs Study Committee of the Kenseihontō prepared draft terms for peace that were much broader than those the party adopted at its meeting on June 28, 1905. *Nihon Bengoshi Kyōkai Rokuji,* No. 88, June 28, 1905, p. 98.

84. *Ibid.,* p. 2. Kobayashi, *Rikken Seiyūkaishi,* Vol. 2, pp. 240–42.

85. Hara, *Hara Kei Nikki,* Vol. 2, June 28, 1905 entry, p. 140.

86. *Ibid.,* Aug. 1, 1905 entry, pp. 142–43.

87. *Ibid.,* Aug. 14, 1905 entry, pp. 143–44. It is not clear whom Katsura had in mind. Maeda Renzan, Hara's biographer, thinks he meant "Yamamoto Gonnohyōe of the Satsuma clan." Maeda, *Hara Takashi Den,* Vol. 2, p. 135.

88. Hara, *Hara Kei Nikki,* Vol. 2, Aug. 14, 1905 entry, p. 143.

89. Hara, *Hara Kei Nikki,* Vol. 2, Aug. 22, 1905 entry, pp. 144–45. On August 23, Ōishi invited Hara to accompany him on a visit to Katsura to discuss the peace negotiations. Hara declined. *Ibid.,* Aug. 23, 1905 entry, p. 145.

90. *Ibid.,* Sept. 1, 1905 entry, p. 147.

91. Ueno Kumazō (ed.), *Nihon Seitō Hattatsushi,* p. 593.

92. *Seiyū,* No. 64, Sept. 25, 1905, pp. 1–2; Kobayashi, *Rikken Seiyūkaishi,* Vol. 2, pp. 243–46. Some scholars have praised Saionji's speech as the brave and frank expression of an "international mind." See Nomura (ed.), *Meiji Taishōshi,* Vol. 6, pp. 250–51. Also Oka, *Kindai Nihon no Seijika,* p. 213.

Takekoshi Yosaburō, a protege of Saionji, wrote in his *Prince Saionji*, p. 218 (Japanese edition, *Saionji Kō*, p. 232.): "Some of the members of the management of the Seiyūkai complained that the publication of such an unpopular address might induce the people to overthrow the Seiyūkai. This greatly angered the Prince. He said, 'Even though one or two such parties as the Seiyūkai were destroyed, if it were for the sake of the country their loss would not be worth notice. The address should be published promptly to enlighten and pacify the minds of the populace.' This moral courage vividly reveals the character of Prince Saionji." The *Japan Chronicle* stated that the views of Marquis Saionji were "eminently wise and statesmanlike," *Japan Chronicle*, Sept. 5, 1905, II, 334. See also Shinobu Junpei, *Gaisei Kantoku to Gaikōkikan*, p. 235.

It has been alleged that Hara drafted Saionji's speech. *Japan Chronicle*, Sept. 19, 1905, II, 354.

93. Kobayashi, *Rikken Seiyūkaishi*, Vol. 2, pp. 30–38; Masumi, *Nihon Seitō Shiron*, Vol. 2, p. 362.

94. Masumi, *Nihon Seitō Shiron*, Vol. 2, p. 335.

95. Kobayashi, *Rikken Seiyūkaishi*, Vol. 2, pp. 170–71.

96. *Ibid.*, p. 246.

97. Hara, *Hara Kei Nikki*, Vol. 2, Sept. 2, 1905 entry, p. 148.

98. Kobayashi, Vol. 2, *Rikken Seiyūkaishi*, pp. 42–43; *Seiyū*, No. 42, Jan. 25, 1904, p. 34; Nakayama Yasuaki, *Shimbun Shūsei Meiji Hennenshi*, Vol. 12, p. 139.

99. *Japan Weekly Mail*, Aug. 24, 1905, p. 213.

100. Ōtsu, *Dai Nihon Kenseishi*, Vol. 5, p. 174; Shinobu Seizaburō, *Taishō Demokurashiishi*, Vol. 1, pp. 34–35; Ueno, *Nihon Seitō Hattatsushi*, p. 590; Kudō, *Teikoku Gikaishi*, Vol. 3, p. 490.

101. Hara, *Hara Kei Nikki*, Vol. 2, Sept. 4, 1905 entry, p. 148.

102. Kudō, *Teikoku Gikaishi*, Vol. 3, p. 491; Ueno, *Nihon Seitō Hattatsushi*, p. 590.

103. *Japan Chronicle*, Sept. 5, 1905, II, 335; Kinkidō (ed.), *The Russo-Japanese War*, Vol. 10, pp. 1413–14.

104. *Seiyū*, No. 62, July 25, 1905, p. 39.

105. Ōishi and Inukai had approached Navy Minister Yamamoto, who they believed would be Katsura's successor. Maeda, *Hara Takashi Den*, Vol. 2, p. 74.

106. Shinobu Seizaburō, *Taishō Demokurashiishi*, Vol. 1, p. 36.

107. Ueno, *Nihon Seitō Hattatsushi*, p. 591; Ōtsu, *Dai Nihon Kenseishi*, Vol. 5, p. 175.

108. Tsurumi Shunsuke, *Nihon no Hyakunen*, Vol. 7, p. 180.

Chapter 8. The Hibiya "Anti-Peace Treaty" Riot

1. Kasai Sakuzō (ed.), *Aa Kugatsu Itsuka*, p. 3; Matsumoto Takehiro, "Iwayuru Hibiya Yakiuchi Jiken no Kenkyū," *Shisō Kenkyū Shiryō*, Special Issue, No. 50, p. 32.

2. During the war, Kōmuchi, as an "uncrowned ambassador" from Japan, was actively engaged in the expansion of Japanese influence in Korea. Kokuryūkai, *Tōa Senkaku Shishi Kiden*, Vol. 1, pp. 860–68.

3. Kasai, *Aa Kugatsu Itsuka*, p. 3.

4. Kasai, *Aa Kugatsu Itsuka*, p. 4; Ōtsu, *Dai Nihon Kenseishi*, Vol. 6, p. 149.

5. Kasai, *Aa Kugatsu Itsuka*, p. 4.

6. This was at No. 3, I-Chome, Uchisaiwaicho, Kōjimachi, Tokyo; *ibid.*; Matsumoto Takehiro, "Iwayuru Hibiya Yakiuchi Jiken no Kenkyū," *Shisō Kenkyū Shiryō*, Special Issue, No. 50, pp. 32–33. Takahashi lists the Mushozoku (Independents) in addition to these eight organizations. Takahashi Yūsai, *Meiji Keisatsushi Kenkyū II: Meiji Sanjū Hachinen no Hibiya Sōjō Jiken*, p. 21. Except for the Kokuryūkai and the Nansa Sō, no details on these organizations are available.

7. These materials include:

    (1) Kasai Sakuzō (ed.), *Aa Kugatsu Itsuka*, a collection of the memoirs of those who actively participated in Rengōkai activities.

    (2) *Kyōto Shūshū Hikokujiken Yoshin Kiroku*, in three parts and a supplement. The records of pretrial investigations of the suspects and witnesses involved in the Hibiya Riot. Neither publisher nor publication date is given. The records total more than 1200 pages.

    (3) "Kyōto Shūshū Jiken Kōhan Bōchō Hikki" in the *Hōritsu Shimbun* (Lawyers' Newspaper), No. 338 (Mar. 5, 1906) to No. 349 (Apr. 25, 1906). Largely unofficial stenographic records of the trial of those involved in the Hibiya Riot.

In addition, the following sources have already been cited: Gaimushō, *Gaikō Bunsho, Nichiro Sensō*, No. 5; the Matsumoto Takehiro Report; the study done by Takahashi Yūsai.

8. Sources from which biographical data on the "active membership" were obtained include: Shūgiin and Sangiin (eds.), *Gikaiseido Shichijūnen Shi: Shūgiin giin Meikan*; Kokuryūkai (ed.), *Tōa Senkaku Shishi Kiden*, Vol. 3; Taishi (ed.), *Taishi Kaikoroku*, Vol. 2; *Nihon Rekishi Daijiten*, 20 vols.; *Dai Jinmei Jiten*, 10 vols.; and Ino Saburō (ed.), *Taishū Jinji Roku*, 2 vols.

9. Sources from which the data on the party affiliations of the Rengōkai

members were obtained include: Shūgiin and Sangiin (eds.), *Gikaiseido Shichijūnen Shi: Shūgiin giin Meikan;* Shūgiin and Sangiin (eds.), *Gikaiseido Shichijūnen Shi: Seitō Kaiha Hen;* and Hayashida Kametarō, *Nihon Seitōshi.*

10. Takahashi Yūsai, *Meiji Keisatsushi Kenkyū II: Meiji Sanjū Hachinen no Hibiya Sōjō Jiken,* p. 20; Gaimushō, *Gaikō Bunsho, Nichiro Sensō,* pp. 782, 784. *Kyōto Shūshū Hikokujiken Yoshin Kiroku,* Part 1, p. 12.

The following works erroneously include Kōmuchi Tomotsune among the Rengōkai leaders: Maejima, *Nihon Seitō Seiji no Shiteki Bunseki,* p. 162; Shinobu Seizaburō, *Taishō Demokurashiishi,* Vol. 1, p. 32; Shinobu Seizaburō, "Meiji Makki no Minshū Undō," p. 350; Fujimura Michio, "Hi-Kōwa Undō," Shinobu Seizaburō and Nakayama Jiichi (eds.), *Nichiro Sensōshi no Kenkyu,* p. 429; *Nihon Rekishi Daijiten,* Vol. 15, p. 280. They also include Tōyama Mitsuru, but no source supports this view. The Matsumoto report does not include Tōyama as a Rengōkai leader.

One source, however, reports that Uchida Ryōhei was on a speaking tour in the northeast region of Japan from June until the end of August 1905. Kokuryūkurabu, *Kokushi Uchida Ryōhei Den,* pp. 299–300.

11. Kasai, *Aa Kugatsu Itsuka,* pp. 4–5. The Rengōkai decided to use the *Niroku Shimpō* as its organ. Beside the fact that a number of Rengōkai members were connected with the newspapers, it was owned by Akiyama Teisuke, an anti-Katsura Diet member who was said to have cooperated with Kōno Hironaka in his memorialization in the nineteenth Diet session. Gaimushō, *Gaikō Bunsho, Nichiro Sensō,* No. 5, p. 782.

The Metropolitan Police Board kept a close watch on the activities of the Rengōkai. The materials on the Rengōkai in the *Gaikō Bunsho* consist almost entirely of reports "from the Metropolitan Police Board to the Ministry of Foreign Affairs."

12. Gaimushō, *Gaiko Bunsho, Nichiro Sensō,* No. 5, pp. 782–83; Takahashi Yūsai, *Meiji Keisatsushi Kenkyū II: Meiji Sanjū Hachinen no Hibiya Sōjō Jiken,* p. 20.

13. Kasai, *Aa Kugatsu Itsuka,* pp. 5–6. See also Ōtsu, *Dai Nihon Kenseishi,* Vol. 6, p. 150.

14. Kasai, *Aa Kugatsu Itsuka,* p. 7.

15. Gaimushō, *Gaikō Bunsho, Nichiro Sensō,* No. 5, p. 783; Takahashi Yūsai, *Meiji Keisatsushi Kenkyū II: Meiji Sanjū Hachinen no Hibiya Sōjō Jiken,* p. 21.

16. Gaimushō, *Gaikō Bunsho, Nichiro Sensō,* No. 5, pp. 783–84, 790; Kasai, *Aa Kugatsu Itsuka,* p. 7; Aomori (ed.), *Aomori Ken Gikaishi,* p. 777.

17. Gaimushō, *Gaikō Bunsho, Nichiro Sensō*, No. 5, pp. 802–803.

18. *Ibid.*, p. 803. This report states that the meeting began at 4:00 p.m. See also Nakayama Yasuaki, *Shimbun Shūsei Meiji Hennenshi*, Vol. 12, p. 470, and Kasai, *Aa Kugatsu Itsuka*, p. 81. Kasai erroneously dates the meeting as having taken place on Aug. 19, 1905.

19. Takahashi Yūsai, *Meiji Keisatsushi Kenkyū II: Meiji Sanjū Hachinen no Hibiya Sōjō Jiken*, p. 22.

20. *Ibid.*, p. 23.

21. Gaimushō, *Gaikō Bunsho, Nichiro Sensō*, No. 5, p. 804.

22. Kasai, *Aa Kugatsu Itsuka*, pp. 13–14. See also "Kyōto Shūshū Hikokujiken Yoshin Kiroku," Part 1, pp. 12, 305; Part 2, pp. 58–59, 136–37; Ōtsu, *Dai Nihon Kenseishi*, Vol. 6, p. 152; Matsumoto Takehiro, "Iwayuru Hibiya Yakiuchi Jiken no Kenkyū," *Shisō Kenkyū Shiryō*, Special Issue, No. 50, p. 41.

23. "Kyōto Shūshū Hikokujiken Yoshin Kiroku," Part 2, pp. 59, 137; Kasai, *Aa Kugatsu Itsuka*, p. 14.

24. "Kyōto Shūshū Hikokujiken Yoshin Kiroku," Part 1, pp. 36–37; Matsumoto Takehiro, "Iwayuru Hibiya Yakiuchi Jiken no Kenkyū," *Shisō Kenkyū Shiryō*, Special Issue, No. 50, p. 42.

25. Matsumoto Takehiro, "Iwayuru Hibiya Yakiuchi Jiken no Kenkyū," *Shisō Kenkyū Shiryō*, Special Issue, No. 50, p. 14; Shinobu Seizaburō, *Taishō Demokurashiishi*, Vol. 1, p. 32; Takahashi Yūsai, *Meiji Keisatsushi Kenkyū II: Meiji Sanjū Hachinen no Hibiya Sōjō Jiken*, p. 24. Takahashi says the letter was distributed on September 3.

26. Kasai, *Aa Kugatsu Itsuka*, pp. 15–16; Nakayama Gisuke, *Kōno Banshū Den*, Vol. 2, pp. 662–63; Ōtsu, *Dai Nihon Kenseishi*, Vol. 6, p. 153.

27. Kasai, *Aa Kagatsu Itsuka*, p. 114; *Hōritsu Shimbun*, No. 341, Mar. 17, 1906, pp. 20–21; Takahashi Yūsai, *Meiji Keisatsushi Kenkyū II: Meiji Sanjū Hachinen no Hibiya Sōjō Jiken*, p. 24.

28. Kasai, *Aa Kugatsu Itsuka*, p. 16; Nakayama Yasuaki, *Shimbun Shūsei Meiji Hennenshi*, Vol. 12, p. 484; "Kyōto Shūshū Hikokujiken Yoshin Kiroku,," Part 1, p. 38.

Kōno stated during the pretrial interrogation: "We were awed at the prospect of troubling His Majesty with our memorial. But we concluded that under the circumstances we had no other way to accomplish our purpose." "Kyōto Shūshū Hikokujiken Yoshin Kiroku," Part I, pp. 37–38.

On his way back from the Imperial Household Ministry, Kōno, "having something to tell," called at the residence of Minister of Finance Sone; Sone, however, was entertaining the American business tycoon E. H. Harriman and Kōno was unable to see him. Nakayama Gisuke, *Kōno Banshū Den,* Vol. 2, p. 674.

29. Gaimushō, *Gaikō Bunsho, Nichiro Sensō,* No. 5, pp. 808–809; Kasai, *Aa Kugatsu Itsuka,* pp. 14–15; Matsumoto Takehiro, "Iwayuru Hibiya Yakiuchi Jiken no Kenkyū," *Shisō Kenkyū Shiryō,* Special Issue, No. 50, pp. 43–44.

30. Gaimushō, *Gaikō Bunsho, Nichiro Sensō,* No. 5, pp. 811–12.

31. Takada Sanroku was a minor member of the Rengōkai, a member of the Kokuryūkai, and a former army officer.

32. "Kyōto Shūshū Hikokujiken Yoshin Kiroku," Part 2, p. 242; Matsumoto Takehiro, "Iwayuru Hibiya Yakiuchi Jiken no Kenkyū," *Shisō Kenkyū Shiryō,* Special Issue, No. 50, p. 44.

33. "Kyōto Shūshū Hikokujiken Yoshin Kiroku," Part 1, p. 22; Supplement, p. 180.

34. "Kyōto Shūshū Hikokujiken Yoshin Kiroku," Part 1, pp. 86–95; Takahashi Yūsai, *Meiji Keisatsushi Kenkyū II: Meiji Sanjū Hachinen no Hibiya Sōjō Jiken,* p. 55.

35. Matsumoto Takehiro, "Iwayuru Hibiya Yakiuchi Jiken no Kenkyū," *Shisō Kenkyū Shiryō,* Special Issue, No. 50, pp. 44–45.

36. Tsukuda, a Nittō Kurabu member and an old China activist, was not a member of the Rengōkai. He had just been released on bail while serving a sentence for blackmail and was closely associated with his lawyers, Ogawa Heikichi and Sakurai Kumatarō. "Kyōto Shūshū Hikokujiken Yoshin Kiroku," Part 1, pp. 214–29.

37. On September 4, Tsukuda requested Yoshizawa by telegram to recruit some day laborers. Yoshizawa went to a flophouse and offered a wage of two yen a day. Since he required the laborers to wear obi sashes and hakama trousers instead of happy coats, and since the rent for an obi and a hakama was one yen a day, only a few were willing to accept Yoshizawa's offer. *Ibid.,* pp. 45–46. See also Takahashi Yūsai, *Meiji Keisatsushi Kenkyū II: Meiji Sanjū Hachinen no Hibiya Sōjō Jiken,* p. 32.

Yoshizawa subsequently became an important figure during the trial of the Rengōkai leaders when, bribed by the prosecuting attorney, he testified against the accused. *Hōritsu Shimbun,* No. 340, Mar. 15, 1906, pp. 14–19. See also Takahashi Yūsai, *Meiji Keisatsushi Kenkyū II: Meiji Sanju Hachinen no Hibiya Sōjō Jiken,* pp. 257–67; Matsumoto Takehiro, "Iwayuru Hibiya Yakiuchi Jiken no Kenkyū," *Shisō Kenkyū Shiryō,* Special Issue, No. 50, pp. 140–43.

It is not known who contributed the funds for the national assembly. It was rumored that Watanabe Kunitake had done so, but there is no evidence to support this. Matsumoto Takehiro, "Iwayuru Hibiya Yakiuchi Jiken no Kenkyū," *Shisō Kenkyū Shiryō*, Special Issue, No. 50, p. 33. See also *Hōritsu Shimbun*, No. 339, Mar. 10, 1906, p. 12; Kaisai, *Aa Kugatsu Itsuka*, pp. 17–18.

38. "Kyōto Shūshū Hikokujiken Yoshin Kiroku," Part 3, p. 4; Ōtsu, *Dai Nihon Kenseishi*, Vol. 6, p. 154. In accordance with the Peace Police Law (*Chian Keisatsuhō*), the authorities prohibited the distribution of the invitations. The order, however, was issued only after the distribution was practically complete. Takahashi Yūsai, *Meiji Keisatsushi Kenkyū II: Meiji Sanjū Hachinen no Hibiya Sōjō Jiken*, p. 32.

39. The most important primary source materials on the Hibiya riot are:

Matsui Shigeru, *Hibiya Sōjō Jiken no Temmatsu*. This is Matsui Shigeru's memoir (he was then Chief of the First Division of the Metropolitan Police Board) and most of it was written immediately after the incident. In this sense, it is very valuable. It gives, however, a record of the incident strictly from the police point of view, and the author defends police actions during the riot very emphatically.

The Matsumoto Report (strictly confidential). This report was written in 1938 as one of the "Thought Studies Series" of the Ministry of Justice. Its author, Matsumoto Takehiro, was then prosecuting attorney at the Osaka Local Court.

Takahashi Yūsai, *Meiji Keisatsushi Kenkyū II: Meiji Sanjū Hachinen no Hibiya Sōjō Jiken*. Takahashi has been in police work for a long time. He has relied very heavily on the above two works.

Nakayama Yasuaki (ed.), *Shimbun Shūsei Meiji Hennenshi*, Vol. 12, pp. 486–89. This gives a detailed story of the riot. We must, however, note that this article was written by the *Tokyo Asahi Shimbun*, the newspaper most critical of the government.

Susukida Zanun, *Meiji Taiheiki*, Vol. 2, pp. 440–57. Detailed, but a record of "indignation."

Hōritsu Shimbun (special issue entitled "A Great Incident: Record of a Blood-Spattered Capital"), No. 303, Sept. 14, 1905, pp. 1–31.

"Kyoto Shūshū Hikokujiken Yoshin Kiroku" and the stenographic record of the trials in the Hibiya Riot case, reprinted in the *Hōritsu Shimbun*, supply some pertinent material.

Major secondary works on the riot are:

Komuro Akiomi, "Hibiya Yakiuchi Jiken no Saikentō," *Kindai Nihonshi Kenkyū*, No. 5 (April 1958).

Nakamura Masanori, Emura Eiichi, and Miyachi Masato, "Nihon Teikokushugi to Jimmin," *Rekishigaku Kenkyū*, No. 327 (August 1967) 1–25, 55.

Nishida Mitsuo, "Meiji Sanjū-Hachi-nen ni okeru Hi-kōwa Undō ni tsuite no ichi Kōsatsu," *Rekishi Kenkyū*, No. 3 (1965).

Shioda Shōbei and Inumaru Giichi, "Hibiya no Yakiuchi," *Rekishi Hyōron*, No. 39 (October 1952).

Takahashi Masao, "Meiji Sanjū Hachinen no Hikōwa Undō," *Nihon Rekishi*, No. 55 (December 1952).

Uesugi Jūjirō, "Hibiya Yakiuchi Jiken no Kenkyū no Tame ni," *Rekishigaku Kenkyū,* No. 6 (June 1955).

40. d'Anethan, *Fourteen Years of Diplomatic Life in Japan,* p. 453; Nakayama Yasuaki, *Shimbun Shūsei Meiji Hennenshi,* Vol. 12, p. 484; Kawae, *Shiryō Kindai Nihonshi,* pp. 49–50.

41. Fujimura Michio, "Hikōwa Undō," Shinobu Seizaburō and Nakayama Jiichi (eds.) *Nichiro Sensōshi no Kenkyū,* p. 430. On the morning of September 5, Tomizu went to Rengōkai headquarters intending to participate in the national rally. Since he was not feeling well, he left and did not participate in the rally after all. Tomizu, *Zoku Kaikoroku,* p. 296.

42. Matsumoto Takehiro, "Iwayuru Hibiya Yakiuchi Jiken no Kenkyū," *Shisō Kenkyū Shiryō,* Special Issue, No. 50, p. 52. Unfortunately, no materials are available on the govenment deliberations leading to this fateful decision. The first clause of Article Eight of the *Chian Keisatsuhō* stipulates that to maintain peace and order, the police may if necessary restrict, prohibit, or disperse outdoor meetings, mass demonstrations, and crowds; if necessary, they may also disperse indoor meetings. *Ibid.,* p. 28.

As already noted, Takada disappeared immediately after presenting the letter of request to the City Office, and other members of the Rengōkai refused to accept the police prohibition on the pretext that they had not requested permission to use the park. "Kyōto Shūshū Hikokujiken Yoshin Kiroku," Part 2, pp. 128–31.

It has been said that Minister of Home Affairs Yoshikawa suggested to the chief of the Metropolitan Police Board that he proclaim martial law before the national assembly took place, but the idea was rejected as unnecessary by the police chief. Matsui, *Hibiya Sōjō Jiken no Temmatsu,* p. 6.

43. In 1905, the total police force in metropolitan Tokyo and its environs numbered 3397. Matsui Shigeru, *Matsui Shigeru Jiden,* p. 190. See Matsumoto Takehiro, "Iwayuru Hibiya Yakiuchi Jiken no Kenkyū," *Shisō Kenkyū Shiryō,* Special Issue, No. 50, p. 52; Takahashi Yūsai, *Meiji Keisatsushi Kenkyū II: Meiji Sanjū Hachinen no Hibiya Sōjō Jiken,* p. 8.

The population of Tokyo was then 1,969,833. The total area of Hibiya Park was 219,344 square yards. Tokyo (ed.), *Dai Hachikai Tokyoshi Tōkei Nempyō,* pp. 111, 46–47.

44. Takahashi Yūsai, *Meiji Keisatsushi Kenkyū II: Meiji Sanjū Hachinen no Hibiya Sōjō Jiken,* p. 49.

45. Kōno later recalled that he "consented to the troublesome request unwillingly." Nakayama Gisuke, *Kōno Banshū Den,* Vol. 2, p. 674.

46. See above.

47. Takahashi Yūsai, *Meiji Keisatsushi Kenkyū II: Meiji Sanjū Hachinen no Hibiya Sōjō Jiken,* p. 50; Matsumoto Takehiro, "Iwayuru Hibiya Yakiuchi Jiken no Kenkyū," *Shisō Kenkyū Shiryō,* Special Issue, No. 50, p. 54; Matsui, *Hibiya Sōjō Jiken no Temmatsu,* pp. 16–17; Susukida, *Meiji Taiheiki,* pp. 443–44; Nakayama Yasuaki, *Shimbun Shūsei Meiji Hennenshi,* Vol. 12, pp. 486–87.

48. Sakuradamon was the place where Tairō Ii Naosuke had been assassinated 45 years before.

49. The Rengōkai leaders were in disagreement about the move toward the Palace. During the pretrial investigations and at the trial, Kōno Hironaka stated that he had acted in accordance with a schedule. However, Ogawa Heikichi stated that there was no such plan. Ogawa did not go to the palace grounds. See *Hōritsu Shimbun,* No. 340, Mar. 15, 1906, p. 5, for Ogawa's statement; No. 341, Mar. 17, 1906, p. 9, for Kōno's statement. Also "Kyōto Shūshū Hikokujiken Yoshin Kiroku," Part 1, pp. 40, 44, for Kōno's statement; Part 1, p. 33 for Ogawa's statement.

50. Takahashi Yūsai, *Meiji Keisatsushi Kenkyū II: Meiji Sanjū Hachinen no Hibiya Sōjō Jiken,* pp. 51–54; Matsumoto Takehiro, "Iwayuru Hibiya Yakiuchi Jiken no Kenkyū," *Shisō Kenkyū Shiryō,* Special Issue No. 50, pp. 55–56; Matsui, *Hibiya Sōjō Jiken no Temmatsu,* p. 18; Nakayama Gisuke, *Kōno Banshū Den,* Vol. 2, pp. 677–78.

51. Takahashi Yūsai, *Meiji Keisatsushi Kenkyū II: Meiji Sanjū Hachinen no Hibiya Sōjō Jiken,* pp. 55–60; Matsui, *Hibiya Sōjō Jiken no Temmatsu,* pp. 19–20; Matsumoto Takehiro, "Iwayuru Hibiya Yakiuchi Jiken no Kenkyū," *Shisō Kenkyū Shiryō,* Special Issue, No. 50, pp. 56–57; Susukida, *Meiji Taiheiki,* pp. 444–45.

52. Tokutomi, *Sohō Jiden,* pp. 397–99; Takahashi Yūsai, *Meiji Keisatsushi Kenkyū II: Meiji Sanjū Hachinen no Hibiya Sōjō Jiken,* pp. 64–72; Matsui, *Hibiya Sōjō Jiken no Temmatsu,* pp. 20–21; Matsumoto Takehiro, "Iwayuru Hibiya Yakiuchi Jiken no Kenkyū," *Shisō Kenkyū Shiryō,* Special Issue, No. 50, pp. 57–59; Susukida, *Meiji Taiheiki,* p. 445.

53. Matsui, *Hibiya Sōjō Jiken no Temmatsu,* p. 31.

54. Matsumoto Takehiro, "Iwayuru Hibiya Yakiuchi Jiken no Kenkyū," *Shisō Kenkyū Shiryō,* Special Issue, No. 50, pp. 59–61; Matsui, *Hibiya Sōjō Jiken no Temmatsu,* pp. 22–32; Takahashi Yūsai, *Meiji Keisatsushi Kenkyū II: Meiji Sanjū Hachinen no Hibiya Sōjō Jiken,* pp. 72–89.

55. Takahashi Yūsai, *Meiji Keisatsushi Kenkyū II: Meiji Sanjū Hachinen no Hibiya Sōjō Jiken,* pp. 95–117; Matsui, *Hibiya Sōjō Jiken no Temmatsu,* pp. 33–55; Matsumoto Takehiro, "Iwayura Hibiya Yakiuchi Jiken no Kenkyū," *Shisō Kenkyū Shiryō,* Special Issue, No. 50, pp. 61–67. An

eyewitness, Yoshikawa Morikuni, one of the leading Meiji socialists, recorded: "I heard an old man who looked like a day-laborer telling the rioters, 'The Ochanomizu police always bother me about the matter of the family registry. Please burn the police box down.'" Yoshikawa, *Keigyaku Seisōshi,* p. 60.

56. *Hōritsu Shimbun,* No. 341, Mar. 17, 1906, p. 10; "Kyōto Shūshū Hikoku Jiken Yoshin Kiroku," Part 1, pp. 40–41. An employee of the insurance company testified during the pretrial investigation that Kōno was president of the company and had been there at around 2 p.m. on the day of the riot. *Ibid.,* p. 120.

57. Nakayama Gisuke, *Kōno Banshū Den,* Vol. 2, pp. 679–80.

58. Kokuryūkurabu, *Kokushi Uchida Ryōhei Den,* pp. 305–307.

59. Kasai, *Aa Kugatsu Itsuka,* pp. 69–70; *Hōritsu Shimbun,* No. 303, Sept. 14, 1905, p. 9.

60. Nakayama Gisuke, *Kōno Banshū Den,* Vol. 2, pp. 678–80. After the meeting, Kōno called on General Nogi and Ōkuma Shigenobu. *Ibid.,* p. 680. Details of their discussions are not available. See also Ōtsu, *Dai Nihon Kenseishi,* Vol. 6, pp. 159–60; Takahashi Yūsai, *Mejii Keisatsushi Kenkyū II: Meiji Sanjū Hachinen no Hibiya Sōjō Jiken,* pp. 61–62.

61. Watanabe, *Meiji Tennō,* Vol. 2, pp. 148–49. The Emperor composed a poem on this occasion (Sasaki, *Meiji Tennō Gyoshū Kinkai,* p. 306):

Kokorozasu
Kata koso kaware kuni o omou,
Tami no makoto wa
Hitotsu naru ran.

Directions may differ,
Their loyalty to the State
is, I believe, one.

62. With the exception of Uchimura Kanzō, the Christian churches cooperated with the national war effort. The churches were, however, in favor of an early termination of the war. Kuyama (ed.), *Kindai Nihon to Kirisutokyō,* p. 279.

There were charges that the rioters intended to embarrass the government by causing diplomatic problems through attacking Christian churches, but it is quite doubtful that they had any such intentions. (Sawa, *Uemura Masahisa to Sono Jidai,* Vol. 5, pp. 898–907.) The attacks did draw immediate protest from American Minister Griscom. Gaimushō, *Gaikō Bunsho, Nichiro Sensō,* No. 5, pp. 885–86.

In 1905, there were 119 Christian churches in Tokyo, with 144 Japanese and 104 foreign Christian ministers, or a total of 248 Christian ministers in all. In 1906, there were 17,178 Christians in Tokyo. Tokyo, *Dai Hachikai Tokyoshi Tōkei Nempyō,* pp. 242–43.

63. For the plight of the ricksha men who were deprived of their jobs by streetcars, see: Rōdō (ed.), *Nihon Rōdō Undo Shiryō,* Vol. 2, pp. 315–19.

64. Matsumoto Takehiro, "Iwayuru Hibiya Yakiuchi Jiken no Kenkyū," *Shisō Kenkyū Shiryō,* Special Issue, No. 50, p. 71. Katsura had assigned policemen and soldiers to guard Okoi's home. Takahashi Yūsai, *Meiji Keisatsushi Kenkyū II: Meiji Sanjū Hachinen no Hibiya Sōjō Jiken,* pp. 93–95. See also Nakayama Yasuaki, *Shimbun Shūsei Meiji Hennenshi,* Vol. 12, p. 490.

65. Griscom, *Diplomatically Speaking,* p. 262.

66. Ōtsu, *Dai Nihon Kenseishi,* Vol. 6, pp. 162–64; Takahashi Yūsai, *Meiji Keisatsushi Kenkyū II: Meiji Sanjū Hachinen no Hibiya Sōjō Jiken,* pp. 162–223; Nakayama Yasuaki, *Shimbun Shūsei Meiji Hennenshi,* Vol. 12, p. 491; Asahi Shimbunsha (ed.), *Asahi Shimbun Shōshi,* p. 46; Yomiuri (ed.), *Yomiuri Shimbun Hachijūnenshi,* pp. 185–86; Ono Hideo, *Nihon Shimbun Hattatsushi,* pp. 304–306; Yamamoto Fumio, *Nihon Shimbunshi,* pp. 214–15.

The martial law was proclaimed in accordance with Article 14 of the Meiji Constitution: "The Emperor declares a state of siege. The condition and effects of a state of seige shall be determined by law." The suggestion that martial law be declared at this point seems to have been made first by Navy Minister Yamamoto Gonnohyōe. Katō Kanji (ed.), *Katō Kanji Taishō Den,* pp. 470–72.

Because the government was slow to proclaim martial law, a rumor quickly spread that the army was dissatisfied with the peace and had refused to cooperate with the government. Komuro, "Hibiya Yakiuchi Jiken no Saikentō," *Kindai Nihonshi Kenkyū,* No. 5 (April 1958), 9–17.

For a complete list of the 37 suspended newspapers and magazines, see Matsumoto Takehiro, "Iwayuru Hibiya Yakiuchi Jiken no Kenkyū," *Shisō Kenkyū Shiryō,* Special Issue, No. 50, pp. 81–84. The major ones were: *Yorozu Chōhō, Miyako Shimbun, Niroku Shimpō, Nihon, Tokyo Asahi Shimbun, Chokugen, Yomiuri Shimbun* and *Osaka Asahi Shimbun.*

67. Komuro, "Hibiya Yakiuchi Jiken no Seikentō," *Kindai Nihonshi Kenkyū,* No. 5 (April 1958), p. 76.

68. *Ibid.,* pp. 71–72.

69. *Ibid.,* pp. 72–74. Many of the policemen were from the samurai class and were veterans of the Satsuma Rebellion. By and large, their attitude toward the people was one of contempt. Takahashi Yūsai, *Meiji Keisatsushi Kenkyū II: Sanjū Hachinen no Hibiya Sōjō Jiken,* pp. 9, 17.

70. Matsumoto Takehiro, "Iwayuru Hibiya Yakiuchi Jiken no Kenkyū," *Shisō Kenkyū Shiryō*, Special Issue, No. 50, pp. 74–76.

71. *Ibid.*, p. 111. It should be noted that at this time the socialists were speaking out in support of the peace treaty. Holding basically anti-war views, they therefore welcomed the peace. Arahata, *Kanson Jiden*, p. 112; Komuro, "Hibiya Yachiuchi Jiken no Saikentō," *Kindai Nihonshi Kenkyū*, No. 5 (April 1958), pp. 13–14. Prosecuting attorney Matsumoto declared: "The observation that some socialist or anarchist planned the riot is totally groundless." Matsumoto Takehiro, "Iwayuru Hibiya Yakiuchi Jiken no Kenkyū," *Shisō Kenkyū Shiryō*, Special Issue, No. 50, p. 22; Matsui, *Hibiya Sōjō Jiken no Temmatsu*, p. 85. Nezu Masashi, himself a "progressive" writer, criticizes those who regard the Hibiya Riot as the forerunner of revolution. See Nezu, *Hihan Gendaishi*, pp. 289–304.

72. Komuro, "Hibiya Yachiuchi Jiken no Saikentō," *Kindai Nihonshi Kenkyū* No. 5 (April 1958), p. 15. Materials on the trials include: *Hōritsu Shimbun*, an unofficial stenographic record; "Kyōto Shūshū Hikokujiken Yoshin Kiroku"; Takahashi Yūsai, "Iwayuru Hibiya Yakiuchi Jiken no Kenkyū," *Shisō Kenkyū Shiryō*, Special Issue, No. 50, pp. 235–303; Matsumoto Takehiro, "Iwayuru Hibiya Yakiuchi Jiken no Kenkyū," *Shisō Kenkyū Shiryō*, Special Issue, No. 50, pp. 117–49; Ōtsu, *Dai Nihon Kenseishi*, Vol. 6, pp. 176–79; Nakayama Gisuke, *Kōno Banshū Den*, Vol. 2, p. 680.

For the defense argument, see Hanai, *Shōtei Ronsō Kokumin Taikai Jiken o ronzu*. Hanai was the chief attorney for the defense of the 139 involved in the case. For a complete list of these 139 lawyers, see Kasai, *Aa Kusatsu Itsuka*, Supplement, pp. 3–6.

For the prosecution argument, see Sugimoto, *Hōsō Yoin*. The prosecution bribed Yoshizawa to testify against the Rengōkai leaders. In the later stages of the trial, Yoshizawa openly recanted his statement and testified in court that he had been bribed by the prosecuting attorney. This naturally impugned the integrity of the prosecution considerably. *Hōritsu Shimbun*, No. 34, Mar. 15, 1906, pp. 14–19.

73. In later years some of the Rengōkai leaders became cabinet ministers. Kōno Hironaka became Minister of Agriculture and Commerce in the Ōkuma Cabinet in 1915 and Minister of Justice in the Katō Takaaki Cabinet in 1925; as Minister of Transportation in the Tanaka Giichi Cabinet Ogawa expressed his extreme nationalism by ordering the removal of all romanized names from signs in train stations throughout Japan. *Nihon Rekishi Daijiten*, Vol. 3, p. 254.

74. For the list of those mass meetings that sent memorials to the Emperor, see Kasai, *Aa Kugatsu Itsuka*, pp. 181–88.

75. Gaimushō *Gaikō Bunsho, Nichiro Sensō*, No. 5, pp. 814–77; Shinobu Seizaburō, *Taishō Demokurashiishi*, Vol. 1, pp. 47–51; Fujimura Michio, "Hikōwa Undō," Shinobu Seizaburō and Nakayama Jiichi (eds.), *Nichiro Sensōshi no Kenkyū*, p. 431; Tomizu, *Zoku Kaikoroku*, pp. 308–13; Ōtsu, *Dai Nihon Kenseishi*, Vol. 6, pp. 168–79. Huntington Wilson, First Secretary of the American Legation in Tokyo, criticized the memorialization of the professors, saying: "It was the not uncommon case of too many professors mixing in foreign policy." Huntington Wilson, *Memoirs of an Ex-Diplomat*, p. 117.

76. Matsui, *Hibiya Sōjō Jiken no Temmatsu*, p. 2; Takahashi Yūsai, *Meiji Keisatsushi Kenkyū II: Meiji Sanjū Hachinen no Hibiya Sōjō Jiken*, pp. 185–88; Matsumoto Takehiro, "Iwayuru Hibiya Yakiuchi Jiken no Kenkyū," *Shisō Kenkyū Shiryō*, Special Issue, No. 50, pp. 86–91; Kōbe (ed.), *Kōbeshi Shi*, pp. 333–34.

77. Hara Takashi did not attend this meeting. Kobayashi, *Rikken Seiyūkaishi*, Vol. 2, pp. 248–49.

78. Ōishi and Inukai expected that Saionji would approach them to enter his cabinet. Ueno, *Nihon Seitō Hattatsushi*, p. 595. See *Seiyū*, No. 65 (Oct. 25, 1905) 44–45.

Upon hearing of the riot in Tokyo, President Roosevelt stated that he did not understand why the Japanese government had allowed the people to expect an enormous indemnity and added that the ruling class in Japan was marvelous but the people, at least those in Tokyo, were as foolish as the Russians. Ueda, *Kindai Nihon Gaikōshi no Kenkyū*, pp. 170–71; Beale, *Theodore Roosevelt and the Rise of America to World Power*, pp. 308–309; Esthus, *Theodore Roosevelt and Japan*, pp. 95–96.

79. Nakayama Gisuke, *Kōno Banshū Den*, Vol. 2, pp. 685–86.

80. Katō Takaaki continued to attack Katsura, not believing Hara's roundabout information on the imminent fall of the Katsura Cabinet. He was appointed Minister of Foreign Affairs in the Saionji Cabinet, an appropriate successor to the Katsura Cabinet that he had so bitterly attacked. Hara, *Hara Kei Nikki*, Feb. 19, 1906 entry, II, 169; Itō Masanori, *Katō Takaaki*, Vol. 1, pp. 543–50.

81. Nakamura Sadako, "Pōtsumasu Kaigiki ni okeru Nihon Gaikō ni taisuru Yoron," *Seishin Joshidaigaku Ronsō*, 7 (December 1955), pp. 26–27; Fujimura Michio, "Hikōwa Undō," Shinobu Seizaburō and Nakayama Jiichi (eds.), *Nichiro Sensōshi no Kenkyū*, pp. 439–40.

82. Tokutomi, *Kōshaku Katsura Tarō Den*, Vol. 2, p. 297.

83. Tokutomi, *Kōshaku Yamagata Aritomo Den*, Vol. 3, p. 713. Meanwhile, the government had sent its representatives in England, the United

States, Korea, and China the following telegrams, signed by Acting Foreign Minister Katsura Tarō:

1. "On the afternoon of September 5 there was a demonstration against the peace terms in Tokyo. The demonstrators started some violence during the night and clashed with policemen once or twice, but they were controlled by the police without any difficulty. There may be further demonstrations, but there is no cause for alarm. I inform you of this in advance, because newspaper correspondents may send exaggerated reports."

2. "September 7. Today we proclaimed martial law in Tokyo and its vicinity, not because any significant incidents occurred, but only to prevent the bad elements in society from harming the good, and from taking advantage of the anti-peace treaty demonstration, and to prevent newspapers from misleading the masses with irresponsible utterances. Last night also there was some noise, but because of our firm control, nothing untoward occurred." Gaimushō, *Gaikō Bunsho, Nichiro Senso*, No. 5, pp. 884–85.

84. The details of the Privy Council deliberations are not known. See Kaigun, *Yamamoto Gonnohyōe to Kaigun*, pp. 221–23. Kudo holds that the Privy Council only reluctantly gave its consent. Kudo, *Meiji Kenseishi*, pp. 833–34. For sources that state that the Privy Council was quite satisfied with the peace, see Gaimushō, *Komura Gaikōshi*, Vol. 2, p. 161; Ko Hakushaku Yamamoto, *Yamamoto Gonnohyōe Den*, Vol. 1, p. 743.

85. Gaimushō, *Gaikō Bunsho, Nichiro Senso*, No. 5, pp. 878–81; Kasai, *Aa Kugatsu Itsuka*, pp. 189–90.

86. Katsura's letter to Itō Hirobumi, dated Oct. 10, 1905, in "Itō [Hirobumi] ke Bunsho." (Unpublished materials.) Also Gaimushō, *Gaikō Bunsho, Nichiro Senso*, No. 5, pp. 556–58; d'Anethan, *Fourteen Years of Diplomatic Life in Japan*, p. 455; Nakayama Yasuaki, *Shimbun Shūsei Meiji Hennenshi*, Vol. 12, p. 504; Kinkidō, *The Russo-Japanese War*, No. 10, pp. 1412–13; *Kokusaihō Zasshi*, 4, No. 5 (January 1906) 74–75.

87. Takahashi Yūsai, *Meiji Keisatsushi Kenkyū II: Menji Sanjū Hachinen no Hibiya Sōjō Jiken*, p. 194. On November 24, Katsura wrote to Yamagata: "The Diet will never approve the Imperial edicts establishing martial law and press control. I therefore consider it wise to rescind these edicts suddenly, before the opening of the next Diet session." Ōtsu, *Dai Nihon Kenseishi*, Vol. 6, pp. 214–15.

88. Hara, *Hara Kei Nikki*, Vol. 2, Jan. 7, 1906 entry, p. 163. Takekoshi, the biographer of Saionji, wrote that after the Hibiya Riot, Katsura approached Saionji and asked him to take the premiership.

"Katsura's idea was that the Prince, who disliked all vexing things, would not accept the difficult position and if he kept away from it he would tell him that, though reluctantly, he would remain in office a little longer and, therefore, the Prince, with the Seiyukai, should assist him. But as the Prince was already resolved on his course, when he had heard what Katsura had to say, he simply replied, 'Very good, for the country's sake I will take upon myself the difficult post,' and contrary to his expectation, Katsura was obliged to resign. At this time Katsura had Yamagata in the hollow of his hand; Itō, who was a thorn in his flesh, had been 'enshrined' in the Presidency-General and sent to Korea, and if Prince Saionji should decline, Katsura could have thought that the world was his, but the move of the Prince brought his reckoning to naught. May it not be truly said Katsura stumbled over his own wisdom and fell?" Takekoshi, *Prince Saionji*, p. 219.

The transfer of power was effected in spite of Yamagata's grumbling. Not only were the Kenseihontō leaders uninformed about the secret agreement, but even some members of the Katsura Cabinet did not know what was coming. Hara, *Hara Kei Nikki*, Vol. 2, Dec. 12, 1905 entry, p. 157; June 29, 1906 entry, p. 184.

The Rengōkai leaders meanwhile interpreted the cabinet change as the successful outcome of their efforts against Katsura. See Yamada Kinosuke's statement in Kasai, *Aa Kugatsu Itsuka*, Preface, p. 2; Komuro, "Hibiya Yakiuchi Jiken no Saikentō," *Kindai Nihonshi Kenkyū*, No. 5 (April 1958) 16.

Hara recorded in his diary on Sept. 24, 1907 (Vol. 2, pp. 260–61) that, while disclaiming any personal aspirations to nobility, he had complained to Itō and Inoue concerning the government's failure to further reward Saionji, despite his great contributions to national unity during the war and the Seiyūkai's cooperation with the government at the time of the Hibiya Riot.

89. Butow, *Tojo and the Coming of the War*, p. 10. See also Dulles, *The Imperial Years*, p. 276; Griswold, *The Far Eastern Policy of the United States*, p. 121; Beale, *Theodore Roosevelt and the Rise of America to World Power*, p. 323; White, *The Diplomacy of the Russo-Japanese War*, p. 324.

90. Griscom, *Diplomatically Speaking*, p. 262.

91. Huntington Wilson, *Memoirs of an Ex-Diplomat*, p. 117.

92. Kennan, "The Sword of Peace in Japan," *The Outlook*, No. 81 (Oct. 14, 1905) 362. See also Kennan, *E. H. Harriman: A Biography*, Vol. 2, pp. 7–8.

93. d'Anethan, *The d'Anethan Dispatches from Japan, 1894–1910*, pp. 209–12.

94. Japan Chronicle, *A Diary of the Russo-Japanese War*, Vol. 2, p. 341.

95. Matsumoto Takehiro, "Iwayuru Hibiya Yakiuchi Jiken no Kenkyū," *Shisō Kenkyū Shiryō*, Special Issue, No. 50, p. 71.

96. Esthus, *Theodore Roosevelt and Japan*, pp. 95–96.

97. Kokuryūkurabu, *Kokushi Uchida Ryōhei Den*, pp. 307–308.

98. Uchida Ryōhei is said to have discussed with Katsura and Itō Hirobumi his plan for a speaking tour and to have received personal approval and some money from Itō before he left for the northeast in June 1905. In late August, when he returned to Tokyo, he is said to have been "compelled to oppose the government's position on the peace treaty." *Ibid.*, pp. 298–300.

99. Ishida Takeshi, *Meiji Seiji Shisō Kenkyū*, pp. 150–80, and Maruyama, "Senzen ni okeru Nihon no Uyoku Undō," in his *Gendai Seiji no Shisō to Kōdō*, pp. 192–94 (English translation in I. I. Morris, *Nationalism and the Right Wing in Japan*, pp. xx–xxi).

100. Minobe Tatsukichi, "Kenryoku no Ranyō to Kore ni taisuru Hankō," *Kokka Gakkai Zasshi*, 19, No. 10 (October 1905), 67–70; Kennan, "The Sword of Peace in Japan," *The Outlook*, No. 81 (Oct. 14, 1905), pp. 360–61; *Japan Chronicle*, Sept. 8, 1905, Vol. 2, p. 361. D'Anethan observed in his Sept. 10, 1905 telegram: "If the chief of police had not, on his own authority, given the unfortunate order to forbid the meeting arbitrarily, no disorder would have occurred. The failure of the police, which did not have the strength to implement its orders, had serious consequences in making possible the very regrettable incidents that followed. The indignation of the mob, which heretofore had been inspired by a perhaps insufficiently thought-through but noble and patriotic feeling, changed in character and turned against the police and the Minister of Home Affairs under whom it was." D'Anethan, *The d'Anethan Dispatches from Japan, 1894–1910*, p. 209.

101. Matsumoto Takehiro, "Iwayuru Hibiya Yakiuchi Jiken no Kenkyū," *Shisō Kenkyū Shiryō*, Special Issue, No. 50, pp. 93–101; Takahashi Yūsai, *Meiji Keisatsushi Kenkyū II: Meiji Sanjū Hachinen no Hibiya Sōjō Jiken*, pp. 304–52.

102. The Home Minister, complaining of being made the scapegoat, asserted that responsibility for the incident was not his alone, but rather the whole cabinet's as well. Genrō Itō was opposed to Katsura's measure, fearing that it would damage the government's prestige. Shumpōkō (ed.), *Itō Hirobumi Den*, Vol. 3, pp. 675–76; and Takahashi Yūsai, *Meiji Keisatsushi Kenkyū II: Meiji Sanjū Hachinen no Hibiya Sōjō Jiken*, pp. 305–307.

One Japanese historian even maintains that Katsura had used the political activists to instigate a mass movement in order to create a pretext for the government to stop growing popular resistance. Uesugi Jūjirō, "Teikokushugi Seiritsuki no Seiji Katei," in Rekishigaku Kenkyūkai and Nihonshi Kenkyūkai (eds.), *Nihon Rekishi Kōza*, Vol. 5, pp. 291–92; also Uesugi's "Hibiya Yakiuchi Jiken no Kenkyū no Tame ni," *Rekishigaku Kenkyū*, No. 6 (June 1955) 27.

103. Smelser, *Theory of Collective Behavior*, pp. 222–69. See also Rudé, *The Crowd in History: 1730–1848*, pp. 237–58; Hobsbawm, *Primitive Rebels*, pp. 108–25; Gurr, "Psychological Factors in Civil Violence," *World Politics*, 20, No. 2 (January 1968) 245–78.

104. For example, Inoue Kiyoshi, *Nihon no Rekishi*, Vol. 2, pp. 79–81; Shinobu Seizaburō, *Taishō Demokurashiishi*, Vol. 1, pp. 53–54; Shioda and Inumaru, "Hibiya no Yakiuchi," *Rekishi Hyōron*, No. 39 (October 1952), p. 11; Inoue Kiyoshi and Suzuki Masashi, *Nihon Kindaishi*, Vol. 1, pp. 243–46; Irimajiri Kōshū, *Seiji Gojūnen*, p. 49; "Seifu no Mōsei o Unagasu," *Chokugen*, No. 32 (Sept. 10, 1905), 251.

105. In the April 1914 issue of the *Chūō Kōron*, Yoshino Sakuzō, the leader of the "Taishō democracy movement," wrote, "I believe it was September 1905 that the masses really began to play a role in [Japanese] politics." He then concluded that the political significance as mass movements of the Hibiya Riot and the Taishō political movements was identical. Ishida, *Kindai Nihon Seiji Kōzo no Kenkyū*, pp. 137–40. See also Matsumoto, *Kindai Nihon no Seiji to Ningen*, pp. 131–33; Hayashi, *Kindai Nihon no Shisōka Tachi*, pp. 248–52; Yamamoto Shirō, "Taishō Seihen," *Iwanami Kōza: Nihon Rekishi*, 18, Gendai I, 248–52.

106. Hasegawa Nyozekan, another exponent of the "Taishō democracy movement," evaluates the Hibiya Riot as follows: "The Hibiya riot was simply a petty scheme on the part of those politicians who opposed the cabinet at the time. It was . . . neither a social nor a political movement. It was a manifestation of the antisocial character of politicians in this country. . . . The riot had little social significance." "Sandai no Seiji," *Bungei Shunjū* (October 1961), p. 326.

BIBLIOGRAPHY

I. English-Language Materials

BOOKS

Abrikossow, Dmitrii I. *Revelations of a Russian Diplomat,* edited by George Alexander Lensen. Seattle: University of Washington Press, 1964.

Adler, Cyrus. *Jacob H. Schiff: His Life and Letters,* Vol. 1. Garden City, N.Y.: Doubleday, Doran and Co., 1928.

Akagi, Roy Hidemichi. *Japan's Foreign Relations, 1542–1936: A Short History.* Tokyo: The Hokuseido Press, 1936.

Akita, George. *Foundations of Constitutional Government in Modern Japan, 1868–1900.* Cambridge: Harvard University Press, 1967.

Almond, Gabriel A. *The American People and Foreign Policy.* New York: Frederick A. Praeger, 1960.

—— and Powell, G. Bingham, Jr. *Comparative Politics: A Developmental Approach.* Boston: Little, Brown and Co., 1966.

Apter, David E., ed. *Ideology and Discontent.* New York: The Free Press, 1964.

Asakawa, Kanichi. *The Russo-Japanese Conflict.* Boston: Houghton Mifflin, 1904.

Baelz, Toku, ed. *Awakening Japan: The Diary of a German Doctor: Erwin Baelz.* New York: The Viking Press, 1932.

Bailey, Thomas A. *The Man in the Street: The Impact of American Public Opinion on Foreign Policy.* Gloucester, Mass.: Peter Smith, 1964.

Beale, Howard K. *Theodore Roosevelt and the Rise of America to World Power.* Baltimore: The Johns Hopkins Press, 1956.

Beasley, W. G. *The Modern History of Japan.* New York: Praeger, 1963.

Beckmann, George M. *The Making of the Meiji Constitution: The Oligarchs and the Constitutional Development of Japan, 1868–1891.* Lawrence: University of Kansas Press, 1957.

Blacker, Carmen. *The Japanese Enlightenment: A Study of the Writings of Fukuzawa Yukichi.* Cambridge: Cambridge University Press, 1964.

Blum, John Morton. *The Republican Roosevelt.* New York: Atheneum, 1962.

Borton, Hugh. *Japan's Modern Century*. New York; The Ronald Press Co., 1955.

Brooke, Lord. *An Eye-Witness in Manchuria*. London: Eveleigh Nash, 1905.

Brown, Delmar M. *Nationalism in Japan: An Introductory Historical Analysis*. Berkeley: University of California Press, 1955.

Brzezinski, Zbigniew and Huntington, Samuel P. *Political Power: USA/ USSR*. New York: The Viking Press, 1967.

Butow, Robert J. C. *Tojo and the Coming of the War*. Princeton: Princeton University Press, 1961.

Causton, E. E. N. *Militarism and Foreign Policy in Japan*. London: George Allen and Unwin, 1936.

Cohen, Bernard C. *The Influence of Non-Governmental Groups on Foreign Policy-Making*. Boston: World Peace Foundation, 1959.

——. *The Political Process and Foreign Policy: The Making of the Japanese Peace Settlement*. Princeton: Princeton University Press, 1957.

——. *The Press and Foreign Policy*. Princeton: Princeton University Press, 1965.

Conroy, Hilary. *The Japanese Seizure of Korea: 1868–1910*. Philadelphia: University of Pennsylvania Press, 1960.

Correspondence: Japan Foreign Office, *Correspondence Regarding the Negotiations between Japan and Russia (1903–1904)* (translation), presented to the Imperial Diet, March 1904.

Crowley, James B. *Japan's Quest for Autonomy: National Security and Foreign Policy, 1930–1938*. Princeton: Princeton University Press, 1966.

Dallin, David J. *The Rise of Russia in Asia*. New Haven: Yale University Press, 1949.

d'Anethan, Baron Albert. *The d'Anethan Dispatches from Japan, 1894–1910*, selected, translated, and edited with a historical introduction by George Alexander Lensen. Tokyo: Sophia University, 1967.

d'Anethan, Baroness Albert. *Fourteen Years of Diplomatic Life in Japan*. New York: McBride and Nast, 1912.

Dennett, Tyler. *Roosevelt and the Russo-Japanese War*. New York: Doubleday, 1925.

de Tocqueville, Alexis. *Democracy in America*, Vol. I. New York: Alfred A. Knopf, 1954.

Dillon, E. J. *The Eclipse of Russia*. New York: G. H. Doran, 1918.

Dulles, Foster Rhea. *The Imperial Years*. New York: Crowell, 1956.

Esthus, Raymond A. *Theodore Roosevelt and Japan*. Seattle: University of Washington Press, 1966.

Fairbank, John K.; Reischauer, Edwin O.; and Craig, Albert M. *East Asia:*

The Modern Transformation. Boston: Houghton Mifflin, 1965.

Falk, Edwin H. *Togo and the Rise of Japanese Sea Power.* New York: Longmans, Green, 1936.

Farrell, R. Barry, ed. *Approaches to Comparative and International Politics.* Evanston: Northwestern University Press, 1966.

Friedrich, Carl J. *Foreign Policy in the Making.* New York: W. W. Norton, 1938.

Garraty, John A. *The Nature of Biography.* New York: Alfred A. Knopf, 1964.

Gelber, L. M. *The Rise of Anglo-American Friendship.* London: Oxford University Press, 1938.

Griscom, Lloyd C. *Diplomatically Speaking.* Boston: Little, Brown, 1940.

Griswold, A. W. *The Far Eastern Policy of the United States.* New Haven and London: Yale University Press, 1962.

Gulick, Sidney Lewis. *The White Peril in the Far East: An Interpretation of the Significance of the Russo-Japanese War.* New York: Fleming H. Revell Co., 1905.

Hamilton, Ian. *A Staff Officer's Scrap-Book during the Russo-Japanese War,* 2 vols. London: Edward Arnold, 1908.

Hilsman, Roger. *To Move a Nation: The Politics of Foreign Policy in the Administration of John F. Kennedy.* Garden City, N.Y.: Doubleday, 1967.

Hishida, Seiji. *Japan among the Great Powers.* New York: Longmans, Green and Co., 1940.

Hobsbawm, E. J. *Primitive Rebels: Studies in Archaic Forms of Social Movement in the 19th and 20th Centuries.* New York: W. W. Norton, 1965.

Hohenberg, John. *Foreign Correspondence: The Great Reporters and Their Times.* New York: Columbia University Press, 1964.

Huddleston, Sisley. *Popular Diplomacy and War.* Rindge, N. H.: Richard R. Smith, 1954.

Ike, Nobutaka. *The Beginnings of Political Democracy in Japan.* Baltimore: The Johns Hopkins Press, 1950.

Ito, Hirobumi. *Commentaries on the Constitution of the Empire of Japan,* translated by Ito Miyoji. Tokyo: Chūō Daigaku, 1906.

Iwasaki, Uichi. *Working Forces in Japanese Politics: 1867–1920.* New York: Columbia University, 1921.

Jansen, Marius B., ed. *Changing Japanese Attitudes toward Modernization.* Princeton: Princeton University Press, 1965.

——. *The Japanese and Sun Yat-sen.* Cambridge: Harvard University Press, 1954.

Japan, Department of Finance. *Report on the War Finance.* 1906.

Japan, Foreign Office. *Correspondence Regarding the Negotiations between Japan and Russia (1903–1904)* (translation). Presented to the Imperial Diet, March 1904.

Japan Chronicle. *A Diary of the Russo-Japanese War: Being an Account of the War as Published Daily in the "Kobe Chronicle,"* Vol. 2. Kobe: Printed and published at the *Chronicle* office, 1904–1906.

Kawabe, Kisaburo. *The Press and Politics in Japan.* Chicago: University of Chicago Press, 1921.

Kennan, George. *E. H. Harriman: A Biography,* Vol. 2. New York: Houghton Mifflin Co., 1922.

Kinkidō, ed. *The Russo-Japanese War,* No. 10. Tokyo: Kinkidō, 1950.

Knorr, Klaus. *The War Potential of Nations.* Princeton: Princeton University Press, 1956.

Kobayashi, Ushisaburo. *Military Industries of Japan.* New York: Oxford University Press, 1922.

——. *War and Armament Loans of Japan.* New York: Oxford University Press, 1922.

——. *War and Armament Taxes of Japan.* New York: Oxford University Press, 1923.

Kublin, Hyman. *Asian Revolutionary: The Life of Sen Katayama.* Princeton: Princeton University Press, 1964.

Kuropatkin, Aleksei N. *The Russian Army and the Japanese War, Being Historical and Critical Comments on the Military Policy and Power of Russia and on the Campaign in the Far East,* translated by Captain A. B. Lindsay and edited by Major F. D. Swinton, 2 vols. London: John Murray, 1909.

Langer, William L. *The Diplomacy of Imperialism, 1890–1902,* 2 vols. New York and London: Alfred A. Knopf, 1935.

LaPalombara, Joseph and Weiner, Myron, eds. *Political Parties and Political Development.* Princeton: Princeton University Press, 1966.

Lawton, Lancelot. *Empires of the Far East,* Vol. 1. London: Grant Richards, 1912.

Le Bon, Gustave. *The Crowd: A Study of the Popular Mind.* New York: The Viking Press, 1963.

Lederer, Ivo J., ed. *Russian Foreign Policy: Essays in Historical Perspective.* New Haven: Yale University Press, 1966.

Lensen, George Alexander. *The Russian Push toward Japan.* Princeton: Princeton University Press, 1959.

Linebarger, Paul M. A., Chu, Djang, and Burks, Ardath W. *Far Eastern*

Governments and Politics: China and Japan. New York: D. van Nostrand Co., 1956.

Lippmann, Walter. *The Public Philosophy.* New York: The New American Library of World Literature, 1960.

Lockwood, William W. *The Economic Development of Japan.* Princeton: Princeton University Press, 1954.

McCormick, Frederick. *The Tragedy of Russia in Pacific Asia,* 2 vols. New York: The Outing Publishing Co., 1907.

McKenzie, Frederick. *From Tokyo to Tiflis: Uncensored Letters from the War.* London: Hurst and Blackett, 1905.

McLaren, Walter Wallace. *A Political History of Japan during the Meiji Era, 1867–1912.* New York: Charles Scribner's Sons, 1916.

Macridis, Roy C., ed. *Foreign Policy in World Politics.* Englewood Cliffs, N.J.: Prentice-Hall, 1967.

Malozemoff, Andrew. *Russian Far Eastern Policy, 1881–1905, with Special Emphasis on the Causes of the Russo-Japanese War.* Berkeley: University of California Press, 1958.

Markel, Lester and Others. *Public Opinion and Foreign Policy.* New York: Harper and Brothers, 1949.

Maruyama, Masao. *Thought and Behaviour in Modern Japanese Politics,* edited by Ivan Morris. London: Oxford University Press, 1963.

Maxon, Yale Candee. *Control of Japanese Foreign Policy: A Study of Civil-Military Rivalry, 1930–1945.* Berkeley: University of California Press, 1957.

Morgenthau, Hans J. *Politics among Nations: The Struggle for Power and Peace.* New York: Alfred A. Knopf, 1967.

Morley, James William. *The Japanese Thrust into Siberia, 1918.* New York: Columbia University Press, 1957.

Morris, I. I. *Nationalism and the Right Wing in Japan.* London: Oxford University Press, 1960.

Morris, J. *Makers of Japan.* Chicago: A. C. McClurg, 1906.

Najita, Tetsuo. *Hara Kei in the Politics of Compromise, 1905–1915.* Cambridge: Harvard University Press, 1967.

Nakano, Tomio. *The Ordinance Power of the Japanese Emperor.* Baltimore: The Johns Hopkins Press, 1923.

Nelson, William H., and Loewenheim, Francis L., eds. *Theory and Practice in American Politics.* Chicago: The University of Chicago Press, 1964.

Neumann, Sigmund, ed. *Modern Political Parties.* Chicago: University of Chicago Press, 1956.

Nish, Ian H. *The Anglo-Japanese Alliance: The Diplomacy of Two Island Empires, 1894–1907.* London: The Athlone Press, 1966.

Norman, E. Herbert. *Japan's Emergence as a Modern State.* New York: Institute of Pacific Relations, 1940.

Ogata, Sadako N. *Defiance in Manchuria: The Making of Japanese Foreign Policy, 1931–1932.* Berkeley: University of California Press, 1964.

Ogawa, Gotaro. *Conscription System in Japan.* New York: Oxford University Press, 1921.

——. *Expenditures of the Russo-Japanese War.* New York: Oxford University Press, 1923.

Okuma, Shigenobu, comp. *Fifty Years of New Japan,* 2 vols. New York: Dutton, 1909.

Ono, Giichi. *Expenditures of the Sino-Japanese War.* New York: Oxford University Press, 1922.

——. *War and Armament Expenditures of Japan.* New York: Oxford University Press, 1922.

Packard, George R., III. *Protest in Tokyo: The Security Treaty Crisis of 1960.* Princeton: Princeton University Press, 1966.

Paige, Glenn D. *The Korean Decision (June 24–30, 1950).* New York: The Free Press, 1968.

Passin, Herbert. *Society and Education in Japan.* New York: Columbia University, Teachers College Bureau of Publications, 1965.

Pittau, Joseph, S. J. *Political Thought in Early Meiji Japan, 1868–1889.* Cambridge: Harvard University Press, 1967.

Polovtseff, P. A. *Glory and Downfall: Reminiscences of a Russian General Staff Officer.* London: G. Bell, 1935.

Pooley, A. M. *Japan at the Cross Roads.* London: George Allen and Unwin, 1917.

——, ed. *The Secret Memoirs of Count Tadasu Hayashi.* New York and London: Putnam, 1915.

Pringle, Henry F. *Theodore Roosevelt: A Biography.* New York: Harcourt, Brace and World, 1956.

Pye, Lucian W. and Verba, Sidney, eds. *Political Culture and Political Development.* Princeton: Princeton University Press, 1965.

Quigley, Harold S. *Japanese Government and Politics: An Introductory Study.* New York: The Century Co., 1932.

Reischauer, Robert Karl. *Japan, Government-Politics.* New York: The Ronald Press, 1939.

Romanov, B. A. *Russia in Manchuria, 1892–1906.* Ann Arbor: The University of Michigan Press, 1952.

Rosen, R. R. *Forty Years of Diplomacy,* 2 vols. New York: Alfred A. Knopf, 1922.

Rosenau, James N., ed. *Domestic Sources of Foreign Policy.* New York: The Free Press, 1967.

——. *Public Opinion and Foreign Policy.* New York: Random House, 1961.

Rudé, George. *The Crowd in History: A Study of Popular Disturbances in France and England, 1730–1848.* New York: John Wiley & Sons, 1964.

Sansom, G. B. *The Western World and Japan.* New York: Alfred A. Knopf, 1958.

Satow, Ernest. *A Diplomat in Japan.* Philadelphia: J. B. Lippincott, 1921.

——. *Korea and Manchuria between Russia and Japan, 1895–1904,* selected and edited with a historical introduction by George Alexander Lensen. Tallahassee: The Diplomatic Press, 1966.

Scalapino, Robert A. *Democracy and the Party Movement in Prewar Japan: The Failure of the First Attempt.* Berkeley: University of California Press, 1953.

—— and Masumi, Junnosuke. *Parties and Politics in Contemporary Japan.* Berkeley: University of California Press, 1962.

Shils, Edward. *Political Development in the New States.* The Hague: Mouton, 1966.

Smelser, Neil J. *Theory of Collective Behavior.* New York: The Free Press of Glencoe, 1963.

Snyder, Richard C. and Furniss, Edgar S., Jr. *American Foreign Policy: Formulation, Principles, and Programs.* New York: Rinehart, 1954.

Stead, Alfred, ed. *Japan by the Japanese.* London: William Heinemann, 1904.

Stokes, Harold Phelps. *Yale, the Portsmouth Treaty and Japan.* Lenox, Mass.: Star Press, 1948.

Storry, Richard. *The Double Patriots: A Study of Japanese Nationalism.* Boston: Houghton Mifflin Co., 1957.

Takekoshi, Yosaburo. *Prince Saionji.* Kyoto: Ritsumeikan University, 1933.

Takeuchi, Tatsuji. *War and Diplomacy in the Japanese Empire.* New York: Doubleday, 1935.

The Times. *The War in the Far East, 1904–1905.* New York: E. P. Dutton and Co., 1905.

Treat, Payson J. *Diplomatic Relations between the United States and Japan: 1895–1905.* Stanford: Stanford University Press, 1938.

Tsunoda, Ryusaku; de Bary, W. Theodore; and Keene, Donald, compilers. *Sources of Japanese Tradition.* New York: Columbia University Press, 1965.

Tupper, Eleanor and McReynolds, G. E. *Japan in American Public Opinion.* New York: Macmillan Co., 1937.

Uyehara, George E. *The Political Development of Japan, 1867–1909.* London, Constable Co., 1910.

Von Laue, Theodore H. *Sergei Witte and the Industrialization of Russia.* New York: Columbia University Press, 1963.

Waltz, Kenneth N. *Foreign Policy and Domestic Politics: The American and British Experience.* Boston and Toronto: Little, Brown and Co., 1967.

Ward, Robert E., ed. *Political Development in Modern Japan.* Princeton: Princeton University Press, 1968.

—— and Rustow, Dankwart A., eds. *Political Modernization in Japan and Turkey.* Princeton: Princeton University Press, 1964.

Weale, B. L. Putnam. *The Coming Struggle in Eastern Asia.* London: Macmillan Co., 1908.

——. *The Re-Shaping of the Far East,* 2 vols. New York: The Macmillan Co., 1911.

——. *The Truce in the East and Its Aftermath.* New York: The Macmillan Co., 1907.

Webb, Herschel. *The Japanese Imperial Institution in the Tokugawa Period.* New York: Columbia University Press, 1968.

White, John Albert. *The Diplomacy of the Russo-Japanese War.* Princeton: Princeton University Press, 1964.

Wilson-Huntington, F. M. *Memoirs of an Ex-Diplomat.* Boston: Bruce Humphries, 1945.

Witte, S. Y. *The Memoirs of Count Witte,* translated and edited by A. Yarmolinsky. New York: Doubleday, 1921.

Wright, Quincy. *The Study of International Relations.* New York: Appleton-Century Croft, 1955.

Yanaga, Chitoshi. *Japan Since Perry.* New York: McGraw-Hill, 1949.

ARTICLES AND PERIODICALS

Almond, Gabriel A. "Democracy and Foreign Policy Making: Some Comparative Observations on the U.S. and Japan," *Bulletin of the International House of Japan,* No. 11, April 1963.

Armstrong, John A. "The Domestic Roots of Soviet Foreign Policy," *International Affairs*, Vol. 41, No. 1, January 1965, pp. 37–47.

Aspaturian, Vernon V. "Internal Politics and Foreign Policy in the Soviet System," in R. Barry Farrell, ed. *Approaches to Comparative and International Politics*. Evanston: Northwestern University Press, 1966, pp. 212–87.

Bailey, Thomas A. "The Dilemma of Democracy," *American Perspective*, Vol. 2, No. 5, October 1948, pp. 211–17.

Benson, Lee. "An Approach to the Scientific Study of Past Public Opinion," *Public Opinion Quarterly*, Vol. 31, No. 4, Winter 1967–1968, pp. 522–67.

Burks, Ardath W. "The Government and Politics of Japan," in Paul M. A. Linebarger, Djang Chu, and Ardath W. Burks. *Far Eastern Governments and Politics: China and Japan*. New York: D. Van Nostrand, 1956, pp. 255–542.

"Can Foreign Policy Be Democratic?" (a Symposium), *American Perspective*, Vol. 2, No. 4, September 1948, pp. 1–33.

Colegrove, Kenneth W. "The Japanese Cabinet," *The American Political Science Review*, Vol. 30, No. 5, October 1936, pp. 903–23.

———. "The Japanese Emperor," *The American Political Science Review*, Vol. 26, No. 4, August 1932, pp. 642–59.

———. "The Treaty-Making Power in Japan," *The American Journal of International Law*, Vol. 25, April 1931, pp. 270–97.

Corbet, R. G. "Japan and the Peace," *Imperial and Asiatic Quarterly Review*, January 1906, pp. 36–42.

Dillon, E. J. "Japan and Russia: The Story of How Peace Was Brought About," *The Contemporary Review*, February 1907, pp. 270–92.

———. "The Story of the Peace Negotiations," *The Contemporary Review*, Vol. 88, October 1905, pp. 457–78.

The Eastern World (Yokohama), 1903–1905.

Elison, George. "Kōtoku Shūsui: The Change in Thought," *Monumenta Nipponica*, Vol. 22, Nos. 3–4, pp. 437–67.

Eltzbacher, O. "The Collapse of Russia: I, The Indemnity Due Japan," *The Nineteenth Century and After* (London), Vol 58, No. 341, July 1905, pp. 1–21.

Farrell, R. Barry. "Foreign Policies of Open and Closed Political Societies," in R. Barry Farrell, ed. *Approaches to Comparative and International Politics*. Evanston: Northwestern University Press, 1966, pp. 167–208.

Friedrich, Carl J. "International Politics and Foreign Policy in Developed (Western) System," in R. Barry Farrell. *Approaches to Comparative and International Politics.* Evanston: Northwestern University Press, 1966, pp. 97–119.

Galai, S. "The Impact of War on the Russian Liberals in 1904–1905," *Government and Opposition,* Vol. 1, No. 1, November 1965, pp. 85–109.

Godwin, Robert K. "Russia and the Portsmouth Peace Conference," *The American Slavic and East European Review,* Vol. 9, No. 4, December 1950, pp. 279–91.

Griffis, W. E. "The Elder Statesmen of Japan: The Power behind the Portsmouth Treaty," *North American Review,* Vol. 18, 1906, pp. 215–27.

Gurr, Ted. "Psychological Factors in Civil Violence," *World Politics,* Vol. 20, No. 2, January 1968, pp. 245–78.

Hackett, Roger F. "Political Modernization and the Meiji Genrō," in Robert E. Ward (ed.), *Political Development in Modern Japan.* Princeton: Princeton University Press, 1968, pp. 65–97.

Iklé, Frank W. "The Triple Intervention: Japan's Lesson in the Diplomacy of Imperialism," *Monumenta Nipponica,* Vol. 22, Nos. 1–2, pp. 122–30.

Jansen, Marius B. "Modernization and Foreign Policy in Meiji Japan," in Robert E. Ward, ed. *Political Development in Modern Japan.* Princeton: Princeton University Press, 1968, pp. 149–88.

Japan Daily Herald (Yokohama), 1903–1905.

Japan Weekly Mail (Yokohama), 1903–1905.

Kennan, G. F. "The Sword of Peace in Japan," *The Outlook,* No. 81, October 14, 1905, pp. 357–65.

Kublin, Hyman. "The Japanese Socialists and the Russo-Japanese War," *Journal of Modern History,* Vol. 22, No. 4, December 1950, pp. 322–39.

McLaren, W. W., ed. "Japanese Government Documents," *Transactions of the Asiatic Society of Japan,* Vol. 42, Part I, 1914, 232–33.

May, Ernest R. "An American Tradition in Foreign Policy: The Role of Public Opinion," in William H. Nelson and Francis L. Loewenheim, eds. *Theory and Practice in American Politics.* Chicago: The University of Chicago Press, 1964, pp. 100–21.

Millard, T. F. "The Financial Prospects of Japan," *Scribner's Magazine,* September 1905, pp. 369–79.

———. "The Fruits of Japan's Victory," *Scribner's Magazine,* Vol. 38, No. 2, August 1905, pp. 240–51.

Miyaoka, Tsunejirō. "Treaty-Making Power under the Constitution of Japan," *International Conciliation,* No. 221, June 1926, pp. 1–17.

Morgenthau, Hans J. "Conduct of American Foreign Policy," *Parliamentary Affairs,* Vol. 3, No. 1, Winter 1949, pp. 147–61.

Nish, Ian H. "Japan's Indecision during the Boxer Disturbances," *Journal of Asian Studies,* Vol. 20, No. 4, August 1961, pp. 449–61.

Norman, E. Herbert. "The Genyōsha: A Study in the Origins of Japanese Imperialism," *Pacific Affairs,* Vol. 17, No. 3, September 1944, pp. 261–84.

Passin, Herbert, "Writer and Journalist in the Transitional Society," in Lucian W. Pye, ed. *Communications and Political Development.* Princeton: Princeton University Press, 1963, pp. 82–123.

Pipes, Richard E. "Domestic Politics and Foreign Affairs," in Ivo J. Lederer, ed. *Russian Foreign Policy: Essays in Historical Perspective.* New Haven: Yale University Press, 1966, pp. 145–69.

Reinsch, Paul S. "An Unfortunate Peace," *The Outlook,* No. 81, September 16, 1905, pp. 117–18.

Scalapino, Robert A. "The Foreign Policy of Modern Japan," in Roy C. Macridis, ed. *Foreign Policy in World Politics.* Englewood Cliffs, N.J.: Prentice-Hall, 1967, pp. 270–313.

———. "Ideology and Modernization—The Japanese Case," in David E. Apter, ed. *Ideology and Discontent.* New York: The Free Press, 1964, pp. 93–127.

Seaman, Louis F. "The Oriental Armistice," *The Outlook,* No. 81, September 16, 1905, pp. 115–17.

Silberman, Bernard S. "Bureaucratic Development and the Structure of Decision-Making in the Meiji Period: The Case of the Genrō," *The Journal of Asian Studies,* Vol. 27, No. 1, November 1967, pp. 81–94.

Stead, Alfred. "Peace in the Far East," *The Fortnightly Review,* Vol. 74 (New Series), July-December 1905, pp. 593–603.

Stead, William T. "How St. Petersburg Received the News of Peace," *The American Monthly Review of Reviews* (New York), Vol. 32, No. 4, October 1905, pp. 426–29.

Thorson, W. B. "American Public Opinion and the Portsmouth Peace Conference," *American Historical Review,* Vol. 53, No. 3, April 1948, pp. 439–64.

Treadgold, Donald W. "Russia and the Far East," in Ivo J. Lederer, ed. *Russian Foreign Policy: Essays in Historical Perspective.* New Haven: Yale University Press, 1966, pp. 531–74.

Ulan, Adam B. "Nationalism, Panslavism, Communism," in Ivo J. Lederer, ed. *Russian Foreign Policy: Essays in Historical Perspective.* New Haven: Yale University Press, 1966, pp. 39–67.

Von Laue, Theodore H. "Problems of Modernization," in Ivo J. Lederer, ed. *Russian Foreign Policy: Essays in Historical Perspective.* New Haven: Yale University Press, 1966, pp. 69–108.

Ward, Robert E. "Japan: The Continuity of Modernization," in Lucian W. Pye and Sidney Verba, eds. *Political Culture and Political Development.* Princeton: Princeton University Press, 1965, pp. 27–82.

UNPUBLISHED MATERIAL

Long, John Wendell. "The Diplomacy of the Portsmouth Conference, 1905." Unpublished Master's essay, Department of History, Columbia University, 1965.

II. Japanese-Language Materials

BOOKS

Andō Teru 安藤照. *Okoi Monogatari* お鯉物語 (Okoi's Story). Tokyo: Fukunaga shoten, 1927.

Aomori Ken Gikaishi Hensan Iinkai 青森県議会史編纂委員会, ed. *Aomori Ken Gikaishi* 青森県議会史. (The History of Aomori Prefectural Assembly.) Aomori: Aomori Kengikai, 1965.

Arahata Kanson 荒畑寒村. *Kanson Jiden* 寒村自伝 (Autobiography of Arahata Kanson). Tokyo: Ronsōsha, 1960.

Araki Riichirō 荒木利一郎. *Kōhon Motoyama Hikoichi Ō Den* 稿本本山彦一翁伝 (Biography of Motoyama Hikoichi). Osaka: Osaka Mainichi Shimbunsha, 1929.

Ariga Nagao 有賀長雄. *Manshū Inin Tōchi Ron* 満洲委任統治論 (On the Japanese Mandate in Manchuria). Tokyo: Waseda Daigaku Shuppanbu, 1905.

Asahi Shimbun Osaka Honsha Shashi Henshū Shitsu 朝日新聞大阪本社社史編修室, ed. *Murayama Ryūhei Den* 村山龍平伝 (Biography of Maruyama Ryūhei). Osaka: Asahi Shimbunsha, 1953.

Asahi Shimbunsha 朝日新聞社, ed. *Asahi Shumbun Shōshi* 朝日新聞小史 (A Short History of the Asahi). Osaka: Asahi Shimbunsha, 1961.

———. *Asahi Shimbun Shakaimen de miru Sesō Shichijūgonen, 1879–1954* 朝日新聞社会面で見る世相75年 1879–1954 (Seventy-Five Years' Social History, 1879–1954, seen through the social section of the Asahi Shimbun). Tokyo: Asahi Shimbunsha, 1954.

Ashizu Uzuhiko 葦津珍彦. *Dai Ajiyashugi to Tōyama Mitsuru* 大アジア主義と頭山満 (Pan-Asianism and Tōyama Mitsuru). Tokyo: Nihon Bunkyōsha, 1965.

Berutsu, Toku (Baelz, Toku), ed. *Berutsu no Nikki* ベルツの日記 (Baelz Diary), 4 vols. Tokyo: Iwanami, 1953.

Dai Jinmei Jiten 大人名辞典 (Biographical Dictionary), 10 vols. Tokyo: Heibonsha, 1953–1955.

Dainihon Teikoku Gikaishi Kankōkai 大日本帝国議会誌刊行会, ed. *Dainihon Teikoku Gikaishi* 大日本帝国議会誌 (Records of the Japanese Diet), Vols. 5–6. Shizuoka: Dainihon Teikoku Gikaishi Kankōkai, 1927–28.

Fujimoto Naonori 藤本尚則. *Kyojin Tōyama Mitsuru Ō* 巨人頭山満翁 (Biography of Tōyama Mitsuru). Tokyo: Seikyōsha, 1922.

Fukuda Eiko 福田英子. *Meiji Shakaishugi Bungakushū (2)* 明治社会主義文学集 (Collection of Socialist Literature of the Meiji Period). Tokyo: Chikuma shoten, 1965.

Furuya Tetsuo 古屋哲夫. *Nichiro Sensō* 日露戦争 (The Russo-Japanese War). Tokyo: Chūōkōronsha, 1966.

Futabatei Shimei 二葉亭四迷. *Futabatei Shimei Zenshū* 二葉亭四迷全集 (The Complete Works of Futabatei Shimei), Vol. 12. Tokyo: Iwanami, 1959.

Gaimushō 外務省 (Japan, Foreign Ministry). *Komura Gaikōshi* 小村外交史 (History of the Komura Diplomacy), 2 vols. Tokyo: Kuretani Shoten, 1953.

———. *Nihon Gaikō Bunsho* 日本外交文書 (Diplomatic Papers of Japan), Vols. 33; 34; 35; 36, No. 1; 37, Nos. 1–2; 38, No. 2; supplementary volumes No. 2 to Vol. 33, Nos. 1, 3, 5 to Vols. 37 and 38 *Nichiro Sensō*. Tokyo: Nihon Kokusairengō Kyōkai, 1957–1960.

———. *Nihon Gaikō Nempyō narabini Shuyō Bunsho* 日本外交年表並主要文書 (Chronological Table of Japanese Diplomacy and Major Documents), 2 vols. Tokyo: Nihon Kokusairengō Kyōkai, 1955.

Genyōshashi Hensankai 玄洋社史編纂会, ed. *Genyōsha shi* 玄洋社史 (History of the Genyōsha). Tokyo: By the editor, 1917.

Gurū Kikin グルー基金, ed. *Kabayama Aisuke Ō* 樺山愛輔翁 (Biography of Kabayama Aisuke). Tokyo: Gurū Kikin, 1955.

Hanai Takuzō 花井卓藏. *Shōtei Ronsō Kokumin Taikai Jiken o ronzu* 訟庭論争国民大会事件を論ず (Record of a Defense Attorney: On the Hibiya Riot Case). Tokyo: Shunjū sha, 1930.

———. *Heiwa no Tsurugi* 平和の剣 (The Sword of Peace). Tokyo: Hibiya Shobō, 1918.

Hara Keiichirō 原奎一郎, ed. *Hara Kei Nikki* 原敬日記 (Hara Takashi Diary), 5 vols. Tokyo: Fukumura Shuppan, 1965.

Hasegawa Shun 長谷川峻. *Tairiku Gaikō no Senku, Yamaza Kōshi* 大陸外交の先駆山座公使 (Pioneer in Asian Continental Diplomacy, Minister Yamaza Enjirō). Tokyo: Ikuseisha, 1938.

Hattori Shisō 服部之総. *Meiji no Seijika Tachi: Hara Takashi ni tsuranaru Hitobito* 明治の政治家たち，原敬につらなる人々 (Meiji Politicians), 2 vols. Tokyo: Iwanami, 1957–1958.

Hayashi Shigeru 林茂. *Kindai Nihon no Shisōka Tachi* 近代日本の思想家たち (Thinkers of Modern Japan). Tokyo: Iwanami, 1961.

Hayashida Kametarō 林田亀太郎. *Meiji Taishō Seikai Sokumenshi* 明治大正政界側面史 (Sidelights on the Political History of the Meiji-Taishō Era). Tokyo: Dainihon Yūbenkai Kōdansha, 1927.

———. *Nihon Seitōshi* 日本政党史 (History of Japanese Political Parties), 2 vols. Tokyo: Dainihon Yūbenkai, 1927.

Hirao Michio 平尾道雄. *Shishaku Tani Tateki Den* 子爵谷干城伝 (Biography of Tani Tateki). Tokyo: Fuzanbō, 1935.

Hiratsuka Atsushi 平塚篤, ed. *Itō Hirobumi Hiroku* 伊藤博文秘録 (Private Record of Itō Hirobumi). Tokyo: Shunjūsha, 1929.

———. *Shishaku Kurino Shinichirō* 子爵栗野慎一郎 (Biography of Kurino Shinichirō). Tokyo: Kōbunsha, 1942.

Hirota Kōki Denki Kankōkai 広田弘毅伝記刊行会, ed. *Hirota Kōki* 広田弘毅 (Biography of Hirota Kōki). Tokyo: Chūō Kōronsha, 1966.

Homma Hisao 本間久雄. *Zoku Meiji Bungakushi* 続明治文学史 (History of Meiji Literature), Vol. 3. Tokyo: Tokyo Dō, 1964.

Honda Kumatarō 本多熊太郎. *Tamashii no Gaikō* 魂の外交 (Diplomacy of Spirit). Tokyo: Chikura, 1938.

Hori Makoto 堀眞琴. *Nichiro Sensō Zengo* 日露戦争前後 (Japan and the Russo-Japanese War). Tokyo: Hakuyōsha, 1940.

Hozumi Yatsuka 穂積八束. *Kempō Teiyō* 憲法提要 (Principles of the Japanese Constitution). Tokyo: Yūhikaku, 1943.

Ichijima Kenkichi 市島謙吉, ed. *Ōkumakō Hachijūgonen Shi* 大隈公八十五年史 (Eighty-Five Years of Ōkuma Shigenobu), Vol. 2. Tokyo: Ōkumakō Hachijūgonen Shi Kankōkai, 1926.

Ienaga Saburō 家永三郎 *et al.*, eds. *Nihon Rekishi: Gendai I* 日本歴史現代 I (History of Japan: Present I). Tokyo: Iwanami, 1963.

———. *Nihon Rekishi: Kindai IV* 日本歴史近代 IV (History of Japan: Modern IV). Tokyo: Iwanami, 1962.

Ijiri Jōkichi 井尻常吉, ed. *Rekidai Kenkan Roku* 歴代顕官録 (Records of High-Ranking Government Officials). Tokyo: Hara Shobō, 1967.

Ikukata Toshirō 生方敏郎. *Meiji Taishō Kenbunshi* 明治大正見聞史 (Personal History of the Meiji-Taishō Era). Tokyo: Shunjūsha, 1926.

Inaba Masao 稲葉正夫, ed. *Daihonei* 大本営 (The Imperial Headquarters). Tokyo: Misuzu Shobō, 1967.

Inada Masatsugu 稲田正次. *Meiji Kempō Seiritsushi* 明治憲法成立史 (History of the Framing of the Meiji Constitution), 2 vols. Tokyo: Yūhikaku, 1960 and 1962.

Ino Saburō 猪野三郎, ed. *Taishū Jinji Roku* 大衆人事録 (Who's Who in Japan). 2 vols. Tokyo: Teikoku Himitsu Tanteisha, 1934.

Inoue Kiyoshi 井上清 *Nihon no Rekishi* 日本の歴史 (A History of Japan), vol. 2 Tokyo: Iwanami, 1966.

Inoue Kiyoshi 井上清 and Suzuki Masashi 鈴木正四, eds. *Nihon Kindaishi* 日本近代史 (Modern History of Japan), 2 vols. Tokyo: Gōdō Shuppan-sha, 1956.

Inoue Masaaki 井上正明, ed. *Hakushaku Kiyoura Keigo Den* 伯爵清浦奎吾伝 (Biography of Count Kiyoura Keigo), 2 vols. Tokyo: Hakushaku Kiyoura Keigo Den Kankōkai, 1935.

Irimajiri Kōshū 入交好脩. *Seiji Gojūnen* 政治五十年 (Fifty Years of Politics). Tokyo: Jiji Tsūshinsha, 1956.

Iriye Kanichi 入江貫一. *Yamagatakō no Omokage* 山県公のおもかげ (Prince Yamagata Aritomo). Tokyo: Kaikōsha, 1930.

Ishida Takeshi 石田雄. *Kindai Nihon Seiji Kozō no Kenkyū* 近代日本政治構造の研究 (Study of Modern Japanese Political Structure). Tokyo: Mirai-sha, 1959.

―――. *Meiji Seiji Shisōshi Kenkyū* 明治政治思想史研究 (Study of Meiji Political Thought). Tokyo: Miraisha, 1961.

Ishii Kikujirō 石井菊次郎. *Gaikō Yoroku* 外交余録 (Diplomatic Commentaries). Tokyo: Iwanami, 1930.

Ishikawa Takuboku 石川啄木. *Takuboku Zenshū* 啄木全集 (Complete Works of Ishikawa Takuboku), Vols. 8, 13. Tokyo: Iwanami, 1953.

Ishimitsu Makiyo 石光眞清. *Kōya no Hana* 曠野の花 (A Flower in the Wilderness). Tokyo: Ryūseikaku, 1965.

Itō Hirobumi 伊藤博文. *Teikoku Kempō Kōshitsu Tempan Gikai* 帝国憲法皇室典範義解 (Commentaries on the Imperial Constitution and the Imperial House Law). Tokyo: Maruzen, 1935.

Itō Jintarō 伊藤仁太郎. *Meiji Rimenshi* 明治裏面史 (Inside History of Meiji), Vol. 2. Tokyo: Seikōkan, 1933.

Itō Masanori 伊藤正徳. *Gunbatsu Kōbōshi* 軍閥興亡史 (Rise and Fall of the Japanese Militarists), Vol. 1. Tokyo: Bungei Shunjūsha, 1958.

———, ed. *Katō Takaaki* 加藤高明 (Biography of Katō Takaaki), 2 vols. Tokyo: Katō Haku Denki Hensan Iinkai, 1929.

Itō Miyoji 伊東巳代治. *Suiusō Nikki* 翠雨荘日記 (Itō's Green Rain-Villa Diary), edited by Kobayashi Tatsuo. Tokyo: Hara Shobō, 1966.

Kaigun Daijin Kanbō 海軍大臣官房, ed. *Yamamoto Gonnohyōe to Kaigun* 山本権兵衛と海軍 (Yamamoto Gonnohyōe and the Navy). Tokyo: Hara Shobō, 1966.

Kajinishi Mitsuhaya 梶西光速 and others. *Nihon Shihonshugi no Hatten* (II) 日本資本主義の成立 (Development of Capitalism in Japan). Tokyo: Tokyo Daigaku Shuppan, 1957.

Kamikawa Hikomatsu 神川彦松, ed. *Nichibei Bunka Kōshōshi* 日米文化交渉史 (History of Cultural Relations between Japan and America), Vol. 1. Tokyo: Tōyōsha, 1956.

Kaneko Kentarō 金子堅太郎. *Nichiro Sensō Hiroku* 日露戦争秘録 (Secret Records of the Russo-Japanese War). Tokyo: Hakubunkan, 1929.

Kasai Sakuzō 笠井作三, ed. *Aa Kugatsu Itsuka* 鳴呼九月五日 (Ah! September 5 [1905]). Tokyo: Nisshinsha, 1909.

Katō Hiroyuki 加藤弘之. *Shinkagaku yori Kansatsu shitaru Nichiro no Unmei* 進化学より観察したる日露の運命 (Japan and Russia from the Viewpoint of the Theory of Evolution). Tokyo: Hakubunkan, 1904.

Katō Kanji Taishō Denki Hensan Kai 加藤寛治大將伝記編纂会, ed. *Katō Kanji Taishō Den* 加藤寛治大將伝 (Biography of Admiral Katō Kanji). Tokyo: By the editor, 1941.

Kawae Suihō 川江水峰, ed. *Shiryō Kindai Nihonshi* 資料近代日本史 (Sources of Modern Japanese History). Chiba: Bōsō Shimbunsha, 1935.

Kawai Eijirō 河合栄治郎. *Meiji Shisōshi no Ichi Danmen* 明治思想史の一断面 (One Phase in the History of Meiji Thought). Tokyo: Nihon Hyōronsha, 1942.

Keishichōshi Hensan Iinkai 警視庁史編纂委員会, ed. *Keishichōshi: Meiji Hen* 警視庁史明治篇 (History of the Metropolitan Police Board: Meiji Period). Tokyo: Keishichōshi Hensan Iinkai, 1959.

Kikichi Takenori 菊地武徳, ed. *Hakushaku Chinda Sutemi Den* 伯爵　珍田捨巳伝 (Biography of Chinda Sutemi). Tokyo: Kyōmei Kaku, 1938.

Kimura Tokio 木村時夫. *Nihon Nashonarizumu no Kenkyū* 日本ナショナリズムの研究 (Study of Japanese Nationalism). Tokyo: Maeno Shoten, 1967.

Kishimoto Eitarō 岸本英太郎, ed. *Meiji Shakai Undō Shisō* 明治社会運動思想 (Ideology of Meiji Social Movements). Tokyo: Aoki, 1955.

Kiyosawa Kiyoshi 清沢洌. *Nihon Gaikōshi* 日本外交史 (Diplomatic History of Japan), 2 vols. Tokyo: Tōyō Keizai Shimpōsha, 1942.

Ko Hakushaku Yamamoto Kaigun Taishō Denki Hensan Kai 故伯爵山本海軍大將伝記編纂会, ed. *Yamamoto Gonnohyōe Den* 山本権兵衛伝 (Biography of Yamamoto Gonnohyōe), 2 vols. Tokyo: Yamamoto Hakushaku Denki Hanpu Kai, 1938.

Kobayashi Yūgo 小林雄吾. *Rikken Seiyūkaishi* 立憲政友会史 (History of the Rikken Seiyūkai), Vol. 2. Tokyo: Rikken Seiyūkaishi Shuppan Kyoku, 1925.

Kobe Shiyakusho 神戸市役所, ed. *Kobeshi Shi* 神戸市史 (History of Kobe City). Hompen: Sōsetsu. Kobe: Kobe Shiyakusho, 1921.

Koizumi Sakutarō 小泉策太郎 *Zuihitsu Saionji Kō* 随筆西園寺公 (Random Notes on Prince Saionji). Tokyo: Iwanami, 1939.

Kojima Kazuo 古島一雄. *Ichi Rōseijika no Kaisō* 一老政治家の回想 (Reminiscences of an Old Statesman). Tokyo: Chūō Kōron sha, 1951.

Kokuryūkai 黒龍会, ed. *Tōa Senkaku Shishi Kiden* 東亞先覚志士記伝 (Biographical Memoirs of Pioneer Patriots in Eastern Asia), 3 vols. Tokyo: Hara Shobō, 1966.

Kokuryūkurabu 黒龍倶楽部, ed. *Kokushi Uchida Ryōhei Den* 国士内田良平伝 (Biography of Uchida Ryōhei). Tokyo: Hara Shobō, 1967.

Kōsaka Masaaki 高坂正顕. *Meiji Bunkashi* (4) *Shisō Genron Hen* 明治文化史思想言論篇 (Cultural History of the Meiji Era, Thought and Opinion). Tokyo: Yōyōsha, 1955.

Koyama Hirotake 小山弘健 and Asada Kōki 浅田光輝. *Nihon Teikokushugi Shi* 日本帝国主義史 (History of Japanese Imperialism), Vol. 1. Tokyo: Aoki, 1958.

Kudō Takeshige 工藤武重. *Konoe Atsumaro Kō* 近衛篤麿公 (Biography of Konoe Atsumaro). Tokyo: Dainichisha, 1938.

———. *Meiji Kenseishi* 明治憲政史 (Constitutional History of the Meiji Era). Tokyo: Yūhikaku, 1934.

———. *Teikoku Gikaishi* 帝国議会史 (History of the Imperial Diet), 3 vols. Tokyo: Yūhikaku, 1906.

Kuno Osamu 久野収 and Sumiya Mikio 隅谷三喜男, eds. *Kindai Nihon Shisōshi Kōza* 近代日本思想史講座 (Series on the History of modern Japanese Thought), vol. 5 Tokyo: Chikuma Shobō, 1963.

Kurahara Korenaga 藏原惟袒. *Nichiro Kaisen ronsan* 日露開戰論纂 (Why Japan Must Fight Russia). Tokyo: Tokyo Kokubunsha, 1903.

Kurihara Hirota 栗原広太. *Hakushaku Itō Miyoji* 伯爵伊東巳代治 (Biography of Count Itō Miyoji), 2 vols. Tokyo: By the author, 1938.

Kurihara Ken 栗原健. *Tennō: Shōwashi Oboegaki* 天皇昭和史覚書 (The Emperor: Memorandum on Shōwa History). Tokyo: Yūshindō, 1955.

Kuroda Kōshirō 黒田甲子郎. *Gensui Terauchi Hakushaku Den* 元帥寺内伯爵伝 (Biography of Field Marshal Terauchi Masatake). Tokyo: Gensui Terauchi Hakushaku Denki Hensanjo, 1920.

Kuroita Katsumi 黒板勝美. *Fukuda Taishō Den* 福田大將伝 (Biography of General Fukuda). Tokyo: Fukuda Taishō Den Kankōkai, 1937.

Kusano Shigematsu 草野茂松 and Namiki Sentarō 並木仙太郎, eds. *Sohō Bunsen* 蘇峰文選 (Writings of Tokutomi Sohō). Tokyo: Minyūsha, 1915.

Kuyama Yasushi 久山康, ed. *Kindai Nihon to Kirisutokyō* 近代日本とキリスト教 (Christianity in Modern Japan). Tokyo: Sōgensha, 1956.

Kuzū Yoshihisa 葛生能久. *Nisshi Kōshō Gaishi* 日支交渉外史 (Unofficial Record of Sino-Japanese Relations), 2 vols. Tokyo: Kokuryūkai Shuppanbu, 1936.

Kyoto Daigaku Bungakubu Kokushi Kenkyū Shitsu 京都大学文学部国史研究室, ed. *Nihon Kindaishi Jiten* 日本近代史辞典 (Dictionary of Modern Japanese History). Tokyo: Tōyōkeizai Shimpōsha, 1964.

Maeda Renzan 前田蓮山. *Hara Takashi* 原敬 (A Biography of Hara Takashi). Tokyo: Jijitsūshinsha, 1958.

————. *Hara Takashi Den* 原敬伝 (Biography of Hara Takashi), 2 vols. Tokyo: Takayama Shoin, 1948.

Maejima Shōzō 前島省三. *Nihon Seitō Seiji no Shiteki Bunseki* 日本政党政治の史的分析 (Historical Analysis of Japanese Party Politics). Kyoto: Hōritsu Bunkasha, 1954.

Mainichi Shimbun Shashi Hensan Iinkai 毎日新聞社史編纂委員会, ed. *Mainichi Shimbun Shichijūnen* 毎日新聞七十年 (Seventy-Year History of the Mainichi Newspaper). Tokyo: Mainichi Shimbunsha, 1952.

Maruyama Masao 丸山眞男. *Gendai Seiji no Shisō to Kōdō* 現代政治の思想と行動 (Thought and Behavior in Modern Politics). Tokyo: Miraisha, 1965.

————. *Nihon no Nashonarizumu* 日本のナショナリズム (Nationalism in Japan). Tokyo: Kawade, 1953.

Masumi Junnosuke 升味準之輔. *Nihon Seitō Shiron* 日本政党史論 (History of Japanese Political Parties), 4 vols. Tokyo: Tokyo Daigaku Shuppankai, 1965–1968.

Masumoto Uhei 升本卯平. *Shizen no Hito Komura Jutarō* 自然の人小村寿太郎 ('A Man of Nature, Komura Jutarō). Tokyo: Takuyōdō, 1914.

Matsui Shigeru 松井茂. *Hibiya Sōjō Jiken no Temmatsu* 日比谷騒擾事件の顛末 (Record of the Hibiya Riot). Tokyo: Matsui Shigeru Sensei Jiden Kankōkai, 1952.

———. *Matsui Shigeru Jiden* 松井茂自伝 (Autobiography). Tokyo: Matsui Shigeru Sensei Jiden Kankōkai, 1952.

Matsumoto Sannosuke 松本三之介. *Kindai Nihon no Seiji to Ningen* 近代日本の政治と人間 (Politics and Man in Modern Japan). Tokyo: Sōbunsha, 1966.

Matsuo Takayoshi 松尾尊允. *Taishō Demokurashii no Kenkyū* 大正デモクラシーの研究 (Study of Taishō Democracy). Tokyo: Aoki Shoten, 1966.

Matsuoka Masao 松岡正男, ed. *Kaigun Taishō Yamashita Gentarō Den* 海軍大將山下源太郎伝 (Biography of Admiral Yamashita Gentarō). Tokyo: Yamashita Taishō Denki Henshū Iinkai, 1941.

Matsushita Yoshio 松下芳男. *Meiji Gunsei Shiron* 明治軍制史論 (Study of the Meiji Military System), 2 vols. Tokyo: Yūhikaku, 1956.

———. *Meiji Taishō Hansen Undōshi* 明治大正反戦運動史 (History of Anti-War Movements During the Meiji and Taishō Periods). Tokyo: Sōbisha, 1949.

———. *Ni-Sshin Sensō Zengo* 日清戦争前後 (Japan and the Sino-Japanese War). Tokyo: Hakuyōsha, 1949.

———. *Sandai Hansen Undōshi* 三代反戦運動史 (History of Anti-War Movements in Modern Japan). Tokyo: Kuroshio Shuppan, 1960.

Matsuura Hakushaku Ke Henshūjo 松浦伯爵家編修所, ed. *Matsuura Atsushi Haku Den Shibunshō* 松浦厚伯伝詩文鈔 (Biography and Poems of Matsuura Atsushi). Tokyo: By the editor, 1936.

Meiji Bunka Shiryō Sōsho Kankōkai 明治文化資料叢書刊行会 ed. *Meiji Bunka Shiryō Sōsho* 明治文化資料叢書 (Collection of Materials on Meiji Culture), Vol. 2. Tokyo: Kazama Shobō, 1959.

Minobe Tatsukichi 美濃部達吉. *Kempō Satsuyō* 憲法撮要 (Essentials of the Meiji Constitution). Tokyo: Yūhikaku, 1932.

Mitani Taichirō 三谷太一郎. *Nihon Seitōseiji no Keisei: Hara Takashi no Seiji Shidō no Tenkai* 日本政党政治の形成原敬の政治指導の展開 (Establishment of Party Politics in Japan: The Development of Hara Takashi's Political Leadership). Tokyo: Tokyo Daigaku Shuppan, 1967.

Miyahara Seiichi 宮原誠一 *Kyōikushi* 教育史 (History of Japanese Education). Tokyo: Tōyō Keizai Shimpōsha, 1965.

Miyajima Hajime 宮島肇. *Meijiteki Shisōkazō no Keisei* 明治的思想家像の形成 (Formation of the Image of the Meiji Thinkers). Tokyo: Miraisha, 1955.

Miyake Setsurei 三宅雪嶺. *Dōjidaishi* 同時代史 (Contemporary History), Vol. 3. Tokyo: Iwanami, 1950.

Mori Kiichi 森喜一. *Nihon Rōdōshakaikyū Jōtaishi* 日本労働者階級状態史 (History of the Condition of the Japanese Laboring Class). Tokyo: Sanichi Shobō, 1961.

Muramatsu Shōfu 村松梢風. *Akiyama Teisuke wa Kataru* 秋山定輔は語る (The Life of Akiyama Teisuke). Tokyo: Dai Nihon Yūbenkai Kōdansha, 1938.

Mutsu Munemitsu 陸奥宗光. *Ken Ken Roku* 蹇蹇録 (Memoirs). Tokyo: Iwanami, 1958.

Myōjō Fukusei Kankōkai 明星複製刊行会, ed. *Myōjō* 明星 (Myōjō). Kyoto: Rinsen Shoten, 1964.

Nakamura Akira 中村哲. *Seijishi* 政治史 (Political History of Modern Japan). Tokyo: Tōyō Keizai Shimpōsha, 1965.

Nakamura Katsunori 中村勝範. *Meiji Shakaishugi Kenkyū* 明治社会主義研究 (Study of Socialism in Meiji Japan). Tokyo: Sekaishoin, 1966.

Nakamura Kikuo 中村菊男. *Itō Hirobumi* 伊藤博文 (Biography of Itō Hirobumi). Tokyo: Jiji Tsūshinsha, 1958.

Nakamura Seiji 中村清二, ed. *Danshaku Yamakawa Sensei Den* 男爵山川先生伝 (Biography of Baron Yamakawa). Tokyo: Iwanami, 1940.

Nakano Tomio 中野登美雄. *Tōsuiken no Dokuritsu* 統帥権の独立 (Independence of the Supreme Command). Tokyo: Yūhikaku, 1934.

Nakayama Gisuke 中山義助. *Kōno Banshū Den* 河野盤州伝 (Biography of Kōno [Banshū] Hironaka), 2 vols. Tokyo: Kōno Banshū Den Kankō Kai, 1923.

Nakayama Yasuaki 中山泰昌, ed. *Shimbun Shūsei Meiji Hennenshi* 新聞集成明治編年史 (Meiji History through Newspapers), Vols. 10–12. Tokyo: Zaisei Keizai Gakkai, 1936.

Nambara Shigeru 南原繁, Royama Masamichi 蠟山政道, and Yabe Teiji 矢部貞治. *Onozuka Kiheiji: Hito to Gyōseki* 小野塚喜平次，人と業績 (Life and Accomplishments of Onozuka Kiheiji). Tokyo: Iwanami, 1963.

Nezu Masashi ねずまさし. *Hihan Gendaishi* 批判現代史 (Critical History of Modern Japan). Tokyo: Nihon Hyōron Shinsha, 1958.

Nihon Kokusei Jiten Kankōkai 日本国政事典刊行会, ed. *Nihon Kokusei Jiten* 日本国政事典 (Dictionary of Japanese Politics), Vol. 3-4. Tokyo: Maruzen, 1955.

Nihon Rekishi Daijiten 日本歴史大辞典 (Encyclopedia of Japanese History), 20 vols. Tokyo: Kawade Shobō, 1956–1960.

Nihonshi Jiten 日本史辞典 (Dictionary of Japanese History). Tokyo, 1963.

Nishi Sawanosuke 西沢之助. *Nichiro Senkyoku Kōwashigi* 日露戦局媾和私議 (My Opinion on the Peace Terms of the Russo-Japanese War). Tokyo: Taiyōsha, 1905.

Nishida Kitarō 西田幾太郎. *Sunshin Nikki* 寸心日記 (Sunshin Diary). Tokyo: Kōbundō, 1948.

Nishida Taketoshi 西田長寿. *Meiji Jidai no Shimbun to Zasshi* 明治時代の新聞と雑誌 (Newspapers and Magazines in the Meiji Period). Tokyo: Shibundō, 1961.

Nomura Hideo 野村秀雄, ed. *Meiji Taishōshi* 明治大正史 (History of the Meiji and Taishō Periods), Vol. 6. Tokyo: Asahi Shimbunsha, 1931.

Nōshōmushō 農商務省 (Ministry of Agriculture and Commerce). *Meiji Sanjū Hachinen no Bukka ni oyoboseshi Sensō no Eikyō* 明治三十八年ノ物價ニ及ボセシ戦争ノ影響 (Effects of the War on Prices in 1905). Tokyo: Nōshōmushō, 1906.

———. *Meiji Sanjū Hachinen no Chingin ni oyoboseshi Sensō no Eikyō* 明治三十八年ノ賃銀ニ及ボセシ戦争ノ影響 (Effects of the War on Wages in 1905). Tokyo: Nōshōmushō, 1906.

———. *Meiji Sanjū Shichinen no Bukka ni oyoboseshi Sensō no Eikyō* 明治三十七年ノ物價ニ及ボセシ戦争ノ影響 (Effects of the War on Prices in 1904). Tokyo: Nōshōmushō, 1905.

———. *Meiji Sanjū Shichinen no Chingin ni oyoboseshi Sensō no Eikyō* 明治三十七年ノ賃銀ニ及ボセシ戦争ノ影響 (Effects of the War on Wages in 1904). Tokyo: Nōshōmushō, 1905.

Numata Takezō 沼田多稼蔵. *Nichiro Rikusen Shinshi* 日露陸戦新史 (New History of Land Battles in the Russo-Japanese War). Tokyo: Iwanami, 1940.

Ogino Chūzaburō 荻野仲三郎, ed. *Sonoda Kōkichi Den* 園田孝吉伝 (Biography of Sonoda Kōkichi). Tokyo: By the author, 1926.

Ōhata Tokushirō 大畑篤四郎. *Kokusai Kankyō to Nihon Gaikō* 国際環境と日

本外交 (The International Situation and Japanese Diplomacy). Tokyo: Azuma Shuppan, 1966.

Oka Yoshitake 岡義武. *Kindai Nihon Seijishi* 近代日本政治史 (Modern Japanese Political History). Tokyo: Sōgensha, 1962.

———. *Kindai Nihon no Seijika* 近代日本の政治家 (Japanese Politicians in Modern Times). Tokyo: Bungei Shunjūshinsha, 1960.

———. *Reimeiki no Meiji Nihon* 黎明期の明治日本 (Meiji Japan at Dawn). Tokyo: Miraisha, 1964.

———. *Yamagata Aritomo* 山県有朋 (Biography of Yamagata Aritomo). Tokyo: Iwanami, 1958.

Okamoto Mitsuzō 岡本光三, ed. *Nihon Shimbun Hyakunenshi* 日本新聞百年史 (One Hundred Years of Japanese Newspapers). Tokyo: Nihon Shimbun Hyakunenshi Kankōkai, 1960.

Ōkochi Kazuo 大河内一男. *Reimeiki no Nihon Rōdōundō* 黎明期の日本労働運動 (Japanese Labor Movements at Dawn). Tokyo: Iwanami, 1965.

Ōkubo Toshiaki 大久保利謙, ed. *Seijishi (III)* 政治史 (Political History). Tokyo: Yamakawa Shuppan, 1962.

Ōmachi Yoshie 大町芳衛 and Igari Matazo 猪狩又藏. *Sugiura Jūkō Sensei* 杉浦重剛先生 (Biography of Sugiura Jūkō). Tokyo: Seikyōsha, 1924.

Ono Hideo 小野秀雄. *Nihon Shimbun Hattatsushi* 日本新聞発達史 (History of Newspapers in Japan). Osaka: Osaka Mainichi Shimbunsha, 1921.

Ono Sanenobu 尾野実信, ed. *Gensui Kōshaku Ōyama Iwao* 元帥公爵大山巌 (Biography of Field Marshal Prince Oyama Iwao). Tokyo: Ōyama Gensui Den Kankō Kai, 1935.

Ōsugi Sakae 大杉栄. *Jijoden* 自叙伝 (Autobiography). Tokyo: Kaizōsha, 1924.

Ōta Azan 太田阿山, ed. *Fukushima Shōgun Iseki* 福島將軍遺績 (Biography of General Fukushima Yasumasa). Tokyo: Tōa Kyōkai, 1941.

Ōtsu Jun'ichirō 大津淳一郎. *Dai Nihon Kenseishi* 大日本憲政史 (History of Constitutional Government in Japan), Vols. 5 and 6. Tokyo: Hōbunkan, 1927.

Ōurashi Kinen Jigyōkai 大浦氏記念事業会, ed. *Ōura Kanetake Den* 大浦兼武伝 (Biography of Ōura Kanetake). Tokyo: Hakubunkan, 1926.

Ōyama Azusa 大山梓, ed. *Yamagata Ikensho* 山県意見書 (Collection of Opinions of Yamagata Aritomo). Tokyo: Hara Shobō, 1966.

Ozaki Yukio 尾崎行雄. *Nihon Kenseishi o Kataru* 日本憲政史を語る (On Constitutional Government in Japan). Tokyo: Nihon Tsūshin Daigaku Hōsei Gakkai, 1941.

Rekishigaku Kenkyūkai 歴史学研究会, ed. *Nihon Shakai no Shiteki Kyū-mei* 日本社会の史的究明 (Historical Study of Japanese Society) Tokyo: Iwanami, 1963.

Rekishigaku Kenkyūkai 歴史学研究会 and Nihon shi Kenkyūkai 日本史研究会, eds. *Nihon Rekishi Kōza* 日本歴史講座 (Lectures on Japanese History), Vol. 5. Tokyo: Tokyo Daigaku Shuppankai, 1958.

Rikugunshō 陸軍省 (Japan, Army Ministry), ed. *Meiji Tennō Godenki Shiryō: Meiji Gunjishi* 明治天皇御伝記資料 明治軍事史 (Biographical Materials on Emperor Meiji: Military History of the Meiji Era), 2 vols. Tokyo: Hara Shobō, 1966.

Rōdō Undō Shiryō Iinkai 労働運動史料委員会, ed. *Nihon Rōdō Undō Shiryō* 日本労働運動史料 (Materials on the Japanese Labor Movement), 10 vols. Tokyo: Tokyo Daigaku Shuppankai, 1963.

Rōyama Masamichi 蠟山政道. *Seijishi* 政治史 (Political History of Japan). Tokyo: Tōyōkeizai Shimpōsha, 1940.

———. *Seitō no Kenkyū* 政党の研究 (Study of Political Parties). Tokyo: Hakujitsu Shoin, 1949.

Sakatani Yoshirō 坂谷芳郎 ed. *Segai Inouekō Den* 世外井上候伝 (Biography of Inoue Kaoru), 5 vols. Tokyo: Naigai Shoseki, 1934.

Sasaki Nobutsuna 佐々木信綱. *Meiji Tennō Gyoshū Kinkai* 明治天皇御集謹解 (Commentaries on the Poems of Emperor Meiji). Osaka: Osaka Asahi Shimbunsha, 1927.

Sawa Wataru 佐波亘. *Uemura Masahisa to Sono Jidai* 植村正久と其の時代 (Uemura Masahisa and His Times), Vol. 5. Tokyo: Kyōbunkan, 1938.

Senki Meicho Kankōkai Henshūbu 戦記名著刊行会編輯部, ed. *Kiji Sono Mama Nichiro Sensō Tōji no Naigai Shimbun Shō* 記事そのまま日露戦争当時の内外新聞抄 (Collection of Newspaper Articles during the Russo-Japanese War). Tokyo: Senki Meicho Kankōkai, 1929.

Shibusawa Keizō 澁沢敬三, ed. *Meiji Bunkashi* (11) *Shakai Keizai Hen* 明治文化史社会経済篇 (Cultural History of the Meiji Era: Society and Economy). Tokyo: Yōyōsha, 1955.

Shibusawa Seien Kinen Zaidan Ryūmonsha 澁沢青淵記念財団龍門社, ed. *Shibusawa Eiichi Denki Shiryō* 澁沢栄一伝記資料 (Biographical Data on Shibusawa Eiichi), Vol. 28. Tokyo: Shibusawa Eiichi Denki Shiryō Kankōkai, 1959.

Shidehara Heiwa Zaidan 幣原平和財団, ed. *Shidehara Kijūrō* 弊原喜重郎 (Biography of Shidehara Kijūrō). Tokyo: By the editor, 1955.

Shidehara Kijūrō 幣原喜重郎. *Gaikō Gojūnen* 外交五十年 (Fifty Years of Diplomacy). Tokyo: Yomiuri Shimbunsha, 1951.

Shimanouchi Toshie 島内登志衛, ed. *Tani Kanjō Ikō* 谷干城遺稿 (Posthumous Manuscripts of Tani Kanjō), Vol. 2. Tokyo: Seikensha, 1912.

Shimomura Fujio 下村富士男. *Kindai no Sensō (II) Nichiro Sensō* 近代の戦争 日露戦争 (Modern Warfare [II]: The Russo-Japanese War). Tokyo: Jinbutsu Ōraisha, 1966.

Shimonaka Yasaburō 下中彌三郎, ed. *Shinsen Daijinmei Jiten* 新撰大人名辞典 (New Biographical Dictionary), 7 vols. Tokyo: Heibonsha, 1937.

Shinobu Junpei 信夫淳平. *Gaisei Kantoku to Gaikōkikan* 外政監督と外交機關 (Supervision of Diplomatic Policy and Diplomatic Organs). Tokyo: Nihon Hyōronsha, 1926.

―――. *Komura Jutarō* 小村寿太郎 (Biography of Komura Jutarō). Tokyo: Shinchōsha, 1942.

―――. *Nidai Gaikō no Shinsō* 二大外交の眞相 (True History of Two Great Diplomatic Events). Tokyo: Banrikaku, 1928.

Shinobu Seizaburō 信夫清三郎. *Kindai Nihon Gaikōshi* 近代日本外交史 (Modern Diplomatic History of Japan). Tokyo: Chūō Kōronsha, 1942.

―――. *Taishō Demokurashiishi* 大正デモクラシー史 (History of Taishō Democracy), Vol. 1. Tokyo: Nihon Hyōron, 1954.

―――. *Taishō Seijishi* 大正政治史 (Political History of the Taishō Period), Vol. 1. Tokyo: Kawade, 1951.

――― and Nakayama Jiichi 中山治一, eds. *Nichiro Sensōshi no Kenkyū* 日露戦争史の研究 (Study of the History of the Russo-Japanese War). Tokyo: Kawade, 1959.

Shinobu Seizaburō, Watabe Tōru 渡部徹, and Koyama Hirotake 小山弘健, eds. *Gendai Hantaisei Undōshi* 現代反体制運動史 (History of Anti-Establishment Movements in Modern Japan). Tokyo: Aoki, 1960.

Shirayanagi Shūko 白柳秀湖. *Meiji Taishō Kokuminshi: Tairiku Shinshutsu* 明治大正国民史，大陸進出 (History of the Japanese People during the Meiji and Taishō Periods). Tokyo: Chikuma Shobō, 1940.

Shūgiin and Sangiin 衆議院，参議院, eds. *Gikaiseido Shichijūnen Shi: Seitō Kaiha Hen* 議会制度七十年史，政党会派編 (Seventy-Year History of the Parliamentary System: Parties). Tokyo: Ōkurashō Insatsukyoku, 1961.

―――, ed. *Gikaiseido Shichijūnen Shi: Shūgiin giin Meikan* 議会制度七十年史，衆議院議員銘鑑 (Seventy-Year History of the Parliamentary System:

Members of the House of Representatives). Tokyo: Ōkurashō Insatsu-kyoku, 1962.

Shukuri Shigeichi 宿利重一. *Kodama Gentarō* 児玉源太郎 (Biography of Kodama Gentarō). Tokyo: Taikyōsha, 1940.

Shumpōkō Tsuishōkai 春畝公追頌会, ed. *Itō Hirobumi Den* 伊藤博文伝 (Biography of Itō Hirobumi), 3 vols. Osaka: Shumpōkō Tsuishōkai, 1940.

Soejima Yasoroku 副島八十六, ed. *Kaikoku Gojūnenshi* 開国五十年史 (Fifty Years of New Japan), 2 vols. Tokyo: Kaikoku Gojūnenshi Hakkōjo, 1907.

Suehiro Kazuo 末広一雄. *Danshaku Kondō Rempei Den* 男爵近藤廉平伝 (Biography of Kondō Rempei). Tokyo: By the author, 1926.

Sugimoto Tokisaburō 杉本時三郎. *Hōsō Yoin* 法窓余韻 (The Memoir of a Prosecuting Attorney). Nagoya: By the author, 1938.

Sumiya Mikio 隅谷三喜男. *Nihon no Rekishi (22) Dai Nippon Teikoku no Shiren* 日本の歴史, 大日本帝国の試煉 (History of Japan [22]: The Trial of Imperial Japan). Tokyo: Chūō Kōronsha, 1966.

————, Kobayashi Kenichi 小林謙一, and Hyōdō Tsutomu 兵藤釗. *Nihon Shihonshugi to Rōdō Mondai* 日本資本主義と労働問題 (Japanese Capitalism and Labor Problems). Tokyo: Tokyo Daigaku Shuppankai, 1967.

Susukida Zanun 薄田斬雲. *Meiji Taiheiki* 明治太平記 (History of the Meiji Era), Vol. 2. Tokyo: Waseda Daigaku Shuppanbu, 1927.

Suzuki Takeo 鈴木武雄. *Zaiseishi* 財政史 (History of Japanese Financial Policy). Tokyo: Tōyōkeizai Shimpō, 1965.

Suzuki Torao 鈴木虎雄, ed. *Katsunan Bunroku* 羯南文録 (Writings of Kuga Katsunan). Tokyo: Dai Nichisha, 1938.

Taguchi Bunta 田口文太, comp. *Teiken Taguchi Ukichi Zenshū* 鼎軒田口卯吉全集 (Complete Works of Taguchi Ukichi), Vol. 5. Tokyo: Teiken Taguchi Ukichi Zenshū Kankō Kai, 1928.

Taishi Kōrōsha Denki Hensankai 対支功労者伝記編纂会, ed. *Taishi Kaikoroku* 対支回顧録 (Memoirs of China Activists), 2 vols. Tokyo: Taishi Kōrōsha Denki Hensankai, 1936.

Takahashi Korekiyo 高橋是清. *Takahashi Korekiyo Jiden* 高橋是清自伝 (Autobiography of Takahashi Korekiyo). Tokyo: Chikura, 1936.

Takahashi Sakue 高橋作衛. *Manshū Mondai no Kaiketsu* 満洲問題之解決 (The Manchurian Question). Tokyo: Shimizu Shoten, 1904.

Takahashi Seigo 高橋清吾. *Seiji Kagaku Genron* 政治科学原論 (Principles of Political Science). Tokyo: Yūhikaku, 1937.

Takahashi Yūsai 高橋雄豺. *Meiji Keisatsushi Kenkyū II: Meiji Sanjū Hachinen no Hibiya Sōjō Jiken* 明治警察史研究，明治三十八年の日比谷騒擾事件 (Study of the History of the Police during the Meiji Era II: The Hibiya Riot of 1905). Tokyo: Reibunsha, 1961.

Takakura Tetsuichi 高倉徹一, ed. *Tanaka Giichi Denki* 田中義一伝記 (Biography of Tanaka Giichi), Vol. 1. Tokyo: Tanaka Giichi Denki Kankōkai, 1958.

Takeda Kiyoko 武田清子. *Tennōsei Shisō to Kyōiku* 天皇制思想と教育 (The Ideology of the Emperor System and Education). Tokyo: Meiji Tosho, 1964.

Takei Sōjūrō 武井宗十郎, ed. *Ōkuma Haku Jikyokudan* 大隈伯時局談 (Count Okuma's Views on Current Events). Tokyo: Hakubunkan, 1905.

Takekoshi Yosaburō 竹越与三郎. *Saionji Kō* (Prince Saionji) 西園寺公 Tokyo: Hōbunshorin, 1947.

Tanaka Asakichi 田中朝吉, ed. *Hara Takashi Zenshū* 原敬全集 (Complete Works of Hara Takashi), Vol. 1. Tokyo: Hara Takashi Zenshū Kankōkai, 1929.

Tani Toshio 谷寿夫. *Kimitsu Nichiro Senshi* 機密日露戦史 (Confidential History of the Russo-Japanese War). Tokyo: Hara Shobō, 1966.

Tatsumi Kijirō 巽来治郎. *Kyokutō Kinji Gaikōshi* 極東近時外交史 (Modern Diplomatic History of the Far East). Tokyo: Waseda Daigaku Shuppanbu, 1914.

Tokutomi Iichirō 德富猪一郎, ed. *Kōshaku Katsura Tarō Den* 公爵桂太郎伝 (Biography of Prince Katsura Tarō), 2 vols. Tokyo: Ko Katsura Kōshaku Kinen Jigyō Kai, 1917.

————, ed. *Kōshaku Matsukata Masayoshi Den* 公爵松方正義伝 (Biography of Prince Matsukata Masayoshi), 2 vols. Tokyo: Kōshaku Matsukata Masayoshi Denki Hakkōsho, 1935.

————, ed. *Kōshaku Yamagata Aritomo Den* 公爵山県有朋伝 (Biography of Prince Yamagata), 3 vols. Tokyo: Yamagata Aritomokō Kinen Jigyōkai, 1933.

————. *Sanjū Shichi-Hachi Nen Eki to Gaikō* 三十七八年役と外交 (The Russo-Japanese War and Diplomacy). Tokyo: Minyūsha, 1925.

————. *Seijika to shite no Katsura Kō* 政治家としての桂公 (Prince Katsura as a Politician). Tokyo: Minyūsha, 1913.

————. *Sohō Jiden* 蘇峰自伝 (Autobiography of Tokutomi Sohō). Tokyo: Chūō Kōronsha, 1935.

————, ed. *Sokū Yamagata Kō Den* 素空山県公伝 (Biography of Prince Yamagata Isaburō). Tokyo: Yamagata Kōshaku Denki Hensankai, 1929.

————. *Taishō Seikyoku Shiron* 大正政局史論 (Taishō Politics). Tokyo: Minyūsha, 1916.

Tokyo Shiyakusho Tōkeika 東京市役所統計課, ed. *Dai Hachikai Tokyoshi Tōkei Nempyō* 第八囘東京市統計年表 (Eighth Statistical Table of the City of Tokyo). Tokyo: Tokyo Shiyakusho Tōkeika, 1911.

Tomizu Kanjin 戸水寛人. *Kaikoroku* 囘顧録 (Memoirs). Tokyo: Shimizu Shoten, 1905.

————. *Zoku Kaikoroku* 続囘顧録 (Memoirs, Part II). Tokyo: Yūhikaku, 1906.

————. *Shin Kokumin* 新国民 (New Nation). Tokyo: Yūhikaku, 1903.

Tōyadate Masao 刀禰館正雄, ed. *Sono Koro o Kataru* その頃を語る (Reminiscences of Those Days). Tokyo: Tokyo Asahi Shimbun, 1928.

Tōyama Shigeki 遠山茂樹 and Adachi Shigeko 安達淑子. *Kindai Nihon Seijishi Hikkei* 近代日本政治史必携 (Handbook for Modern Japanese Political History). Tokyo: Iwanami, 1961.

Tozawa Tetsuhiko Kyōju Kanreki Kinenronbunshū Kankōkai 戸澤鉄彦教授還暦記念論文集刊行会, ed. *Burujoa Kakumei no Kenkyū* ブルジョア革命の研究 (Study of Bourgeois Revolutions). Tokyo: Nihon Hyōron Shinsha, 1954.

Tsukada Masao 塚田昌夫, ed. *Rikken Minseitōshi* 立憲民政党史 (History of Rikken Minseitō), Vol. I. Tokyo: Rikken Minseitōshi Hensankyoku, 1935.

Tsunoda Jun 角田順. *Manshū Mondai to Kokubō Hōshin* 満洲問題と国防方針 (The Manchurian Question and Japan's National Defense Policy). Tokyo: Hara Shobō, 1967.

Tsurumi Shunsuke 鶴見俊輔. *Nihon no Hyakunen* 日本の百年 (A Century of Japan), Vol. 7. Tokyo: Chikuma, 1962.

Tsurumi Yūsuke 鶴見祐輔. *Gotō Shimpei* 後藤新平 (Biography of Gotō Shimpei), Vol. 2. Tokyo: Gotō Shimpei Haku Denki Hensankai, 1937.

Uchimura Kanzō 内村鑑三. *Uchimura Kanzō Zenshū* 内村鑑三全集 (Complete Works of Uchimura Kanzō), Vol. 14. Tokyo: Iwanami, 1932.

Uchiyama Shōzō 内山省三, ed. *Aizan Bunshū* 愛山文集 (Collection of Writings by Yamaji Aizan). Tokyo: Minyūsha, 1917.

Ueda Toshio 植田捷雄, ed. *Kindai Nihon Gaikōshi no Kenkyū* 近代日本外交史の研究 (Study of Modern Japanese Diplomatic History). Tokyo: Yūhikaku, 1956.

Uehara Etsujirō 植原悦二郎. *Nihon Minken Hattatsushi* 日本民権発達史 (History of the Development of Civil Rights in Japan), Vol. 1. Tokyo: Nihon Minshu Kyōkai, 1958.

Ueno Kumazō 上野熊藏, ed. *Nihon Seitō Hattatsushi* 日本政党発達史 (History of Political Parties in Japan). Tokyo: Hakuaikan, 1918.

Uesugi Shinkichi 上杉慎吉. *Kempō Jutsugi* 憲法述義 (Lectures on the Japanese Constitution). Tokyo: Yūhikaku, 1944.

Watanabe Ikujirō 渡辺幾治郎. *Meiji Tennō* 明治天皇 (Emperor Meiji), 2 vols. Tokyo: Meiji Tennō Shōtokukai, 1958.

————. *Nihon Kinsei Gaikōshi* 日本近世外交史 (Recent Japanese Diplomatic History). Tokyo: Chikura, 1938.

Yamaji Aizan 山路愛山. *Yamaji Aizan Shū* 山路愛山集 (Collected Writings of Yamaji Aizan). Tokyo: Chikuma Shobō, 1965.

Yamamoto Fumio 山本文雄. *Nihon Shimbunshi* 日本新聞史 (History of Japanese Newspapers). Osaka: Kokusai Shuppan, 1948.

Yamazaki Tanshō 山崎丹照. *Tennōsei no Kenkyū* 天皇制の研究 (Studies on the Emperor System). Tokyo: Teikoku Chihōgyōsei Gakkai, 1959.

Yanaihara Tadao 矢内原忠雄, ed. *Gendai Nihon Shōshi* 現代日本小史 (Short History of Contemporary Japan), 3 vols. Tokyo: Misuzu, 1952.

Yano Fumio 矢野文雄. *Yasuda Zenjirō* 安田善次郎 (Biography of Yasuda Zenjirō). Tokyo: Yasuda Hozensha, 1930.

Yomiuri Shimbun 讀賣新聞, ed. *Yomiuri Shimbun Hachijūnenshi* 讀賣新聞八十年史 (Eighty Years of the Yomiuri). Tokyo: Yomiuri Shimbunsha, 1955.

Yoshikawa Morikuni 吉川守圀. *Keigyaku Seisōshi* 荊逆星霜史 (History of Struggles). Tokyo: Aoki, 1957.

ARTICLES AND PERIODICALS

Andō Minoru 安藤実. "Nichi-Ro Sensō no Seijiteki Kiketsu (I)" 日露戦争の政治的帰結 (Political Consequences of the Russo-Japanese War), *Nitchū Mondai* 日中問題 (Sino-Japanese Problems), No. 6, May 1961, pp. 1–26.

Fujii Shōichi 藤井松一. "Teikokushugi no Seiritsu to Nichiro Sensō" 帝国主義の成立と日露戦争 (Establishment of Imperialism and the Russo-Japanese War), in Rekishigaku Kenkyūkai 歴史学研究会, ed. *Jidai Kubunjō no Rironteki Shomondai* 時代区分上の理論的諸問題 (Theoretical Problems of Periodization). Tokyo: Iwanami, 1956.

Fujimura Michio 藤村道生. "Hikōwa Undō 非講和運動 (Anti-Peace Movements) in Shinobu Seizaburō 信夫清三郎 and Nakayama Jiichi 中山治一 (eds.), *Nichiro Sensōshi no Kenkyū* 日露戦争史の研究 (Study of the History of the Russo-Japanese War), Tokyo: Kawade, 1959, pp. 418–46.

————. "Kaisen Yoron no Kōzō," 開戦世論の構造 (Nature of the Pro-War Public Opinion) in Shinobu Seizaburō 信夫清三郎 and Nakayama Jiichi 中山治一 (eds.), *Nichiro Sensōshi no Kenkyū* 日露戦争史の研究 (Study of the History of the Russo-Japanese War). Tokyo: Kawade 1959, pp. 179–216.

————. "Nichiro Sensō ni tsuite" 日露戦争について (On the Russo-Japanese War), *Rekishi Kyōiku* 歴史教育 (History Education), Vol. 5, No. 1, 1957, pp. 20–25.

————. "Nichiro Sensō no Seikaku ni yosete" 日露戦争の性格によせて (On the Nature of the Russo-Japanese War), *Rekishigaku Kenkyū* 歴史学研究 (Historical Studies), Vol. 5, No. 195, May 1956, pp. 1–13.

Fujita Takeo 藤田武夫. "Nichiro Sensō to Chihō Zaisei" 日露戦争と地方財政 (The Russo-Japanese War and Local Finance), *Keizaishi Kenkyū* 経済史研究 (Study of Economic History), Vol. 16, No. 6, February 1936, pp. 73–90.

Furukawa Kiyohiko 古川清彦. "Meiji Bungaku to Shakai I: Nichiro Sensō" 明治文学と社会, 日露戦争 (Meiji Literature and Society: The Russo-Japanese War), in Utsunomiya Daigaku Gakugei Gakubu, ed. *Kenkyū Ronshū* 研究論集 (Studies), No. 14, Part I, March 1965, pp. 34–45.

Gaikō Jihō 外交時報 (Diplomatic Review), 1900–1906.

Hōritsu Shimbun 法律新聞 (Lawyers Newspaper), 1903–1906.

Inada Masatsugu 稲田正次. "Taiheiyō Sensō Boppatsu to Tennō Genrō oyobi Jūshin no Chii" 太平洋戦争勃発と天皇元老及び重臣の地位 (The Outbreak of the Pacific War and the Emperor, the Genrō, and the Senior Ministers), in Ueda Toshio 植田捷雄, ed. *Taiheiyō Sensō Geninron* 太平洋戦争原因論 (Studies of the Causes of the Pacific War). Tokyo: Shimbun Gekkan Sha, 1953.

Inoue Kiyoshi 井上清. "Nichiro Sensō ni tsuite" 日露戦争について (On the Russo-Japanese War), *Nihonshi Kenkyū* 日本史研究 (Study of Japanese History), No. 38. 1958, pp. 1–16.

Ishida Hideo 石田栄雄. "Pōtsumasu Jōyaku to Hoppō Ryōdo Mondai" ポーツマス條約と北方領土問題 (The Portsmouth Treaty and the Northern Territories), *Kokusaihō Gaikō Zasshi* 国際法外交雑誌 (Journal of International Law and Diplomacy), Vol. 60, Nos. 4–6, March 1962, pp. 68–98.

Iyenaga Saburō 家永三郎. "Meiji Kempō Seitei Tōsho no Kempō Shisō" 明治憲法制定当初の憲法思想 (Ideas on the Constitution at the Time of the Promulgation of the Meiji Constitution), in Iyenaga Saburō, ed. *Meiji Kokka no Hō to Shisō* 明治国家の法と思想 (Laws and Thoughts of the State during the Meiji Period). Tokyo: Ochanomizu Shobō, 1966.

——. "Nihon ni Okeru Heiwa Shisō no Dentō" 日本における平和思想の伝統 (The Tradition of Anti-War Thought in Japan), *Shisō no Kagaku* 思想の科学 (Science of Ideas), Vol. 8, No. 2, 1964, pp. 76–84.

Katsura Tarō 桂太郎. "Jiden" 自伝 (Autobiography of Katsura Tarō), *Meiji Shiryō* 明治史料 (Meiji Historical Materials), No. 7, June 1961, pp. 1–48.

Kogiro Teruyuki 小木曾照行. "Pōtsumasu Kōwa Kaigi," ポーツマス講和会議 (Portsmonth Peace Conference) in Shinobu Seizaburō 信夫清三郎 and Nakayama Jiichi 中山治一 (eds.) *Nichiro Sensōshi no Kenkyū* 日露戦争史の研究 (Study of the History of the Russo-Japanese War). Tokyo: Kawade, 1959, pp. 377–417.

Kokkei Shimbun 滑稽新聞, No. 103, September 5, 1905.

Kokusaihō Zasshi 国際法雑誌 (Journal of International Law), Vol. 4, No. 5, January 1906.

Komuro Akiomi 小室晃臣. "Hibiya Yakiuchi Jiken no Saikentō" 日比谷焼打事件の再検討 (Reexamination of the Hibiya Riot), *Kindai Nihonshi Kenkyū* 近代日本史研究 (Study of Modern Japanese History), No. 5, April 1958, pp. 9–17.

Kunikida Tetsuo 国木田哲夫, ed. *Senji Gahō* 戦時画報 (Wartime Pictorial News). Tokyo: Kinji Gahōsha 1904–1905.

Maruyama Masao 丸山眞男. "Chūsei to Hangyaku" 忠誠と反逆 (Loyalty and Treason), *Kindai Nihon Shisōshi Kōza* 近代日本思想史講座 (Series on the History of Modern Japanese Thought), Vol. 6, pp. 379–471. Tokyo: Chikuma Shobō, 1963.

————. "Kuga Katsunan to Kokumin Shugi" 陸羯南と国民主義 (Kuga Katsunan and Nationalism), in Meiji Shiryō Kenkyū Renrakukai 明治史料研究連絡会, ed. *Minkenron kara Nashionarisumu e* 民権論からナショナリズムへ (From Civil Rights Movement to Nationalism). Tokyo: Ochanomizu Shobō, 1957.

————. "Meiji Kokka no Shisō" 明治国家の思想 (Ideology of the Meiji State), in Rekishigaku Kenkyūkai 歴史学研究会, ed. *Nihon Shakai no Shiteki Kyūmei* 日本社会の史的究明 (Historical Study of Japanese Society). Tokyo: Iwanami, 1963.

Nakamura Masanori 中村政則, Emura Eiichi 江村栄一, and Miyachi Masato 宮地正人. "Nihon Teikokushugi to Jimmin" 日本帝国主義と人民 (Japanese Imperialism and the People), *Rekishigaku Kenkyū* 歴史学研究 (Historical Studies), No. 327, August 1967, pp. 1–22 and 55.

Nakamura Sadako 中村貞子. "Pōtsumasu Kaigiki ni okeru Nihon Gaikō ni taisuru Yoron" ポーツマス会議期における日本外交に対する世論 (Japanese Public Opinion on Foreign Relations during the Portsmouth Conference), *Seishin Joshidaigaku Ronsō* 聖心女子大学論叢 (Seishin Studies), Vol. 7, December 1955, pp. 1–39.

Nakayama Jiichi 中山治一. "Gaikō Kakumei ni okeru Furansu no Sekkyokuteki Yakuwari" 外交革命におけるフランスの積極的役割 (Positive Role of France in the Diplomatic Revolution), *Nagoya Daigaku Bungakubu Kenkyū Ronshū* 名古屋大学文学部研究論集 (Nagoya University Studies: Literature Department), Vol. 14 (History V), 1956, pp. 65–71.

Nihon Bengoshi Kyōkai Rokuji 日本辯護士協会録事 (Records of the Japan Lawyers Association), 1903–1906.

Nihon Kokusai Seiji Gakkai 日本国際政治学会, ed. "Nichiro Ni-sso Kankei no Tenkai" 日露日ソ関係の展開 (Development of Imperial and Soviet Russian-Japanese Relations), *Kokusai Seiji* 国際政治 (International Relations), No. 2, October 1966.

————, ed. "Nihon Gaikōshi Kenkyū: Meiji Jidai" 日本外交史研究, 明治時代 (Study of Japanese Diplomatic History: The Meiji Period), *Kokusai Seiji* 国際政治 (International Relations), Fall 1957.

————, ed. "Nihon Gaikōshi Kenkyū: Ni-Sshin Nichiro Sensō" 日本外交史研究, 日清日露戦争 (Study of Japanese Diplomatic History: Sino-Japanese and Russo-Japanese Wars), *Kokusai Seiji* 国際政治 (International Relations), No. 3, April 1962.

Nishida Mitsuo 西田光男. "Meiji Sanjū-hachi-nen ni okeru hi-kōwa undō ni tsuite no ichi kōsatsu" 明治三十八年における非講和運動についての

一考察 (Study of the Anti-Peace Movement in 1905), *Rekishi Kenkyū* 歴史研究 (Historical Studies), No. 3, 1965, pp. 39–54.

Nishida Taketoshi 西田長寿. "Heimin Shimbun to Sono Jidai: Hisenron o chūsin to shite" 平民新聞とその時代, 非戦論を中心として (The Heimin Shimbun and Its Times: Its Anti-War Activities), *Bungaku* 文学 (Literature), Vol. 21, No. 10, 1953, pp. 976–82.

Nōshōmushō 農商務省 (Ministry of Agriculture and Commerce). "Meiji Sanjū Hachinen no Bukka ni Oyoboseshi Sensō no Eikyō" 明治三十八年ノ物價二及ホセシ戦争ノ影響 (Effect of the War on Prices in 1905) (Tokyo, 1906), reprinted in Meiji Bunka Shiryō Sōsho Kankōkai 明治文化資料叢書刊行会, ed. *Meiji Bunka Shiryō Sōsho* 明治文化資料叢書 (Collected Materials on Meiji Culture), Vol. 2. Tokyo: Kazama Shobō, 1959.

———. "Meiji Sanjū Shichinen no Bukka ni Oyoboseshi Sensō no Eikyō" 明治三十七年ノ物價二及ホセシ戦争ノ影響 (Effects of the War on Prices in 1904 (Tokyo, 1905), reprinted in Meiji Bunka Shiryō Sōsho Kankōkai 明治文化資料叢書刊行会, ed. *Meiji Bunka Shiryō Sōsho* 明治文化資料叢書 (Collected Materials on Meiji Culture), Vol. 2. Tokyo: Kazama Shobō, 1959.

———. "Meiji Sanjū Shichinen no Chingin ni Oyoboseshi Sensō no Eikyō" 明治三十七年ノ賃金二及ホセシ戦争ノ影響 (Effect of the War on Wages in 1904) (Tokyo, 1905), reprinted in Meiji Bunka Shiryō Sōsho Kankōkai 明治文化資料叢書刊行会, ed. *Meiji Bunka Shiryō Sōsho* 明治文化資料叢書 (Collected Materials on Meiji Culture), Vol. 2. Tokyo: Kazama Shobō, 1959.

Ōhata Tokushirō 大畑篤四郎. "Nichiro Kaisen Gaikō" 日露開戦外交 (Prewar Diplomacy between Japan and Russia), *Kokusai Seiji* 国際政治 (International Relations), No. 3, April 1962, pp. 102–18.

———. "Nichiro Sensō to Mankan Mondai: II" 日露戦争と満韓問題 (The Russo-Japanese War and the Question of Manchuria and Korea), *Kindai Nihonshi Kenkyū* 近代史研究 (Studies on Modern Japanese History), No. 6, September 1958, pp. 9–16.

Oka Yoshitake 岡義武. "Gaikenteki Rikkensei ni okeru Seitō: Seitō Seijika to shite no Hara Takashi" 外見的立憲政における政党, 政党政治家としての原敬 (Political Parties under Spurious Constitutional Government: Hara Takashi as a Party Politician), *Shisō* 思想 (Thought), No. 333, March 1952, pp. 32–37.

———. "Jōyaku Kaisei Rongi ni Arawareta Tōji no Taigai Ishiki" 條約改正論議に現われた当時の対外意識 (Attitudes toward Foreign Powers Manifested in the Treaty Revision Debates), *Kokka Gakkai Zasshi* 国家学会雑誌 (Journal of Political Science), Vol. 67, Nos. 1–4, August–September 1953, pp. 1–24 and 183–206.

———. "Kindai Nihon Seiji no Tokuisei" 近代日本政治の特異性 (Peculiarities of Modern Japanese Politics), in Oka Yoshitake and others. *Kindai Nihon no Tokuisei* 近代日本の特異性 (Peculiarities of Modern Japan). Tokyo: Hakujitsu Shoin, 1948, pp. 1–43.

———. "Kokuminteki Dokuritsu to Kokka Risei" 国民的独立と国家理性 (National Independence and National Interests), *Kindai Nihon Shisōshi Kōza* 近代日本思想史講座 (Series on the History of Modern Japanese Thought), Vol. 8, pp. 9–79. Tokyo: Chikuma Shobō, 1961.

———. "Meiji Kokka, Sono Seikaku to Isan" 明治国家その性格と遺産 (The Meiji State, its Nature and Legacy), *Kokka Gakkai Zasshi* 国家学会雑誌 (Journal of Political Science), Vol. 80, Nos. 9–10, pp. 509–18.

———. "Meiji Shoki no Jiyū Minken Ronsha no Me ni Eijitaru Tōji no Kokusai Jōsei" 明治初期の自由民権論者の眼に映じたる当時の国際情勢 (The International Situation Seen by Civil Rights Movement Activists in the Early Meiji Era), in Meiji Shiryō Kenkyū Renrakukai 明治史料研究連絡会, ed. *Minken Ron Kara Nashionarizumu e* 民権論からナショナリズムへ (From Civil Rights Movement to Nationalism). Tokyo: Ochanomizu Shobō, 1957.

———. "Nisshin Sensō to Tōji ni okeru Taigai Ishiki" 日清戦争と当時における対外意識 (The Sino-Japanese War and Our Contemporary Attitude toward Foreign Powers), *Kokka Gakkai Zasshi* 国家学会雑誌 (Journal of Political Science), Vol. 68, Nos. 3–4, December 1954, pp. 223–54; Nos. 5–6, February 1955, pp. 101–29.

Onabe Teruhiko 尾鍋輝彦. "Nichiro Sensō no Seikakuron ni Yosete" 日露戦争の性格論によせて (On the Nature of the Russo-Japanese War), *Rekishi Hyōron* 歴史評論 (History Review), No. 112, December 1959, pp. 11–18.

Rōdō Undōshi Kenkyūkai 労働運動史研究会, ed. *Chokugen* 直言 (Speaking Straightforwardly). Tokyo: Meiji Bunken Shiryō Kankōkai, 1960.

———, ed. *Shūkan Heimin Shimbun* 週刊平民新聞 (Heimin Shimbun, Weekly Edition), 2 vols. Tokyo: Meiji Bunken Shiryō Kankōkai, 1962.

Sakamoto Natsuo 坂本夏男. "Nichiro Sensō ni okeru Kōwa e no Michi"

日露戦争における講和への道 (The Way to Peace during the Russo-Japanese War), *Nihon Kindai Shigaku* 日本近代史学 (Modern History of Japan), No. 1, 1958, pp. 41–51.

Satō Saburō 佐藤三郎. "Nisshin Nichiro Sensō no Seikaku" 日清日露戦争の性格 (On the Nature of the Sino-Japanese and the Russo-Japanese Wars), *Rekishi Kyōiku* 歴史教育 (History Education), Vol. 2, No. 2, 1954, pp. 90–96.

Seiyū 政友 (Organ of the Seiyūkai), 1903–1906.

Shimomura Fujio 下村富士男. "Nichiro Sensō no Seikaku" 日露戦争の性格 (The Nature of the Russo-Japanese War), *Kokusai Seiji* (International Relations), Fall 1957, pp. 137–52.

————. "Nichiro Sensō to Manshū Shijō" 日露戦争と満洲市場 (The Russo-Japanese War and the Manchurian Market), *Nagoya Daigaku Bungakubu Kenkyū Ronshū* 名古屋大学文学部研究論集 (Nagoya University Studies: Literature Department), Vol. 14 (History V), 1956, pp. 1–16.

————. "Nichiro Sensō zen Seron Keisei no Ichi Kyokumen: Kōtoku Shūsui o Chūshin ni Shite" 日露戦争前世論形成の一局面, 幸徳秋水を中心にして (One Aspect of the Formulation of Public Opinion prior to the Russo-Japanese War: Kōtoku Shūsui), *Kokushigaku* 国史学 (Study of Japanese History), No. 71, March 1959, pp. 1–15.

————. "Seron no Atsuryoku to Shihon no Atsuryoku: Nichiro Sensō no Baai" 世論の圧力と資本の圧力, 日露戦争の場合 (Pressure of Public Opinion or Pressure of Capital: The Case of the Russo-Japanese War), *Rekishi Kyōiku* 歴史教育 (History Education), Vol. 10, No. 2, 1962, pp. 45–50.

Shinobu Seizaburō 信夫清三郎. "Meiji Makki no Minshū Undō," 明治末期の民衆運動 (Mass movements in the late Meiji Period) in Tozawa Tetsuhiko Kyōju Kanreki Kinenronbunshū Kankōkai 戸澤鉄彦教授還暦記念論文集刊行会, ed. *Burujoa Kakumei no Kenkyū* ブルジョア革命の研究 (Study of Bourgeois Revolutions). Tokyo: Nihon Hyōron shinsha, 1954, pp. 343–86.

Shioda Shōbei 塩田庄兵衛 and Inumaru Giichi 犬丸義一. "Hibiya no Yaki-uchi" 日比谷の焼打 (The Hibiya Riot), *Rekishi Hyōron* 歴史評論 (History Review), No. 39, October 1952, pp. 1–12.

Somura Yasunobu 曾村保信. "Nihon no Shiryō kara mita Nichiro sen zen no Manshū, Shiberia Mondai" 日本の資料から見た日露戦前の満洲, シベリア問題 (The Manchurian and Siberian Questions Seen through

Japanese Materials), *Kokusaihō Gaikō Zasshi* 国際法外交雑誌 (Journal of International Law and Diplomacy), Vol. 57, Nos. 1–2, April/June 1958, pp. 1–27 and 29–60.

Sugano Tadashi 菅野正. "Giwadan Jihen to Nihon no Yoron" 義和団事変と日本の与論 (The Boxer Rebellion and Public Opinion in Japan), *Hisutoria* ヒストリア (Historical Study), Nos. 44–45, June 1966, pp. 26–50.

Sumiya Mikio 隅谷三喜男. "Heimin Shimbun to Sono Kōzokushi" 平民新聞とその後続紙 (The Heimin Shimbun and Its Successors), *Shisō* 思想 (Thought), No. 461, November 1962, pp. 131–41.

Tachi Sakutarō 立作太郎. "Meiji Sanjū Shichi Hachinen Sen'eki to Yōroppa oyobi Amerika Kyōkoku no Gaikō" 明治三十七八年戦役とヨーロッパ及びアメリカ強国の外交 (The Russo-Japanese War and the Diplomacy of European and American Powers), in Tachi Sakutarō Hakushi Ronkō Iinkai 立作太郎博士論行委員会, ed. *Tachi Hakushi Gaikōshi Ronbunshū* 立博士外交史論文集 (Collection of Essays on Diplomatic History by Tachi Sakutarō). Tokyo: Nihon Hyōronsha, 1946.

Taiyō 太陽 (Sun), 1903–1906.

Takahashi Masao 高橋昌郎. "Meiji Sanjū Hachinen no Hi-Kōwa Undō" 明治三十八年の非講和運動 (The Anti-Peace Treaty Movement in 1905), *Nihon Rekishi* 日本歴史 (Japanese History), No. 55, December 1952, pp. 20–25.

"Terauchi Ke Bunsho" 寺内家文書 (The Terauchi Papers), reprinted in *Seiji Keizaishigaku* 政治経済史学 (Studies on Politics and Economics), No. 15, April 1964, pp. 26–30; No. 17, June 1964 p. 35; No. 22, November 1964, pp. 16–19.

Tokyo Ginkō Shūkaijo 東京銀行集会所. "Sengo Keizai ni kansuru Sho Meiryū Iken" 戦後経済に関する諸名流意見 (Opinions of Business Leaders on the Postwar Economy), in Meiji Bunka Shiryō Sōsho Kankōkai, ed. *Meiji Bunka Shiryō Sōsho* 明治文化資料叢書 (Collection of Materials on Meiji Culture), Vol. 2. Tokyo: Kazama Shobō, 1959, pp. 321–86.

Tokyo Pakku 東京パック, 1903–1905.

Tōyō Keizai Shimpō 東洋経済新報 (Oriental Economist), 1903–1905.

Tsunoda Jun 角田順. "Nihon Gendaishi eno Ichi Shikaku (I): Seisen Ryōryaku no Kōsatsu" 日本現代史への一視角, 政戦両略の考察 (One Angle to the Study of Modern Japanese History (I): A Study of Civil-Military Relations in Policy Making), *Gaikō Jihō* 外交時報 (Diplomatic Review), No. 1028, May 1966, pp. 81–91.

Uchiyama Masakuma 内山正熊. "Kasumigaseki Seitō Gaikō no Seiritsu" 霞ケ関正統外交の成立 (Establishment of Orthodoxy in Kasumigaseki Diplomacy), *Kokusai Seiji* 国際政治 (International Relations), No. 2, 1964, pp. 1-16.

―――. "Komura Gaikō Hihan" 小村外交批判 (Critical Study of Komura Diplomacy), *Hōgaku Kenkyū* 法学研究 (Studies of Law and Politics), Vol. 41, No. 5, May 1968, pp. 123-50.

Uesugi Jūjirō 上杉重二郎. "Hibiya Yakiuchi Jiken no Kenkyū no Tame ni" 日比谷焼打事件の研究のために (For Study of the Hibiya Riot), *Rekishigaku Kenkyū* 歴史学研究 (Historical Studies), No. 6, June 1955, pp. 23-29.

―――. "Teikokushugi Seiritsuki no Seiji Katei" 帝国主義成立期の政治過程 (Political History during the Development of Imperialism in Japan), in Rekishigaku Kenkyūkai 歴史学研究会 and Nihonshi Kenkyūkai 日本史研究会, eds. *Nihon Rekishi Kōza* 日本歴史講座 (Lecture Series on Japanese History), Vol. 5. Tokyo: Tokyo Daigaku Shuppankai, 1958.

Yamamoto Shirō 山本四郎. "Taishō Seihen" 大正政変 (Taishō Change), *Iwanami Kōza: Nihon Rekishi*, 18, *Gendai I* 日本歴史現代 I (Iwanami Series: Japanese History), pp. 245-85. Tokyo: Iwanami, 1963.

Yasunaka Satoshi 安中聰. "Nichiro Sensō no Seikaku o Meguru Saikin no Dōkō ni Tsuite" 日露戦争の性格をめぐる最近の動向について (On Recent Trends in Scholarship on the Nature of the Russo-Japanese War), *Rekishi Kyōiku* 歴史教育 (History Education), Vol. 7, No. 1, 1959, pp. 65-70.

Yoshimura Michio 吉村道男. "Nichiro Kōwa Mondai no Ichisokumen" 日露講和問題の一側面 (One Phase of the Russo-Japanese Peace Negotiations), *Kokusai Seiji* 国際政治 (International Politics), No. 3, 1961, pp. 122-33.

UNPUBLISHED MATERIAL

Gaimushō 外務省. Nichiro Jiken Gaihyō Ippan: VIII 日露事件外評一般 (General Foreign Opinions on the Russo-Japanese War). Japanese Army and Navy Archives 1868-1945, Reel No. 44.

"Itō (Hirobumi) ke Bunsho" 伊藤(博文)家文書 (Itō Hirobumi Family Papers). Kensei Shiryōshitsu, Kokuritsu Kokkai Toshokan.

"Kensei Shiryō Kōhon. Meiji Sanjū-hachi nen Shiryō" 憲法資料稿本, 明治三十八年資料 (Manuscripts on the History of Parliamentary Government, 1905). Tokyo: Kensei Shiryōshitsu, Kokuritsu Kokkai Toshokan.

"Kensei Shiryō Kōhon. Meiji Sanjū-shichi nen Shiryō" 憲政資料稿本, 明治三十七年資料 (Manuscripts on the History of Parliamentary Government, 1904). Tokyo: Kensei Shiryōshitsu, Kokuritsu Kokkai Toshokan.

"Kyōto Shūshū Hikokujiken Yoshin Kiroku" 兇徒聚衆被告事件予審記録 (Records of the Pre-Trial Investigations of the Hibiya Riot), 3 parts and 1 supplement. n.d., n.p.

Matsumoto Takehiro 松本武祐. "Iwayuru Hibiya Yakiuchi Jiken no Kenkyū" 所謂日比谷焼打事件の研究 (Study of the Hibiya Riot), *Shisō Kenkyū Shiryō* 思想研究資料 (Materials on Thought Studies), Special Issue, No. 50 (strictly confidential). Shihōshō Keiji Kyoku, 1939.

INDEX

Diet (*Continued*)
227, 235; relation to Cabinet, 23-24; wartime, 24, 39, 131-39, 241; *ingai-dan* in, 50, 88, 193; 19th session, 84, 89, 90, 131, 134, 197; 20th session, 131, 135, 198; 21st session, 131, 132, 135, 187, 198; 18th session, 133; Saionji-Matsuda-Hara triumvirate, 134, 136; *Kei-En Jidai* (Katsura-Saionji era), 138; 22d session, 198
Dillon, E. J., 282
Dōshi Kisha Kurabu (Fellow Newspapermen's Club), 197

Education, 53; Imperial Rescript of *1890,* 16, 53
Emperor, 38, 48, 76, 101, 131, 258, 265, 299; prerogatives and powers of, 11, 12-13, 21, 33; and war, 13, 108, 110-11, 117, 120, 123-24; relation to Genrō, 13, 14-21, 25, 54; as commander-in-chief, 16, 33, 170, 182; right of direct access (*iakū jōsō*), 34; *Sonnō Jōi* slogan (to revere the Emperor and expel the barbarians), 44; as father, 53; inviolability of, 53; *kunsoku no kan* (evil advisers surrounding the Emperor), 54; and negotiations with Russia, 76, 78, 84-85, 87, 90, 100, 101 (*see also* Imperial Conferences); loyalty to, 129; and Portsmouth Conference, 154, 169; and anti-peace treaty movement, 205, 207, 212; Imperial Order on restoration of peace, 218
England, 60, 70, 79
Enjōji Kiyoshi, 87, 199, 211

Farrell, R. Barry, quoted, 2
Finance Minister, 38
Foreign Minister, 38
Foreign Ministry, and Russian activities in Manchuria, 72, 73
Foreign policy: oligarchic control of, 1, 2, 3, 4, 6, 8, 11-54 *passim,* 227-32 (*see also* Oligarchic system); role of

Emperor in, 12-13; Imperial Conferences and oligarchs, 37-40
Foreign policy makers during Russo-Japanese War, 38-39, 42, 46, 57, 75, 80, 94, 99, 101, 228-30, 232; *see also* Oligarchic government
Foreign relations, 6, 7, 8; differences in attitudes on, 41-54; Imperial Proclamation on the Opening of International Intercourse, 33; Triple Intervention of Russia, Germany and France (1895), 47, 48, 49, 52, 53, 61, 68, 105
France, relations with Japan, 47, 54
Friedrich, Carl J., quoted, 2
Fuan no heiwa (uneasy peace), 92
Fujita Denzaburō, 184
Fukien, 77
Fukoku kyōhei (enrich the nation and strengthen its army) policy, 43
Fukuda Masatarō, 73, 250
Fukushima, Yasumasa, Gen., 71, 250
Fukuzawa Yukichi, 30, 47, 67
Fushimi, Prince, 147
Futabatei Shimei, 95, 177

Gaikō Jihō (periodical), 143
Gaikō mondai (diplomatic question), 67-68
Gashin shōtan (suffer privation for revenge), 48-49
Genrō (elder statesmen), 24, 25, 30-31, 37, 38, 39, 40, 118, 162, 169, 170, 188, 227, 236, 237, 238, 257, 258; function of, 5, 13, 14-21, 230; weakness and decline of, 5, 230, 232; qualification for membership, 14; five in *1904,* 14-21; and negotiations with Russia, 69, 71, 74, 78, 79-81, 84, 95, 97, 99; and war, 112, 116, 117, 120, 122, 123, 124
Genrō conferences, 25, 35, 36, 37, 38, 72, 98-99, 101, 120, 122
Genrōin (Senate), 18
Gensuifu (Board of Field Marshals and Fleet Admirals), 17, 19, 35, 235
Genyōsha (Dark Ocean Society), 28, 50-51, 52, 58, 61, 247

STUDIES OF THE EAST ASIAN INSTITUTE

The Ladder of Success in Imperial China, by Ping-ti Ho. New York: Columbia University Press, 1962.

The Chinese Inflation, 1937-1949, by Shun-hsin Chou. New York: Columbia University Press, 1963.

Reformer in Modern China: Chang Chien, 1853-1926, by Samuel Chu. New York: Columbia University Press, 1965.

Research in Japanese Sources: A Guide, by Herschel Webb with the assistance of Marleigh Ryan. New York: Columbia University Press, 1965.

Society and Education in Japan, by Herbert Passin. New York: Bureau of Publications, Teachers College, Columbia University, 1965.

Agricultural Production and Economic Development in Japan, 1873-1922, by James I. Nakamura. Princeton, N. J.: Princeton University Press, 1966.

Japan's First Modern Novel: Ukigumo of Futabatei Shimei, by Marleigh Ryan. New York: Columbia University Press, 1967.

The Korean Communist Movement, 1918-1948, by Dae-Sook Suh. Princeton, N. J.: Princeton University Press, 1967.

The First Vietnam Crisis, by Melvin Gurtov. New York: Columbia University Press, 1967.

Cadres, Bureaucracy and Political Power in Communist China, by A. Doak Barnett. New York: Columbia University Press, 1967.

The Japanese Imperial Institution in the Tokugawa Period, by Herschel Webb. New York: Columbia University Press, 1968.

The Recruitment of University Graduates in Big Firms in Japan, by Koya Azumi. New York: Teachers College Press, Columbia University, 1968.

The Communists and Chinese Peasant Rebellion: A Study in the Rewriting of Chinese History, by James P. Harrison, Jr. New York: Atheneum Publishers, 1969

How the Conservatives Rule Japan, by Nathaniel B. Thayer. Princeton, N. J.: Princeton University Press, 1969.

Aspects of Chinese Education, edited by C. T. Hu. New York: Teachers College Press, Columbia University, 1969.

Economic Development and the Labor Market in Japan, by Koji Taira. New York: Columbia University Press, 1970.

The Japanese Oligarchy and the Russo-Japanese War, by Shumpei Okamoto. New York: Columbia University Press 1970.

Imperial Restoration in Medieval Japan, by Paul Varley, New York: Columbia University Press (forthcoming).

Li Tsung-Jen, A Memoir. Edited by T. K. Tong. University of California Press (forthcoming).

Documents on Korean Communism, by Dae-Sook Suh. Princeton, N. J.: Princeton University Press (forthcoming).

Japan's Postwar Defense Policy, 1947-1968, by Martin E. Weinstein. New York: Columbia University Press (forthcoming).

DATE DUE
